GCSE AQA
Geography

There's been a seismic shift in AQA GCSE Geography, and the latest Grade 9-1 course is tougher than ever. Luckily, this CGP book has it all covered...

It's packed with brilliant study notes, clear diagrams and cracking case studies — plus plenty of exam-style practice to test how much you've *really* learned.

We've also included top advice for the exams (including the new Geographical Applications paper), so there won't be any earth-shattering shocks on the day.

How to access your free Online Edition

This book includes a free Online Edition to read on your PC, Mac or tablet.
You'll just need to go to **cgpbooks.co.uk/extras** and enter this code:

0125 6249 9400 9091

By the way, this code only works for one person. If somebody else has used this book before you, they might have already claimed the Online Edition.

Complete
Revision & Practice
<u>Everything</u> you need to pass the exams!

Contents

Unit 2: Challenges in the Human Environment

Unit 3: Geographical Applications

Geographical Skills

Practice Exams

Don't Forget

You <u>don't</u> need to study <u>all</u> of the content in Units 1B, 1C and 2C — some of the themes are optional. See page 1 for more details.

Published by CGP

Contributors:
Nick Anderson, Sophie Anderson, Jack Gillett, Meg Gillett, Barbara Melbourne.

Editors:
Claire Boulter, David Maliphant, Claire Plowman, David Ryan.

Proofreading:
Karen Wells.

ISBN: 978 1 78294 613 7

With thanks to Ana Pungartnik for the copyright research.

Printed by Elanders Ltd, Newcastle upon Tyne.
Clipart from Corel®

Based on the classic CGP style created by Richard Parsons.

Structure of the Course

'Know thy enemy', 'forewarned is forearmed'... There are many boring quotes that just mean <u>being prepared is a good thing</u>. <u>Don't</u> stumble <u>blindly</u> into a GCSE course — find out what you're facing.

You'll have to do **Three Exams**

See pages 164-175 for more on geographical skills.

GCSE Geography's divided into <u>four units</u> — <u>Unit 1: Living with the Physical Environment</u>, <u>Unit 2: Challenges in the Human Environment</u>, <u>Unit 3: Geographical Applications</u> and <u>Unit 4: Geographical Skills</u>.

You'll have to do <u>three exams</u> — <u>one</u> on each of <u>units 1, 2 and 3</u>. <u>Unit 4</u> is assessed in <u>all three</u> exams. <u>All</u> your <u>exams</u> will take place at the <u>end of the course</u>.

Unit 1: Physical Environment

Unit 1 is divided into <u>three sections</u> (A, B and C) and <u>twelve themes</u>. You <u>don't</u> have to study <u>all</u> of the themes in <u>Sections B</u> and <u>C</u>.

<u>Section A: The Challenge of Natural Hazards</u>
* Natural Hazards
* Tectonic Hazards
* Weather Hazards
* Climate Change

<u>Section B: The Living World</u>

If you're not sure which of the optional themes to revise, check with your teacher.

* Ecosystems
* Tropical Rainforests
* EITHER Hot Deserts OR Cold Environments

<u>Section C: Physical Landscapes in the UK</u>
* UK Physical Landscapes
* TWO FROM Coastal Landscapes, River Landscapes OR Glacial Landscapes in the UK

Here's how <u>Paper 1</u> is structured:

1 hour 30 minutes	88 marks in total	35% of your final mark

Unit 2: Human Environment

Unit 2 is divided into <u>three sections</u> (A, B and C). Section C is split into <u>four themes</u>. You <u>don't</u> have to study <u>all</u> of the themes in <u>Section C</u>.

<u>Section A: Urban Issues and Challenges</u>

<u>Section B: The Changing Economic World</u>

<u>Section C: The Challenge of Resource Management</u>
* Resource Management
* EITHER Food OR Water OR Energy

Here's how <u>Paper 2</u> is structured:

1 hour 30 minutes	88 marks in total	35% of your final mark

This book follows the same <u>structure</u> as the course. For example:

<u>Unit 1B — Hot Deserts</u> covers everything in:
* <u>Unit 1</u>: Living with the Physical Environment,
* <u>Section B</u>: The Living World,
* Theme: <u>Hot Deserts</u>.

Unit 3: Geographical Applications

There <u>isn't</u> any <u>new content</u> for you to learn in Unit 3, it's all about <u>applying</u> what you <u>already know</u>.

It's divided into <u>two sections</u>:

<u>Section A: Issue Evaluation</u>
* You'll get some material <u>12 weeks before</u> the exam. You have to <u>analyse</u> and <u>interpret</u> it, then answer questions in the exam on a <u>related issue</u>.

<u>Section B: Fieldwork</u>
* In the exam, you'll have to write about general <u>fieldwork techniques</u>, as well as <u>geographical enquiries</u> (i.e. fieldwork) that you have <u>done yourself</u>.

You have to answer <u>all the questions</u> in this exam. Here's how <u>Paper 3</u> is structured:

1 hour 15 minutes	76 marks in total	30% of your final mark

There's more information about this paper on pages 160-163.

Be clear on what you've got to do in your exams

It's worthwhile knowing all of this stuff so nothing comes as a shock to you. It also stops you from being the person who tried to answer every single question in the exam — there's a fine line between bravery and self-sabotage...

Natural Hazards

You often see <u>natural hazards</u> on the <u>news</u> — but that's <u>not</u> an excuse to watch telly instead of revising.

A **Natural Hazard** is a **Threat** to **People or Property**

1) A natural hazard is a <u>natural process</u> which <u>could</u> cause <u>death</u>, <u>injury</u> or <u>disruption</u> to humans, or <u>destroy property</u> and possessions.

2) A <u>natural disaster</u> is a natural hazard that has actually <u>happened</u>.

3) Extreme events which do not pose <u>any</u> threat to human activity are <u>not</u> counted as hazards (e.g. a <u>drought</u> in an <u>uninhabited</u> desert or an <u>avalanche</u> in <u>Antarctica</u>).

There are **Two Main Types** of **Natural Hazard**

Most natural hazards can be divided up into <u>two main categories</u>:

1 Geological Hazards

Geological hazards are caused by <u>land</u> and <u>tectonic</u> (see next page) processes.

Examples of geological hazards include <u>volcanoes</u> and <u>earthquakes</u> (see p.3-8), <u>landslides</u> and <u>avalanches</u>.

2 Meteorological Hazards

Meteorological hazards are caused by <u>weather</u> and <u>climate</u>.

Examples of meteorological hazards include <u>tropical storms</u> (p.11-15), other <u>extreme weather</u> (p.16-17) including heatwaves and cold spells, and <u>climate change</u> (p.20-24).

Different **Factors** Affect the **Hazard Risk** from Natural Hazards

<u>Hazard risk</u> is the <u>probability</u> (chance) that a natural hazard <u>occurs</u>. There are several <u>factors</u> affecting hazard risk:

Vulnerability

1) The <u>more people</u> that are <u>in areas exposed</u> to <u>natural hazards</u>, the <u>greater</u> the <u>probability</u> they will be <u>affected</u> by a natural hazard — so the <u>hazard risk</u> is <u>higher</u>.

2) For example, an area with high population density on a <u>flood plain</u> (like <u>Bangladesh</u>) is very vulnerable to <u>flooding</u> caused by extreme weather, and a city at the base of a <u>volcano</u> (like <u>Naples</u>, Italy) is very vulnerable to <u>volcanic eruptions</u>.

Capacity To Cope

1) Natural hazards have to <u>affect human activities</u> to count as a <u>hazard</u>. The <u>better</u> a population can <u>cope</u> with an extreme event, the <u>lower</u> the <u>threat</u>.

2) For example, <u>higher income countries</u> (HICs) are <u>better</u> able to <u>cope</u> with <u>flooding</u> because they can afford to build <u>flood defences</u>, <u>evacuate</u> people in a disaster and <u>repair</u> damage afterwards.

Nature of Natural Hazards

1) <u>Type</u> — the <u>hazard risk</u> from <u>some</u> hazards is <u>greater</u> than <u>others</u>. E.g. <u>tropical storms</u> can be <u>predicted</u> and monitored, giving people time to <u>evacuate to safety</u>. But <u>earthquakes</u> happen <u>very suddenly</u>, with no warning, so it's <u>much harder</u> to protect people.

2) <u>Frequency</u> — some natural hazards occur <u>more often</u> than <u>others</u>, <u>increasing</u> the <u>hazard risk</u>.

3) <u>Magnitude</u> — <u>more severe</u> natural hazards cause <u>greater effects</u> than <u>less severe</u> natural hazards. E.g. a <u>magnitude 9.0</u> earthquake struck Japan in 2011 and <u>killed</u> over <u>15 000 people</u>. When a <u>6.3 magnitude</u> earthquake struck L'Aquila, Italy, around <u>300 people died</u> (see p.7).

Natural hazards are extreme events that pose a threat to people

If you can get your head around the definitions on this page it will set you up well for the rest of the topic. Remember, not all hazards were created equal — the risk from natural hazards is affected by a range of factors.

Tectonic Plates

The <u>Earth's surface</u> is made of <u>huge floating plates</u> that are constantly moving...

The Earth's Surface is Separated into **Tectonic Plates**

1) The <u>core</u> of the Earth is a ball of solid (inner) and liquid (outer) <u>iron and nickel</u>.

2) Around the core is the <u>mantle</u>, which is <u>semi-molten rock</u> that <u>moves very slowly</u>.

3) The <u>outer layer</u> of the Earth is the <u>crust</u>.

4) The crust is <u>divided</u> into slabs called <u>tectonic plates</u> (they float on the mantle). Plates are made of <u>two types</u> of crust — <u>continental</u> and <u>oceanic</u>:

- <u>Continental crust</u> is <u>thicker</u> (30-50 km) and <u>less dense</u>.

- <u>Oceanic crust</u> is <u>thinner</u> (5-10 km) and <u>more dense</u>.

5) The <u>plates</u> are <u>moving</u> because of convection currents in the <u>mantle underneath</u> the crust.

6) The places where plates meet are called <u>plate margins</u> or <u>plate boundaries</u>.

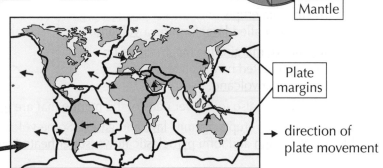

Crust
Outer core
Inner core
Mantle

Plate margins

→ direction of plate movement

There are **Three Types** of **Plate Margin**

1 Destructive Margins

Destructive margins are where two plates are <u>moving towards</u> each other, e.g. along the west coast of South America.

Where an <u>oceanic plate</u> meets a <u>continental plate</u>, the denser <u>oceanic</u> plate is <u>forced down</u> into the mantle and <u>destroyed</u>. This often creates <u>volcanoes</u> and <u>ocean trenches</u> (very deep sections of the ocean floor where the oceanic plate goes down).

Where <u>two continental plates</u> meet, the plates <u>collide</u>, and the ground is <u>folded</u> and <u>forced upwards</u> to create <u>mountain ranges</u>.

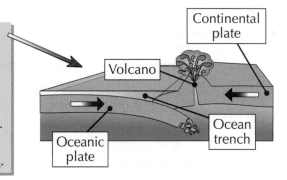

Continental plate
Volcano
Ocean trench
Oceanic plate

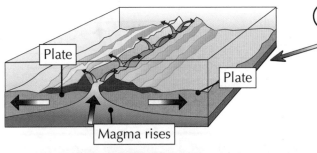

Plate
Plate
Magma rises

2 Constructive Margins

Constructive margins are where two plates are <u>moving away</u> from each other, e.g. at the mid-Atlantic ridge. <u>Magma</u> (molten rock) <u>rises</u> from the mantle to fill the gap and <u>cools</u>, <u>creating new crust</u>.

3 Conservative Margins

Conservative margins are where two plates are <u>moving sideways</u> past each other, or are moving in the <u>same direction</u> but at <u>different speeds</u>, e.g. along the west coast of the USA. Crust <u>isn't created</u> or <u>destroyed</u>.

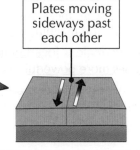

Plates moving sideways past each other

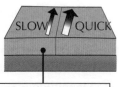

SLOW QUICK

Plates moving in the same direction at different speeds

REVISION TIP

Earth's structure = core, then mantle, then crust on the outside

Make sure you understand the Earth's structure and what tectonic plates are. Practise sketching and labelling the diagrams at the bottom of the page to learn the types of margin too.

Volcanoes and Earthquakes

Where plates meet, <u>volcanoes</u> and <u>earthquakes</u> can occur.

Volcanoes are Found at **Destructive** and **Constructive Plate Margins**

1) At <u>destructive plate margins</u> the <u>oceanic plate</u> goes <u>under</u> the <u>continental plate</u> because it's <u>more dense</u>.

- The <u>oceanic plate</u> moves down into the <u>mantle</u>, where it's <u>melted</u> and <u>destroyed</u>.
- A <u>pool</u> of <u>magma</u> forms.
- The <u>magma rises</u> through <u>cracks</u> in the crust called <u>vents</u>.
- The magma <u>erupts</u> onto the surface (where it's called <u>lava</u>) forming a <u>volcano</u>.

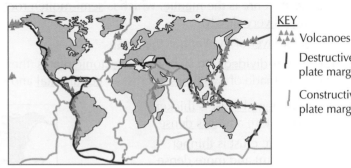

KEY
▲▲▲ Volcanoes
| Destructive plate margin
| Constructive plate margin

2) At <u>constructive margins</u> the magma <u>rises up</u> into the <u>gap</u> created by the plates moving apart, forming a <u>volcano</u>.

3) Some volcanoes also form over parts of the <u>mantle</u> that are <u>really hot</u> (called <u>hotspots</u>), e.g. in Hawaii.

4) When a volcano erupts, it emits <u>lava</u> and <u>gases</u>. Some volcanoes emit <u>lots</u> of <u>ash</u>, which can <u>cover land</u>, <u>block out</u> the <u>sun</u> and form <u>pyroclastic flows</u> (<u>super-heated</u> currents of <u>gas</u>, <u>ash</u> and <u>rock</u>).

Earthquakes Occur at **All Three** Types of **Plate Margin**

1) Earthquakes are caused by the <u>tension</u> that builds up at <u>all three</u> types of <u>plate margin</u>:

<u>Destructive margins</u> — <u>tension builds up</u> when one plate gets <u>stuck</u> as it's moving down past the other into the mantle.

<u>Constructive margins</u> — <u>tension builds</u> along <u>cracks within the plates</u> as they move away from each other.

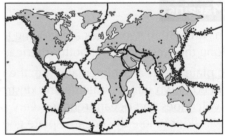

KEY
⠿ Earthquakes
| Plate margin

<u>Conservative margins</u> — tension builds up when plates that are grinding past each other get <u>stuck</u>.

2) The plates eventually <u>jerk past each other</u>, sending out <u>shock waves</u> (vibrations). These vibrations are the <u>earthquake</u>.

3) The shock waves <u>spread out</u> from the <u>focus</u> — the point <u>in</u> the Earth where the earthquake <u>starts</u>. Near the focus the waves are <u>stronger</u> and cause <u>more damage</u>.

4) The <u>epicentre</u> is the point <u>on the Earth's surface</u> <u>straight above</u> the <u>focus</u>.

5) Earthquakes are measured using the <u>moment magnitude scale</u>:

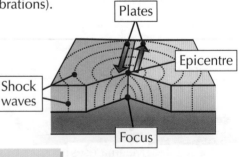

Plates
Epicentre
Shock waves
Focus

- The moment magnitude scale measures the amount of <u>energy released</u> by an earthquake (called the <u>magnitude</u>).
- The moment magnitude scale is <u>logarithmic</u> — so a magnitude 7 earthquake is <u>ten times more powerful</u> than a magnitude 6 earthquake.
- <u>Magnitude 6</u> and below earthquakes normally only cause <u>slight damage</u> to <u>buildings</u>, although they can be <u>worse</u> in very built up areas.
- <u>Magnitude 7</u> and above earthquakes can cause <u>major damage</u> and <u>deaths</u>.

Damage after the magnitude 7.8 earthquake in Nepal in 2015

Learn how and where volcanoes and earthquakes form

You'll never have to draw a map like those above, but you should have some idea of where tectonic hazards occur.

Earthquakes — Effects and Responses

Earthquakes have a load of really <u>serious effects</u>, as well as being pretty exciting to learn about.

Earthquakes have **Primary** and **Secondary Effects...**

The <u>primary effects</u> of an <u>earthquake</u> are the <u>immediate impacts</u> of the ground shaking.
The <u>secondary effects</u> happen <u>later on</u>, often as a <u>result</u> of the primary effects.

1 Primary Effects

1) <u>Buildings</u> and <u>bridges collapse</u>, and <u>homes</u> are <u>destroyed</u>.
2) People are <u>injured</u> or <u>killed</u> by <u>collapsed buildings</u> and <u>falling debris</u>.
3) <u>Roads</u>, <u>railways</u>, <u>ports</u> and <u>airports</u> are <u>damaged</u>.
4) <u>Electricity cables</u>, <u>gas</u> and <u>water pipes</u> and <u>communications networks</u> are damaged, <u>cutting off</u> supplies.

2 Secondary Effects

1) Earthquakes can <u>trigger landslides</u> and <u>tsunamis</u> — these <u>destroy more</u> buildings and cause <u>more injuries</u> and <u>deaths</u>.
2) <u>Leaking gas</u> can be <u>ignited</u>, <u>starting fires</u>.
3) People are left <u>homeless</u> and could <u>die</u>, e.g. from <u>cold</u>.
4) There's a <u>shortage</u> of <u>clean water</u> and a <u>lack</u> of proper <u>sanitation</u> — this makes it <u>easier</u> for <u>diseases</u> to <u>spread</u>.
5) Due to <u>blocked</u> or <u>destroyed</u> roads, <u>aid</u> and <u>emergency vehicles</u> can't get through, and <u>trade</u> is difficult.
6) <u>Businesses</u> are <u>damaged</u> or <u>destroyed</u>, causing <u>unemployment</u> and <u>lost income</u>, and tourists can be put off visiting the area.
7) <u>Repairs</u> and <u>reconstruction</u> can be <u>very expensive</u>, so can <u>weaken</u> a country's <u>economy</u>.

> Tsunamis are a series of enormous waves caused when huge amounts of water get displaced, e.g. by an earthquake under the ocean floor.

Roads can buckle and crack.

...Which Trigger **Immediate** and **Long-Term** Responses

Some effects of earthquakes have to be dealt with <u>immediately</u> to stop <u>further loss of life</u>, <u>injuries</u> or <u>damage to property</u>. Others are dealt with in the <u>longer term</u>:

Immediate Responses

1) <u>Rescue</u> people <u>trapped</u> by <u>collapsed buildings</u>, and <u>treat injured people</u>.
2) <u>Recover dead bodies</u> to prevent spread of <u>disease</u>.
3) Put out <u>fires</u>.
4) Set up <u>temporary shelters</u> for people whose <u>homes</u> have been <u>damaged</u> or <u>destroyed</u>.
5) Provide temporary supplies of <u>water</u>, <u>food</u>, <u>electricity</u>, gas and <u>communications systems</u> if regular supplies have been <u>damaged</u>.
6) <u>Foreign governments</u> or <u>charities</u> may send <u>aid workers</u>, <u>supplies</u>, <u>equipment</u> or <u>financial donations</u> to the areas affected.
7) <u>Tech companies</u> may set up <u>disaster response tools</u>, allowing damage to be <u>recorded</u> and people to <u>confirm</u> their <u>safety</u>, e.g. Google Crisis Response™ service.

Long-Term Responses

1) <u>Re-house</u> people who lost their homes.
2) <u>Repair</u> or <u>rebuild</u> damaged <u>buildings</u>, <u>roads</u>, <u>railways</u> and <u>bridges</u>.
3) <u>Reconnect</u> broken electricity, water, gas and communications connections.
4) If necessary, <u>improve building regulations</u> so that buildings are <u>more resistant</u> to damage from earthquakes.
5) Set up <u>initiatives</u> to help <u>economic recovery</u>, e.g. by <u>promoting tourism</u>.

Primary effects are ones caused directly by the ground shaking

Secondary effects are the ones that happen later on. Earthquakes cause various nasty impacts and you should be clear on which are primary and which are secondary. It's a good idea to learn a few of each for the exams.

Volcanoes — Effects and Responses

People living near a volcano can be <u>seriously affected</u> if it erupts — and <u>not</u> all the effects happen <u>straight away</u>. If an eruption does occur, there are lots of ways that people <u>respond</u> to try and help those affected.

Volcanic Eruptions also have Primary and Secondary Effects...

1 Primary Effects

1) <u>Buildings</u> and <u>roads</u> are <u>destroyed</u> by <u>lava flows</u> and <u>pyroclastic flows</u>. <u>Buildings</u> may also <u>collapse</u> if <u>enough ash falls on them</u>.

2) <u>People</u> and <u>animals</u> are <u>injured</u> or <u>killed</u> by <u>pyroclastic flows</u>, <u>lava flows</u> and <u>falling rocks</u>.

3) <u>Crops</u> are <u>damaged</u> and <u>water supplies</u> are <u>contaminated</u> when <u>ash</u> falls on them.

4) <u>People</u>, <u>animals</u> and <u>plants</u> are <u>suffocated</u> by <u>volcanic gases</u>.

2 Secondary Effects

1) <u>Mudflows</u> (also called <u>lahars</u>) form when <u>volcanic material mixes</u> with <u>water</u>, e.g. from <u>heavy rainfall</u> or <u>snow melt</u>. Mudflows and <u>landslides</u> cause more <u>destruction</u>, <u>death</u> and <u>injury</u>.

2) <u>Flooding</u> can be caused by <u>hot</u> rock, ash and gas <u>melting ice</u> and <u>snow</u> on the volcano. Rock and ash can <u>clog up rivers</u> and <u>dams</u>, making <u>flooding worse</u>.

3) <u>Transport networks</u> are blocked or destroyed so <u>aid</u> and <u>emergency vehicles can't get through</u>, and <u>trade</u> is <u>difficult</u>.

4) People are left <u>homeless</u>. <u>Damaged</u> or <u>destroyed</u> businesses cause <u>unemployment</u> and loss of income.

5) <u>Tourism</u> can be <u>disrupted</u> straight after an eruption — but often it can <u>increase afterwards</u> with tourists interested in seeing volcanoes.

6) <u>Ash</u> makes fields <u>more fertile</u> once it's broken down.

7) <u>Recovering</u> after an eruption can take a <u>very long time</u> and cost a <u>huge amount</u> of money, weakening a country's economy.

Montserrat's capital city had to be abandoned after an eruption.

...Which also lead to Immediate and Long-Term Responses

Immediate Responses

1) <u>Evacuate</u> people before the eruption, if it was <u>predicted</u>, or evacuate <u>as soon as possible</u> after the eruption starts.

2) Provide <u>food</u>, <u>drink</u> and <u>shelter</u> for evacuated people.

3) Treat people <u>injured</u> by the eruption, e.g. from falling debris or ash inhalation.

4) <u>Rescue</u> anyone cut off by <u>damage</u> to <u>roads</u> or <u>bridges</u>.

5) Provide temporary supplies of <u>electricity</u>, <u>gas</u> and <u>communications</u> systems if regular supplies have been <u>damaged</u>.

6) <u>Foreign governments</u> or <u>charities</u> may send <u>aid workers</u>, <u>supplies</u>, <u>equipment</u> or <u>financial donations</u> to the areas affected.

7) <u>Tech companies</u> may set up <u>disaster response tools</u> allowing damage to be <u>recorded</u> and people to <u>confirm</u> their <u>safety</u>, e.g. Google Crisis Response™ service.

Long-Term Responses

1) <u>Repair</u> and <u>rebuild</u> if possible, or <u>resettle</u> affected people elsewhere.

2) <u>Repair</u> and <u>reconnect</u> <u>infrastructure</u> (<u>roads</u>, <u>rail</u>, <u>power lines</u> and <u>communication networks</u> etc.).

3) <u>Improve</u>, <u>repair</u> and <u>update</u> monitoring and evacuation plans.

4) <u>Boost the economy</u> if possible, e.g. by attracting <u>tourists</u> to see the volcano and its effects.

EXAM TIP

Immediate responses are those that happen straight away

Make sure you read the questions in the exam carefully — it's no good writing all about treating injured people and providing emergency aid if the question asks you for the long-term responses.

Tectonic Hazards

And you thought I'd forgotten all about the real-world examples.

Tectonic Hazards Affect **Wealthy** and **Less Wealthy** Countries **Differently**

The effects of earthquakes and the responses to them are different in different parts of the world.
A lot depends on how wealthy the part of the world is.

1) Earthquake in Italy, a higher income country:

Place: L'Aquila, Italy
Date: 6th April, 2009
Size: 6.3 on the moment magnitude scale

2) Earthquake in Pakistan, a lower income country:

Place: Kashmir, Pakistan
Date: 8th October, 2005
Size: 7.6 on the moment magnitude scale

Primary Effects

- Around 300 deaths, mostly from collapsed buildings.
- 1500 people were injured.
- Tens of thousands of buildings were damaged or destroyed.
- Over 60 000 people were made homeless.
- A bridge near the town of Fossa collapsed, and a water pipe was broken near the town of Paganica.

- Around 80 000 deaths, mostly from collapsed buildings.
- Tens of thousands of people were injured.
- Hundreds of thousands of buildings were damaged or destroyed, including whole villages.
- Around 3 million people were made homeless.
- Water pipelines and electricity lines were broken, cutting off supply.

Secondary Effects

- Aftershocks hampered rescue efforts and caused more damage.
- Fires in some collapsed buildings caused more damage.
- The broken water pipe near the town of Paganica caused a landslide.
- Electricity and phone services were interrupted, although most were repaired within a day.

- Landslides buried buildings and people. They also blocked access roads and cut off water supplies, electricity supplies and telephone lines.
- Diarrhoea and other diseases spread due to little clean water.
- Freezing winter conditions shortly after the earthquake caused more casualties and meant rescue and rebuilding operations were difficult.

Immediate Responses

- Camps were set up for people made homeless, providing water, food and medical care.
- Ambulances, fire engines and the army were sent in to rescue survivors.
- Cranes and diggers were used to remove rubble.
- Free mobile phones and SIM cards were provided for people who had lost their homes.
- Money was provided by the government to pay rent, and gas and electricity bills were suspended.

- International aid and equipment such as helicopters and rescue dogs were brought in, as well as teams of people from other countries.
- Despite this, help didn't reach many areas for days or weeks, and many people had to be rescued by hand without any equipment or help from emergency services.
- Tents, blankets and medical supplies were distributed, although it took up to a month for them to reach most areas.

Long-Term Responses

- New settlements were built to accommodate over 20 000 residents who used to live in the damaged city centre.
- Most of the city centre is being rebuilt, but there have been criticisms over delays.
- An investigation was set up into why modern buildings weren't built to withstand earthquakes.

- 40 000 people from one destroyed town have been relocated to a new settlement.
- Aid was given to rebuild schools, and government money was given to people to rebuild their homes.
- However, many people had to use the government money to buy food. After 3 years, thousands of people were still living in temporary tents. Some schools were still not rebuilt 10 years after the earthquake, with pupils being taught outside.

The effects of tectonic hazards are not as severe in wealthy areas

The amount of damage an earthquake does, and the number of people that get hurt, are different in different parts of the world. Learn as many facts and figures as you can for a tectonic hazard in a rich and in a poor country.

Living With Tectonic Hazards

Plenty of people live in areas affected by tectonic hazards because, most of the time, the hazards keep pretty quiet...

Lots of **People Live** in Areas at **Risk** from **Tectonic Hazards**

There are a few reasons why people choose to live close to volcanoes or in areas vulnerable to earthquakes:

1) They've always lived there — moving away may mean leaving friends and family.
2) They're employed in the area. If people move they would have to find new jobs.
3) They're confident of support from their government after an earthquake or volcanic eruption, e.g. to help rebuild houses.
4) Some people think that severe earthquakes or eruptions won't happen again in the area.
5) The soil around volcanoes is fertile because it's full of minerals from volcanic ash and lava. This makes it good for growing crops, which attracts farmers.
6) Volcanoes are tourist attractions — loads of tourists visit volcanoes so lots of people live around volcanoes to work in the tourist industry.

Management can **Reduce** the **Effects** of **Tectonic Hazards**

Management strategies can reduce the number of people killed, injured, made homeless or made unemployed.

Monitoring
1) Networks of seismometers and lasers monitor earth movements, and can be used in early warning systems to give a small but vital amount of warning before a large earthquake occurs.
2) Scientists can monitor the tell-tale signs that come before a volcanic eruption. Things such as tiny earthquakes, escaping gas, and changes in the shape of the volcano (e.g. bulges in the land where magma has built up under it) all mean an eruption is likely.

Prediction
1) Earthquakes cannot be reliably predicted, but by monitoring the movement of tectonic plates scientists can forecast which areas should be prepared for one to occur.
2) Volcanic eruptions can be predicted if the volcano is well-monitored. Predicting when a volcano is going to erupt gives people time to evacuate — this reduces the number of injuries and deaths.

Protection
1) Buildings can be designed to withstand earthquakes, e.g. by using materials like reinforced concrete or building special foundations that absorb an earthquake's energy.
2) Existing buildings and bridges can be strengthened (e.g. by wrapping pillars in steel frames) so they're less likely to collapse under the weight of falling ash or due to shaking from an earthquake.
3) Automatic shut-off switches can be fitted that turn off gas and electricity supplies to prevent fires if an earthquake is detected by a monitoring system.

Planning
1) Future developments can be planned to avoid the areas most at risk from tectonic hazards.
2) Emergency services can train and prepare for disasters, e.g. by practising rescuing people from collapsed buildings or setting up shelters. This will reduce the number of people killed.
3) People can be educated so that they know what to do if an earthquake or eruption happens.
4) Governments can plan evacuation routes to get people out of dangerous areas quickly and safely in case of an earthquake or volcanic eruption. This reduces the number of people killed or injured by things like fires, pyroclastic flows or mudflows.
5) Emergency supplies like blankets, clean water and food can be stockpiled. If a natural hazard is predicted the stockpiles can be moved close to areas likely to be affected.

Predicting a volcanic eruption gives people time to evacuate
Make sure you know how monitoring, prediction, protection and planning can reduce the risks from earthquakes and volcanoes. It's easy to get them muddled up, so try writing out a few points for each.

Worked Exam Questions

Exam questions are the best way to practise what you've learnt. After all, they're exactly what you'll have to do on the big day — so work through this worked example very carefully.

1 Study **Figure 1**, which shows the Earth's tectonic plates and the distribution of volcanoes.

1.1 Describe the global distribution of volcanoes.

Volcanoes are most commonly found along destructive plate margins, but they also occur at constructive and conservative plate margins. Some are also found away from plate margins, e.g. in Hawaii.

[2]

Figure 1

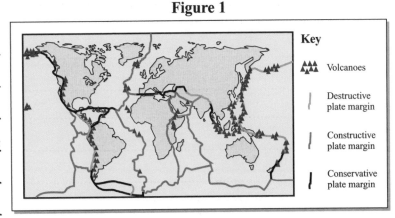

Key

▲▲▲ Volcanoes

| Destructive plate margin

| Constructive plate margin

| Conservative plate margin

1.2 Outline **one** reason for this distribution.

Volcanoes are found at constructive margins because as the plates pull apart, a gap forms between them. Magma rises into this gap, and erupts at the surface, forming volcanoes.

[2]

[Total 4 marks]

2 **Figure 2** shows the effects of two tectonic hazards in different parts of the world. Hazard A occurred in a low-income country and Hazard B in a high-income country.

2.1 Outline **one** possible reason why Hazard B killed fewer people than Hazard A in the first 24 hours after the event.

Hazard B occurred in a high-income country, which would have had more money available to evacuate people from the area, so fewer people would have been killed as the hazard struck.

[2]

Figure 2

	Hazard A	Hazard B
Number of deaths in first 24 hours after event	9084	208
Number of deaths in first 30 days after event	19 790	221
Cost of rebuilding (US $)	4 billion	16 billion

2.2 Explain why the number of deaths **after** the first 24 hours might have increased more significantly in the area affected by Hazard A than Hazard B.

There may not have been money to repair roads and transport systems in the area affected by Hazard A because it has a lower income than the country in which Hazard B occurred. This would have made it difficult for aid and medical care to reach those affected. It may also have taken longer to repair damaged water and sewage systems after Hazard A, causing disease to spread and increasing the death toll.

[4]

[Total 6 marks]

Exam Questions

1   **Figure 1** shows Yokohama, a city in Japan. Yokohama is close to Mount Fuji, an active volcano, and is also prone to earthquakes.

Figure 1

1.1   Explain how buildings and other structures shown in **Figure 1** might have been designed to reduce the effects of earthquakes or volcanic eruptions in the area.

....

....

....

....

....

[4]

1.2   Outline **one** other way in which the effects of tectonic hazards in Yokohama could be reduced.

....

....

[2]

[Total 6 marks]

2   Study **Figure 2**, which shows some of the effects of a volcanic eruption in Montserrat in 1997, and **Figure 3**, which shows some of the effects of an earthquake in Nepal in 2015.

Figure 2

Figure 3

2.1   Using **Figure 2** or **Figure 3** and your own knowledge, outline **two** primary effects of **either** volcanic eruptions **or** earthquakes. Tick the circle of the hazard you have chosen.

Volcanic eruptions ◯   Earthquakes ◯

Effect 1:..

....

Effect 2:..

....

[Total 2 marks]

Global Atmospheric Circulation

There's an overall <u>movement</u> of air between the <u>equator</u> and the <u>poles</u> that affects the Earth's <u>climate</u>.

Air **Circulates** between **High** and **Low Pressure Belts** as **Surface Winds**

1) <u>Winds</u> are <u>large scale movements of air</u> caused by <u>differences in air pressure</u>.

2) Differences in air pressure are caused by <u>differences in temperature</u> between the <u>equator</u> and the <u>poles</u>. Winds move <u>FROM</u> the areas of <u>high</u> pressure <u>TO</u> the areas of <u>low pressure</u>.

3) Winds are part of <u>global atmospheric circulation</u> loops (or <u>cells</u>). These loops have <u>warm rising air</u> which creates a <u>low pressure belt</u>, and <u>cool falling air</u> which creates a <u>high pressure belt</u>.

4) There are three loops in each hemisphere. Here's how it all works:

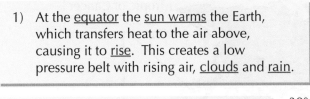

1) At the <u>equator</u> the <u>sun warms</u> the Earth, which transfers heat to the air above, causing it to <u>rise</u>. This creates a low pressure belt with rising air, <u>clouds</u> and <u>rain</u>.

2) As the air rises it <u>cools</u> and <u>moves out</u> to 30° north and south of the equator.

3) <u>30° north and south</u> of the equator the <u>cool air sinks</u>, creating a <u>high pressure belt</u> with <u>cloudless skies</u> and <u>very low rainfall</u>.

4) The cool air reaches the ground surface and moves as surface winds either <u>back to the equator</u> or <u>towards the poles</u>:

- Surface winds blowing towards the <u>equator</u> are called <u>trade winds</u>.

- They blow from the SE in the southern hemisphere and from the NE in the northern hemisphere. At the equator, these <u>trade winds meet</u> and are heated by the sun. This causes them to rise and form <u>clouds</u>.

- Surface winds blowing towards the <u>poles</u> are called <u>westerlies</u>. They blow from the NW in the southern hemisphere and from the SW in the northern hemisphere.

5) <u>60° north and south of the equator</u> the warmer surface winds meet colder air from the poles. The warmer air is less dense than the cold air so it <u>rises</u>, creating <u>low pressure</u>.

6) Some of the air <u>moves back</u> towards the equator, and the rest moves towards the <u>poles</u>.

7) At the <u>poles</u> the <u>cool air sinks</u>, creating <u>high pressure</u>. The high pressure air is drawn back towards the equator as <u>surface winds</u>.

<u>Global atmospheric circulation</u> causes areas to have some types of weather more often than others — it affects the Earth's <u>climate</u>. For example, the UK has a lot of <u>low pressure</u> weather systems that are <u>blown in</u> from the <u>Atlantic Ocean</u> on <u>westerly</u> winds. These bring <u>wet</u> and <u>windy weather</u>.

Pressure belts and surface winds are determined by global circulation

Air moves in loops (called cells) from the equator to the poles and back. This gives us surface winds and creates belts of high and low pressure that affect the climate — they're why deserts are so dry and rainforests are so wet.

Tropical Storms

Tropical storms are <u>intense low pressure</u> weather systems with <u>heavy rain</u> and <u>strong winds</u> that spiral around the <u>centre</u>. They have a few different names (<u>hurricanes</u>, <u>typhoons</u>, and <u>cyclones</u>), but they're all the <u>same thing</u>.

Tropical Storms **Develop** over **Warm Water**

1) Tropical storms develop when the <u>sea temperature</u> is <u>27 °C or higher</u> and when the <u>wind shear</u> (the <u>difference</u> in <u>windspeed</u>) between <u>higher</u> and <u>lower</u> parts of the atmosphere is <u>low</u>.

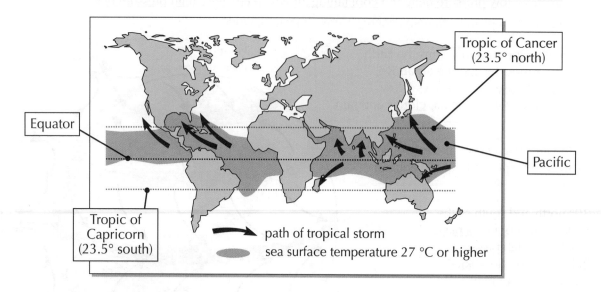

Equator

Tropic of Cancer (23.5° north)

Pacific

Tropic of Capricorn (23.5° south)

→ path of tropical storm

⬭ sea surface temperature 27 °C or higher

2) <u>Warm</u>, <u>moist</u> air <u>rises</u> and <u>condensation</u> occurs. This releases huge amounts of <u>energy</u>, which makes the storms <u>powerful</u>. The <u>rising air</u> creates an area of <u>low pressure</u>, which increases <u>surface winds</u>.

3) Tropical storms <u>move towards the west</u> because of the <u>easterly winds</u> near the equator.

4) The Earth's <u>rotation</u> deflects the paths of the winds, which causes the storms to <u>spin</u>.

5) The storm <u>gets stronger</u> due to <u>energy</u> from the warm <u>water</u>, so <u>wind speeds increase</u>. They <u>lose strength</u> when they move over <u>land</u> or <u>cooler water</u> because the energy supply from the warm water is <u>cut off</u>.

6) Most tropical storms occur between <u>5°</u> and <u>30°</u> north and south of the equator — any further from the equator and the water <u>isn't warm enough</u>. The <u>majority</u> of storms occur in the <u>northern hemisphere</u> (especially over the <u>Pacific</u>), in <u>late summer</u> and <u>autumn</u>, when sea temperatures are <u>highest</u>.

Tropical storms form at low latitudes — between 5° and 30° N & S

Since even the top scientists haven't worked it out yet, you don't need to know exactly how tropical storms form, but you might be asked to outline the main steps in their formation in the exam.

Tropical Storms

Tropical storms have a <u>distinctive shape</u> and <u>structure</u>. This makes them quite easy to spot on <u>satellite images</u>...

Learn the **Features** and **Structure** of a Tropical Storm

Tropical storms are <u>circular</u> in shape, <u>hundreds of kilometres wide</u> and usually last <u>7-14 days</u>. They spin <u>anticlockwise</u> in the <u>northern</u> hemisphere, and <u>clockwise</u> in the <u>southern</u> hemisphere.

The <u>centre</u> of the storm is called the <u>eye</u> — it's up to <u>50 km across</u> and is caused by <u>descending air</u>. There's very <u>low pressure</u>, <u>light winds</u>, <u>no clouds</u>, <u>no rain</u> and a <u>high temperature</u> in the eye.

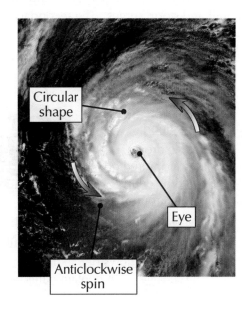

Circular shape

Eye

Anticlockwise spin

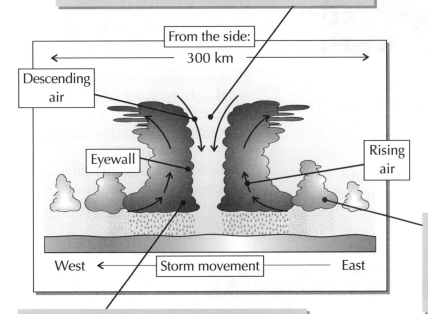

From the side:

300 km

Descending air

Eyewall

Rising air

West

Storm movement

East

Towards the <u>edges</u> of the storm the <u>wind speed falls</u>, the <u>clouds</u> become <u>smaller</u> and more <u>scattered</u>, the <u>rain</u> becomes <u>less intense</u> and the <u>temperature increases</u>.

The eye is surrounded by the <u>eyewall</u>, where there's <u>spiralling rising air</u>, very <u>strong winds</u> (around 160 km per hour), <u>storm clouds</u>, <u>torrential rain</u> and a <u>low temperature</u>.

Climate Change May Affect Tropical Storms

1) <u>Global temperatures</u> are expected to <u>rise</u> as a result of climate change. This means that <u>more</u> of the world's oceans could be <u>above 27 °C</u>, so <u>more places</u> in the world may experience tropical storms.

2) Oceans will <u>stay</u> at 27 °C or higher for <u>more of the year</u> — so the <u>number</u> of tropical storms each year could <u>increase</u>.

3) Higher temperatures also mean tropical storms will be <u>stronger</u>, meaning they could cause <u>more damage</u>.

Rising temperatures mean warmer oceans, which might mean more storms

Climate change could mean that tropical storms occur over a larger area, and their strength and frequency may increase too. You should learn the features and structure of a tropical storm, so you won't be fazed by anything the examiners throw at you. Try testing yourself by sketching out the diagram above — remember the labels.

Tropical Storms — Effects and Responses

When tropical storms hit land, they can have serious effects on people and the environment.

Tropical Storms have Primary and Secondary Effects...

The primary effects of a tropical storm are the immediate impacts of strong winds, high rainfall and storm surges. The secondary effects are the effects that happen later on.

> Storm surges are large rises in sea level caused by the low pressure and high winds of a storm.

1 Primary Effects

1) Buildings and bridges are destroyed.
2) Rivers and coastal areas flood.
3) People drown, or they're injured or killed by debris that's blown around.
4) Roads, railways, ports and airports are damaged.
5) Electricity cables are damaged, cutting off supplies.
6) Sewage overflows due to flooding. The sewage often contaminates water supplies.

The more settlements built and businesses set up in an area, the greater the effect because there are more people and properties to be affected by a tropical storm.

2 Secondary Effects

1) People are left homeless, which can cause distress, poverty and ill health or death due to lack of shelter.
2) There's a shortage of clean water and a lack of proper sanitation — this makes it easier for diseases to spread.
3) Roads are blocked or destroyed so aid and emergency vehicles can't get through.
4) Businesses are damaged or destroyed, causing unemployment.
5) There can be shortages of food if crops are damaged, livestock are killed or supply lines are blocked.

...Which Trigger Immediate and Long-Term Responses

Immediate responses happen when a storm is forecast to hit a populated area, while it is happening, and immediately afterwards.

Long-term responses are to do with restoring the area to the condition it was before the storm struck, and reducing the impact of future storms.

Immediate Responses

1) Evacuate people before the storm arrives.
2) Rescue people who have been cut off by flooding and treat injured people.
3) Set up temporary shelters for people whose homes have been flooded or damaged.
4) Provide temporary supplies of water, food, electricity, gas and communications systems if regular supplies have been damaged.
5) Recover any dead bodies to prevent the spread of disease.
6) Foreign governments or NGOs may send aid workers, supplies, equipment or financial donations to the area.
7) Tech companies may set up disaster response tools, allowing damage to be recorded, people to confirm their safety and alerts about areas at risk from the storm to be shared.

Long-Term Responses

1) Repair homes or rehouse people who have been displaced due to damaged buildings.
2) Repair or replace damaged infrastructure.
3) Repair and improve flood defence systems, e.g. levees and flood gates.
4) Improve forecasting techniques to give people more warning in the future.
5) Provide aid, grants or subsidies to residents to repair and strengthen homes.
6) Promote economic recovery in the area and encourage people to return to the area, e.g. with tax breaks or other incentives.
7) Improve building regulations so more buildings withstand hurricanes, or change planning rules so homes can't be built in the most risky areas.

Tropical Storms — Effects and Responses

Hurricane Katrina struck Mississippi & Louisiana, USA, in August 2005

The effects of Hurricane Katrina were severe, particularly in New Orleans where flood defences failed.

Primary Effects

1) More than 1800 people were killed.
2) 300 000 houses were destroyed.
3) Large areas were flooded, including 80% of New Orleans.
4) 3 million people were left without electricity.
5) Some bridges collapsed.
6) Coastal habitats were damaged.

Secondary Effects

1) Hundreds of thousands of people were made homeless.
2) 230 000 jobs were lost from damaged businesses.
3) Water supplies were polluted with sewage and chemicals.
4) The total cost of the damage was estimated at $150 billion.

There were immediate and longer term responses to the effects:

Immediate Responses

1) 70-80% of New Orleans residents were evacuated before the hurricane reached land.
2) Mississippi and Louisiana declared states of emergency — they set up control centres and emergency shelters, and stockpiled supplies.
3) The coastguard, police, fire service and army rescued over 50 000 people.
4) Charities collected donations and provided aid, including millions of hot meals.

Longer Term Responses

1) The US government provided over 16 billion dollars for the rebuilding of homes, and provided funds to repair other essential infrastructure.
2) The US Army recommended that buildings are rebuilt on stilts or not rebuilt at all in very low-lying areas.
3) Repaired and improved flood defences for New Orleans costing 14.5 billion dollars were completed in 2013.

There are Many Ways of Reducing the Effects of Tropical Storms

Prediction

1) Scientists use data from things like radar, satellites and aircraft to monitor storms. Computer models are then used to calculate a predicted path for the storm.
2) Predicting where and when a tropical storm is going to happen gives people time to evacuate and protect their homes and businesses, e.g. by boarding up windows.

Planning

1) Future developments, e.g. new houses, can be planned to avoid the areas most at risk.
2) Emergency services can train and prepare for disasters, e.g. by practising rescuing people from flooded areas with helicopters. This reduces the number of people killed.
3) Governments can plan evacuation routes to get people away from storms quickly.

Protection

1) Buildings can be designed to withstand tropical storms, e.g. by using reinforced concrete. Buildings can also be put on stilts so they're safe from floodwater.
2) Flood defences can be built along rivers (e.g. levees) and coasts (e.g. sea walls).
3) All of these reduce the number of buildings destroyed, so fewer people will be killed, injured, made homeless and made unemployed.

The facts on Katrina make for grim reading

 If you concentrate on learning the specific details of the effects and responses to Hurricane Katrina, you'll find you've also learned some of the general effects and responses from the previous page.

UK Weather Hazards

Weather hazards are quite common in the UK — and it's not just about rain, either...

The UK Experiences Lots of Different Weather Hazards

Rain

1) Too much rain in too short a time can cause flooding, which can damage homes and possessions, disrupt transport networks and cause death by drowning.

2) It can also force businesses to close, and recovering from flooding can cost millions of pounds.

Wind

1) Strong winds (gales) can damage properties and cause disruption to transport.

2) Uprooted trees and debris can injure or kill people.

3) Forests can be damaged when trees are blown over.

4) Winds are strongest in coastal areas of the UK, particularly the west coast, and in upland areas.

Snow and Ice

1) Snow and ice can cause injuries due to slipping and deaths due to the cold.

2) Schools and businesses can be forced to shut, and major disruption to road, rail and air travel can occur causing economic impacts.

3) Cold snaps can damage crops and other plants.

Thunderstorms

1) Heavy rain, lightning and strong winds occur in thunderstorms.

2) They are most common in summer in the south and east of the UK.

3) Lightning can occasionally cause death and can cause fires that damage property or the environment.

Hailstorms

Hailstorms make driving very dangerous and can damage property and destroy crops.

Heat Waves

1) Sometimes the UK can have long periods of hot weather. This can cause deaths from heat exhaustion or breathing difficulties as pollution builds up in the air.

2) Disruption to transport from rails buckling or roads melting can cause economic impacts — but the tourism industry may benefit from the better weather.

Drought

1) Drought is a lack of precipitation (i.e. not enough rain or snow).

2) Water supplies can run low during a drought, causing economic impacts such as crop failures. Rules to conserve water (like banning hosepipe use) have to be introduced.

Weather in the UK is Becoming More Extreme

1) Temperatures have become more extreme in recent years — December 2010 was the coldest for over 100 years, with severe snow and ice causing several deaths, and school and road closures. But just four months later, April 2011 was the warmest April on record.

2) It's raining more — more rainfall records have been broken in 2010-2014 than in any decade on record, even after only half a decade. 2013 was one of the wettest years on record, and December 2015 was the wettest month ever recorded.

3) Major flooding occurs often — e.g. there was major flooding caused by storms and high rainfall in the Somerset Levels during the winter of 2013-2014, in west Wales in 2012, in Cumbria in 2005, 2009 and 2015-2016 (along with large parts of northern England and parts of Scotland).

The UK has lots of different weather hazards

The weather hazards affecting the UK might not seem as bad as volcanoes, earthquakes or hurricanes. But the effects on people can still be pretty severe — and there's some evidence that weather is getting worse.

Extreme UK Weather

On the whole, UK weather isn't that extreme, but it has its <u>moments</u>. You need to know an <u>example</u> of an <u>extreme weather event</u>, and how <u>management strategies</u> reduced the <u>risk</u> from it.

November 2010 and December 2010 were Extremely Cold

When: <u>25 November 2010</u> to <u>26 December 2010</u>

What: A <u>long</u> period of <u>heavy snow</u> and <u>very cold</u> weather <u>across the UK</u>.

Why: <u>Cold air</u> from <u>northern Europe</u> and <u>Siberia</u> caused <u>two long</u> <u>periods</u> of very cold weather with a brief thaw in between.

Snow covered much of the UK on 8 December 2010.

Social Impacts

- <u>Several</u> people <u>died</u> from <u>hypothermia</u> or <u>accidents</u> due to losing control on <u>icy roads</u>.
- Lots of water pipes <u>froze</u> in the cold weather and <u>burst</u>. When they <u>thawed</u>, the pipes started to <u>leak</u>. <u>40 000 homes</u> and <u>businesses</u> across Northern Ireland were left <u>without water</u>, in some cases for <u>over a week</u>.
- <u>Schools closed</u> on several occasions, including 7000 schools on 2 December, meaning that many parents had to take <u>time off work</u> (if they could get there) to look after their children.

Economic Impacts

- <u>Transport networks</u> were severely <u>disrupted</u>. Some <u>motorways</u> were <u>shut</u>, e.g. part of the <u>M8</u> was <u>closed</u> for <u>two days</u>. Some drivers were <u>trapped</u> in their cars for over <u>15 hours</u>. <u>Trains</u> and <u>flights</u> were also cancelled.
- As a result some people were <u>unable</u> to get to <u>work</u>, affecting the UK's economy.
- The run up to <u>Christmas</u> is a <u>busy</u> time for shops. In 2010 their <u>sales</u> were <u>down</u> as shoppers were <u>put off</u> by the <u>weather</u>.
- The <u>overall economic impact</u> of the cold period was around <u>£1.6 billion</u> — enough to <u>reduce</u> the UK's <u>GDP</u> by about <u>0.5%</u>.

Roads were badly affected.

Environmental Impacts

- <u>Snow</u> covered <u>almost all</u> of the UK on several occasions — to a depth of <u>over 50 cm</u> in some hilly locations.
- The frost <u>damaged crops</u>, especially <u>sugar beet</u>.
- Use of <u>gas</u> and <u>electricity</u> was <u>more than double</u> a normal December, <u>increasing CO_2</u> emissions.

Management Strategies can Reduce the Risk from Weather Hazards

The 2010 cold snap was bad, but it could have been worse if there weren't strategies to reduce the risk:

1) PREDICTION — <u>warning systems</u> gave people <u>time to prepare</u> for extreme weather.
   For example, the Met Office first warned about the cold weather at the <u>start</u> of November.

2) PROTECTION — <u>individuals</u> and <u>local authorities</u> prepared for extreme weather <u>before it happened</u>.
   For example, councils stocked up on <u>gritters</u> and <u>salt supplies</u> to keep roads <u>safe</u> and <u>open</u> in cold weather — although there were some <u>shortages</u> as the cold spell went on.

3) PLANNING — <u>emergency services</u> and <u>local councils</u> planned how to deal with extreme weather events in advance, e.g. they made plans to <u>close schools</u> when it would be too dangerous for people to get there.

REVISION TIP

Cold weather caused problems in November and December 2010

Seriously cold weather causes serious disruption, and so do other weather hazards. You may have studied a different example in class — whichever example you learn, make sure you know the causes and impacts, as well as strategies to reduce the risk of that particular extreme weather event in the UK.

Worked Exam Questions

These exam questions are just like the type you'll get in the exam — except they've got the answers written in for you already. Have a look to see the sorts of things you should be writing.

1 Study **Figure 1**, a photograph of Slidell, Louisiana after Hurricane Katrina in 2005.

1.1 Give **two** primary effects of the tropical storm shown in **Figure 1**.

Figure 1

Effect 1: Buildings were destroyed.

Effect 2: Roads were damaged.

[2]

1.2 Outline **two** immediate responses that could help reduce the effects of an event such as that shown in **Figure 1**.

Response 1:

Evacuate people before the storm arrives.

Response 2: Rescue people who have been cut off by flooding.

[2]

1.3 Outline **two** long-term responses that could help reduce the effects of an event such as that shown in **Figure 1**.

Response 1: Repair homes or rehouse people who have been displaced due to damaged buildings.

Response 2: Repair and improve flood defence systems, e.g. levees and floodgates.

[2]

[Total 6 marks]

2 Study **Figure 2**, a graph showing global temperature change between 1960 and 2015.

2.1 Suggest how the distribution of tropical storms could change in the future if the trend in temperature change shown in **Figure 2** continues.

Tropical storms only form in areas where the

sea temperature is 27 °C or higher.

The graph shows an average global

temperature increase of 0.5 °C over 50 years.

Figure 2

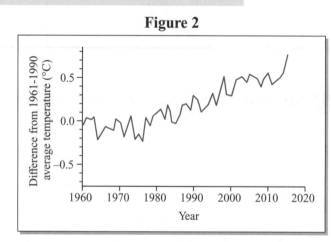

This may have caused ocean temperatures to increase. If the warming continues, larger areas of ocean

will be 27 °C or warmer. This means the area affected by tropical storms will increase in size, with

areas at higher latitudes affected.

[Total 4 marks]

Exam Questions

1   Study **Figure 1**, a photograph of a weather hazard experienced in the UK.

1.1   Outline **two** possible effects of the weather hazard shown in **Figure 1**.

Figure 1

Effect 1:..

....

Effect 2:..

....
[2]

1.2   Suggest **two** possible effects of heat waves in the UK.

Effect 1:...

Effect 2:...
[2]

[Total 4 marks]

2   Study **Figure 2**, a forecast map showing the predicted path of a hurricane over Cuba, approaching Miami, Florida.

Figure 2

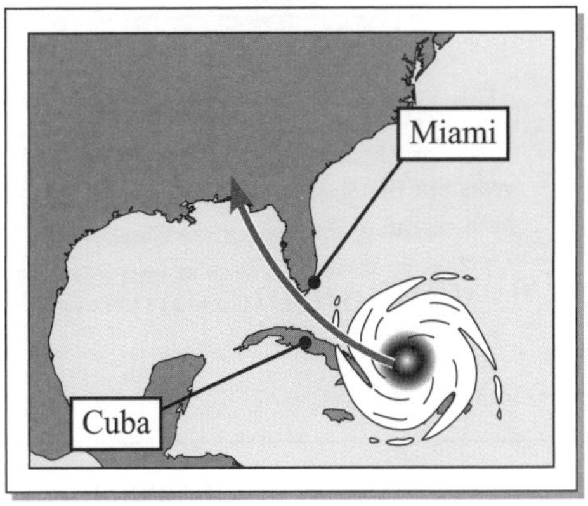

2.1   Explain how this prediction could help to reduce the effects of the storm in Miami.

....

....

....

....
[2]

2.2   Using an example of a tropical storm that you have studied, discuss how immediate and long-term responses helped to reduce its effects.

....

....

....

....

....

....

....
[6]

[Total 8 marks]

Climate Change — The Evidence

We British like to talk about the weather, so global climate change should give us plenty to go on...

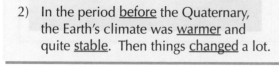

The Earth is **Getting Warmer**

Climate change is any significant change in the Earth's climate over a long period.
The climate constantly changes, it always has, and it always will.

1) The Quaternary period is the most recent geological time period, spanning from about 2.6 million years ago to the present day.

The Quaternary period includes the whole of human history.

2) In the period before the Quaternary, the Earth's climate was warmer and quite stable. Then things changed a lot.

3) During the Quaternary, global temperature has shifted between cold glacial periods that last for around 100 000 years, and warmer interglacial periods that last for around 10 000 years.

This graph shows the last 400 000 years but the glacial-interglacial cycles have been repeating throughout the Quaternary period — there have been at least 20.

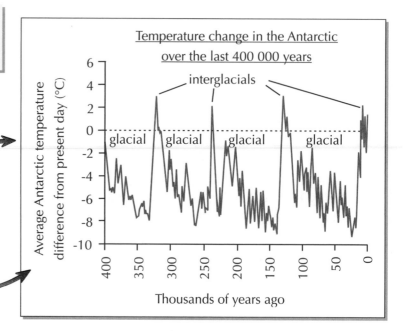

Temperature change in the Antarctic over the last 400 000 years

4) The last glacial period ended around 15 000 years ago. Since then the climate has been warming.

5) Global warming is the term used to describe the sharp rise in global temperatures over the last century. It's a type of climate change.

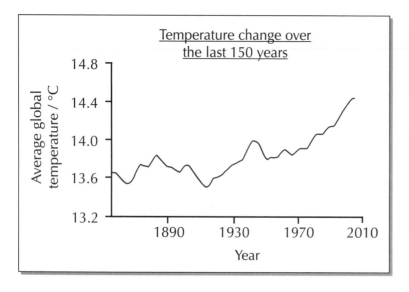

Temperature change over the last 150 years

Temperature has increased rapidly over the last 100 years

These graphs may look complicated, but the main thing to remember is that during the Quaternary period the climate repeatedly went from warm to cold, and then back to warm again. And now it's getting rapidly warmer.

Climate Change — The Evidence

There's information stored in thick <u>ice sheets</u>, deep layers of <u>sediment</u> and in <u>tree rings</u> that scientists can use to find out what the Earth's <u>climate</u> was like <u>thousands of years ago</u>.

Evidence for **Climate Change** Comes from **Many Sources**

Scientists can <u>work out</u> how the climate has <u>changed over time</u> using a range of <u>methods</u>. For example:

Ice and Sediment Cores

1) Ice sheets are made up of <u>layers</u> of ice — <u>one</u> layer is formed each <u>year</u>.
2) Scientists drill into ice sheets to get <u>long cores</u> of ice.
3) By analysing the <u>gases</u> trapped in the layers of ice, they can tell what the <u>temperature</u> was each year.
4) One ice core from <u>Antarctica</u> shows the temperature changes over the last <u>400 000 years</u> (see graph on previous page).
5) The <u>remains</u> of <u>organisms</u> found in cores taken from <u>ocean sediments</u> can also be analysed. These can extend the temperature record back at least <u>5 million years</u>.

Temperature Records

1) Since the <u>1850s</u> global temperatures have been measured accurately using <u>thermometers</u>. This gives a <u>reliable</u> but <u>short-term record</u> of temperature change.
2) <u>Historical records</u> (e.g. harvest dates, newspaper weather reports) can extend the record of climate change a bit <u>further back</u>.

Pollen Analysis

1) <u>Pollen</u> from plants gets <u>preserved</u> in <u>sediment</u>, e.g. at the bottom of lakes or in peat bogs.
2) Scientists can <u>identify</u> and <u>date</u> the preserved pollen to show which <u>species</u> were living at that time.
3) Scientists know the <u>conditions</u> that plants live in <u>now</u>, so preserved pollen from <u>similar plants</u> shows that <u>climate conditions</u> were <u>similar</u>.

Tree Rings

1) As a tree grows it forms a <u>new ring</u> each year — the tree rings are <u>thicker</u> in <u>warm</u>, <u>wet conditions</u>.
2) Scientists take <u>cores</u> and <u>count</u> the rings to find the <u>age</u> of a tree. The <u>thickness</u> of each ring shows what the <u>climate</u> was like.
3) Tree rings are a reliable source of evidence of climate change for the past <u>10 000 years</u>.

Learn the evidence for climate change

There were no thermometers 2.6 million years ago but scientists can reconstruct climates using these clever methods. Climate change is a hot topic, so make sure you learn this stuff inside out before your exam.

Climate Change — Causes

Climate change goes back long before humans roamed this Earth. Some natural factors cause climate change, but in the last 150 years or so human activities have begun to change the climate too.

Some **Natural Factors** are Possible **Causes** of **Climate Change...**

1 Orbital Changes

1) The way the Earth moves round the Sun changes. For example, the path of the Earth's orbit around the Sun changes from an almost perfect circle to an ellipse (an oval) and back again about every 96 000 years.

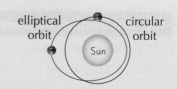

2) These changes affect the amount of solar radiation (how much energy) the Earth receives. If the Earth receives more energy, it gets warmer.

3) Orbital changes may have caused the glacial and interglacial cycles of the Quaternary period.

2 Volcanic Activity

1) Major volcanic eruptions eject large quantities of material into the atmosphere.

2) Some of these particles reflect the Sun's rays back out to space, so the Earth's surface cools.

3) Volcanoes also release CO_2 (a greenhouse gas — see below) but not enough to cause warming.

4) Volcanic activity may cause short-term changes in climate, e.g. the cooling that followed the eruption of Mount Pinatubo in 1991.

3 Solar Output

1) The Sun's output of energy isn't constant — it changes in short cycles of about 11 years, and possibly also in longer cycles of several hundred years.

2) Periods when solar output is reduced may cause the Earth's climate to become cooler in some areas.

3) Most scientists think that changes in solar output don't have a major effect on global climate change.

...and so are **Human Activities**

1) The rate of the recent rise in global temperature (global warming) is unheard of.

2) There's a scientific consensus (general agreement) that human activities are causing global warming by making the greenhouse effect stronger.

3) The greenhouse effect is where greenhouse gases, such as carbon dioxide (CO_2) and methane, absorb outgoing heat, so less is lost to space. It's essential for keeping the planet warm.

4) Too much greenhouse gas in the atmosphere means too much energy is trapped and the planet warms up.

5) Humans are increasing the concentration of greenhouse gases by:

Cement Production

Cement is made from limestone, which contains carbon. When cement is produced, lots of CO_2 is released into the atmosphere.

Burning Fossil Fuels

CO_2 is released into the atmosphere when fossil fuels like coal, oil, natural gas and petrol are burnt, e.g. in thermal power stations or in cars.

Farming

1) Farming of livestock produces a lot of methane — cows love to fart...

2) Rice paddies contribute to global warming, because flooded fields emit methane.

Deforestation

1) Plants remove CO_2 from the atmosphere and convert it into organic matter using photosynthesis.

2) When trees and plants are chopped down, they stop taking in CO_2.

3) CO_2 is also released into the atmosphere when trees are burnt as fuel or to make way for agriculture.

REVISION TIP — Global warming is caused by a stronger greenhouse effect

You may have to explain the causes of climate change in your exam — try writing an explanation (in your own words) of how natural factors and human activities can cause global temperature change.

Effects of Climate Change

Whether it's <u>human</u> or <u>natural</u> factors to blame, scientists are <u>pretty sure</u> climate change is having an <u>impact</u>...

Climate Change Affects the Environment...

Temperatures are <u>expected</u> to <u>rise</u> by <u>0.3-4.8 °C</u> between <u>2005</u> and <u>2100</u>.
This is <u>already</u> causing some <u>major effects</u> on the <u>environment</u>, and will <u>continue</u> to do so:

Environmental Effects

1) <u>Warmer</u> temperatures are causing <u>glaciers</u> to <u>shrink</u> and <u>ice sheets</u> like Greenland to <u>melt</u>. The <u>melting</u> of ice on <u>land</u>, especially from the <u>Greenland</u> and <u>Antarctic ice sheets</u>, means that water <u>stored on land</u> as ice <u>returns</u> to the <u>oceans</u>. This causes <u>sea level rise</u>.

2) <u>Sea ice</u> is also <u>shrinking</u>, leading to the loss of polar habitats.

3) Rising sea levels means <u>low-lying</u> and <u>coastal areas</u>, like the <u>Maldives</u>, will be <u>flooded</u> more <u>regularly</u>. <u>Coastal erosion</u> will <u>increase</u> with sea level rise and some coastal areas will be <u>submerged</u>, so habitats will be <u>lost</u>.

4) Other species are <u>declining</u> due to warming, e.g. some <u>coral reefs</u> are suffering from <u>bleaching</u> due to increasing sea water temperatures.

5) <u>Precipitation patterns</u> are <u>changing</u> — warming is affecting <u>how much rain</u> areas get.

6) The <u>distribution</u> and <u>quantity</u> of some species could change and <u>biodiversity</u> could <u>decrease</u>:
   - Some species are now found in <u>higher latitudes</u> due to warming temperatures.
   - Some <u>habitats</u> are being <u>damaged</u> or <u>destroyed</u> due to climate change — species that are specially <u>adapted</u> to these areas may become <u>extinct</u>.

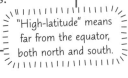

"High-latitude" means far from the equator, both north and south.

...and it Affects People Too

<u>Rising temperatures</u> and <u>climate change</u> don't only affect the environment — there are <u>impacts</u> on <u>people too</u>.

Effects on People

1) In some places <u>deaths</u> due to <u>heat</u> have <u>increased</u> — but deaths due to <u>cold</u> have <u>decreased</u>.

2) Some areas could become so <u>hot and dry</u> that they're <u>difficult</u> or <u>impossible</u> to inhabit. <u>Low-lying coastal areas</u> could be <u>lost</u> to the <u>sea</u> or <u>flood</u> so often that they also become <u>impossible</u> to inhabit. This could lead to <u>migration</u> and <u>overcrowding</u> in other areas.

3) Some areas are <u>struggling</u> to supply <u>enough</u> water for their residents due to <u>problems</u> with <u>water availability</u> caused by changing rainfall patterns. This can lead to <u>political tensions</u>, especially where rivers <u>cross borders</u>.

4) Climate change is affecting <u>farming</u> in <u>different ways</u> around the <u>world</u>:
   - <u>Globally</u>, some crops have <u>suffered</u> from climate change (e.g. <u>maize crops</u> have got <u>smaller</u> due to <u>warming</u> in recent years).
   - But some farmers in <u>high-latitude countries</u> are finding that crops <u>benefit</u> from warmer conditions.

5) <u>Lower crop yields</u> could <u>increase malnutrition</u>, <u>ill health</u> and <u>death</u> from starvation, particularly in lower latitudes.

6) Climate change means the <u>weather</u> is getting <u>more extreme</u>. This means <u>more money</u> has to be <u>spent</u> on <u>predicting</u> extreme weather events, <u>reducing their impacts</u> and <u>rebuilding after</u> them.

Rising temperatures are affecting rainfall patterns and causing ice sheets to melt

Scientists still don't know what the exact impacts of climate change will be, but some effects are already being seen. Make sure you know how climate change could affect both people and the environment.

Managing Climate Change

You've just seen the <u>effects</u> of climate change — some of them are pretty <u>worrying</u>. People have come up with a variety of ways of <u>coping</u>, though, and you need to know about them.

Mitigation Strategies aim to Reduce the Causes of Climate Change

Various strategies aim to <u>reduce</u> the <u>causes</u> of climate change, by <u>reducing</u> the concentration of <u>greenhouse gases</u> in the atmosphere:

Carbon Capture

1) <u>Carbon Capture and Storage</u> (<u>CCS</u>) is a new technology designed to reduce climate change by <u>reducing emissions</u> from <u>fossil fuel</u> burning <u>power stations</u>.

2) CCS involves <u>capturing CO_2</u> and <u>transporting it</u> to places where it can be stored safely, e.g. deep underground.

Planting Trees

Planting trees <u>increases</u> the amount of <u>carbon dioxide</u> that is <u>absorbed</u> from the atmosphere through photosynthesis.

Alternative Energy Production

1) <u>Replacing</u> fossil fuels with nuclear power and renewable energy can help reduce climate change by <u>reducing</u> greenhouse gas emissions from <u>power stations</u>.

2) In the UK, more <u>offshore wind farms</u> are being built, several <u>wave</u> and <u>tidal power projects</u> are planned, and new <u>nuclear power plants</u> are also being planned.

International Agreements

1) From 1997, <u>most countries</u> in the world agreed to <u>monitor</u> and <u>cut greenhouse gas emissions</u> by signing an <u>international agreement</u> called the <u>Kyoto Protocol</u>.

2) Each country was set a <u>target</u>, e.g. the <u>UK</u> agreed to reduce emissions by <u>12.5%</u> by 2012. The UK met the target, actually reducing emissions by an average of <u>22%</u>.

3) The <u>EU</u> has now agreed to cut emissions by <u>20%</u> from their 1990 levels by 2020.

Adaptation Means Responding to Changes Caused by Climate Change

Here are some of the ways that people are <u>adjusting</u> to the effects of <u>climate change</u>:

Changing Agricultural Systems

Changing <u>rainfall patterns</u> and <u>higher temperatures</u> will affect the <u>productivity</u> of existing systems.

1) It may be necessary to plant <u>new crop types</u> that are more <u>suitable</u> to the <u>new climate conditions</u> in an area, e.g. soya, peaches and grapes may be grown in southern England.

2) In some regions, <u>biotechnology</u> is being used to create <u>new crop varieties</u> which are <u>more resistant</u> to extreme weather events, e.g. drought resistant millet is being grown in Kenya.

Managing Water Supply

<u>Dry areas</u> are predicted to get <u>drier</u>, leading to more <u>water shortages</u> — so people need to use water resources more <u>efficiently</u>.

1) <u>Water meters</u> can be installed in people's homes to <u>discourage</u> them from using a lot of water.

2) <u>Rainwater</u> can be <u>collected</u> and <u>waste water</u> can be <u>recycled</u> to make more water available.

Coping with Rising Sea Levels

<u>Sea levels</u> are predicted to <u>rise</u> by up to 82 cm by 2100, which would <u>flood</u> many <u>islands</u> and <u>coastal areas</u>.

1) <u>Physical defences</u> such as <u>flood barriers</u> are being built and better <u>flood warning systems</u> are being put in place. E.g. the <u>Thames Barrier</u> in London can be closed to prevent sea water flooding the city.

2) In areas that can't afford expensive flood defences, e.g. Bangladesh, people are <u>building</u> their <u>houses</u> on top of <u>earth embankments</u> and building raised <u>flood shelters</u> to use in emergencies.

It's possible to reduce the causes and effects of climate change

Make sure you get the difference between mitigation and adaptation — don't let the examiners catch you out. Mitigation means reducing the risk, and adaptation means adjusting to extreme events.

Worked Exam Questions

Working through exam questions is a great way of testing what you've learned and practising for the exam. This worked example will give you an idea of the kind of answers examiners are looking for.

1 Study **Figure 1**, which shows data on sea level rise between 1900 and 2100.

1.1 What is the average predicted rise in sea level between 2050 and 2100?

.... 30 .... cm

[1]

Figure 1

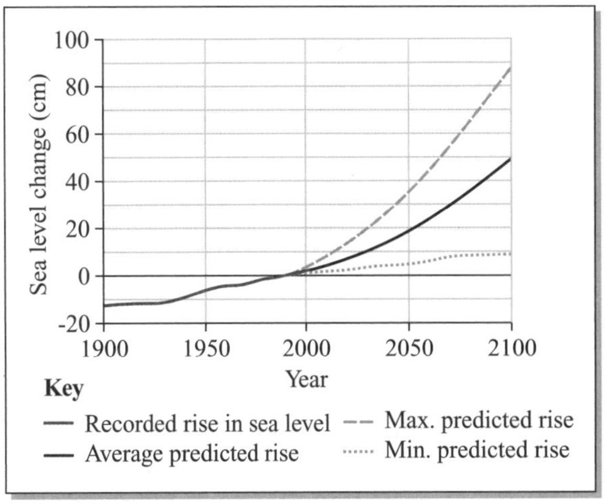

Key
— Recorded rise in sea level   -- Max. predicted rise
— Average predicted rise   ...... Min. predicted rise

1.2 Suggest **one** way in which the rise in sea level might affect the environment.

Low-lying and coastal areas may be flooded more regularly.

[1]

1.3 Apart from sea level rise, outline **two** possible environmental effects of climate change.

Effect 1: Warmer temperatures may cause glaciers to shrink and ice sheets like Greenland to melt, leading to the loss of polar habitats.

Effect 2: Some species that are adapted to particular climates may decline if they don't adapt to the changing climate.

[2]

[Total 4 marks]

2 Study **Figure 2**, a photograph showing an adaptation to rising sea levels.

Figure 2

2.1 Explain how the response shown in **Figure 2** may help people to cope with rising sea levels.

Building houses on stilts means that people can continue to live in areas that are flooded by rising sea levels. This means that people can remain safe and don't lose their homes or possessions.

[2]

2.2 Describe **one** other way that people could adapt to rising sea levels.

Physical defences such as flood barriers could be built to cope with rising sea levels.

[1]

[Total 3 marks]

Exam Questions

1   Study **Figure 1**, which shows global temperature between 1860 and 2000.

1.1   How much did global temperature rise by between 1860 and 2000?

.... °C
[1]

Figure 1

1.2   Describe the change in average global temperature shown by the graph.

....

....

....

....

....

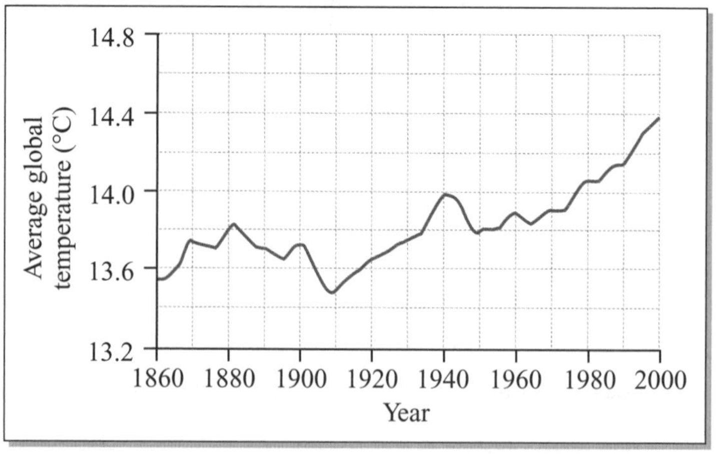

[2]

[Total 3 marks]

2   Study **Figure 2**, a graph showing temperature changes during the Quaternary period.

Figure 2

2.1   The temperature changes shown in **Figure 2** were worked out from ice core records. Explain how ice cores provide evidence for past climate change.

....

....

....

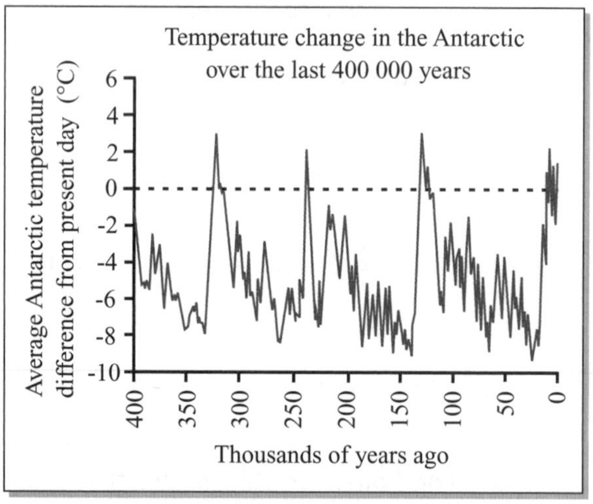

....
[2]

2.2   Explain **two** possible causes of the changes in temperature between 400 000 and 100 000 years ago shown in **Figure 2**.

Cause 1: ....

....

....

Cause 2: ....

....

....

[4]

[Total 6 marks]

Revision Summary

That wraps up <u>Unit 1A</u> — time to put yourself to the test and find out <u>how much you really know</u>.
- Try these questions and <u>tick off each one</u> when you <u>get it right</u>.
- When you've done <u>all the questions</u> for a topic and are <u>completely happy</u> with it, tick off the topic.

Natural Hazards (p.2) ☑
1) What is a natural hazard?
2) Give three factors affecting hazard risk.

Tectonic Plates (p.3-4) ☑
3) Name the type of plate boundary where two plates are moving towards each other.
4) Name the type of plate boundary where two plates are moving sideways against each other.
5) Why do volcanoes form at destructive plate boundaries?
6) At which types of plate boundaries can earthquakes occur?

Effects of Tectonic Hazards (p.5-8) ☑
7) Give two secondary effects of a volcanic eruption.
8) a) Give an example of an earthquake in a wealthier part of the world.
   b) Describe two effects of the earthquake and two responses to it.
9) a) Give an example of an earthquake in a less wealthy part of the world.
   b) Describe two responses to the earthquake.
10) Why do people live in areas prone to tectonic hazards?
11) Name the four management strategies that can be used to reduce the effects of tectonic hazards.

Global Atmospheric Circulation and Tropical Storms (p.11-15) ☑
12) How does global atmospheric circulation lead to high and low pressure belts?
13) Describe the distribution of tropical storms.
14) What conditions are required for a tropical storm to develop?
15) In what direction does a tropical storm move? Which way does it rotate?
16) What can cause a tropical storm to lose strength?
17) Describe two characteristics of the eye of a tropical storm.
18) True or false: there are likely to be more tropical storms each year if climate becomes warmer.
19) Describe four secondary effects of tropical storms.
20) Give two immediate and two long-term responses to tropical storms.

Extreme Weather in the UK (p.16-17) ☑
21) List the types of extreme weather that can be experienced in the UK.
22) Give one piece of evidence for the weather becoming more extreme in the UK.
23) a) Give an example of one extreme UK weather event and explain what caused it.
   b) Describe the social, economic and environmental impacts of the extreme weather event.

Climate Change (p.20-24) ☑
24) What is the Quaternary period?
25) Give four sources of evidence for climate change over the Quaternary period.
26) True or false: the Sun's output remains the same all the time.
27) What is the greenhouse effect?
28) How can human activities increase the concentration of greenhouse gases in the atmosphere?
29) Give one possible effect of climate change on people.
30) How might alternative energy production reduce the causes of climate change?

Ecosystems

Welcome to a lovely new topic — get ready to learn all about <u>ecosystems</u>.

An **Ecosystem** Includes all the **Living** and **Non-Living Parts** in an **Area**

1) An <u>ecosystem</u> is a unit that includes all the <u>biotic (living) parts</u> (e.g. plants and animals) and the <u>abiotic (non-living) parts</u> (e.g. soil and climate) in an <u>area</u>.

2) The <u>organisms</u> in ecosystems can be classed as <u>producers</u>, <u>consumers</u> or <u>decomposers</u>.

3) A <u>producer</u> is an organism that uses <u>sunlight energy</u> to <u>produce food</u>.

4) A <u>consumer</u> is an organism that gets its energy by <u>eating other organisms</u> — it eats <u>producers</u> or <u>other consumers</u>.

5) A <u>food chain</u> shows <u>what eats what</u>. A <u>food web</u> shows <u>lots of food chains</u> and how they <u>overlap</u>.

6) A <u>decomposer</u> is an organism that gets its energy by <u>breaking down dead material</u>, e.g. <u>dead producers</u>, <u>dead consumers</u> or <u>fallen leaves</u>. <u>Bacteria</u> and <u>fungi</u> are decomposers.

7) When <u>dead material</u> is <u>decomposed</u>, <u>nutrients</u> are <u>released</u> into the <u>soil</u>. The nutrients are then <u>taken up</u> from the soil <u>by plants</u>. The plants may be eaten by <u>consumers</u>. When the plants or consumers <u>die</u>, the <u>nutrients are returned</u> to the <u>soil</u>. This <u>transfer of nutrients</u> is called <u>nutrient cycling</u>.

Example of a small scale ecosystem

- A <u>hedgerow</u> ecosystem includes the <u>plants</u> that make up the hedgerow, the <u>organisms that live in it</u> and <u>feed on it</u>, the <u>soil</u> in the area and the <u>rainfall</u> and <u>sunshine</u> it receives.

- The <u>producers</u> include <u>hawthorn bushes</u> and <u>blackberry bushes</u>.

- The <u>consumers</u> include <u>thrushes</u>, <u>ladybirds</u>, <u>spiders</u>, <u>greenfly</u>, <u>sparrows</u> and <u>sparrowhawks</u>.

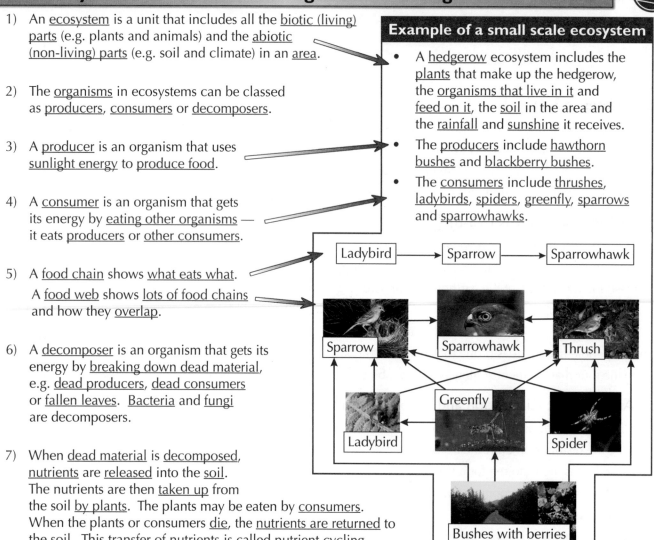

A **Change** to **One Part** of an **Ecosystem** has an **Impact** on **Other Parts**

<u>Some parts</u> of an ecosystem <u>depend on the others</u>, e.g. consumers depend on producers for a <u>source of food</u> and some depend on them for a <u>habitat</u> (a place to live). So, if <u>one part changes</u> it <u>affects all the other parts</u> that depend on it. Here are two <u>hedgerow examples</u>:

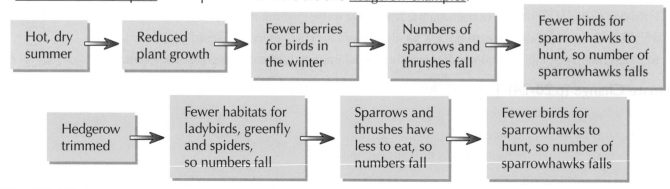

Food webs show multiple interlinked food chains

You may be asked how a change in an ecosystem affects the other parts. To help you figure out the answer, draw a food web for the ecosystem so you can easily see what will have more food, less food, no habitat and so on.

Global Ecosystems

There are loads of different <u>ecosystems</u> in the world. Time for a whistle-stop tour...

You Need to Know the **Characteristics** of **Global Ecosystems**

1) The <u>climate</u> in an area determines <u>what type</u> of <u>ecosystem forms</u>. So <u>different parts</u> of the <u>world</u> have <u>different ecosystems</u> because they have <u>different climates</u>.

2) The map shows the <u>global distribution</u> of six <u>types of ecosystem</u> — there are a lot more, but these are some of the major ones.

Grassland

There are <u>two types</u> of grassland. <u>Savannah grasslands</u> are found <u>between</u> the <u>tropics</u>. There are <u>distinct dry</u> and <u>wet</u> seasons, although <u>rainfall</u> is still relatively <u>low</u>. Most of the vegetation is <u>grasses</u> with a <u>few scattered trees</u>. <u>Temperate grasslands</u> are found at <u>higher latitudes</u> where there is <u>more variation</u> in <u>temperature</u> and <u>less rainfall</u>. There are <u>no trees</u> here — just <u>grasses</u>.

Tundra

Found at high latitudes (above 60° N) in northern <u>Europe</u>, <u>Alaska</u> and northern <u>Canada</u>. <u>Winters</u> are very <u>cold</u>, <u>summers</u> are <u>brief</u> and there is <u>little rainfall</u>. There are hardly any <u>trees</u> — vegetation includes <u>mosses</u>, <u>grasses</u> and <u>low shrubs</u>. There's a layer of permanently frozen ground called <u>permafrost</u> (see p.47).

Temperate Deciduous Forest

Found mainly in the <u>mid latitudes</u> where there are <u>four distinct seasons</u>. Summers are <u>warm</u>, winters are relatively <u>mild</u> and there's <u>rainfall</u> all year round. <u>Deciduous</u> trees <u>lose their leaves</u> in winter to cope with the colder weather.

Tropic of Cancer, 23.5° N

Equator

Tropic of Capricorn, 23.5° S

Tropical Rainforest

Found around the <u>equator</u>, between the tropics, where it's <u>hot</u> and <u>wet all year</u> round. This is an area of <u>lush forest</u>, with <u>dense canopies</u> of vegetation forming <u>distinct layers</u>. There's <u>more</u> about tropical rainforests on the <u>next page</u>.

Polar

Found around the <u>north</u> and <u>south poles</u>. They are very <u>cold</u>, <u>icy</u> and <u>dry</u>. Not much <u>grows</u> at all (see p.47). They remain <u>dark</u> for several months each year so the <u>growing season</u> is very <u>short</u> — about 2 months.

Hot Desert

Found between <u>15°</u> and <u>35° north</u> and <u>south</u> of the equator where there's <u>little rainfall</u> (see p.39). It's very <u>hot</u> during the <u>day</u> and very <u>cold</u> at <u>night</u>. <u>Shrubs</u> and <u>cacti</u> are <u>sparsely distributed</u> in the sandy soil.

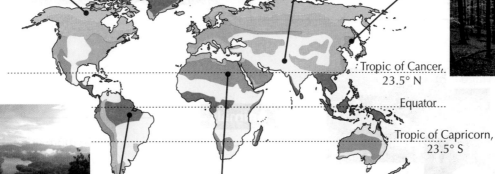

The climate in an area determines the type of ecosystem found there

Don't panic — you don't need to learn this map off by heart. You should know roughly where the different ecosystems are found though, as well as their basic characteristics. There's more on some of them coming up next.

Tropical Rainforests

Let's have an in-depth look at tropical rainforests...

Tropical Rainforests are Hot and Wet All Year Round

Climate

- The climate is the same all year round — there are no definite seasons.
- It's hot (the temperature is generally between 20-28 °C and only varies by a few degrees over the year). This is because near the equator, the sun is overhead all year round.
- Rainfall is very high, around 2000 mm per year. It rains every day, usually in the afternoon.

Soil

The soil isn't very fertile as heavy rain washes nutrients away. There are nutrients at the surface due to decayed leaf fall, but this layer is very thin as decay is fast in the warm, moist conditions.

Plants

Most trees are evergreen (i.e. they don't drop their leaves in a particular season) to take advantage of the continual growing season. Many trees are really tall and the vegetation cover is dense — very little light reaches the forest floor. There are lots of epiphytes (plants that grow on other living plants and take nutrients and moisture from the air), e.g. orchids and ferns.

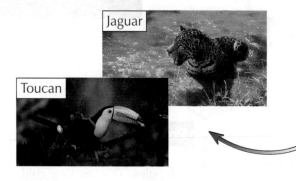

Jaguar

Toucan

Animals

Rainforests are believed to contain more animal species than any other ecosystem. Gorillas, jaguars, anacondas, tree frogs and sloths are all examples of rainforest animals. There are also loads of species of insects and birds. Many animals are brightly coloured and make a lot of noise.

People

The rainforests are home to many people, who have adapted to life there over many generations. They make a living by hunting and fishing, gathering nuts and berries and growing vegetables in small garden plots.

Rainforests are hot and wet with dense vegetation

Make sure you know the characteristics of the rainforest ecosystem — it'll help with the rest of the topic as well as getting you easy marks in the exam. Cover the page and scribble down what you know to check you've got it all.

Tropical Rainforests — Biodiversity

All the <u>parts</u> in ecosystems are all <u>linked together</u>, so if one part changes it can have major consequences. <u>Tropical rainforests</u> are no exception — especially because <u>biodiversity</u> is so <u>high</u>.

Rainforests are **Interdependent Ecosystems**

All the parts of the rainforest (climate, water, soils, plants, animals and people) are <u>dependent</u> on one another — if any <u>one</u> of them <u>changes</u>, <u>everything</u> else is <u>affected</u>. For example:

1) The warm and wet <u>climate</u> means that dead plant material is <u>decomposed</u> quickly by <u>fungi and bacteria</u> on the forest floor. This makes the surface <u>soil</u> high in <u>nutrients</u>, meaning plants can grow <u>quickly and easily</u>.

2) Plants pass on their <u>nutrients</u> when they are eaten by <u>animals</u>. The dense vegetation provides lots of food, so <u>animal populations</u> are <u>high</u>. Many plant and animal species have formed <u>symbiotic relationships</u> (where they each <u>depend</u> on the other for <u>survival</u>). For example:

> <u>Agouti</u> (a rodent) are one of the <u>only</u> animals who can <u>crack open</u> the hard seed pod of the <u>Brazil nut</u> to eat the nut inside. Sometimes, the agouti <u>bury</u> the nuts — these can <u>sprout</u> into <u>new seedlings</u>. If the agouti became <u>extinct</u>, the Brazil nut trees would <u>decline</u> and so could all the other <u>animals</u> who <u>live in</u> or <u>feed on</u> the Brazil nut trees. <u>People</u> who <u>sell</u> Brazil nuts to make a living may also be affected.

3) <u>Changes</u> to the rainforest ecosystem, such as <u>people</u> reducing <u>tree cover</u> by <u>deforestation</u> (see p.33-34), can have <u>knock-on effects</u> on the whole ecosystem. For example, by <u>reducing</u> the amount of CO_2 being absorbed from the atmosphere, adding to the <u>greenhouse effect</u> and changing the <u>climate</u> (see p.22).

4) Trees also <u>intercept</u> and take up lots of <u>water</u>, and release it back into the atmosphere, providing moisture for further rainfall. <u>Deforestation</u> means the <u>climate</u> may change, and the risk of <u>drought increases</u>, affecting the <u>plants</u> and <u>animals</u> that live in the ecosystem.

Rainforests Have **Very High Biodiversity**

1) <u>Biodiversity</u> is the <u>variety</u> of organisms living in a particular area — both <u>plants</u> and <u>animals</u>.

2) Rainforests have extremely <u>high biodiversity</u> — they contain around <u>50%</u> of the world's <u>plant</u>, <u>animal</u> and <u>insect species</u>, and may contain <u>around half</u> of <u>all life</u> on Earth.

3) Rainforests are <u>stable</u> and <u>productive</u> environments because it's <u>hot</u> and <u>wet all year round</u>. Plants and animals don't have to cope with <u>changing conditions</u> and there is always <u>plenty</u> to <u>eat</u>.

4) Many organisms have <u>evolved</u> to <u>depend</u> on just a <u>few species</u> for survival — they are very <u>specific</u> to a particular <u>habitat</u> and <u>food source</u>, and many species are only found in a <u>small area</u>.

5) <u>Deforestation</u> (cutting down trees) and <u>uncontrolled development</u> of the rainforest are likely to lead to the <u>extinction</u> of many species and the <u>loss</u> of <u>biodiversity</u>. The number of <u>endangered species</u> in Brazil increased from <u>218</u> in <u>1989</u> to <u>628</u> in <u>2008</u>.

Interdependence means everything affects everything else

To revise interdependence try thinking of a scenario that might happen, e.g. it gets hotter, then draw a flow diagram showing how that change impacts the plants, animals, people etc. in the rainforest. If you follow each step logically you should be able to figure out what might happen to each part.

Tropical Rainforests — Adaptations

You may be wondering how <u>plants</u> and <u>animals</u> are able to <u>survive</u> in this <u>hot</u>, <u>steamy</u> environment...

Plants and Animals have Adapted to the Physical Conditions

<u>Plants</u> in the rainforest are <u>adapted</u> to cope with the <u>high rainfall</u>, <u>high temperatures</u> and competition for <u>light</u>:

1) <u>Tall trees</u> competing for sunlight have big roots called <u>buttress roots</u> to <u>support</u> their trunks.

2) Plants have <u>thick</u>, <u>waxy leaves</u> with <u>pointed tips</u>. The pointed tips (called <u>drip-tips</u>) channel the water to a point so it <u>runs off</u> — that way the <u>weight</u> of the <u>water doesn't damage</u> the plant, and there's no standing water for <u>fungi</u> and <u>bacteria</u> to grow in. The waxy coating of the leaves also helps <u>repel</u> the rain.

3) Many trees have <u>smooth</u>, <u>thin bark</u> as there is no need to <u>protect</u> the trunk from cold temperatures. The smooth surface also allows water to <u>run off easily</u>.

4) The rainforest has <u>four distinct layers</u> of plants with different adaptations. For example, plants in the highest layer (<u>emergents</u>) <u>only</u> have branches at their <u>crown</u> (where <u>most light</u> reaches them), and plants in the <u>undercanopy</u> have <u>large leaves</u> to absorb as <u>much light</u> as possible.

5) <u>Climbing plants</u>, such as lianas, <u>use</u> the <u>tree trunks</u> to <u>climb</u> up to the sunlight.

6) Plants <u>drop</u> their <u>leaves</u> gradually throughout the year, meaning they can go on growing <u>all year round</u>.

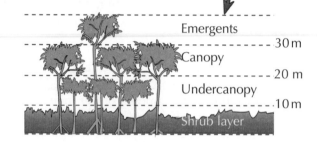

Emergents
- - - - - - - 30 m
Canopy
- - - - - - - 20 m
Undercanopy
- - - - - - 10 m
Shrub layer

<u>Animals</u> are <u>adapted</u> in different ways so that they can <u>find food</u> and <u>escape predators</u>:

1) Many animals spend their <u>entire lives</u> high up in the <u>canopy</u>. They have <u>strong limbs</u> so that they can spend all day <u>climbing</u> and <u>leaping</u> from tree to tree, e.g. howler monkeys.

2) Some animals have <u>flaps of skin</u> that enable them to <u>glide</u> between trees, e.g. flying squirrels. Others have <u>suction cups</u> for <u>climbing</u>, e.g. red-eyed tree frogs.

3) Some <u>birds</u> have <u>short</u>, <u>pointy wings</u> so that they can easily <u>manoeuvre</u> between the <u>dense</u> tangle of branches in the trees, e.g. the harpy eagle has a short wingspan.

4) Some animals are <u>camouflaged</u>, e.g. leaf-tailed geckos look like leaves so they can <u>hide</u> from <u>predators</u>.

5) Many animals are <u>nocturnal</u> (active at <u>night</u>), e.g. sloths. They <u>sleep</u> through the day and <u>feed</u> at night when it's <u>cooler</u> — this helps them to <u>save energy</u>.

6) Some animals are adapted to the <u>low light levels</u> on the rainforest floor, e.g. anteaters have a sharp sense of <u>smell</u> and <u>hearing</u>, so they can <u>detect predators</u> without seeing them.

7) Many rainforests animals can <u>swim</u>, e.g. jaguars. This allows them to cross <u>river channels</u>.

EXAM TIP

Adaptations help animals and plants to thrive in the hot, wet conditions

You may be given a picture of a plant or animal in the exam and asked to describe how it's adapted to its environment. Don't panic if you have no idea what species it is — just think about the conditions in the rainforest and how the features shown in the picture might be adaptations to help it survive.

Tropical Rainforests — Deforestation

Removal of trees from forests is called deforestation. It's happening on a huge scale in many tropical rainforests. Deforestation has many impacts — some good, some bad and some downright ugly.

Deforestation is the Main Threat to Tropical Rainforests

There are lots of reasons why tropical rainforests are chopped down:

Population pressure — as the population in the area increases, trees are cleared to make land for new settlements.

Mineral extraction — minerals (e.g. gold and iron ore) are mined and sold to make money.

Energy development — building dams to generate hydro-electric power floods large areas of forest.

Commercial logging — trees are felled to make money. Road building for logging also requires more tree clearance.

Commercial farming — forest is cleared to make space for cattle grazing, or for huge palm oil or soya plantations.

Subsistence farming — forest is cleared so farmers can grow food for themselves and their families.

Deforestation has Environmental and Economic Impacts

Environmental Impacts

1) With no trees to hold the soil together, heavy rain washes away the soil (soil erosion). This can lead to landslides and flooding.

2) Without a tree canopy to intercept (catch) rainfall and tree roots to absorb it, more water reaches the soil. This reduces soil fertility as nutrients in the soil are washed away, out of reach of plants.

3) Trees remove CO_2 from the atmosphere. Also, burning vegetation to clear forest produces CO_2. So deforestation means more CO_2 in the atmosphere, which adds to the greenhouse effect. Deforestation is responsible for at least 15% of global CO_2 emissions each year — more than all of the world's annual transport emissions combined.

Economic Impacts

1) Logging, farming and mining create jobs.

2) A lot of money is made from selling timber, mining and commercial farming.

3) In the long term, deforestation can destroy the resources that countries depend on, e.g. timber, and reduce the attractiveness of the area to tourists.

4) The livelihoods of some local people are destroyed — deforestation can cause the loss of the animals and plants that they rely on to make a living.

The Rate of Deforestation is Changing

1) The rate of rainforest deforestation is very high — roughly 300 000 km² per year from 2000-2010.

2) Globally the rate seems to be slowing down but there are still hotspots where the rate of deforestation is increasing, e.g. in Borneo and Nigeria.

3) Overall, deforestation in Brazil and Indonesia accounted for almost half of the global total between 2001 and 2014, though Brazil has reduced its deforestation rate since 1990.

Deforestation can bring wealth into an area

A bit of a serious page this one, but an important one nonetheless — you should know the six main causes of deforestation like the back of your hand. And remember that rates of deforestation vary across the world.

Deforestation

The Amazon is the largest rainforest on Earth, but it's shrinking fast due to deforestation.

Case Study — Deforestation is a Problem in the Amazon

1) The Amazon is the largest rainforest on Earth — covering an area of around 8 million km², including parts of Brazil, Peru, Colombia, Venezuela, Ecuador, Bolivia, Guyana, Suriname and French Guiana.

2) Since 1978, over 750 000 km² (more than three times the size of the UK) has been destroyed by deforestation.

3) There are lots of causes — for example, between 2000 and 2005:

- 65-70% was caused by commercial (cattle) ranching.
- 20-25% was caused by small-scale subsistence farming — many farmers have been settled by the Brazilian government along the Trans-Amazonian Highway.
- 5-10% was caused by other commercial farming — mostly soy farming, but rice, corn and sugar cane are also grown.
- 2-3% was caused by logging, including lots of illegal logging. New roads have opened up areas of the forest that were previously too hard to get to.
- 1-2% was caused by other activities such as mineral extraction (e.g. gold mining), road building, energy development and building new settlements.

4) Population growth and migration to the area is also putting pressure on the Amazon rainforest, especially as the Brazilian government offers land in the rainforest to poor people from overcrowded cities.

5) There are many more small-scale subsistence farmers now, and people who have no land or whose land has become unproductive are opening up more areas of the forest.

Amazon Rainforest

South America

Deforestation in the Amazon has Many Impacts

Environmental

1) The Amazon stores around 100 billion tonnes of carbon — deforestation will release some of this as carbon dioxide, which causes global warming.

2) Brazil is losing 55 million tons of topsoil every year because of soil erosion caused by soy farming.

Economic

1) Economic development has brought wealth to countries that were very poor.

2) Farming makes a lot of money for countries in the rainforest, e.g. in 2008, Brazil made $6.9 billion from trading cattle. It is also the world's second biggest exporter of soy beans.

3) The mining industry creates jobs for loads of people, e.g. the Buenaventura mining company in Peru employs over 3100 people.

4) Logging contributes a huge amount to Brazil's economy.

5) Local Brazilian rubber tappers who extract natural rubber from rubber trees have lost their livelihoods as trees have been cut down.

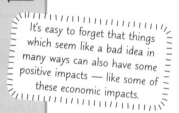

It's easy to forget that things which seem like a bad idea in many ways can also have some positive impacts — like some of these economic impacts.

The Amazon rainforest is being rapidly deforested

If you've learned the information from the previous page, there shouldn't be anything too surprising here. But make sure you also learn plenty of case study facts — you'll need them in the exam.

Tropical Rainforests — Sustainable Management

It's not all doom and gloom for rainforests. In fact, this page is dedicated to the ways to manage them.

It's Important to Protect Tropical Rainforests

1) It's important to protect the rainforest, in order to preserve its biodiversity — maintaining the high diversity of plants and animals is valuable to both people and the environment.

2) Many products including rubber, coffee, chocolate and medicines are sourced from the rainforest. If species become extinct, the chance to discover new medicines and develop new products is reduced.

3) Sustainable development also allows for long-term economic benefits, e.g. through developing ecotourism.

4) Protecting the rainforests may help reduce the greenhouse effect (p.22), by reducing CO_2 emissions (from burning etc.), and allowing the trees to continue absorbing CO_2.

5) Some of the impacts of rainforest destruction, e.g. climate change, could affect all countries, not just the countries where the deforestation is happening.

6) Rainforests also help regulate the climate and water cycle — without them the risks of drought and flooding in certain areas can increase.

Tropical Rainforests can be Sustainably Managed

Rainforests can be managed in a way that's sustainable, i.e. in a way that allows people today to get the things they need, but without stopping people in the future from getting what they need. Here's how:

Selective Logging

1) Only some trees (e.g. just the older or inferior ones) are felled — most trees are left standing.

2) This is less damaging to the forest than felling all the trees in an area. If only a few trees are taken from each area the overall forest structure is kept — the canopy's still there and the soil isn't exposed. This means the forest will be able to regenerate so it can be used in the future.

3) The least damaging forms are 'horse logging' and 'helicopter logging' — dragging felled trees out of the forest using horses or removing them with helicopters instead of huge trucks.

EXAMPLE: Helicopter logging is used in the Malaysian state of Sarawak.

Replanting

1) This is when new trees are planted to replace the ones that are cut down.

2) This means there will be trees for people to use in the future.

3) It's important that the same types of tree are planted that were cut down, so that the variety of trees is kept for the future.

4) In some countries there are laws to make logging companies replant trees when they clear an area.

See the next page for more ways to manage rainforests sustainably.

Ecotourism

1) Ecotourism is tourism that minimises damage to the environment and benefits the local people.

2) Only a small number of visitors are allowed into an area at a time. Environmental impacts are minimised, e.g. by making sure waste and litter are disposed of properly to prevent land and water contamination.

3) Ecotourism provides a source of income for local people, e.g. they act as guides, provide accommodation and transport. It can also raise awareness of conservation issues and bring in more money for rainforest conservation.

4) If local people are employed in tourism, they don't have to log or farm to make money, meaning fewer trees are cut down. If a country's economy relies on ecotourism, there's an incentive to conserve the environment.

5) Ecotourism has been very successful in Costa Rica (a country in Central America). It is the largest source of income for the country and has led to 21% of the country being protected from development.

Tropical Rainforests — Sustainable Management

A few more <u>sustainable ways</u> to manage rainforests...

International Hardwood Agreements

1) <u>Hardwood</u> is a general term for wood from <u>certain tree species</u>, e.g. <u>mahogany</u> and <u>teak</u>. The wood tends to be <u>fairly dense</u> and <u>hard</u> — it's used to make things like <u>furniture</u>.

2) <u>High demand</u> for hardwood from <u>consumers</u> in <u>richer countries</u> means that <u>some tropical hardwood trees</u> are becoming <u>rarer</u> as people are chopping them down and selling them.

3) There are <u>international agreements</u> in place to try to <u>reduce illegal logging</u>, and <u>promote</u> hardwood from <u>sustainably managed forests</u>.

EXAMPLE: The <u>Forest Stewardship Council</u>® is an organisation made up of <u>businesses</u>, <u>non-governmental organisations</u> (such as Greenpeace) and <u>individuals</u> from all over the world.

They <u>mark</u> sustainably-sourced timber products with their <u>logo</u> so that <u>consumers</u> can choose products that are not <u>contributing</u> to unsustainable deforestation.

Education

1) Education of the <u>international community</u> about the <u>impacts</u> of deforestation can <u>encourage people</u> to buy products that are <u>certified</u> from <u>sustainably managed sources</u>.

2) Some <u>local people don't know</u> what the <u>environmental impacts</u> of deforestation are. Local people try to make <u>money</u> in the <u>short-term</u> (e.g. by illegal logging) to <u>overcome</u> their own <u>poverty</u>.

3) Educating local people about the <u>impacts</u> of deforestation and <u>ways to reduce the impacts decreases damage</u> to the rainforest environment.

4) Also, educating local people about <u>alternative ways to make money</u> that <u>don't damage</u> the <u>environment</u> as much, e.g. ecotourism, means they aren't <u>dependent</u> on <u>unsustainable</u> options in order to make a <u>living</u>.

Reducing Debt

1) A lot of tropical rainforests are in <u>lower income countries</u>.

2) Lower income countries often <u>borrow money</u> from <u>wealthier countries</u> or <u>organisations</u> (e.g. the World Bank) to fund <u>development schemes</u> or <u>cope with emergencies</u> like floods.

3) This <u>money</u> has to be <u>paid back</u> with <u>interest</u>.

4) These countries often <u>allow logging</u>, <u>farming</u> and <u>mining in rainforests</u> to <u>make money</u> to <u>pay back the debt</u>.

5) So <u>reducing debt</u> means countries <u>don't have to do this</u> and the rainforests can be <u>conserved for the future</u>.

6) Debt can be <u>cancelled</u> by countries or organisations, but there's <u>no guarantee</u> the <u>money</u> that would have been spent on repayments <u>will be spent on conservation</u> instead.

7) A better solution is a <u>conservation swap</u>, where part of a country's debt is paid off in exchange for a guarantee that the <u>money is spent on conservation</u>.

EXAMPLE: In <u>2008</u> the USA reduced Peru's debt by <u>$25 million</u> in exchange for <u>rainforest conservation</u>.

Conservation

1) Many <u>countries</u> have set up <u>national parks</u> and <u>nature reserves</u> within rainforests. In these areas <u>damaging activities</u>, e.g. logging, are <u>restricted</u>. However, a <u>lack</u> of <u>funds</u> can make it <u>difficult</u> to <u>police</u> the restrictions.

2) As a result, some countries have set up <u>funds</u> which <u>overseas governments</u> and <u>businesses</u> can <u>invest in</u>. The countries get the money <u>in exchange</u> for rainforest <u>conservation</u>.

3) The money can be used to <u>enforce restrictions</u> on <u>damaging activities</u> and to <u>promote sustainable use</u> of the rainforests.

EXAMPLE: <u>Norway</u> has paid <u>$1 billion</u> into Brazil's <u>Amazon Fund</u> to be used for conservation.

Sustainable management of rainforests protects their biodiversity

This may seem like a lot of information, but you don't have to learn every detail — think about how each strategy enables people to get the things they need without stopping people in the future from doing so.

Worked Exam Questions

Read through this page carefully — it shows you the sorts of things the examiners are looking for in your answers. Then have a bash at the questions on the next page on your own.

1   Study **Figure 1**, which shows part of a food web for a coastal ecosystem.

Figure 1

1.1 Which of the organisms in the food web shown in **Figure 1** is a producer? Shade **one** oval only.

A   Sea otter   ○

B   Crab   ○

C   Sea snail   ○

D   Seaweed   ●

[1]

1.2 Give **one** example of a consumer from the food chain shown in **Figure 1**.

Sea urchin

[1]

1.3 Describe how nutrients are cycled in a land-based ecosystem.

When dead material decomposes, nutrients are released into the soil. The nutrients are then taken

up from the soil by plants. The plants may be eaten by consumers, so the nutrients they contain are

transferred to the consumers. When the plants or consumers die, the nutrients are returned to the

soil, and the cycle continues.

[4]

[Total 6 marks]

2   Study **Figure 2**, a diagram showing layers of vegetation in a tropical rainforest.

2.1 Using **Figure 2**, describe the physical conditions in the layers labelled A and B.

A: There is lots of light but it is exposed

to wind and heavy rainfall.

B: It is sheltered and quite dark because

of the trees above.

[2]

Figure 2

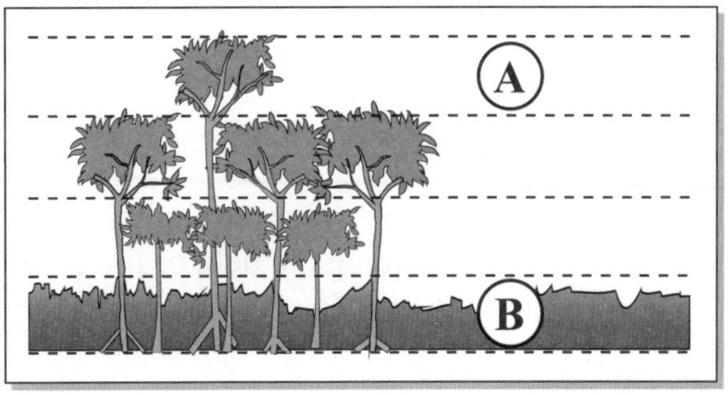

2.2 Describe the climate of tropical rainforests.

The climate is the same all year round.

It's hot (the temperature is generally between 20 and 28 °C and only varies by a few degrees over

the year). Rainfall is very high (around 2000 mm per year) and it rains every day.

[3]

[Total 5 marks]

Exam Questions

1   Study **Figure 1**, a series of maps showing the extent of deforestation in an
       area of tropical rainforest in a lower income country between 1966 and 2016.

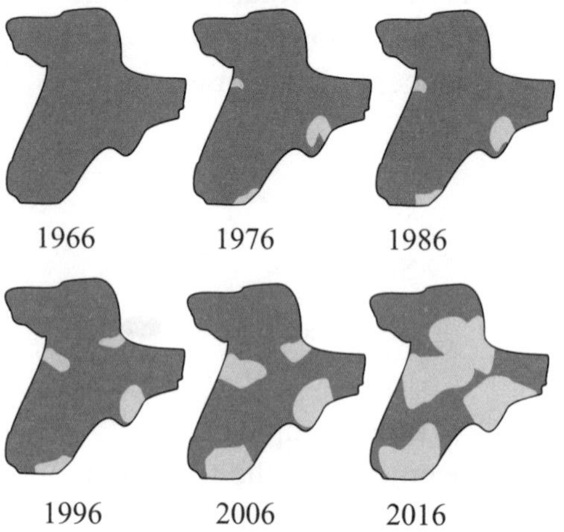

1.1   Outline **two** possible causes of deforestation in the
       area shown in **Figure 1**.

Figure 1

Cause 1: ....

....

....

Cause 2: ....

....

....
[2]

1.2   Outline **one** positive economic impact of deforestation.

....

....
[1]

1.3   Outline **one** environmental impact of deforestation.

....

....

....
[2]

1.4   Explain how selective logging can help to make tropical rainforest use more sustainable.

....

....

....

....
[3]

1.5   Explain how reducing the debt of the country shown in **Figure 1** might help to reduce
       deforestation there.

....

....

....
[2]

[Total 10 marks]

Hot Deserts

Hot deserts are <u>hot</u> and also very <u>dry</u>. This affects the <u>plants</u> and <u>animals</u> that can live there.

Hot Deserts Are Found in **Hot, Dry Climates**

Climate
There's very <u>little rainfall</u> — <u>less than 250 mm</u> per year.
<u>When</u> it rains also <u>varies a lot</u> — it might only rain <u>once</u> every
two or three years. Temperatures are <u>extreme</u> — they range from
very <u>hot</u> in the <u>day</u> (e.g. 45 °C) to very <u>cold</u> at <u>night</u> (e.g. 5 °C).

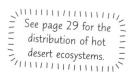
See page 29 for the distribution of hot desert ecosystems.

Soil
It's usually <u>shallow</u> with a <u>coarse</u>, <u>gravelly texture</u>. There's <u>hardly any leaf fall</u> so the
soil <u>isn't very fertile</u>. Lack of <u>rainfall</u> and <u>plant material</u> mean the soil is often <u>dry</u>.

Plants
Plant growth is pretty <u>sparse</u> due to the <u>lack of rainfall</u>.
Plants that do grow include <u>cacti</u> and <u>thornbushes</u>.
The plants are usually quite <u>short</u> (e.g. low shrubs or
short woody trees) though cacti can grow fairly tall.
Many plants have a <u>short life cycle</u>, only appearing
when it <u>rains</u> (see page 41).

Animals
1) Hot deserts contain animals <u>adapted</u> to
survive in the <u>harsh</u> environment. There are
lots of <u>lizards</u>, <u>snakes</u>, <u>insects</u> and <u>scorpions</u>.
2) <u>Mammals</u> tend to be <u>small</u> and <u>nocturnal</u>,
e.g. kangaroo rats. Most <u>birds leave</u> the desert
during the harshest conditions but some,
e.g. roadrunners, can live there <u>all year round</u>.

People
1) <u>Many</u> people living in the desert
grow a few <u>crops</u> where there are
natural springs or wells to supply
water, usually in the desert <u>fringes</u>.
2) Indigenous people are often <u>nomadic</u>
— they <u>travel</u> all the time in search of
food and water for their <u>herds</u>, which
are mostly goats and sheep.

Hot deserts have shallow soils and sparse vegetation

Hot deserts are pretty much what you'd expect them to be — hot, dry and sandy, with low populations of plants,
animals and people. Study this page closely, then cover it up and write down what you can remember.

Hot Deserts — Biodiversity

Everything is <u>connected</u> to everything else in the <u>hot desert ecosystem</u>.

Hot Deserts are Fragile, Interdependent Ecosystems

The <u>biotic</u> (living) components of hot deserts (plants, animals and people) and the <u>abiotic</u> (non-living) components (climate, water, soils) are <u>closely related</u> — if <u>one</u> of them <u>changes</u>, <u>the others</u> are <u>affected</u>.

1) <u>Plants</u> gain their <u>nutrients</u> from the <u>soil</u>, and <u>provide nutrients</u> and <u>water</u> to the <u>animals</u> that eat them. In turn, animals spread <u>seeds</u> through their <u>dung</u>, helping the plants to <u>reproduce</u>.

2) The hot and dry <u>climate</u> affects the soil in deserts. Soils are salty due to <u>high evaporation</u>, and relatively low in nutrients because there is little <u>decomposition</u> of dead plant material by <u>fungi</u> and <u>bacteria</u>. This means that plants <u>struggle to grow</u>.

3) The <u>sparse</u> vegetation <u>limits</u> the amount of <u>food</u> available, so the desert can only support <u>low-density</u> populations of <u>animals</u>.

4) <u>Water</u> supplies in deserts can be extremely <u>scarce</u>. Rainfall is <u>very low</u>, and the coarse desert soil means that any rain that does fall <u>quickly drains away</u>. <u>Animals</u> and <u>people</u> have to find ways of <u>coping</u>, e.g. by <u>constantly moving</u> to new places, or digging <u>deep wells</u>.

5) <u>People</u> have to <u>irrigate</u> (artificially water) the land in order to be able to <u>grow crops</u>. Drawing <u>unsustainable</u> amounts of water from wells <u>lowers the level</u> of water underground — <u>reducing</u> the amount available to other plants. Some <u>plant species</u> and the <u>animals</u> that <u>depend</u> on them can struggle to survive as a result.

6) <u>Changes</u> to components of the ecosystem, such as allowing cattle to <u>overgraze</u> vegetation, can have <u>knock-on effects</u> on the <u>whole ecosystem</u>, e.g. by causing <u>soil erosion</u>. Without plant roots to <u>stabilise</u> the soil, the wind can <u>blow</u> fine sand/soil particles away. Soil erosion can lead to clouds of <u>dust</u> in the atmosphere, which can change the <u>climate</u> of deserts — <u>reducing rainfall</u>, making them even <u>drier</u>.

Biodiversity is Higher in Areas with Water

1) <u>Hot deserts</u> have relatively low biodiversity (compared with tropical rainforests). <u>Small areas</u> around <u>ephemeral</u> (temporary) <u>ponds</u> or <u>rivers</u> or along the desert <u>margins</u> have the highest levels of biodiversity, and contain a <u>high proportion</u> of species that are <u>endemic</u> (unique) to the desert.

2) Areas with water also have the <u>highest density</u> of <u>human</u> populations. Human <u>development</u> threatens biodiversity by increasing <u>desertification</u> (see p.44) and by <u>over-using</u> or <u>contaminating</u> water supplies.

3) <u>Development</u> around the <u>desert margins</u> also means that <u>habitats</u> are being <u>divided</u> up by <u>roads</u>. This is <u>threatening</u> animals that <u>migrate</u> over <u>large distances</u> to find food and water, e.g. desert bighorn sheep.

4) <u>Global warming</u> is generally making hot deserts <u>hotter</u> and <u>drier</u>. This is forcing some species, e.g. lizards, to move to cooler areas to cope with the rising temperatures. However, species that are <u>already</u> at the <u>limits</u> of their environment don't have <u>anywhere else</u> to go, so are at risk of <u>decline</u> or <u>extinction</u>.

5) <u>Low biodiversity</u> and <u>pressure</u> from <u>development</u> and <u>climate change</u> mean that deserts contain many <u>biodiversity hotspots</u> — places where there are a <u>high proportion</u> of endemic species that are threatened with <u>extinction</u>.

Biodiversity in hot deserts is low and many species are threatened
You don't have to learn these examples of interdependence, if there are others that you have studied. Just make sure you can say what might happen to the other parts of the ecosystem if something changes.

Hot Deserts — Adaptations

<u>Plants</u> and <u>animals</u> can only <u>survive</u> in the desert because they have some clever <u>adaptations</u>.

Plants and Animals are Adapted to the Hot, Dry Conditions

<u>Desert plants</u> have <u>adaptations</u> to help them cope with the <u>hot</u>, <u>dry</u> conditions.

1) Plant <u>roots</u> are either extremely <u>long</u> to reach very <u>deep water</u> supplies, or spread out very <u>wide near the surface</u> to <u>catch</u> as <u>much water</u> as <u>possible</u> when it <u>rains</u>.

2) Many plants, e.g. cacti, are <u>succulents</u>. They have <u>large</u>, <u>fleshy</u> <u>stems</u> for <u>storing water</u> and <u>thick waxy skin</u> to <u>reduce water loss</u> (water loss from plants is called <u>transpiration</u>). Some also have sharp <u>spines</u> and <u>toxins</u> to stop animals <u>stealing water</u> from their stems.

3) Some plants have <u>small leaves</u> or <u>spines</u> — this gives them a <u>low surface area</u>, reducing transpiration.

4) The <u>seeds</u> of some plants <u>only germinate when it rains</u> — the plants <u>grow</u>, <u>flower</u> and <u>release seeds</u> in just a <u>few weeks</u>, which makes sure they <u>only grow</u> when there's <u>enough water to survive</u>.

<u>Desert animals</u> are also <u>adapted</u> to cope with the high <u>temperatures</u> and <u>limited</u> supply of <u>water</u>.

1) Being <u>nocturnal</u> means that animals can <u>stay cool</u> in burrows during the <u>day</u> or sit still in the <u>shade</u> whilst it's <u>hottest</u>, e.g. fennec foxes. Desert animals also often have <u>long limbs</u> or <u>ears</u>, providing a <u>large surface area</u> to <u>lose heat</u> from.

2) <u>Lizards</u> and <u>snakes</u> are able to tolerate <u>high body temperatures</u>, e.g. desert iguanas can <u>survive</u> temperatures up to 42 °C.

Fennec foxes

Lizard

3) Some bigger animals <u>store</u> large amounts of <u>fat</u> which they can break down into <u>water</u> when needed, e.g. camels' humps.

4) Some animals get all the <u>water</u> they need from what they <u>eat</u>, e.g. cactus mice get water from cactus fruits and insects, and most desert animals <u>minimise</u> water loss from <u>sweat</u> and <u>urine</u>.

5) Adaptations to cope with the <u>sand</u> are common. For example, camels <u>keep sand out</u> of their eyes and nose during sand storms by having <u>triple eyelids</u>, <u>long eyelashes</u> and being able to <u>close their nostrils</u>. They also have <u>large</u>, <u>flat feet</u> so that they don't <u>sink</u> into the sand.

Many desert plants have fleshy stems, spiny leaves and waxy skin

Plant adaptations are about trying to get as much water as possible and animals need to be able to stay cool and get enough water. Keep these key ideas in mind if you get asked about an organism you don't recognise in the exam.

Development in Hot Deserts

It's time to learn about the <u>economic opportunities</u> in a real desert...

There are Lots of **Development Opportunities** in the **Sahara**

The <u>Sahara</u> is Earth's <u>largest</u> desert — it's almost the size of the United States. It stretches across parts of <u>many countries</u> in <u>north Africa</u>. Opportunities for <u>economic development</u> in the Sahara include:

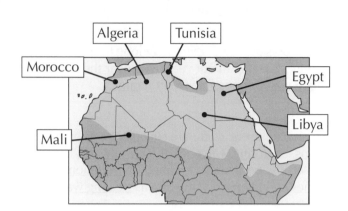

Morocco | Algeria | Tunisia | Egypt | Libya | Mali

1) <u>Mineral resources</u> — <u>Morocco</u> is now the world's <u>largest exporter</u> of <u>phosphate</u> (which is used in fertilisers, cleaning products, batteries etc.).

2) <u>Oil and gas</u> — <u>Algeria</u> is a leader in <u>oil exploration</u> and <u>extraction</u> in the Sahara Desert. <u>60%</u> of its <u>income</u> comes from the oil and gas industry. It has many oil fields, including <u>Hassi Messaoud</u>, and the industry employs over <u>40 000 people</u>.

3) <u>Solar energy</u> — 12 or more hours of bright sunshine and <u>cloudless skies</u> every day are ideal for generating <u>solar power</u>. A 100 km² area solar energy development in <u>Tunisia</u> is planned to supply enough <u>electricity</u> to meet the needs of 2 million homes in Western Europe by 2018.

4) <u>Tourism</u> — many people are fascinated by <u>remote</u> and <u>exotic</u> desert locations. Sandboarding, carting and cross-desert treks are popular <u>tourist activities</u> in the Sahara, e.g. <u>camel trekking</u> in <u>Morocco</u>. Tourism in the Sahara itself remains on a <u>small scale</u>, though many people visit <u>cities</u> on the <u>outskirts</u>, e.g. <u>Marrakech</u>.

5) <u>Farming</u> — water is essential for plant growth so commercial agriculture in the Sahara is only possible where there is enough <u>irrigation water</u> — e.g. the <u>Aswan Dam</u> provides a year-round water supply in <u>Egypt</u>.

The Sahara isn't just sand — there's economic development too

The different opportunities in the Sahara may surprise you, but you might need to write about them in detail in the exam — make sure you learn plenty of facts and figures, including specific locations.

Development in Hot Deserts

There may be lots of <u>opportunities</u> in hot deserts but they come with some pretty tough <u>challenges</u> too.

The **Extreme Climate** and **Inaccessibility** Make **Development Challenging**

1) The harsh conditions mean that the Sahara's <u>population</u> is only about <u>2 million</u>. Most people live in small <u>fertile</u> areas, where <u>water</u> from a spring or well is used to <u>irrigate</u> the ground so that crops, e.g. dates, can be grown. Others are <u>nomadic</u>, constantly searching for <u>fresh grazing</u> for their herds of goats, sheep and camels.

2) <u>Development</u> in the Sahara is <u>challenging</u> — trying to <u>locate</u> and <u>exploit</u> resources in the <u>hot</u>, <u>dry</u> and <u>remote desert</u>:

Extreme Temperatures

1) Due to the lack of <u>cloud cover</u>, daily temperatures can <u>range</u> from over <u>40 °C</u> during the day to <u>below freezing</u> at night. Exposure to high temperatures can cause <u>illness</u> or <u>death</u>, and <u>healthcare</u> may be a <u>long distance</u> away.

2) The hot season is often <u>too hot</u> for <u>tourists</u> so employment in the tourism industry can be <u>seasonal</u>.

Inaccessibility

1) The Sahara is <u>huge</u> — people and materials have to travel <u>long distances</u> — often by <u>air</u>, which is <u>expensive</u>.

2) It's difficult to provide <u>services</u>, e.g. medical care, to <u>remote regions</u>, making it hard for them to develop.

3) <u>Expensive pipelines</u> have to be built to transport <u>oil</u> and <u>gas</u> from remote areas.

4) It takes <u>5 days</u> by <u>truck</u> to transport <u>salt</u> from salt mines in <u>Mali</u> out of the desert.

Water Supply

1) The Sahara has very <u>low annual rainfall</u> (less than 70 mm in places). Rainfall is <u>unpredictable</u> and most <u>rivers</u> only flow during <u>part</u> of the year.

2) Providing enough water for <u>workers</u>, <u>industry</u> or <u>irrigation</u> is extremely hard.

3) <u>Deep boreholes</u> are used to extract water <u>stored</u> naturally <u>under the Sahara</u> but this <u>isn't sustainable</u> because the supply isn't being replenished.

4) Some desert resources are so <u>valuable</u> that <u>new developments</u> find ways of supplying the water they need, e.g. the phosphate mines in <u>Morocco</u> pipe water from a <u>dam</u> in <u>central Morocco</u>.

The Sahara is very hot, inaccessible and lacking water

Don't worry if you've studied a different hot desert environment. As long as you know the opportunities and challenges for development and you've got some good, specific examples from that place, you'll be sorted.

Desertification

Like most places, deserts have their <u>problems</u> and <u>desertification</u> is a big one, but there are ways to <u>manage</u> it too.

Desertification is Caused by **Human** and **Physical** Factors

1) <u>Desertification</u> is the <u>degradation</u> of land so that it becomes more desert-like
   — it becomes <u>drier</u> and <u>less productive</u>. A <u>third</u> of the world's land surface
   is at <u>risk</u> of desertification, particularly at the <u>margins</u> of <u>deserts</u>.

2) <u>Soil erosion</u> is a key part of desertification. Soil that is <u>exposed</u> (not covered by plants) is easily <u>removed</u>
   by <u>wind</u> or <u>water</u>. <u>Nutrients</u> in the soil (e.g. from fallen leaves and dead plants) are <u>lost</u>, making soil
   <u>unproductive</u>. Eventually the ground becomes <u>sandy</u>, <u>dusty</u>, <u>stony</u> or just <u>bare rock</u>.

3) The main <u>causes</u> of desertification are:

Climate Change

1) <u>Rainfall</u> — climate change is
   expected to <u>reduce rainfall</u> in areas
   that are already quite <u>dry</u>. Less rain
   means that <u>less water</u> is available for
   <u>plant growth</u>, so plants <u>die</u>. Plant
   <u>roots</u> hold the soil together. If the
   plants <u>die</u>, the soil is easily <u>eroded</u>.

2) <u>Temperatures</u> — global temperatures
   are expected to <u>increase</u>. Higher
   temperatures mean that more <u>water</u>
   <u>evaporates</u> from the land and from
   plants. This makes soils <u>drier</u> and
   means that plants <u>die</u> (so their roots
   no longer hold the soil together).

Human Activities

1) <u>Removal of fuel wood</u> — many people in arid (dry)
   areas rely on <u>wood</u> for fuel for <u>cooking</u>. Removal of
   trees leaves the soil <u>exposed</u> so it is more <u>easily eroded</u>.

2) <u>Overgrazing</u> — <u>too many</u> cattle or sheep eat the plants
   <u>faster</u> than they can <u>re-grow</u>. This leads to more <u>soil</u>
   <u>erosion</u> because the plants no longer hold the soil
   together. <u>Trampling</u> by animals also erodes the soil.

3) <u>Over-cultivation</u> — if crops are planted in the <u>same area</u>
   continually, all the <u>nutrients</u> in the soil get <u>used up</u>.
   This means that plants can <u>no longer be grown</u> in those
   soils and, without plants, <u>soil erosion</u> increases.

4) <u>Population growth</u> — this puts <u>pressure</u> on the land,
   leading to more <u>deforestation</u> (for firewood), more
   <u>overgrazing</u> and more <u>over-cultivation</u>.

The **Risk** of **Desertification** can be **Reduced**

There are lots of <u>different strategies</u> for <u>reducing the risk</u> of desertification, for example:

1) WATER MANAGEMENT — growing <u>crops</u> that don't need much <u>water</u> (e.g. millet, sorghum or
   olives) can <u>reduce</u> water use. Using <u>drip irrigation</u> on crops instead of surface irrigation means
   that the soil isn't <u>eroded</u> by lots of water being added all in one go.

2) TREE PLANTING — <u>trees</u> can be planted to act as <u>windbreaks</u> to protect soil from
   <u>wind erosion</u>. Trees can also be used to <u>stabilise</u> the <u>sand</u> to prevent the desert from
   <u>encroaching</u> on farm land. Growing trees <u>in amongst</u> crops <u>protects</u> the crops (and
   soil) by providing shade, which <u>reduces temperatures</u> and <u>evaporation rates</u>.

3) SOIL MANAGEMENT — <u>leaving</u> areas of land to <u>rest</u> in between grazing or planting lets them
   <u>recover</u> their nutrients. <u>Rotating crops</u> that use <u>different nutrients</u> from the soil means that the same
   nutrients don't keep being <u>removed</u>. <u>Compost</u> can be used to <u>add extra nutrients</u> to the soil.

4) APPROPRIATE TECHNOLOGY — this involves using <u>cheap</u>, <u>sustainable</u> and <u>easily available materials</u>
   that are <u>easy</u> for local people to <u>maintain</u>. For example, <u>sand fences</u> (barriers to trap windblown sand)
   or <u>terraces</u> can be constructed to <u>stabilise</u> the soil and reduce erosion. The rate of deforestation can be
   reduced by using <u>solar cookers</u>, which use the <u>sun's energy</u> to heat food. They are <u>cheap</u> and <u>easy</u> to
   make, and don't require fuel wood to work.

Desertification is when productive land turns into desert

There's a lot to learn here — but the key thing is that the loss of plants means that the soil is more easily eroded,
making it less fertile and so less able to support plants. Management strategies aim to reverse this process.

Worked Exam Questions

Here's a typical exam question with the answers filled in to help. They won't be there on the real exam though, so you'd better learn how to answer them yourself...

1 Study **Figure 1**, a photograph of a water source in Libya.

Figure 1

1.1 Using **Figure 1**, describe where biodiversity in hot deserts is highest.

> Biodiversity is highest around water sources, such as the
>
> oasis shown in Figure 1.
>
> *[1]*

1.2 Explain why biodiversity in hot desert environments is particularly vulnerable to human activity.

> Most species of plants and animals live near water sources, and this is also where human populations
>
> are highest. Human activity in these areas is therefore likely to have a negative effect on biodiversity.
>
> If water sources are used up (e.g. for irrigation) or contaminated (e.g. by livestock), there is no
>
> water available for plants and animals, so they may die. Also, human activities are thought to be
>
> contributing to climate change. Climate change may make some desert environments hotter and
>
> drier, so species that are adapted to particular conditions may move or die out.
>
> *[4]*
>
> *[Total 5 marks]*

2 Study **Figure 2**, a map of a hot desert region showing some of the sources of income in different locations.

Figure 2

2.1 Using **Figure 2**, describe the economic opportunities at location A.

> Economic opportunities
>
> at location A may
>
> include mining and
>
> commercial farming.
>
> There are mineral
>
> resources to the north of the settlement, which could encourage mining companies to extract them
>
> for export. The settlement is also situated on the river, so there is water for irrigation, creating
>
> opportunities for commercial farming, e.g. to the south of the settlement.
>
> *[Total 3 marks]*

Exam Questions

1   Study **Figure 1**, a diagram showing interdependence in a hot desert environment.

1.1   Using **Figure 1**, describe and explain the interdependence between the climate and the soil in a hot desert environment.

Figure 1

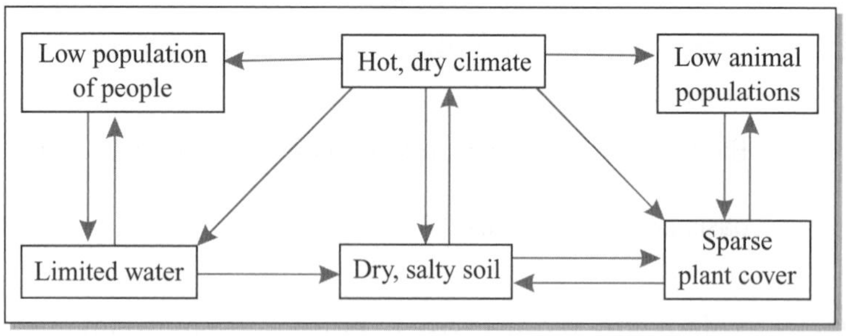

Low population of people ← Hot, dry climate → Low animal populations

Low population of people ↓

Hot, dry climate ↓

Low animal populations ↓

Limited water → Dry, salty soil ← Sparse plant cover

....

....

....

....

....

[3]

1.2   Using **Figure 1**, outline **two** ways that water extraction for crop irrigation may affect hot desert environments.

1:...

....

2:...

....

[2]

[Total 5 marks]

2   Study **Figure 2**, a photograph of an area of hot desert in Morocco.

2.1   Suggest how human activity may contribute to desertification in areas on the fringes of hot deserts.

Figure 2

....

....

....

....

....

....

....

....

....

[Total 6 marks]

Cold Environments — Tundra and Polar

It's time for a foray into the <u>ice cold</u> world of <u>tundra</u> and <u>polar environments</u>...

Tundra and Polar Environments are found in Cold Climates

Climate

1) Polar areas are very cold, temperatures are <u>never</u> normally above 0 °C. Winters are <u>normally</u> below <u>–40 °C</u> and can reach <u>–90 °C</u>.

2) Tundra areas are also <u>cold</u> — temperatures in the <u>warmest</u> month are a maximum of only <u>10 °C</u>, and winters can reach around <u>–50 °C</u>.

3) Rainfall (and snowfall) is <u>low</u> — no more than <u>100 mm</u> a year in <u>polar</u> areas and <u>380 mm</u> or less in <u>tundra</u> areas (mainly in the summer).

4) There are <u>clearly defined</u> seasons — <u>cold summers</u> and <u>even colder winters</u>.

Soil

1) Polar environments are <u>covered by ice sheets</u>, so there is <u>no soil</u> exposed and <u>few</u> plants or animals.

2) Soil in <u>tundra</u> environments is <u>thin</u> and <u>acidic</u> and <u>not very fertile</u>.

3) There is normally a layer of <u>permanently frozen ground</u> called <u>permafrost</u> beneath the thin soil — the permafrost layer contains large amounts of trapped greenhouse gas.

Plants

1) There are <u>very few</u> plants in polar areas — some <u>lichens</u> and <u>mosses</u> are found on rocks, and there are a few <u>grasses</u> on the <u>coast</u> of Antarctica where it's <u>warmer</u>.

2) Plants grow <u>slowly</u> and <u>don't</u> grow <u>very tall</u> — <u>grasses</u> are the most common plants. Further north, only <u>mosses</u> and <u>lichens</u> can survive.

3) Some <u>small</u>, <u>short</u> trees grow in <u>warmer</u>, <u>sheltered</u> areas.

Animals

1) There are <u>relatively few</u> different species of animals compared with <u>other ecosystems</u>.

2) <u>Polar bears</u>, <u>penguins</u> and marine mammals like <u>whales</u>, <u>seals</u> and <u>walrus</u> are examples of animals found in <u>polar</u> regions. <u>Lemmings</u>, Arctic <u>hares</u>, <u>wolves</u> and <u>reindeer</u> are all animals that live in <u>tundra</u> areas.

People

1) Polar environments are <u>almost uninhabited</u>. A few <u>scientists</u> live on <u>Antarctica</u> for short periods. Some <u>indigenous</u> people live in <u>Arctic</u> areas.

2) Tundra environments are home to many people, including <u>indigenous peoples</u>, and <u>oil</u> and <u>gas workers</u> in larger towns.

Cold Environments are Fragile, Interdependent Ecosystems

The <u>biotic</u> (living) components of cold environments (plants, animals and people) and the <u>abiotic</u> (non-living) components (climate, soils, permafrost) are <u>closely related</u> — if <u>one</u> of them <u>changes</u>, <u>the others</u> are <u>affected</u>.

1) <u>Plants</u> gain their <u>nutrients</u> from the <u>soil</u>, and <u>provide nutrients</u> to the animals that eat them. In turn, animals spread <u>seeds</u> through their <u>dung</u>, helping the plants to <u>reproduce</u>.

2) <u>Plant cover</u> is <u>low</u> — the cold climate causes plants to <u>grow slowly</u> and also to <u>decompose very slowly</u>. This means that the soil is relatively <u>low in nutrients</u> — further <u>reducing</u> the ability of plants to <u>grow</u>.

3) <u>Herbivores</u> like reindeer that rely on plants like <u>mosses</u> to survive must migrate to areas where plants are <u>able to grow</u> to find food. <u>Carnivores</u> like wolves have to <u>follow</u> the <u>herbivores</u>.

4) In <u>summer</u>, when the tundra has greater <u>plant cover</u>, the surface plants <u>absorb heat</u> from the sun, and prevent the permafrost below from <u>thawing</u>. The permafrost provides <u>water</u> for plants.

5) Changes to components of the ecosystem, such as vehicles <u>damaging plant cover</u>, can have <u>knock-on effects</u> on the <u>whole ecosystem</u>, e.g. by causing permafrost to <u>melt</u>. Melting permafrost can <u>flood land</u>, preventing plants from growing. It also <u>releases</u> trapped <u>greenhouse gases</u> — leading to increased <u>global warming</u>, and changes to the <u>climate</u> of cold environments, threatening <u>plants and animals</u>.

REVISION TIP

Cold environments are often frozen, but they're not lifeless

Knowing the characteristics of cold environments will help you understand how the components are related, so make sure you're clear on the details then draw a diagram showing all the connections.

Cold Environments — Biodiversity

Cold environments are <u>difficult</u> to <u>survive</u> in — even well-equipped polar explorers can get it <u>wrong</u>.
Plants and animals have some <u>clever adaptations</u> to help them <u>survive</u> in the harsh conditions.

The **Plants** and **Animals** have **Adapted** to the **Cold, Dry Climate**

<u>Plants</u> in tundra environments have <u>adapted</u> to survive the <u>extreme cold</u> and <u>strong winds</u>.
They must also adapt to the <u>dry winter</u> conditions when all moisture is <u>frozen</u>, and <u>wet summer</u>
conditions when the <u>top layer</u> of soil <u>thaws</u> and the ground becomes <u>boggy</u> and <u>waterlogged</u>.

1) Most plants become <u>dormant</u> (stop trying to grow) to survive the <u>cold</u>, <u>dark winters</u>.

2) Plants are <u>small</u> and <u>round-shaped</u> to provide protection from the <u>wind</u>.

3) Most plants have <u>shallow roots</u> because of the layer of <u>permafrost</u> beneath the soil layer.

4) Leaves are generally <u>small</u> to limit the amount of <u>moisture lost</u>
through <u>transpiration</u>.

5) The warmer, wetter summer is <u>very short</u>, so most plants have
adapted to have a <u>growing season</u> of just <u>50-60 days</u>.

6) Many plants use <u>underground runners</u> or <u>bulbs</u> instead of <u>seeds</u>
to <u>reproduce</u> because the growing season is so <u>short</u>.

Tundra vegetation

<u>Animals</u> in cold environments have also <u>adapted</u> to the cold, dry, snowy conditions:

1) Animals in cold environments tend to be <u>well-insulated</u> — they might
have a <u>thick fur coat</u> like polar bears or a <u>layer of blubber</u> like seals.
This reduces the amount of <u>energy</u> they have to use to keep <u>warm</u>.

2) Some animals <u>hibernate</u> to conserve energy and survive the <u>winter</u>,
e.g. Arctic <u>ground squirrels</u> hibernate for 7-8 months of the year and
can survive even if their <u>body temperature drops</u> below freezing.

3) Animals that <u>don't hibernate</u> have adapted to survive on
the <u>limited food</u> sources available in winter. For example,
<u>reindeer</u> have adapted to eat <u>lichens</u> in winter.

4) Many birds <u>migrate</u> to <u>warmer</u> areas during <u>winter</u> — for example,
<u>Arctic terns</u> live in the <u>Arctic</u> during the <u>northern</u> hemisphere summer,
then fly to the <u>Antarctic</u> for the <u>southern</u> hemisphere summer.

5) Many animals have <u>white coats</u> in <u>winter</u> for <u>camouflage</u> — this helps
predators to <u>sneak up</u> on prey, and prey to <u>hide</u> in the snow. E.g. <u>Arctic</u>
<u>hares</u> are <u>white</u> so they are harder for predators to <u>spot</u> in the <u>snow</u>.

An Arctic tern

A camouflaged
Arctic hare

Cold Environments have **Low Biodiversity**

1) Cold environments have very <u>low biodiversity</u> (particularly <u>Antarctica</u>) — there are <u>fewer species</u>
of plants and animals in cold environments than most other environments.

2) <u>Low biodiversity</u> means when the population of one species <u>changes</u> it can affect
the population of <u>dependent species</u> — e.g. <u>changes</u> in the number of <u>lemmings</u>
affects the number of <u>Arctic foxes</u> (their predators).

3) <u>Global warming</u> is causing some species to move <u>towards</u> the poles, where it is <u>cooler</u>, to cope with
<u>temperature rises</u> elsewhere. Species already adapted to polar environments <u>can't</u> go anywhere
colder, so are at <u>risk</u> of <u>decline</u> or <u>extinction</u> if <u>climate change</u> causes the polar areas to <u>warm up</u>.

Arctic hares have white coats because they're adapted to wintry conditions

If you've chosen to study Cold Environments, you'll need to do a cracking good job of learning how plants and
animals adapt to the conditions, and why biodiversity is low. Knowing this will set you up for the exam nicely.

Development in Cold Environments

CASE STUDY

Alaska is one example of a cold environment where the extreme climate creates challenges to development.

There are **Development Opportunities** in **Alaska...**

Alaska is a cold environment that's part of the USA.
The northern parts of Alaska are inside the Arctic circle.
Opportunities for economic development include:

1) Oil and gas — over half Alaska's income comes from the oil and gas industry. Most oil fields are around Prudhoe Bay, and the Trans-Alaska oil pipeline links the oil fields with Valdez, from where the oil can be shipped to customers.

2) Mineral resources — gold, silver, iron ore and copper are mined, particularly in the Tintina gold belt. It contributed $2.2 billion to Alaska's GDP in 2013.

3) Fishing — salmon, crab and pollock are fished. Fishing employs 79 000 people and contributes over $5bn to Alaska's economy.

4) Tourism — tourists are attracted by Alaska's wilderness scenery. Around 2 million tourists visit Alaska each year, bringing in money and creating opportunities for employment.

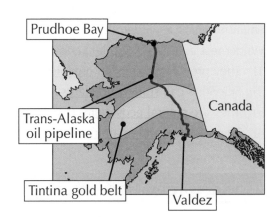

...but there are also **Challenges to Development**

1) Alaska's state population is one of the smallest in the US, despite being the largest state by area. Most people live in the south and southeast of the state, near the coast, where it is warmer and less remote.

2) Development in Alaska can present challenges — getting access to resources and finding a workforce to exploit them, as well as providing buildings, infrastructure and protection from the extreme weather.

Extreme Temperature

1) It's really cold — in Prudhoe Bay the mean annual temperature is around −9 °C. Extreme weather such as snow and strong winds are common. Exposure to the extreme cold can cause injury or death, and healthcare may be a long distance away.

2) As well as extreme temperature and weather, Alaska is subject to extremes in the amount of daylight it gets — in winter, it can be dark nearly all the time.

Inaccessibility

1) Alaska is a long way from the rest of the US. Some areas are extremely remote, and the mountainous terrain makes access difficult and expensive.

2) In winter, the only way to get to some towns is via air or dangerous ice roads. In summer, there are no roads to some towns because the ground is too soft.

3) The population of Alaska is small and scattered — people in small towns may be a long way from employment opportunities or services.

Buildings and Infrastructure

1) Providing buildings and infrastructure that can cope with the ground and weather conditions is difficult and expensive.

2) Most construction work can only take place in summer, when the days are longer and temperatures are warmer.

3) The value of some resources means that people find ways to overcome the challenges, e.g. some parts of the Trans-Alaska oil pipeline are raised on stilts, to prevent it melting the permafrost, which would make the ground unstable.

Cold environments have opportunities, but exploiting them can be difficult

Cold environments can be full of challenges — it's what happens when you combine beautiful, frozen wildernesses with useful economic development opportunities. You might be asked about them in the exam, so get learning...

Cold Environments — Sustainable Management

Cold environments are <u>fragile</u> areas that need to be <u>protected</u> from damage by <u>sustainable management</u>.

Cold Environments are **Valuable Wilderness Areas** worth **Conserving**

<u>Wilderness</u> areas are wild, natural environments that haven't been changed significantly by people. They are mainly <u>undeveloped</u>, <u>uninhabited</u> and <u>undisturbed</u>. <u>Large parts</u> of cold environments are wilderness areas.

Wilderness areas are <u>important</u> and worth <u>protecting</u> for the future because:

1) They provide <u>habitats</u> for <u>organisms</u>, so help to protect <u>biodiversity</u>.

2) Scientists can <u>study wild plants</u> and <u>animals</u> in their <u>natural habitats</u>.

3) They are <u>natural ecosystems</u> that are useful to <u>compare</u> to <u>managed</u> ecosystems.

4) They are the <u>last remaining</u> areas that <u>haven't</u> been <u>altered</u> by human activity.

Cold Environments are **Fragile** and Take a **Long Time** to **Recover**

Cold environments are very <u>fragile</u> — if they are <u>interfered</u> with, it can take a <u>long time</u> for them to return to their <u>original state</u>.

1) Plant <u>growth</u> is very <u>slow</u> — if plants are <u>damaged</u> (e.g. by vehicle tyres) they take a <u>long time</u> to regrow.

2) Species are <u>highly specialised</u> so find it difficult to <u>adapt to change</u> — e.g. polar bears are adapted to hunt on ice and their numbers are <u>decreasing</u> as sea ice melts <u>earlier</u> each year.

Strategies are Needed to **Balance** Economic Development with **Conservation**

There are lots of <u>different strategies</u> that can help balance <u>conservation</u> with <u>economic development</u>:

Use of Technology

1) Development can cause <u>problems</u> that can be <u>solved</u> by <u>modern technology</u>. E.g. heated buildings can <u>melt permafrost</u>, leading to <u>subsidence</u> which may cause <u>roads</u> and <u>buildings</u> to <u>collapse</u> and <u>pipes to crack</u>.

2) Modern <u>construction methods</u> can minimise environmental impacts, for example <u>elevating buildings</u> on piles or building on <u>gravel beds</u> can prevent buildings <u>warming the ground</u>.

Conservation Groups

1) Conservation groups <u>pressure governments</u> to <u>protect</u> cold environments that are <u>at risk</u> or have been <u>damaged</u>.

2) E.g. the <u>World Wild Fund for Nature</u> and <u>Greenpeace</u> encourage <u>sustainable management</u> of cold environments and argue for <u>governments</u> to prevent actions that would cause <u>damage</u>.

Role of Governments

1) If development is allowed <u>without regulation</u>, it can cause <u>damage</u> to the environment. E.g. <u>mineral</u> and <u>energy mining</u> can cause ground and water <u>pollution</u> and logging activities <u>destroy habitats</u>.

2) Governments can make <u>laws</u> to <u>protect</u> cold environments, such as the <u>1964 Wilderness Act</u> that designated <u>wilderness areas</u> and <u>protected</u> them from development, including large parts of <u>Alaska</u>.

International Agreements

1) Some cold environments are protected by <u>international agreements</u>, e.g. Antarctica.

2) The <u>1959 Antarctic Treaty</u>, signed by <u>12 nations</u>, <u>limits visitors</u> landing at one site to <u>100</u> at a time, ensures peaceful <u>non-military</u> activities, prohibits <u>nuclear activities</u> and prevents <u>cruise ships</u> of over <u>500 passengers</u> stopping.

EXAM TIP

Development can cause damage that takes a very long time to recover

Balancing the benefits of economic development against the need to protect cold environments from being damaged could well come up in your exam. To ace a question on this topic, you need to make sure you know both sides of the argument and be ready to write about a few strategies that can be used.

Worked Exam Questions

It's not enough just to learn some facts for the exam, you'll also need to know how to put them into a good exam answer. So here are some worked examples to help you on the way.

1 Study **Figure 1**, a diagram showing interdependence in cold environments.

Figure 1

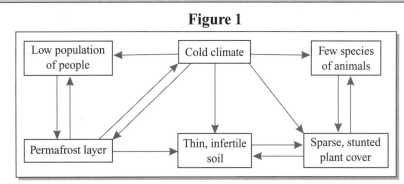

1.1 Using **Figure 1** and your own knowledge, describe how the climate can affect the soil fertility in a cold environment.

The cold climate causes plants to decompose very slowly. This means that the soil is relatively low in nutrients.

[2]

1.2 Explain how damage to the plants in a tundra environment could affect the climate there.

Damaging plant cover can cause permafrost to melt. Melting permafrost can release trapped greenhouse gases. These contribute to global warming, leading to changes in the climate of cold environments.

[3]

1.3 To what extent can the needs of economic development be balanced with the need for conservation in cold environments?

People living in cold environments need to be able to exploit economic opportunities to provide jobs and earn money, e.g. from mining, tourism and mineral extraction. However, cold environments are fragile and often pristine natural ecosystems that are worth conserving and can take a long time to recover. Governments can introduce laws (e.g. the 1964 Wilderness Act in the USA) to protect parts of cold environments from development and regulate potentially damaging economic activities. International agreements can be made between countries to protect uninhabited areas, for example the 1959 Antarctic Treaty limits visitors to Antarctica and prohibits nuclear activities. Technology can be used to prevent or minimise environmental problems caused by development, for example using modern construction methods like elevating buildings on piles or building on gravel beds can prevent buildings warming the ground and melting the permafrost. In conclusion, although any development in cold environments can cause damage, it is possible to use strategies like regulation and modern technology to reduce the damage to an acceptable amount and contain it within a limited area.

[6]

[Total 11 marks]

Exam Questions

1 Study **Figure 1**, a photograph of an Arctic fox.

Figure 1

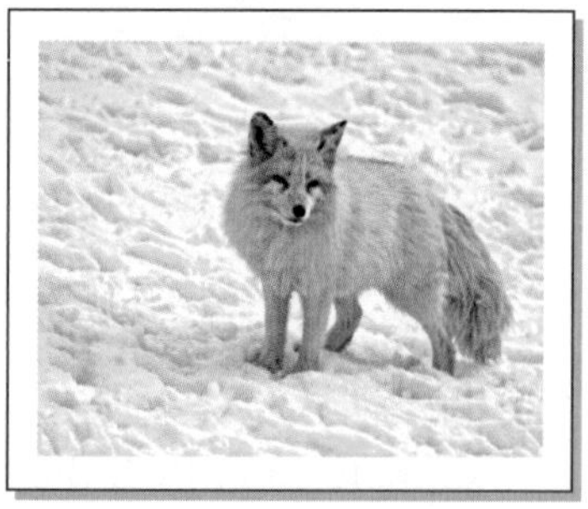

1.1 Outline **one** way in which the Arctic fox shown in **Figure 1** is adapted to its habitat.

[2]

1.2 Suggest how a warming climate could affect the Arctic fox shown in **Figure 1**.

[2]

[Total 4 marks]

2 Study **Figure 2**, a map of a cold environment.

Figure 2

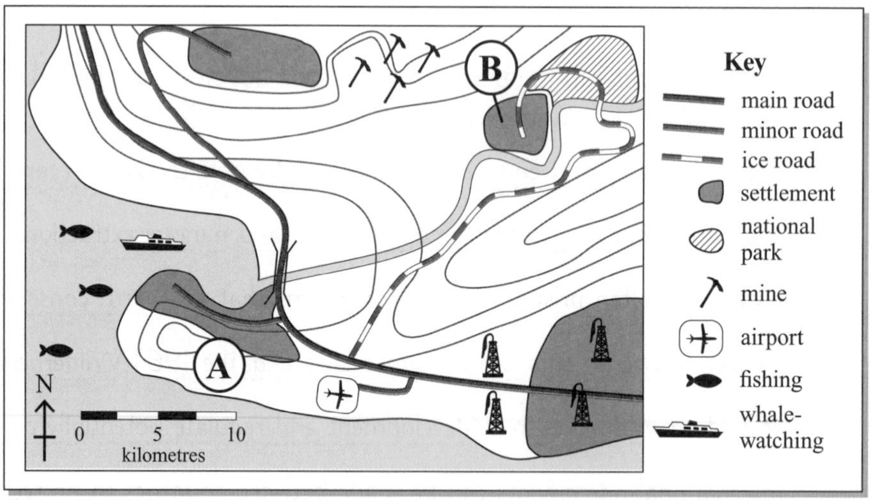
A
B
N
0
5
10
kilometres
Key
main road
minor road
ice road
settlement
national park
mine
airport
fishing
whale-watching

2.1 Using **Figure 2**, describe the economic opportunities at location A.

[3]

2.2 Using evidence from **Figure 2**, outline **one** challenge to the economic development of location B.

[2]

[Total 5 marks]

Revision Summary

That's just about it for Unit 1B — so now's an excellent moment to test your knowledge with some questions.

- Try these questions and tick off each one when you get it right.
- When you've done all the questions for a topic and are completely happy with it, tick off the topic.

Remember that you only need to learn one out of Hot Deserts and Cold Environments for the exam.

Ecosystems (p.28-29) ☑

1) What is an ecosystem?
2) Give two abiotic features of ecosystems.
3) What is a producer?
4) Describe the role of decomposers in ecosystems.
5) Where are temperate deciduous forests found?
6) What type of ecosystem is nearly always found between the Tropics of Cancer and Capricorn?

Tropical Rainforests (p.30-36) ☑

7) Describe the vegetation of tropical rainforests.
8) Give an example of an interdependent relationship in the tropical rainforest ecosystem.
9) Describe three ways that plants are adapted to living in tropical rainforests.
10) What is biodiversity?
11) Give six causes of deforestation in tropical rainforests.
12) a) Give an example of a tropical rainforest.
    b) Describe one negative economic impact of deforestation in that rainforest.
13) Why is it important to protect tropical rainforests?
14) What is selective logging?
15) What is ecotourism?
16) How do international hardwood agreements help in the sustainable management of rainforests?
17) Outline one way that education can help to make rainforest management more sustainable.

Hot Deserts (p.39-44) ☑

18) Describe the climate in hot deserts.
19) What is the soil like in hot deserts?
20) Describe two ways that people cope with the lack of water in hot deserts.
21) Give two adaptations of plants to hot desert environments.
22) Give two adaptations of animals to hot desert environments.
23) Describe one issue related to biodiversity in hot deserts.
24) Describe how inaccessibility can make development challenging in hot desert environments.
25) Explain how tree planting can reduce the risk of desertification.
26) Give one strategy, other than tree planting, that can reduce the risk of desertification.

Cold Environments (p.47-50) ☑

27) Describe the climate of cold environments.
28) How are polar and tundra environments different?
29) Give two adaptations of plants to cold environments.
30) How does hibernating during winter help animals in cold environments to survive?
31) Describe one issue related to biodiversity in cold environments.
32) How can extreme temperatures make development challenging in a cold environment?
33) a) What is a wilderness area?
    b) Why are these areas worth protecting?

The UK Physical Landscape

Ah, the UK landscape. Majestic <u>mountains</u>, cracking <u>coasts</u> and raging <u>rivers</u> — I could go on all day...

The UK has large **Upland** and **Lowland** Areas, and Important **Rivers**

The UK's main <u>upland</u> areas (orange and red on the map below) tend to be in the <u>north</u> and <u>west</u> of the country, and <u>lowland</u> areas (green on the map) to the <u>south</u> and <u>east</u>.

Most <u>cities</u> are in <u>lowland</u> areas and often on the UK's main <u>rivers</u> — such as <u>London</u> (on the <u>Thames</u>), <u>Liverpool</u> (on the <u>Mersey</u>) and <u>Cardiff</u> (on the <u>Severn Estuary</u>).

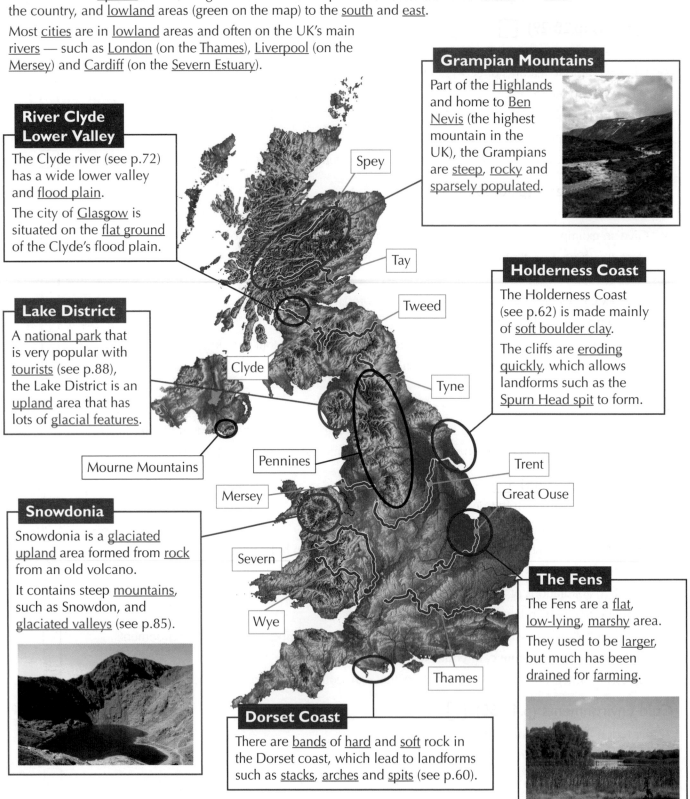

Grampian Mountains

Part of the <u>Highlands</u> and home to <u>Ben Nevis</u> (the highest mountain in the UK), the Grampians are <u>steep</u>, <u>rocky</u> and <u>sparsely populated</u>.

River Clyde Lower Valley

The Clyde river (see p.72) has a wide lower valley and <u>flood plain</u>.

The city of <u>Glasgow</u> is situated on the <u>flat ground</u> of the Clyde's flood plain.

Holderness Coast

The Holderness Coast (see p.62) is made mainly of <u>soft boulder clay</u>.

The cliffs are <u>eroding quickly</u>, which allows landforms such as the <u>Spurn Head spit</u> to form.

Lake District

A <u>national park</u> that is very popular with <u>tourists</u> (see p.88), the Lake District is an <u>upland</u> area that has lots of <u>glacial features</u>.

Snowdonia

Snowdonia is a <u>glaciated</u> <u>upland</u> area formed from <u>rock</u> from an old volcano.

It contains steep <u>mountains</u>, such as Snowdon, and <u>glaciated valleys</u> (see p.85).

The Fens

The Fens are a <u>flat</u>, <u>low-lying</u>, <u>marshy</u> area.

They used to be <u>larger</u>, but much has been <u>drained</u> for <u>farming</u>.

Dorset Coast

There are <u>bands</u> of <u>hard</u> and <u>soft</u> rock in the Dorset coast, which lead to landforms such as <u>stacks</u>, <u>arches</u> and <u>spits</u> (see p.60).

Map labels: Spey, Tay, Tweed, Clyde, Tyne, Trent, Great Ouse, Mourne Mountains, Pennines, Mersey, Severn, Wye, Thames

You don't need to memorise this map

This is a lovely little introduction to the rest of the UK physical landscapes section. You don't need to learn the exact locations of all these areas, but make sure you have a rough idea of the UK's main geographical features.

Coastal Weathering and Erosion

Weathering is the breakdown of rocks where they are, erosion is when the rocks are broken down and carried away by something, e.g. by seawater.

Rock is Broken Down by Mechanical and Chemical Weathering

1) Mechanical weathering is the breakdown of rock without changing its chemical composition. There's one main type of mechanical weathering that affects coasts — freeze-thaw weathering:

> 1) It happens when the temperature alternates above and below 0 °C (the freezing point of water).
> 2) Water gets into rock that has cracks, e.g. granite.
> 3) When the water freezes it expands, which puts pressure on the rock.
> 4) When the water thaws it contracts, which releases the pressure on the rock.
> 5) Repeated freezing and thawing widens the cracks and causes the rock to break up.

2) Chemical weathering is the breakdown of rock by changing its chemical composition. Carbonation weathering is a type of chemical weathering that happens in warm and wet conditions:

> 1) Rainwater has carbon dioxide dissolved in it, which makes it a weak carbonic acid.
> 2) Carbonic acid reacts with rock that contains calcium carbonate, e.g. carboniferous limestone, so the rocks are dissolved by the rainwater.

Mass Movement is when Material Falls Down a Slope

1) Mass movement is the shifting of rocks and loose material down a slope, e.g. a cliff. It happens when the force of gravity acting on a slope is greater than the force supporting it.

2) Mass movements cause coasts to retreat rapidly.

3) They're more likely to happen when the material is full of water — it acts as a lubricant, and makes the material heavier.

4) You need to know about THREE types of mass movement.

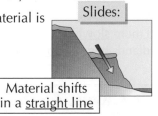

Slides:
Material shifts in a straight line

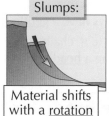

Slumps:
Material shifts with a rotation

Rockfalls:
Material breaks up and falls down slope

Waves Wear Away the Coast Using Three Processes of Erosion

> 1) Hydraulic power — waves crash against rock and compress the air in the cracks. This puts pressure on the rock. Repeated compression widens the cracks and makes bits of rock break off.
> 2) Abrasion — eroded particles in the water scrape and rub against rock, removing small pieces.
> 3) Attrition — eroded particles in the water smash into each other and break into smaller fragments. Their edges also get rounded off as they rub together.

1) The waves that carry out erosional processes are called destructive waves:

2) Destructive waves have a high frequency (10-14 waves per minute).

3) They're high and steep.

4) Their backwash (the movement of the water back down the beach) is more powerful than their swash (the movement of the water up the beach). This means material is removed from the coast.

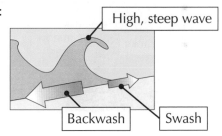

High, steep wave

Backwash   Swash

Practise sketching the three types of mass movement

This page is packed full of information, but it's just about how the coast is worn away and rocks are broken down into smaller pieces. Make sure you can sketch the diagrams without looking at the page.

Coastal Landforms Caused by Erosion

Erosion by waves forms many coastal landforms over long periods of time.

Waves Erode Cliffs to Form Wave-cut Platforms

1) Waves cause most erosion at the foot of a cliff (see diagrams below).
2) This forms a wave-cut notch, which is enlarged as erosion continues.
3) The rock above the notch becomes unstable and eventually collapses.
4) The collapsed material is washed away and a new wave-cut notch starts to form.
5) Repeated collapsing results in the cliff retreating.
6) A wave-cut platform is the platform that's left behind as the cliff retreats.

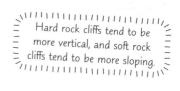
Hard rock cliffs tend to be more vertical, and soft rock cliffs tend to be more sloping.

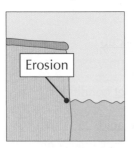
Erosion

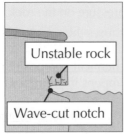
Unstable rock
Wave-cut notch

Collapsed material

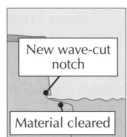
New wave-cut notch
Material cleared

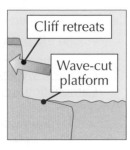
Cliff retreats
Wave-cut platform

Headlands and Bays Form Where Erosion Resistance is Different

1) Soft rocks or rocks with lots of joints have low resistance to erosion. Hard rocks with a solid structure have a high resistance to erosion.
2) Headlands and bays form where there are alternating bands of resistant and less resistant rock along a coast.
3) The less resistant rock (e.g. clay) is eroded quickly and this forms a bay — bays have a gentle slope.
4) The resistant rock (e.g. chalk) is eroded more slowly and it's left jutting out, forming a headland — headlands have steep sides.

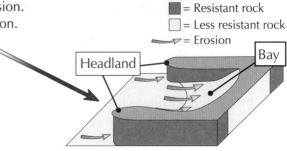
= Resistant rock
= Less resistant rock
= Erosion
Headland
Bay

Headlands are Eroded to form Caves, Arches and Stacks

1) Headlands are usually made of resistant rocks that have weaknesses like cracks.
2) Waves crash into the headlands and enlarge the cracks — mainly by hydraulic power and abrasion.
3) Repeated erosion and enlargement of the cracks causes a cave to form.
4) Continued erosion deepens the cave until it breaks through the headland — forming an arch, e.g. Durdle Door in Dorset.
5) Erosion continues to wear away the rock supporting the arch, until it eventually collapses.
6) This forms a stack — an isolated rock that's separate from the headland, e.g. Old Harry in Dorset.

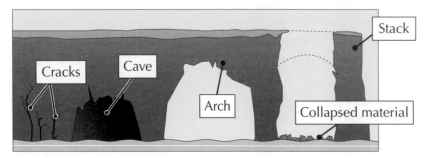
Cracks
Cave
Arch
Stack
Collapsed material

Arch
Durdle Door, Dorset

Caves are eroded to arches, which are eroded to stacks

This might seem a bit of a complicated page to begin with but take your time to learn how each landform is created. You could be asked about any individual landform in the exam, or about the whole process of formation.

Coastal Transportation and Deposition

The material that's been eroded is moved around the coast and deposited by waves.

Transportation is the Movement of Material

Material is transported along coasts by a process called longshore drift:

1) Waves follow the direction of the prevailing (most common) wind.

2) They usually hit the coast at an oblique angle (any angle that isn't a right angle).

3) The swash carries material up the beach, in the same direction as the waves.

4) The backwash then carries material down the beach at right angles, back towards the sea.

5) Over time, material zigzags along the coast.

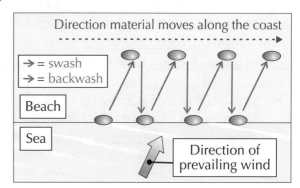

There are four other processes of transportation:

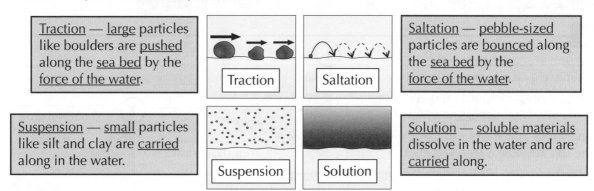

Traction — large particles like boulders are pushed along the sea bed by the force of the water.

Saltation — pebble-sized particles are bounced along the sea bed by the force of the water.

Suspension — small particles like silt and clay are carried along in the water.

Solution — soluble materials dissolve in the water and are carried along.

Deposition is the Dropping of Material

1) Deposition is when material being carried by the seawater is dropped on the coast. It occurs when water carrying sediment slows down so that it isn't moving fast enough to carry so much sediment.

2) Coasts are built up when the amount of deposition is greater than the amount of erosion.

3) The amount of material that's deposited on an area of coast is increased when:

   • There's lots of erosion elsewhere on the coast, so there's lots of material available.

   • There's lots of transportation of material into the area.

4) Low energy waves (i.e. slow waves) carry material to the coast but they're not strong enough to take a lot of material away — this means there's lots of deposition and very little erosion.

Waves that deposit more material than they erode are called constructive waves.

1) Constructive waves have a low frequency (6-8 waves per minute).

2) They're low and long.

3) The swash is powerful and it carries material up the coast.

4) The backwash is weaker and it doesn't take a lot of material back down the coast. This means material is deposited on the coast.

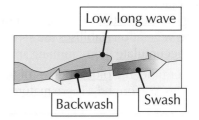

The amount of erosion affects the amount of deposition elsewhere

More processes for you to learn here but none of them are tricky. You might find it useful to draw yourself a diagram of how longshore drift works — you'll get a feel for how the material is moved along the coast in a zigzag pattern.

Coastal Landforms Caused by Deposition

Here are some more <u>landforms</u> for you to learn about. This time it's all about <u>deposition</u>.

Beaches are formed by Deposition

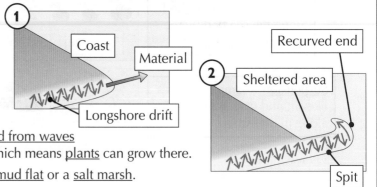

High water mark

Low water mark

Constructive wave

Beach

1) Beaches are found on coasts <u>between</u> the <u>high water mark</u> (the <u>highest point on the land</u> the <u>sea level</u> gets to) and the <u>low water mark</u> (the <u>lowest point</u> on the land the <u>sea level</u> gets to).

2) They're formed by <u>constructive waves</u> (see p.57) depositing material like <u>sand</u> and <u>shingle</u>.

3) <u>Sand</u> and <u>shingle beaches</u> have different <u>characteristics</u>:

- <u>Sand</u> beaches are <u>flat</u> and <u>wide</u> — sand particles are <u>small</u> and the weak backwash <u>can</u> move them <u>back down</u> the beach, creating a <u>long, gentle slope</u>.
- <u>Shingle</u> beaches are <u>steep</u> and <u>narrow</u> — shingle particles are <u>large</u> and the weak backwash <u>can't</u> move them back down the beach. The shingle particles <u>build up</u> and create a <u>steep slope</u>.

Deposited Sediment forms Spits, Bars and Sand Dunes

Spits

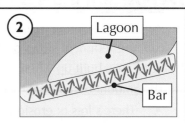

1) Spits form at <u>sharp bends</u> in the coastline, e.g. at a <u>river mouth</u>.

2) <u>Longshore drift</u> transports sand and shingle <u>past</u> the bend and <u>deposits</u> it in the sea.

3) Strong winds and waves can <u>curve</u> the end of the spit (forming a <u>recurved end</u>).

4) The <u>sheltered area</u> behind the spit is <u>protected from waves</u> — lots of material <u>accumulates</u> in this area, which means <u>plants</u> can grow there.

5) <u>Over time</u>, the sheltered area can become a <u>mud flat</u> or a <u>salt marsh</u>.

1 Coast — Material — Longshore drift

2 Recurved end — Sheltered area — Spit

Bars

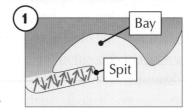

1) A bar is formed when a spit <u>joins two headlands together</u>.

2) The bar <u>cuts off</u> the bay between the headlands <u>from the sea</u>.

3) This means a <u>lagoon</u> can form <u>behind</u> the bar.

1 Bay — Spit

2 Lagoon — Bar

Sand Dunes

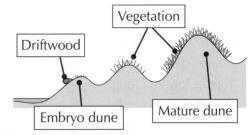

1) <u>Sand dunes</u> are formed when <u>sand</u> deposited by <u>longshore drift</u> is moved <u>up</u> the beach by the <u>wind</u>.

2) <u>Obstacles</u> (e.g. driftwood) cause wind speed to <u>decrease</u> so sand is <u>deposited</u>. This sand is <u>colonised</u> by <u>plants</u> and <u>grasses</u>. The vegetation <u>stabilises</u> the sand and encourages more sand to <u>accumulate</u> there, forming small dunes called <u>embryo dunes</u>.

3) Over time, the <u>oldest</u> dunes <u>migrate</u> inland as newer embryo dunes are formed. These <u>mature dunes</u> can reach heights of <u>up to 10 m</u>.

Driftwood — Vegetation — Embryo dune — Mature dune

Bars are just spits that join two headlands together

In the exam, you might have to identify coastal landforms caused by deposition on photographs or diagrams. It's not too tricky — just make sure you're familiar with the main features of each landform before the exam.

Identifying Coastal Landforms

Map skills will come in very useful in your exam so it's worth practising them now.

Identifying Landforms Caused by Erosion

You might be asked to identify coastal landforms on a map in the exam. The simplest thing they could ask is whether the map is showing erosional or depositional landforms, so here's how to identify a few erosional landforms to get you started:

Have a look at pages 170-171 for more on reading maps.

Caves, Arches and Stacks

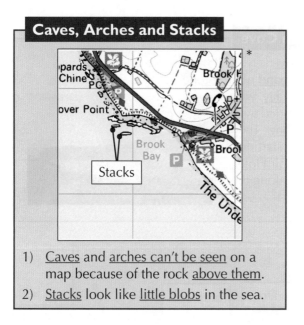

1) Caves and arches can't be seen on a map because of the rock above them.
2) Stacks look like little blobs in the sea.

Cliffs and Wave-cut Platforms

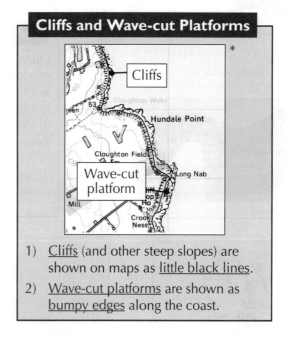

1) Cliffs (and other steep slopes) are shown on maps as little black lines.
2) Wave-cut platforms are shown as bumpy edges along the coast.

Identifying Landforms Caused by Deposition

Identifying depositional landforms is easy once you know that beaches are shown in yellow on maps. Here's how to identify a couple of depositional landforms:

Beaches

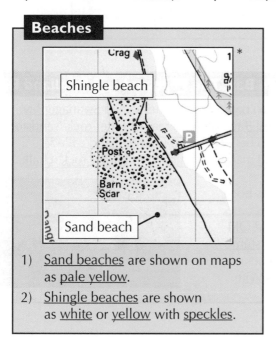

1) Sand beaches are shown on maps as pale yellow.
2) Shingle beaches are shown as white or yellow with speckles.

Spits

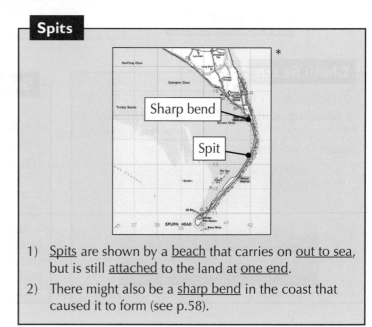

1) Spits are shown by a beach that carries on out to sea, but is still attached to the land at one end.
2) There might also be a sharp bend in the coast that caused it to form (see p.58).

Make sure you can identify each landform on a map

There are some easy marks up for grabs with map questions, so learn this page. Practise looking for landforms on any maps you can get hold of. Don't forget though, caves and arches can't be seen.

UK Coastal Landscape

The <u>Dorset coast</u> has lots of landforms — <u>headlands</u>, <u>bays</u>, <u>arches</u>, <u>stacks</u>, <u>coves</u>, <u>tombolos</u>, <u>lagoons</u>...

The **Dorset Coast** has Examples of many **Coastal Landforms**

The Dorset coast is made from bands of <u>hard rock</u> (like limestone and chalk) and <u>soft rock</u> (like clay). The rocks have been <u>eroded at different rates</u> giving <u>headlands</u> and <u>bays</u> and lots of other exciting coastal landforms.

Durdle Door

<u>Durdle Door</u> is a great example of an <u>arch</u>. <u>Erosion by waves</u> opened up a <u>crack</u> in the limestone <u>headland</u>, which became a <u>cave</u> and then developed into an arch.

Lulworth Cove

<u>Lulworth Cove</u> is a small bay formed after a gap was eroded in a <u>band of limestone</u>. Behind the limestone is a band of <u>clay</u>, which has been eroded away to form the <u>bay</u>. The same is now starting to happen at <u>Stair Hole</u> further west along the coast.

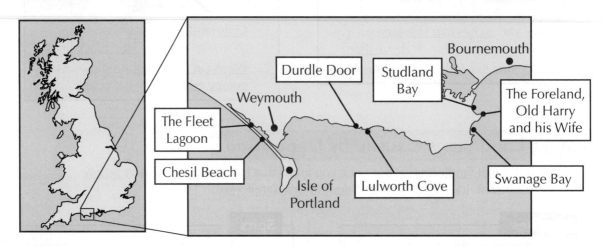

Chesil Beach

<u>Chesil Beach</u> is a <u>tombolo</u> (a type of <u>bar</u>) formed by <u>longshore drift</u>. It joins the <u>Isle of Portland</u> to the mainland. Behind Chesil Beach is a shallow <u>lagoon</u> called <u>The Fleet Lagoon</u>.

Swanage Bay, The Foreland and Studland Bay

There are two <u>bays</u> with beaches called <u>Swanage Bay</u> and <u>Studland Bay</u>. They're areas of <u>softer rock</u> (<u>sandstone</u> and <u>clay</u>). In between them is a <u>headland</u> called <u>The Foreland</u> made from a band of <u>harder rock</u> (<u>chalk</u>). The end of the headland has been eroded to become a <u>stack</u> called <u>Old Harry</u> and a <u>stump</u> (a collapsed stack) called <u>Old Harry's Wife</u>.

You might have studied a different coastal landscape in class

If you've learnt about a different area, you can choose whether to revise that or the Dorset coastline for your exam. Whichever example you decide to revise, make sure you know the names of all the landforms for that bit of coast.

Coastal Management Strategies

The aim of coastal management is to protect people and the environment from the impacts of erosion and flooding. Not all coastal areas can be managed though — the amount of money available is limited.

Coastal Defences Include Hard and Soft Engineering

Hard Engineering
Man-made structures built to control the flow of the sea and reduce flooding and erosion.

Soft Engineering
Schemes set up using knowledge of the sea and its processes to reduce the effects of flooding and erosion.

	Defence	What it is	Benefits	Costs
Hard Engineering	**Sea Wall**	A wall made out of a hard material like concrete that reflects waves back to sea.	It prevents erosion of the coast. It also acts as a barrier to prevent flooding.	It creates a strong backwash, which erodes under the wall. Sea walls are very expensive to build and to maintain.
	Gabions	A wall of wire cages filled with rocks usually built at the foot of cliffs.	The gabions absorb wave energy and so reduce erosion. They're cheap and easy to build.	They're ugly to look at and the wire cages can corrode over time.
	Rock Armour	Boulders that are piled up along the coast. (It's also sometimes called rip-rap.)	The boulders absorb wave energy and so reduce erosion and flooding. It's a fairly cheap defence.	Boulders can be moved around by strong waves, so they need to be replaced.
	Groynes ← longshore drift	Wooden or stone fences that are built at right angles to the coast. They trap material transported by longshore drift.	They create wider beaches which slow the waves. This gives greater protection from flooding and erosion. They're a fairly cheap defence.	They starve beaches further down the coast of sand, making them narrower. Narrower beaches don't protect the coast as well, leading to greater erosion and floods.
Soft Engineering	**Beach Nourishment and Reprofiling**	Sand and shingle from elsewhere (e.g. from the seabed) or from lower down the beach that's added to the upper part of beaches.	It creates wider beaches which slow the waves. This gives greater protection from flooding and erosion.	Taking material from the seabed can kill organisms like sponges and corals. It's a very expensive defence. It has to be repeated.
	Dune Regeneration	Creating or restoring sand dunes by either nourishment, or by planting vegetation to stabilise the sand.	Sand dunes provide a barrier between the land and the sea. Wave energy is absorbed which prevents flooding and erosion. Stabilisation is cheap.	The protection is limited to a small area. Nourishment is very expensive.

Another Option is to just do Nothing — Managed Retreat

1) Managed retreat (also called coastal realignment) involves removing current defences and allowing the sea to flood the land behind.

2) Over time the land will become marshland, which then protects the land behind from flooding and erosion.

3) It is a cheap and easy strategy, and it doesn't need maintaining. The marshland can also create new habitats for plants and animals.

Breach in old defences

New marshland

4) Because land is lost to the sea, choosing areas to flood can cause conflicts, e.g. flooding farmland would affect the livelihood of farmers. The saltwater can also have a negative effect on existing ecosystems.

REVISION TIP

You might be asked to identify management strategies from a photo
Don't just learn the names of the different engineering strategies — make sure you know exactly what they look like, how they work and a couple of benefits and disadvantages of each one.

Coastal Management

The Holderness coast in North East England has one of the highest rates of coastal erosion in Europe. Coastal management schemes are used to protect some areas from erosion.

The **Holderness Coast** is **Retreating**

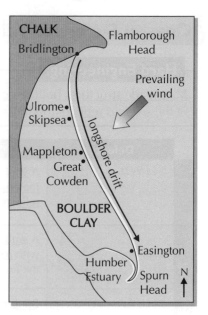

1) Erosion is causing the cliffs to collapse along the Holderness coastline. The cliffs are made from soft, easily eroded boulder clay.

2) The prevailing winds mean that the eroded material is moved south along the coast by longshore drift instead of staying in the place it came from, exposing a new area of cliff to erosion and causing the coastline to retreat.

3) About 1.8 m of land is lost to the sea every year — in some places, e.g. Great Cowden, the rate of erosion has been over 10 m per year in recent years. Farms, businesses and homes are threatened by the erosion.

4) Over 11 km of the Holderness coastline is managed using hard engineering strategies because:

- There are towns and villages like Hornsea (population: over 8000), Withernsea (population: over 6000) and Mappleton where people live.

- There is important infrastructure like the B1242 road which links many of the towns and businesses along the coast.

- The gas terminal at Easington supplies 25% of the UK's gas and is right on the edge of the cliff.

Parts of **Holderness** are **Protected** by **Rock Armour** and **Groynes**

In 1991, 450 m of coastline around Mappleton had to be protected at a cost of £2 million, and using over 61 000 tonnes of rocks.

Coastal management at Mappleton involved two types of hard engineering:

1) Placing rock armour (granite boulders) along the base of the cliff to absorb the power of the waves.

2) Building two rock groynes to trap sand and create a beach to absorb the power of the waves.

There are also defences at Hornsea (where there is a sea wall and some groynes), and at Withernsea (where there is a sea wall, groynes and rock armour).

The Defences **Saved Mappleton...** but **Still Caused Conflicts**

The coastal management scheme was successful — the village of Mappleton and the B1242 road are no longer at risk from erosion.

However, the management strategy has caused conflicts. The rock groynes prevented sediment moving south along the coast by longshore drift. This has caused increased erosion south of Mappleton, and led to:

1) Loss of land to the south of Mappleton — especially around Great Cowden's farms and caravan park.

2) The operation of coastguard and lifeboat services from Spurn Head being under threat due to erosion.

3) A loss of habitat for wildlife on Spurn Head — less material is coming down the coast to collect at Spurn Head, so it is at risk of being washed away.

4) In 1999, a 1 km stretch of coast near the gas terminal at Easington having to be protected by rock armour — at a cost of £6.6 million.

5) Bays forming between the protected areas, and the protected areas becoming headlands. Maintaining the defences in the protected areas is becoming more expensive and may cause conflict.

The hard engineering strategies are moving the problems elsewhere

Holderness really is taking a battering from the sea. Cover the page and see if you can remember the impacts of the rapid erosion, the strategies used to manage it and the results of these strategies.

Worked Exam Questions

Have a read of these worked answers — they'll give you a good idea of what you need to write in the exam.

1 Study **Figure 1**, a photograph showing coastal landforms.

Figure 1

1.1 Name the type of landform labelled A in **Figure 1**.

Headland

[1]

1.2 Explain how the landforms shown in **Figure 1** are formed.

Headlands and bays form where there are alternating bands of resistant and less resistant rock along the coast. The less resistant rock is eroded quickly and this forms a bay. The resistant rock is eroded more slowly, forming a headland.

[3]

[Total 4 marks]

2 Study **Figure 2**, a graph showing how the width of a beach varied along its length in the years 2010 and 2015.

Figure 2

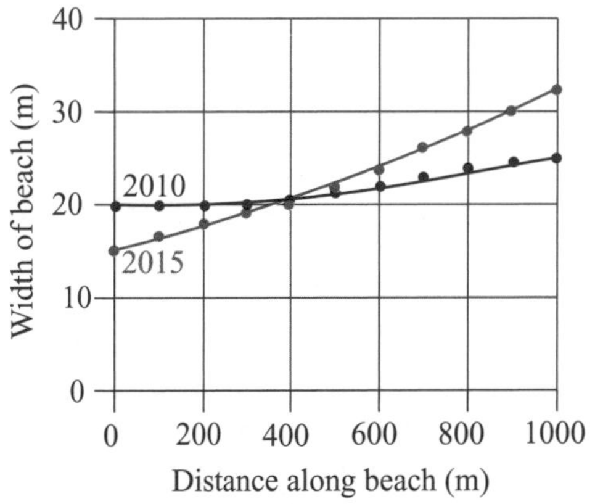

2.1 Name and describe the process of sediment transport that caused these changes in beach width.

The sediment was transported by longshore drift. Waves follow the direction of the prevailing wind, hitting the coast at an oblique angle. The swash carries material up the beach, in the same direction as the waves. The backwash then carries material down the beach at right angles to the beach, back towards the sea. Over time, material zigzags along the coast. The beach becomes narrower where material is transported away and wider where it is deposited.

[4]

2.2 Name the type of wave acting on the stretch of coast shown in **Figure 2**.

Constructive waves

[1]

2.3 Give **two** characteristics of this type of wave.

1: Constructive waves are low frequency.

2: They have a powerful swash.

[2]

[Total 7 marks]

Exam Questions

1   Study **Figure 1**, an Ordnance Survey® map of a coastal area in Devon.

1.1   The end of the spit is marked X on **Figure 1**. Give the six figure grid reference for the end of the spit.

....

.... *[1]*

Figure 1

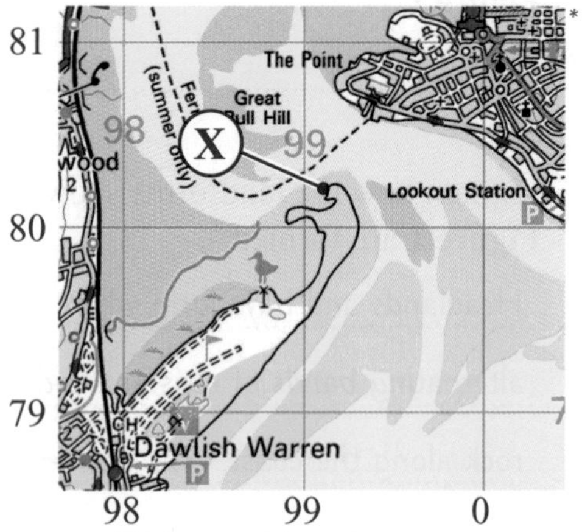

2 centimetres to 1 kilometre (one grid square)

Kilometres

0   1   2

1.2   What is the distance between the end of the spit and Dawlish Warren station at 979786?

> You'll need to use a ruler and the scale at the bottom of Figure 1 to work this out.

.... km

[1]

1.3   Explain how the spit shown in **Figure 1** was formed.

....

....

....

....

....

[2]

[Total 4 marks]

2   Study **Figure 2**, a news article about coastal defences in Cliffall, a UK coastal town.

Figure 2

HOPE FOR CLIFFALL'S COASTLINE

Work is due to start next week on new defences for the Cliffall coastline. The town has been suffering from the effects of coastal erosion over the last few years but it's hoped the new defences will prevent further problems. The scheme will use a combination of defences, including groynes, dune regeneration and beach nourishment. The work will be completed gradually over the next four years, with the groynes the top priority.

2.1   Describe **one** soft engineering strategy mentioned in **Figure 2**.

....

....

[1]

2.2   Give **one** advantage and **one** disadvantage of this soft engineering strategy.

Advantage:...

Disadvantage:...

[2]

[Total 3 marks]

Revision Summary

That wraps up <u>Coastal Landscapes in the UK</u> — time to test yourself and find out <u>how much you really know</u>.

- Try these questions and <u>tick off each one</u> when you <u>get it right</u>.
- When you've done <u>all the questions</u> for a topic and are <u>completely happy</u> with it, tick off the topic.

Remember, you only need to learn <u>two</u> from Coasts, Rivers and Glacial Landscapes, so if you're not a coasts sort of a person, you don't need to answer these questions — you can go straight onto rivers instead.

Weathering and Erosion (p.55-56) ☑

1) How does freeze-thaw weathering break up rock?
2) Describe the process of chemical weathering.
3) What are the three types of mass movement?
4) What are the three types of erosion caused by waves? Explain how they work.
5) Give the characteristics of destructive waves.
6) How does a wave-cut platform form?
7) Describe how erosion can turn a crack in a cliff into a cave.
8) What is a stack?

Transportation and Deposition (p.57-58) ☑

9) Apart from longshore drift, what are the four other processes of transport?
10) a) When does deposition occur?
    b) What can increase the amount of material that is deposited?
11) True or false: constructive waves have a weaker backwash than swash.
12) What are the characteristics of shingle beaches?
13) How do bars form?
14) How do sand dunes form?

Coastal Landforms (p.59-60) ☑

15) Why can't cracks, caves and arches be seen on a map?
16) What do stacks look like on a map?
17) How are cliffs shown on a map?
18) On maps, what do speckles on top of yellow shading tell you?
19) a) Name a coastal area which has erosional and depositional landforms.
    b) Name one erosional landform in that area.
    c) Name one depositional landform in that area.

Coastal Management (p.61-62) ☑

20) Describe the difference between hard engineering and soft engineering coastal management strategies.
21) What is a disadvantage of using sea walls as a coastal defence?
22) What are gabions?
23) What is rock armour?
24) What is managed retreat?
25) a) For a named coastline, explain why coastal management is needed.
    b) Give examples of conflicts caused by coastal management along this coastline.

The River Valley

You need to know <u>what</u> happens to the <u>shape</u> of a <u>river valley</u> and a <u>river's gradient</u> as it flows downhill.

A River's **Long Profile** and **Cross Profile Vary** Over its Course

1) The <u>path</u> of a river as it <u>flows downhill</u> is called its <u>course</u>.

2) Rivers have an <u>upper course</u> (closest to the <u>source</u> of the river), a <u>middle course</u> and a <u>lower course</u> (closest to the <u>mouth</u> of the river).

3) Rivers form <u>channels</u> and <u>valleys</u> as they <u>flow downhill</u>.

4) They <u>erode</u> the landscape — <u>wear it down</u>, then <u>transport</u> the material to somewhere else where it's <u>deposited</u>.

5) The <u>shape</u> of the <u>valley</u> and <u>channel changes</u> along the river depending on whether <u>erosion</u> or <u>deposition</u> is having the <u>most impact</u> (is the <u>dominant process</u>).

6) The <u>long profile</u> of a river shows you how the <u>gradient</u> (steepness) <u>changes</u> over the different courses.

7) The <u>cross profile</u> shows you what a <u>cross-section</u> of the river looks like.

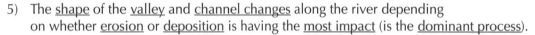

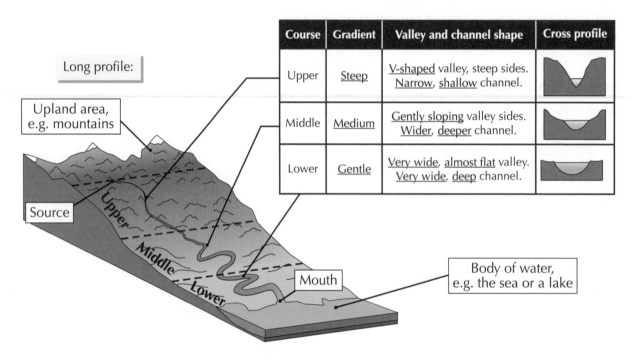

Course	Gradient	Valley and channel shape	Cross profile
Upper	<u>Steep</u>	<u>V-shaped</u> valley, steep sides. <u>Narrow</u>, <u>shallow</u> channel.	
Middle	<u>Medium</u>	<u>Gently sloping</u> valley sides. <u>Wider</u>, <u>deeper</u> channel.	
Lower	<u>Gentle</u>	<u>Very wide</u>, almost flat valley. Very wide, <u>deep</u> channel.	

Vertical and **Lateral Erosion** Change the **Cross Profile** of a River

Erosion can be <u>vertical</u> or <u>lateral</u> — both types happen at the <u>same time</u>, but one is usually <u>dominant</u> over the other at <u>different points</u> along the river:

There's more on the processes of erosion on the next page.

Vertical erosion

This <u>deepens</u> the river valley (and channel), making it <u>V-shaped</u>. It's dominant in the <u>upper course</u> of the river. High <u>turbulence</u> causes the <u>rough, angular particles</u> to be scraped along the river bed, causing intense <u>downwards</u> erosion.

Lateral erosion

This <u>widens</u> the river valley (and channel) during the formation of <u>meanders</u> (see page 69). It's dominant in the <u>middle</u> and <u>lower courses</u>.

Long profile = gradient, cross profile = a cross-section of the river
Try sketching the cross profile diagrams and describing the shape of the valley and channel, just to check you've got it all memorised. Make sure you learn where vertical and lateral erosion are more dominant.

Erosion, Transportation and Deposition

As rivers flow, they <u>erode</u> material, <u>transport</u> it and then <u>deposit</u> it further <u>downstream</u>.

There are **Four Processes** of **Erosion**

1) <u>Hydraulic action</u>

> The <u>force</u> of the water <u>breaks rock particles away</u> from the <u>river channel</u>.

2) <u>Abrasion</u>

> Eroded <u>rocks</u> picked up by the river <u>scrape</u> and <u>rub</u> against the <u>channel</u>, wearing it away. <u>Most erosion</u> happens by <u>abrasion</u>.

3) <u>Attrition</u>

> Eroded <u>rocks</u> picked up by the river <u>smash into each other</u> and break into <u>smaller fragments</u>. Their <u>edges</u> also get <u>rounded off</u> as they rub together. The <u>further</u> material travels, the more <u>eroded</u> it gets — attrition causes <u>particle size</u> to <u>decrease</u> between a river's <u>source</u> and its <u>mouth</u>.

4) <u>Solution</u>

> River water <u>dissolves</u> some types of rock, e.g. <u>chalk</u> and <u>limestone</u>.

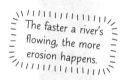
The faster a river's flowing, the more erosion happens.

Transportation is the **Movement** of **Eroded Material**

The <u>material</u> a river has <u>eroded</u> is <u>transported downstream</u>.
There are <u>four processes</u> of transportation:

Traction
<u>Large</u> particles like boulders are <u>pushed</u> along the <u>river bed</u> by the <u>force of the water</u>.

Suspension
<u>Small</u> particles like silt and clay are <u>carried along</u> by the water.

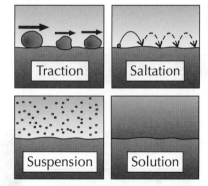
Traction | Saltation
Suspension | Solution

Saltation
<u>Pebble-sized</u> particles are <u>bounced along</u> the <u>river bed</u> by the <u>force of the water</u>.

Solution
<u>Soluble materials dissolve</u> in the water and are <u>carried along</u>.

Deposition is When a River **Drops Eroded Material**

Deposition is when a river <u>drops</u> the <u>eroded material</u> it's <u>transporting</u>.
It happens when a river <u>slows down</u> (<u>loses velocity</u>).

There are a <u>few reasons</u> why rivers
slow down and deposit material:

1) The <u>volume</u> of <u>water</u> in the river <u>falls</u>.
2) The <u>amount</u> of <u>eroded material</u> in the water <u>increases</u>.
3) The water is <u>shallower</u>, e.g. on the <u>inside of a bend</u>.
4) The river <u>reaches</u> its <u>mouth</u>.

Learn the four processes of erosion and the four processes of transportation

There are lots of very similar names to remember here — try not to confuse saltation, solution and suspension.
And yes, solution is both a process of erosion and transportation. Get them fixed in your head before moving on.

River Landforms — Erosion

The <u>processes</u> of erosion on the previous page <u>change the landscape</u> and create <u>distinctive landforms</u>.
Now's your chance to find out all about them, starting with <u>waterfalls</u>...

Waterfalls and Gorges are Found in the Upper Course of a River

1) <u>Waterfalls</u> form where a river flows over an area of <u>hard rock</u> followed by an area of <u>softer rock</u>.

2) The <u>softer rock</u> is <u>eroded</u> (by <u>hydraulic action</u> and <u>abrasion</u>) <u>more</u> than the <u>hard rock</u>, creating a '<u>step</u>' in the river.

3) As water goes over the step it <u>erodes more and more</u> of the softer rock.

4) A <u>steep drop</u> is eventually created, which is called a <u>waterfall</u>.

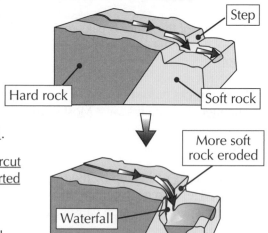

Step

Hard rock

Soft rock

5) The <u>hard rock</u> is eventually <u>undercut</u> by erosion. It becomes <u>unsupported</u> and <u>collapses</u>.

6) The collapsed rocks are <u>swirled around</u> at the foot of the waterfall where they <u>erode</u> the softer rock by <u>abrasion</u> (see previous page). This creates a deep <u>plunge pool</u>.

7) Over time, <u>more undercutting</u> causes <u>more collapses</u>. The waterfall will <u>retreat</u> (move back up the channel), leaving behind a steep-sided <u>gorge</u>.

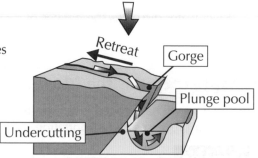

More soft rock eroded

Waterfall

Retreat

Gorge

Plunge pool

Undercutting

Some Rivers Wind around Interlocking Spurs

1) In the <u>upper course</u> of a river most of the <u>erosion</u> is <u>vertically downwards</u>. This creates <u>steep-sided</u>, <u>V-shaped valleys</u>.

2) The rivers <u>aren't powerful enough</u> to <u>erode laterally</u> (sideways) — they have to <u>wind around</u> the <u>high hillsides</u> that stick out into their paths on either side.

3) The <u>hillsides that interlock</u> with each other (like a zip if you were looking from above) as the river winds around them are called <u>interlocking spurs</u>.

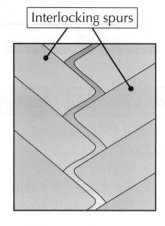

Interlocking spurs

Interlocking spurs along a river in Shropshire

Waterfalls, gorges and interlocking spurs are landforms resulting from erosion

Step over the hard rock and plunge into the pool — that's how I remember how waterfalls are formed.
Geography examiners love river landforms (they're a bit weird like that) so make sure you learn how they form.

River Landforms — Meanders

When a river's <u>eroding</u> and <u>depositing</u> material, <u>meanders</u> and <u>ox-bow lakes</u> can form.

Meanders are Formed by **Erosion** and **Deposition**

Rivers develop <u>large bends</u> called <u>meanders</u> in their <u>middle</u> and <u>lower courses</u>, in areas where there are both <u>shallow</u> and <u>deep</u> sections in the channel:

1) The <u>current</u> (the flow of the water) is <u>faster</u> on the <u>outside</u> of the bend because the river channel is <u>deeper</u> (there's <u>less friction</u> to <u>slow</u> the water down).

2) So more <u>erosion</u> takes place on the <u>outside</u> of the bend, forming <u>river cliffs</u>.

3) The <u>current</u> is <u>slower</u> on the <u>inside</u> of the bend because the river channel is <u>shallower</u> (there's <u>more friction</u> to <u>slow</u> the water down).

4) So eroded material is <u>deposited</u> on the <u>inside</u> of the bend, forming <u>slip-off slopes</u>.

> Erosion of the outside bend takes place by the processes of abrasion and hydraulic action (see page 67).

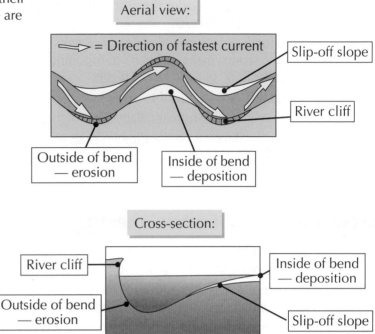

Aerial view:

⟹ = Direction of fastest current

Slip-off slope

River cliff

Outside of bend — erosion

Inside of bend — deposition

Cross-section:

River cliff

Inside of bend — deposition

Outside of bend — erosion

Slip-off slope

Ox-Bow Lakes are Formed from **Meanders**

Meanders get <u>larger</u> over time — they can eventually turn into an <u>ox-bow lake</u>:

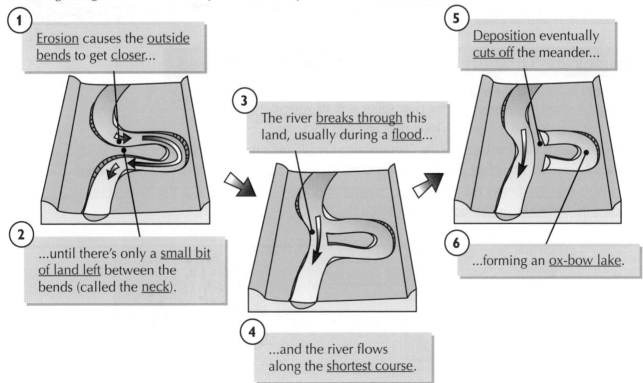

1 <u>Erosion</u> causes the <u>outside bends</u> to get <u>closer</u>...

2 ...until there's only a <u>small bit of land left</u> between the bends (called the <u>neck</u>).

3 The river <u>breaks through</u> this land, usually during a <u>flood</u>...

4 ...and the river flows along the <u>shortest course</u>.

5 <u>Deposition</u> eventually <u>cuts off</u> the meander...

6 ...forming an <u>ox-bow lake</u>.

The features of meanders are formed by erosion and deposition

In the exam, don't be afraid to draw diagrams of river landforms — examiners love a good diagram and they can help make your answer clear. Don't spend forever making them into works of art though...

River Landforms — Deposition

When rivers <u>flow fast</u>, they <u>erode</u> the landscape. As they <u>slow down</u>, they make <u>landforms</u> through <u>deposition</u>.

Flood Plains are Flat Areas of Land that Flood

1) The <u>flood plain</u> is the <u>wide valley floor</u> on either side of a river which occasionally <u>gets flooded</u>.

2) When a river <u>floods</u> onto the flood plain, the water <u>slows down</u> and <u>deposits</u> the <u>eroded material</u> that it's <u>transporting</u>. This <u>builds up</u> the flood plain (makes it <u>higher</u>).

3) <u>Meanders migrate</u> (move) <u>across</u> the flood plain, making it <u>wider</u>.

4) Meanders also migrate <u>downstream</u>, <u>flattening</u> out the valley floor.

5) The <u>deposition</u> that happens on the <u>slip-off slopes</u> of meanders also <u>builds up</u> the flood plain.

Flood plain

All these landforms are found in the lower course of a river.

Levees are Natural Embankments

1) Levees are <u>natural embankments</u> (raised bits) along the <u>edges</u> of a <u>river channel</u>.

2) During a flood, <u>eroded material</u> is <u>deposited</u> over the whole flood plain.

3) The <u>heaviest material</u> is <u>deposited closest</u> to the river channel, because it gets <u>dropped first</u> when the river <u>slows down</u>.

4) <u>Over time</u>, the <u>deposited material builds up</u>, creating <u>levees</u> along the edges of the channel, e.g. along the Yellow River in China.

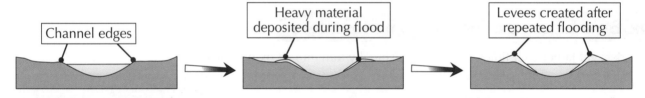

Channel edges | Heavy material deposited during flood | Levees created after repeated flooding

Estuaries are Tidal Areas Where the River Meets the Sea

1) <u>Estuaries</u> are found at the <u>mouth</u> of a river, where it meets the <u>sea</u>. The land is close to <u>sea level</u> and the river <u>valley</u> is at its <u>widest</u>.

2) The water here is <u>tidal</u> — the river level <u>rises</u> and <u>falls</u> each day.

3) The water <u>floods</u> over the <u>banks</u> of the river carrying the <u>silt</u> and <u>sand</u> onto the valley floor.

4) As the tide reaches its <u>highest point</u>, the water is moving very <u>slowly</u> so the sediment is <u>deposited</u>.

5) Over time, more and more mud builds up, creating large areas of <u>mudflats</u>, e.g. the Severn estuary.

6) At <u>low tide</u>, the <u>wide</u>, <u>muddy banks</u> are exposed.

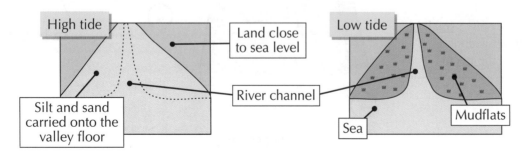

High tide | Land close to sea level | Low tide
Silt and sand carried onto the valley floor | River channel | Sea | Mudflats

Deposition is common in the lower course of a river

Last few landforms to learn, I promise. These ones are all about the water slowing down and dropping stuff. Make sure you know the characteristics of these landforms and you can describe the process of their formation.

Identifying River Landforms

You can know all the facts about <u>rivers</u>, but if you don't know what their <u>features</u> look like on <u>maps</u> then some of the exam questions will be a wee bit tricky. Here's something I prepared earlier...

Contour Lines Tell you the **Direction** a **River Flows**

<u>Contour lines</u> are the <u>orange lines</u> drawn all over maps. They tell you about the <u>height</u> of the land (in metres) by the numbers marked on them, and the <u>steepness</u> of the land by how <u>close together</u> they are (the <u>closer</u> they are, the <u>steeper</u> the slope).

It sounds obvious, but rivers <u>can't</u> flow uphill. Unless gravity's gone screwy, a river flows <u>from higher</u> contour lines <u>to lower</u> ones. Have a look at this map of Cawfell Beck:

Take a peek at pages 170-171 for more on reading maps.

1 The <u>height values</u> get <u>smaller</u> towards the <u>west</u> (left), so west is <u>downhill</u>.

2 Cawfell Beck is flowing from <u>east</u> to <u>west</u> (right to left).

3 A <u>V-shape</u> is formed where the contour lines <u>cross</u> the river. The V-shape is <u>pointing uphill</u> to where the river came from.

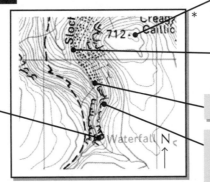

Maps contain **Evidence** for **River Landforms**

Exam questions might ask you to look at a <u>map</u> and give the <u>evidence</u> for a <u>landform</u>. Remember, different landforms are found in the <u>upper</u> and <u>lower course</u> — you can use this evidence to help you <u>identify</u> them.

Evidence for the Upper Course

<u>Waterfalls</u> are marked on maps, but the <u>symbol for a cliff</u> (black, blocky lines) and the <u>close contour lines</u> are evidence for an upper-course waterfall.

The nearby land is <u>high</u> (712 m).

The river <u>crosses lots</u> of <u>contour lines</u> in a <u>short distance</u>, which means it's <u>steep</u>.

The river's <u>narrow</u> (a <u>thin</u> blue line).

The <u>contour lines</u> are very <u>close together</u> and the valley floor is narrow. This means the river is in a <u>steep-sided V-shaped</u> valley.

Evidence for the Lower Course

The nearby land is <u>low</u> (less than 15 m).

The river doesn't <u>cross any contour lines</u> so it's <u>very gently sloping</u>.

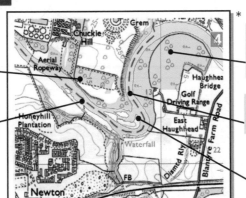

The river meanders across a large flat area (<u>no contours</u>), which is the <u>flood plain</u>.

The river's <u>wide</u> (a <u>thick</u> blue line).

The river has <u>large meanders</u> and an <u>ox-bow lake</u> may be formed here.

Pay close attention to contour lines, height values and symbols

Map questions can be a goldmine of easy marks — all you have to do is say what you see. You just need to understand what the maps are showing, so read this page carefully, then see if you can remember it all.

UK River Landscape

You can see many of the <u>landforms</u> of <u>erosion</u> and <u>deposition</u> from pages 68-70 along the <u>River Clyde</u>.

The **River Clyde** Flows Through **Scotland**

1) The River Clyde is about <u>160 km long</u>.

2) Its <u>source</u> is in the <u>Southern Uplands region</u> of <u>Scotland</u> and the river <u>flows north-west</u> through <u>Motherwell</u> and <u>Glasgow</u>.

3) The <u>mouth</u> of the River Clyde is an <u>estuary</u> on the <u>west coast</u> of Scotland.

4) Here are some of the <u>features</u> and <u>landforms</u> in the <u>valley</u> that the <u>River Clyde</u> flows through:

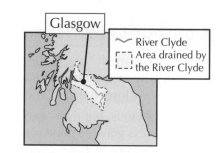

Glasgow

~ River Clyde
Area drained by the River Clyde

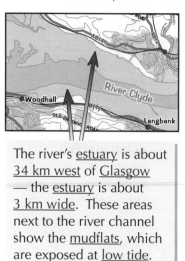

The River Clyde's flood plain

The river's <u>estuary</u> is about <u>34 km west</u> of <u>Glasgow</u> — the <u>estuary</u> is about <u>3 km wide</u>. These areas next to the river channel show the <u>mudflats</u>, which are exposed at <u>low tide</u>.

<u>Glasgow</u> is <u>built on</u> the <u>flood plain</u> of the River Clyde. The land is about <u>5 m above sea level</u> on <u>either side of the river</u>.

There's also a <u>gorge</u> along this part of the river, formed by the <u>waterfalls retreating</u>. There are <u>steep cliffs</u> along the banks of the river, then at the <u>top</u> of the gorge the land <u>flattens</u> out.

The river <u>meanders</u> <u>between</u> <u>Motherwell</u> and <u>Glasgow</u>.

Glasgow

Motherwell

Lanark

direction of flow

The <u>Falls of Clyde</u> are <u>four</u> waterfalls near <u>Lanark</u>. The <u>highest fall</u> is <u>Corra Linn</u> — it's about <u>27 m high</u>.

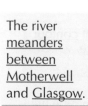

There are <u>interlocking spurs</u> at <u>Crawford</u>. The spurs are between <u>300</u> and <u>500 m high</u>.

Crawford

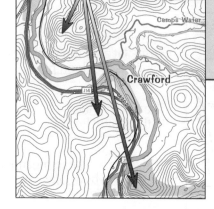

Corra Linn

There's an <u>ox-bow lake</u> starting to form from a meander in the <u>New Lanark</u> area.

The River Clyde's got it all

Almost all of the landforms you've studied so far in this section are found at some point along the River Clyde. You need to know and be able to identify the landforms of a named UK river valley, so get learnin' about one.

River Discharge and Flooding

We've not really talked much about the actual <u>water</u> in a river. Well, all that's about to change — hooray.

River Discharge is the Volume of Water Flowing in a River

<u>River discharge</u> is just the <u>volume of water</u> that flows in a river <u>per second</u>. It's measured in <u>cumecs</u> — cubic metres per second (m³/s). <u>Hydrographs</u> show how the discharge at a <u>certain point</u> in a river <u>changes</u> over time in relation to <u>rainfall</u>:

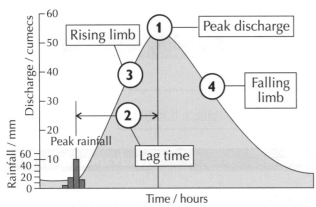

① <u>Peak discharge</u>: The <u>highest discharge</u> in the period of time you're looking at.

② <u>Lag time</u>: The <u>delay</u> between <u>peak rainfall</u> and <u>peak discharge</u>.

③ <u>Rising limb</u>: The <u>increase</u> in river discharge as <u>rainwater</u> flows into the river.

④ <u>Falling limb</u>: The <u>decrease</u> in river discharge as the river returns to its <u>normal level</u>.

Lag time happens because most rainwater <u>doesn't land directly</u> in the river channel — there's a <u>delay</u> as rainwater <u>gets to the channel</u>. It gets there by <u>flowing quickly overland</u> (called <u>surface runoff</u>, or just <u>runoff</u>), or by <u>soaking into the ground</u> (called <u>infiltration</u>) and flowing <u>slowly underground</u>.

Rivers Flood due to Physical and Human Factors

<u>Flooding happens</u> when the level of a river gets <u>so high</u> that it <u>spills</u> over its banks. The <u>river level</u> <u>increases</u> when the <u>discharge increases</u> because a high discharge means there's <u>more water</u> <u>in the channel</u>. This means the factors that <u>increase discharge</u> can <u>cause flooding</u>:

Prolonged Rainfall

After a <u>long period</u> of rain, the soil becomes <u>saturated</u>. Any further rainfall <u>can't infiltrate</u>, which <u>increases runoff</u> into rivers. This increases discharge quickly, so flooding is more likely.

Heavy Rainfall

Heavy rainfall means the water arrives <u>too rapidly</u> for <u>infiltration</u>, so there's <u>a lot of runoff</u>. This <u>increases</u> <u>discharge quickly</u>, increasing the risk of a flood.

Geology (rock type)

<u>Clay soils</u> and some <u>rocks</u>, e.g. <u>granite</u> and <u>shale</u>, are <u>impermeable</u> (i.e. they <u>don't</u> allow <u>infiltration</u>) so <u>runoff</u> is <u>increased</u>. When it rains, <u>discharge</u> <u>increases quickly</u>, which can cause a flood.

Relief (change in the height of the land)

If a river is in a <u>steep-sided valley</u>, water will reach the river channel <u>much faster</u> because water <u>flows</u> <u>more quickly</u> on <u>steeper slopes</u>. <u>Discharge increases</u> <u>rapidly</u>, increasing the flood risk.

Changing the <u>land use</u>, e.g. by <u>building</u> on it or <u>removing trees</u>, can also <u>increase</u> the <u>flood risk</u>.

Land use

1) Buildings are often made from <u>impermeable materials</u>, e.g. concrete, and they're surrounded by <u>roads</u> made from <u>tarmac</u> (also impermeable). Impermeable surfaces <u>increase runoff</u> and <u>drains</u> quickly take runoff to rivers — <u>discharge increases quickly</u>, so there's a <u>greater risk</u> of flooding.

2) Trees <u>intercept</u> rainwater on their leaves, which then <u>evaporates</u>. Trees also <u>take up water</u> from the ground and <u>store it</u>. This means <u>cutting down</u> trees <u>increases</u> the <u>volume</u> of water that <u>reaches</u> the river channel, which <u>increases discharge</u> and makes flooding <u>more likely</u>.

You get lag time because rainwater doesn't fall directly into the river channel

Hydrographs are a good way of showing the changes in river discharge when there is a storm or lots of rainfall. Make sure you know how the factors shown affect peak discharge and lag time and how this can cause flooding.

Hard vs Soft Engineering

Floods can be <u>devastating</u>, but there are a number of different <u>strategies</u> to stop them or lessen the blow.

Strategies can be classed as **Hard Engineering** or **Soft Engineering**

There's <u>debate</u> about <u>which strategies are best</u>, so you'll need to know the <u>benefits</u> and <u>costs</u> of a few of them.

Hard Engineering Strategies can **Reduce** the **Risk** of **Flooding** Occurring

Hard Engineering

<u>Man-made structures</u> built to <u>control the flow</u> of rivers and <u>reduce flooding</u>.

Method	What it is	Benefits	Disadvantages
Dams and reservoirs	<u>Dams</u> (huge walls) are built <u>across</u> the rivers, usually in the <u>upper course</u>. A <u>reservoir</u> (artificial lake) is formed <u>behind</u> the dam.	Reservoirs <u>store water</u>, especially during periods of prolonged or heavy rain, <u>reducing</u> the <u>risk of flooding</u>. The water in the reservoir can be used as <u>drinking water</u> and to <u>generate hydroelectric power</u> (HEP).	Dams are <u>very expensive</u> to build. Creating a reservoir can <u>flood existing settlements</u>. Eroded material is <u>deposited</u> in the <u>reservoir</u> and <u>not</u> along the river's <u>natural course</u> so <u>farmland</u> downstream can become <u>less fertile</u>.
Channel straightening	The river's <u>course</u> is <u>straightened</u> — <u>meanders</u> are <u>cut out</u> by building <u>artificial straight channels</u>.	Water moves out of the area <u>more quickly</u> because it doesn't travel as far — <u>reducing</u> the <u>risk</u> of flooding.	<u>Flooding</u> may happen <u>downstream</u> instead, as water is <u>carried there faster</u>. There's <u>more erosion downstream</u> because the water's <u>flowing faster</u>.
Embankments	<u>Raised walls</u> are built <u>along</u> the river banks.	The river can hold <u>more water</u> so it will flood <u>less frequently</u>, protecting buildings on the flood plain.	They're quite <u>expensive</u> and there's a risk of <u>severe flooding</u> if the water rises <u>above</u> the level of the embankments or if they <u>break</u>.
Flood relief channels	<u>Channels</u> are built that <u>divert</u> the water around important areas or take it elsewhere if the water level in the river gets <u>too high</u>.	Flooding is prevented because <u>river discharge</u> is <u>reduced</u>. <u>Gates</u> on the flood relief channels mean that the <u>release</u> of water can be <u>controlled</u>.	There will be <u>increased discharge</u> where the relief channel rejoins the river (or joins another river) which could cause <u>flooding</u> in that area. If the water level gets <u>too high</u> for the <u>relief channels</u> they could also <u>flood</u>.

Make sure you know the disadvantages as well as the benefits of each strategy

Flooding can be a nightmare. But, as luck would have it, there are plenty of strategies to reduce the impacts. What's less lucky is that they might come up in the exam, so get learning what they are, and their pros and cons.

Hard vs Soft Engineering

The table on the previous page gives some of the <u>disadvantages</u> of <u>hard engineering</u> strategies. Because of these drawbacks, <u>soft engineering</u> strategies can sometimes be a <u>better solution</u>.

Soft Engineering Strategies can Reduce the Effects of Flooding

Soft Engineering

Schemes set up using <u>knowledge</u> of a <u>river</u> and its <u>processes</u> to <u>reduce the effects of flooding</u>.

Method	What it is	Benefits	Disadvantages
Flood warnings	The <u>Environment Agency</u> warns people about possible flooding through <u>TV</u>, <u>radio</u>, <u>newspapers</u> and the <u>internet</u>.	The <u>impact</u> of flooding is <u>reduced</u> — warnings give people time to <u>move possessions upstairs</u>, put <u>sandbags</u> in position and to <u>evacuate</u>.	Warnings <u>don't stop</u> a <u>flood</u> from happening. People may <u>not</u> hear or have <u>access</u> to the <u>warnings</u>.
Preparation	Buildings are <u>modified</u> to <u>reduce</u> the amount of <u>damage</u> a flood could cause. People make <u>plans</u> for what to do in a flood — they keep items like <u>torches</u> and <u>blankets</u> in a <u>handy place</u>.	The <u>impact</u> of flooding is <u>reduced</u> — <u>buildings</u> are <u>less damaged</u> and people <u>know what to do</u> when a flood happens. People are also <u>less likely to worry</u> about the threat of floods.	Preparation <u>doesn't guarantee safety</u> from a flood and it could give people a <u>false sense of security</u>. It's <u>expensive</u> to modify homes and businesses.
Flood plain zoning	Restrictions <u>prevent building</u> on parts of a flood plain that are <u>likely to be affected</u> by a flood.	The <u>risk of flooding</u> is <u>reduced</u> — <u>impermeable surfaces aren't created</u>, e.g. buildings and roads. The <u>impact</u> of flooding is also <u>reduced</u> — there aren't any buildings to damage.	The <u>expansion</u> of an <u>urban area</u> is <u>limited</u> if there aren't any other suitable building sites. It's no help in areas that have <u>already been built on</u>.
Planting trees	Planting trees in the river valley <u>increases interception</u> of rainwater and also increases the <u>lag time</u>.	<u>Discharge</u> and <u>flood risk</u> are <u>reduced</u>. Vegetation <u>reduces soil erosion</u> in the valley and provides <u>habitats</u> for <u>wildlife</u>.	<u>Less land</u> is available for <u>farming</u>.
River restoration	River restoration involves making the river <u>more natural</u>, e.g. by removing man made levees, so that the <u>flood plain</u> can <u>flood naturally</u>.	There is <u>less risk</u> of <u>flooding downstream</u> because <u>discharge</u> is <u>reduced</u>. <u>Little maintenance</u> is needed as the river is left in its natural state and there are <u>better habitats</u> for <u>wildlife</u>.	<u>Local flood risk</u> can <u>increase</u>, especially if nothing's done to prevent major flooding.

Another big table of costs and benefits to learn

Soft engineering strategies work with the river's natural processes, so they tend to be more environmentally friendly than hard engineering strategies. They do have drawbacks though — a big one is that they may not prevent flooding.

Flood Management

Time for a real-world <u>example</u> of <u>flood management</u>, and it's off to Cornwall...

Severe Flash Floods showed the need for Flood Defences in Boscastle

1) The village of <u>Boscastle</u> on the north coast of <u>Cornwall</u> was devastated by a <u>flash flood</u> on 16th August 2004, which caused <u>millions of pounds</u> worth of <u>damage</u>. Despite being <u>vulnerable to flash flooding</u>, it had <u>no modern</u> flood defences.

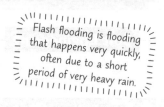
Flash flooding is flooding that happens very quickly, often due to a short period of very heavy rain.

2) The village is surrounded by <u>steep valley sides</u>, and land <u>upstream</u> of the village has been <u>cleared</u> of <u>trees and vegetation</u>. This <u>increases</u> surface <u>runoff</u> and means that during periods of heavy rain, river <u>discharge increases quickly</u>.

Steep sides
Narrow channel

3) The <u>old bridge</u> in the village had a <u>low arch</u> over a very <u>narrow river channel</u>. The flooding in 2004 was <u>made worse</u> because trees and vehicles in the floodwater became <u>trapped</u> under the bridge, forming a <u>dam</u>.

4) The village is a popular <u>tourist destination</u> and <u>90%</u> of the local economy <u>relied on tourism</u>. After 2004, the number of tourists <u>dropped</u> significantly, increasing the <u>demand for protection</u> against future floods.

A Flood Management Scheme is Now in Place

A <u>flood management scheme</u> for Boscastle was completed in <u>2008</u>. It includes both <u>hard</u> and <u>soft</u> engineering strategies...

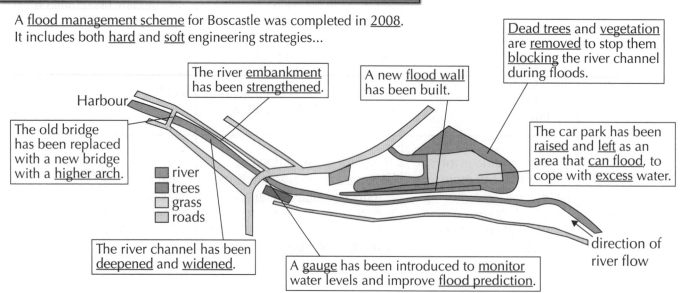

The river <u>embankment</u> has been <u>strengthened</u>.

A new <u>flood wall</u> has been built.

<u>Dead trees</u> and <u>vegetation</u> are <u>removed</u> to stop them <u>blocking</u> the river channel during floods.

Harbour

The old bridge has been replaced with a new bridge with a <u>higher arch</u>.

The car park has been <u>raised</u> and <u>left</u> as an area that <u>can flood</u>, to cope with <u>excess</u> water.

■ river
■ trees
■ grass
■ roads

The river channel has been <u>deepened</u> and <u>widened</u>.

A <u>gauge</u> has been introduced to <u>monitor</u> water levels and improve <u>flood prediction</u>.

direction of river flow

The devastating floods in 2004 showed the need for management in Boscastle

Whether you've studied Boscastle or a different flood management scheme in the UK, make sure you know details of why the scheme was needed and what the management strategy was. Then move on to the next page...

Flood Management

On the whole, the flood management scheme in Boscastle was a success, but there were still some issues with it...

The Scheme has **Social, Economic** and **Environmental** Issues

Social Issues

1) Residents' lives were disrupted for years by rebuilding projects and the construction of flood defences.

2) The new defences have made Boscastle a safer place to live.

3) However, they'll only protect against a 1 in 75 year flood — they won't prevent flooding of the same size as the 2004 flood. The defences needed for this would spoil the character of the village.

4) Many residents do not like the new bridge, and think that it's not in keeping with the character of the village.

Economic Issues

1) Homes and businesses are now less at risk of flooding. So there is less risk of expensive damage to property, loss of stock and business, and rising insurance costs.

2) The flood management scheme cost over £4 million but the scheme isn't as good as it could be — some options were still considered too expensive.

Environmental Issues

1) Vegetation and river habitats in the area are now continuously managed. Biodiversity and river habitats have been improved.

2) The new channel has been engineered to look natural and to function as a normal river.

EXAM TIP

You need to know the issues surrounding a flood management scheme

Make sure you don't get your social, environmental and economic issues mixed up in the exam — you may lose marks. Have a quick read through your answer when you're done and check for mistakes.

Worked Exam Questions

Time to put your knowledge to the test... We've made life easier for you by giving you the answers to the first page of practice exam questions. Read over them to get an idea of what your exam answers should be like.

1 Study **Figure 1**, which shows the long profile of a river.

Figure 1

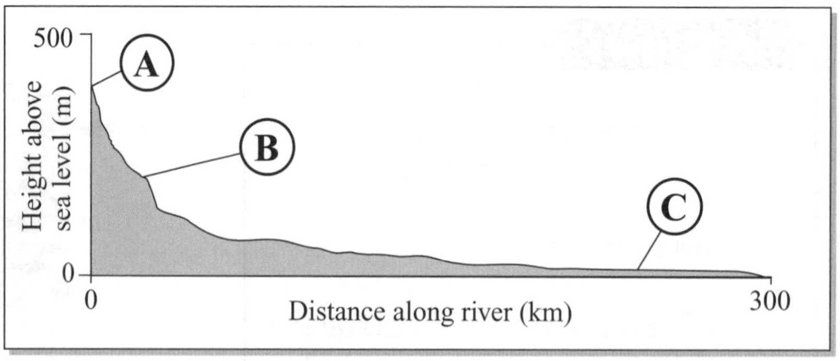

1.1 Which part of the river is labelled A in **Figure 1**? Shade one oval only.

A Mouth ⬭

B Source ⬤

C Lower course ⬭

D Channel ⬭

[1]

1.2 Describe the cross profile at the points labelled B and C in **Figure 1**.

Cross profile at point B: The valley is V-shaped with steep sides. The channel is narrow and shallow.

Cross profile at point C: The valley is very wide and almost flat. The channel is very wide and deep.

[4]

1.3 Explain why the upper course of a river valley has a different cross profile from the lower course.

In the upper course, high turbulence causes rough, angular particles to be scraped along the river bed,

causing intense vertical erosion. This deepens the river valley (and channel), making it V-shaped.

In the lower course of a river, lateral erosion is dominant, widening the river valley (and channel).

[4]

[Total 9 marks]

2 Study **Figure 2**, which shows some of the engineering strategies used to combat flooding along the River Joiner.

Figure 2

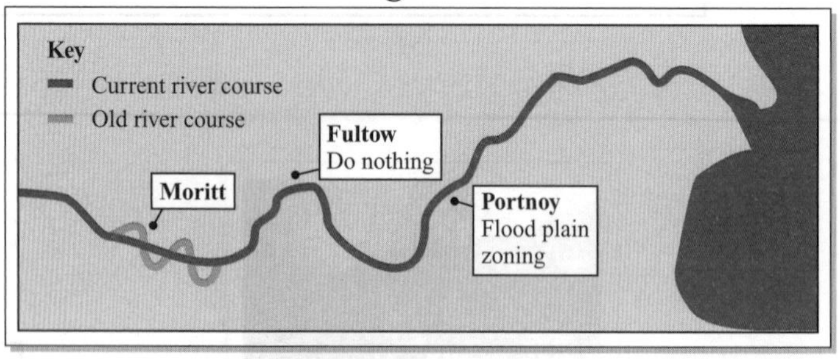

Key
■ Current river course
■ Old river course

Fultow Do nothing

Moritt

Portnoy Flood plain zoning

2.1 What engineering strategy has been used to protect Moritt?

Channel straightening

[1]

2.2 Explain how the engineering strategy at Moritt could cause problems in Fultow.

Channel straightening may cause

flooding or increased erosion at Fultow because flood water is carried there faster.

[2]

2.3 Describe the engineering strategy being used at Portnoy and explain its benefits.

Flood plain zoning prevents people building on parts of a flood plain that are likely to flood.

It reduces the risk of flooding because impermeable surfaces aren't created, e.g. buildings and roads.

It also reduces the impact of flooding because there aren't any houses or roads to be damaged.

[3]

[Total 6 marks]

Exam Questions

1 Study **Figure 1**, which shows storm hydrographs for two rivers.

Figure 1

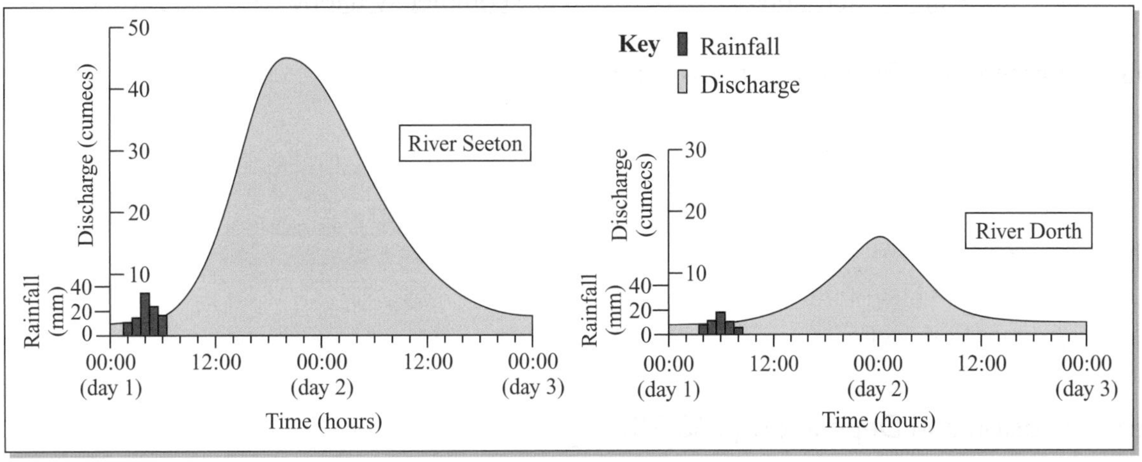

1.1 Peak rainfall around the River Dorth was at 06:00 on day 1. What was the lag time?

....
[1]

1.2 Which river is more likely to flood? Outline **one** reason for your answer.

....

....

....
[2]

1.3 The land around the River Seeton has been paved and built on. Suggest how land use in the catchment of the River Seeton might affect the shape of the hydrograph in **Figure 1**.

....

....

....
[2]

[Total 5 marks]

2 Study **Figure 2**, which shows a landform that is likely to be found in the upper course of a river.

Figure 2

2.1 Explain the formation of this landform.

....

....

....

....

....

....
[Total 4 marks]

Revision Summary

That's it for <u>River Landscapes</u>. Now it's time to see how much information your brain has <u>soaked up</u>.
- Try these questions and <u>tick off each one</u> when you <u>get it right</u>.
- When you've done <u>all the questions</u> for a topic and are <u>completely happy</u> with it, tick off the topic.

River Valley Profiles and Processes (p.66-67) ☑

1) What does a river's long profile show?
2) Describe the cross profile of a river's middle course.
3) Name the part of the river course where vertical erosion is dominant.
4) What's the difference between abrasion and attrition?
5) Name two processes of transportation.
6) When does deposition occur?

Features of Erosion and Deposition (p.68-70) ☑

7) Where do waterfalls form?
8) How is a gorge formed?
9) What are interlocking spurs?
10) a) Where is the current fastest on a meander?
    b) What feature of a meander is formed where the flow is fastest?
11) Name the landform created when a meander is cut off by deposition.
12) What is a flood plain?
13) Where are estuaries found?
14) Outline the main features of a river estuary.

Evidence for River Landforms (p.71-72) ☑

15) What do the contour lines on a map show?
16) Give two pieces of map evidence for a waterfall.
17) Give two pieces of map evidence for a river's lower course.
18) Suggest what you might look for to identify an estuary on a map.
19) What features would you expect to see in a photo of a flood plain?
20) List the main landforms of a named river landscape.

Flooding and Flood Defences (p.73-77) ☑

21) What is river discharge?
22) What is lag time?
23) Describe two physical factors that can cause floods.
24) Explain how cutting down trees can increase flooding.
25) Define hard engineering.
26) Define soft engineering.
27) Describe how channel straightening reduces the risk of a flood.
28) Describe the disadvantages of flood warnings.
29) Describe the advantages of river restoration.
30) a) Using a named example of a flood management scheme, explain why the scheme was needed.
    b) Give two features of the scheme and explain how they reduce the flood risk.
    c) Describe the social issues caused by the scheme.

Glacial Erosion

Glaciers are masses of ice that fill valleys and hollows and slowly move downhill. The UK might not have any glaciers any more, but it did in the past, and they can seriously carve up the landscape through erosion.

Much of the UK Used to be Covered in Ice

1) There have been lots of glacial (cold) periods during the last 2.6 million years.

2) During some glacial periods, parts of the UK were covered in a massive ice sheet.

3) The map shows the maximum extent of ice cover during the last ice age, 20 000 years ago.

4) Ice covered most of Scotland, Ireland and Wales and came as far south as the Bristol channel in England.

5) The erosion, transport and deposition of material by ice has been very important in shaping the landscape of the UK.

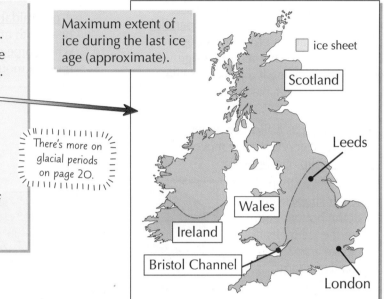

Maximum extent of ice during the last ice age (approximate).

There's more on glacial periods on page 20.

ice sheet

Scotland

Leeds

Wales

Ireland

Bristol Channel

London

Glaciers Erode the Landscape as They Move

1) The weight of the ice in a glacier makes it move downhill (advance), eroding the landscape as it goes.

2) The moving ice erodes the landscape in two ways:

- Plucking occurs when meltwater at the base, back or sides of a glacier freezes onto the rock. As the glacier moves forward it pulls pieces of rock out.

- Abrasion is where bits of rock stuck in the ice grind against the rock below the glacier, wearing it away (it's a bit like the glacier's got sandpaper on the bottom of it).

3) At the top end of the glacier the ice doesn't move in a straight line — it moves in a circular motion called rotational slip. This can erode hollows in the landscape and deepen them into bowl shapes.

4) The rock above glaciers is also weathered (broken down where it is) by the conditions around glaciers.

5) Freeze-thaw weathering is where water gets into cracks in rocks. The water freezes and expands, putting pressure on the rock. The ice then thaws, releasing the pressure. If this process is repeated it can make bits of the rock fall off.

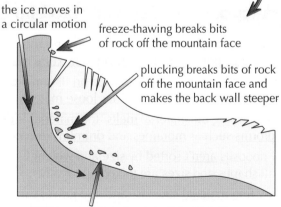

the ice moves in a circular motion

freeze-thawing breaks bits of rock off the mountain face

plucking breaks bits of rock off the mountain face and makes the back wall steeper

abrasion grinds and gouges the valley floor

Glaciers erode valleys in two ways — by plucking and abrasion

You don't have know every detail on the map above, but you should know roughly how far south the ice got. Make sure you also know the difference between plucking, abrasion (types of erosion) and freeze-thaw weathering.

Glacial Landforms

The landscape of most upland areas in the UK have been massively affected by ice. Here are some of the landforms that are created by glacial erosion that you can see in the UK...

Glacial Erosion Produces **Seven Different Landforms**

An arête is a narrow, steep-sided ridge formed when two glaciers flow in parallel valleys. The glaciers erode the sides of the valleys, which sharpens the ridge between them giving it a jagged profile. (E.g. Striding Edge, Lake District)

A pyramidal peak is a pointed mountain peak with at least three sides. It's formed when three or more back-to-back glaciers erode a mountain. (E.g. Snowdon, Wales)

Corries begin as hollows containing a small glacier. As the ice moves by rotational slip, it erodes the hollow into a steep-sided, armchair shape with a lip at the bottom end. When the ice melts it can leave a small circular lake called a tarn. (E.g. Red Tarn, Lake District)

Truncated spurs are cliff-like edges on the valley side formed when ridges of land (spurs) that stick out into the main valley are cut off as the glacier moves past.

Hanging valleys are valleys formed by smaller glaciers (called tributary glaciers) that flow into the main glacier. The glacial trough is eroded much more deeply by the larger glacier, so when the glaciers melt the valleys are left at a higher level.

Ribbon lakes are long, thin lakes that form after a glacier retreats. They form in hollows where softer rock was eroded more than the surrounding hard rock. (E.g. Windermere, Lake District)

Glacial troughs are steep-sided valleys with flat bottoms. They start off as a V-shaped river valley but change to a U-shape as the glacier erodes the sides and bottom, making it deeper and wider. (E.g. Nant Ffrancon, Snowdonia)

Glaciers **Transport** and **Deposit Material called Till**

1) Glaciers can move material (such as sand, clay and rocks) over very large distances — this is called transportation. This unsorted mixture of material is called till.

2) The material is frozen in the glacier, carried on its surface, or pushed in front of it. It's called bulldozing when the ice pushes loose material in front of it.

3) When the ice carrying the material melts, the material is deposited (dropped) on the valley floor, forming landforms such as moraines and drumlins (see next page).

4) Most glacial deposits aren't sorted by size and weight like river deposits — rocks of all shapes and sizes are mixed up together.

5) However, very fine material such as sand and gravel can get washed away from the front of the glacier by small meltwater streams. The streams sort the material by size and deposit it in layers (called outwash) in front of the glacier.

Learn how ice produces these seven landforms

Make sure you know what each of these landforms looks like — and also make sure you know why they look the way they do. You might be asked to spot them on a map in the exam, or from a photo — see pages 84-85.

Glacial Deposition

Glaciers <u>transport</u> a lot of material — and that material has to <u>end up somewhere</u>.

Glaciers **Deposit Material** as **Different Types** of **Moraine**

<u>Moraines</u> are <u>landforms</u> made out of <u>till</u> dropped by a <u>glacier</u> as it melts.
There are four <u>different types</u>, depending on their <u>position</u>:

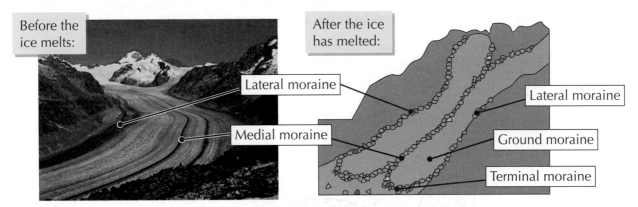

1) <u>Lateral</u> moraine is a <u>long mound</u> of material deposited where the <u>side</u> of the glacier was. It's formed by material eroded from the <u>valley walls</u> and carried along on the <u>ice surface</u> at the <u>sides</u> of the glacier.

2) <u>Medial</u> moraine is a <u>long ridge</u> of material deposited along the <u>centre</u> of a valley floor. When <u>two glaciers meet</u>, the <u>lateral moraines</u> from the two edges <u>join</u> and form a line of material running along the <u>centre</u> of the <u>new glacier</u>.

3) <u>Terminal</u> moraine builds up at the <u>snout</u> of the glacier — marking the <u>furthest point</u> reached by the ice. Material that's <u>abraded</u> and <u>plucked</u> from the valley floor is transported at the front of the glacier, and then deposited as <u>semicircular mounds</u> as the ice retreats.

4) <u>Ground moraine</u> is eroded material that was dragged along the <u>base</u> of the glacier and is deposited over a <u>wide area</u> on the <u>valley floor</u> as the ice melts.

Material can also be **Deposited** as **Drumlins and Erratics**

Drumlins

1) <u>Drumlins</u> are <u>elongated hills</u> of <u>glacial deposits</u> — the largest ones can be <u>over 1000 m</u> long, <u>500 m</u> wide and <u>50 m</u> high.

2) They're <u>round</u>, <u>blunt</u> and <u>steep</u> at the <u>upstream</u> end, and <u>tapered</u>, <u>pointed</u> and <u>gently sloping</u> at the <u>downstream</u> end.

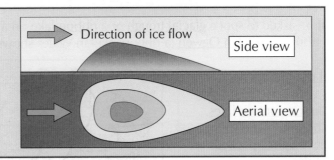

Erratics

1) <u>Erratics</u> are <u>rocks</u> that have been <u>picked up</u> by a glacier, <u>carried along</u> and <u>dropped</u> in an area that has a completely <u>different rock type</u>.

2) Erratics often look <u>out of place</u>, e.g. a large boulder on its <u>own</u>.

Glaciers deposit material when the ice melts

All those different types of moraine can get a bit confusing when you're just reading about them. To get them memorised, try sketching the diagram from the top of the page and labelling the four different types.

Identifying Glacial Landforms

In the exam you might be asked to spot glacial landforms on an OS® map. It's no problem when you know how, so here are a few tips for you...

Use Contour Lines to Spot Pyramidal Peaks, Corries and Arêtes on a Map

Contour lines are the orange lines drawn all over maps. They tell you about the height of the land by the numbers marked on them, and the steepness of the land by how close together the lines are (the closer they are, the steeper the slope). Here are a few tips on how to spot pyramidal peaks, arêtes and corries on a map:

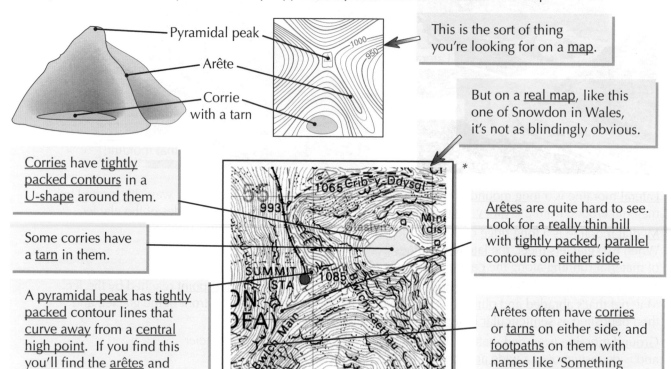

Pyramidal peak
Arête
Corrie with a tarn

This is the sort of thing you're looking for on a map.

But on a real map, like this one of Snowdon in Wales, it's not as blindingly obvious.

Corries have tightly packed contours in a U-shape around them.

Some corries have a tarn in them.

A pyramidal peak has tightly packed contour lines that curve away from a central high point. If you find this you'll find the arêtes and corries around it.

Arêtes are quite hard to see. Look for a really thin hill with tightly packed, parallel contours on either side.

Arêtes often have corries or tarns on either side, and footpaths on them with names like 'Something Edge', e.g. 'Striding Edge'.

You can also use Maps to Spot Glacial Troughs and Ribbon Lakes

You might be asked to spot a glacial trough or a ribbon lake on a map extract. This map of Nant Ffrancon (a glacial trough) and Llyn Ogwen (a ribbon lake) in Wales shows the classic things to look out for:

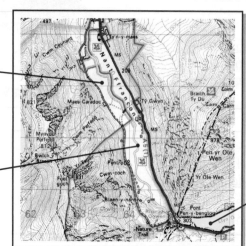

Glacial troughs are flat valleys with very steep sides. There are no contour lines on the bottom of the valley but they're tightly packed on the sides.

Look for a wide, straight valley in a mountainous area with a river that looks too small to have formed the valley.

Many glacial troughs have ribbon lakes in them. Look for a flat valley with steep sides surrounding a long straight lake.

Contour lines are the key to spotting glacial landforms on maps

EXAM TIP: Don't panic if you're given map extracts in the exam — just study them carefully and try to picture the landforms. Make sure you refer to the map in your answer, and give details about what's shown.

UK Glacial Landscape

Snowdonia is a great place to look for glacial landforms. It may not be covered in ice now, but it has seen a lot of ice in the past. Here's an example of some of the landforms that are found there.

Snowdonia is a Glacial Landscape in North Wales

1) Snowdonia is an area in north Wales. It has been repeatedly covered by ice during glacial periods (see page 20).

2) The upland areas of Snowdonia (e.g. the Glyders — mountains to the north-east of Snowdon) show many of the landforms from pages 82-83.

3) Here are some of the glacial features that are found on the Glyders and the surrounding area:

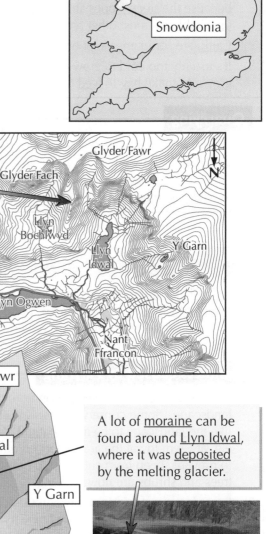

The sharp ridge between the two corries, known as Y Gribin, is an example of an arête. At its lower end, it is cut off by the Ogwen valley leaving a truncated spur.

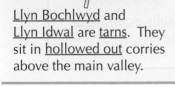

Llyn Bochlwyd and Llyn Idwal are tarns. They sit in hollowed out corries above the main valley.

Glyder Fach

Llyn Bochlwyd

Glyder Fawr

Llyn Idwal

A lot of moraine can be found around Llyn Idwal, where it was deposited by the melting glacier.

Llyn Ogwen

Y Garn

Nant Ffrancon

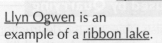

Llyn Ogwen is an example of a ribbon lake.

Nant Ffrancon is a glacial trough. You can see the large U-shaped valley and the River Ogwen that looks too small to have created it.

There are lots of different glacial landforms in Snowdonia

This is just an example of some of the glacial landforms that can be seen in Snowdonia. You may have studied a different example — that's fine, as long as you can spot and describe the landforms there from maps and photos.

Land Use in Glacial Landscapes

People <u>use</u> glaciated areas in loads of different ways. Unfortunately, these different activities create <u>conflicts</u>.

Glaciated Areas have Many Economic Uses

Farming

1) <u>Sheep farming</u> is common in <u>upland</u> glaciated areas because the <u>steep slopes</u> and <u>poor soils</u> make it <u>unsuitable</u> for most other types of farming.
2) <u>Cattle</u> are sometimes kept on the flatter <u>valley floors</u>.
3) It's usually too cold to grow <u>crops</u>, but <u>grass</u> is grown to make <u>hay</u> to <u>feed</u> the <u>animals</u>.

Forestry

1) <u>Coniferous (evergreen) forests</u> are often planted in upland areas because they can <u>cope</u> with the <u>cold</u> weather and high <u>rainfall</u>.
2) The trees are used for <u>timber</u>, e.g. for <u>building materials</u>.

Quarrying

1) The <u>erosion</u> by glaciers left lots of <u>rock exposed</u>, making it easy to get to.
2) Glacial landscapes are often quarried for <u>slate</u>, <u>granite</u>, and <u>limestone</u>.

Tourism

1) Glaciated areas have <u>dramatic</u> landscapes, making them <u>attractive</u> places to visit.
2) People take part in a <u>variety of activities</u> including hiking, climbing, boating, mountain biking and skiing.

Economic Activity Causes Conflict in Glacial Landscapes

Most <u>upland glacial landscapes</u> in the <u>UK</u> are very <u>attractive</u> areas. Conservationists want to <u>preserve</u> the <u>environmental value</u> of the landscapes, but <u>development</u> is needed to provide <u>employment</u> (e.g. in farming, quarrying, forestry or tourism) and to provide <u>roads</u> and <u>facilities</u> for the many <u>visitors</u> to glacial areas. This creates <u>conflict</u> between <u>conservation</u> and <u>development</u>. For example:

See pages 87-88 for more on the impacts of tourism.

Conflicts caused by Farming

1) Grazing sheep remove <u>vegetation</u> from the landscape. Some conservationists would like the landscape to be more <u>natural</u> — e.g. at Cwm Idwal the area is fenced off to prevent sheep from entering, so more <u>trees</u> and <u>shrubs</u> are now growing.
2) Some farmers don't want lots of tourists <u>walking</u> through their land, and may try to <u>block footpaths</u> or <u>deter walkers</u>.

Conflicts caused by Tourism

1) <u>Conservationists</u> may object to the <u>development</u> of <u>infrastructure</u> to support the tourism industry, e.g. the visitor centre on the top of Snowdon.
2) Tourists can <u>damage stone walls</u>, <u>scare sheep</u>, leave <u>gates</u> open and <u>trample</u> on crops, causing conflict with <u>farmers</u>.

Conflicts caused by Forestry

1) <u>Harvesting</u> trees means <u>chopping</u> forests down, which affects conservation efforts because it can <u>scare off wildlife</u> and <u>damage habitats</u>.
2) Coniferous forests don't support as many different types of <u>species</u> as mixed woodland. This may make the area <u>less attractive</u> to tourists and there may be <u>limited access</u> when the trees are being chopped down.

Conflicts caused by Quarrying

1) Conservationists object to the <u>destruction</u> of <u>habitats</u> and the <u>damage</u> to <u>local wildlife</u>.
2) Quarrying makes the environment <u>less attractive</u> to tourists so they may be discouraged from visiting. This could have <u>economic impacts</u> on <u>local businesses</u> who depend on the tourists.
3) Local residents may object to the <u>large trucks</u> that transport the quarried stone <u>passing</u> close to their homes, and the <u>noise</u> from the quarry itself.

Different land uses in glacial landscapes can cause conflict
If you get a question about conflict between different groups of people in the exam, make sure you write about both points of view. If you're stuck, try putting yourself in the shoes of the groups involved.

Tourism in Glacial Landscapes

Glacial landscapes in the UK are visited by millions of people every year — but popularity comes at a price...

Tourism has Social, Economic and Environmental Impacts

Glacial landscapes are very popular with tourists. This has a number of impacts:

Economic Impacts

1) Tourism can have a positive economic impact on glacial landscapes as it is often the main industry.
2) Tourism offers employment to local people (e.g. in hotels, shops, cafés and the outdoor industry). However, jobs are often seasonal and low paid.
3) Less positive impacts include extremely high house prices due to demand for holiday and second homes. This can often mean that local people are unable to buy houses and so are forced out of the area.
4) The price of goods and services is often higher because tourists are willing to pay more.

Social Impacts

1) Increased traffic causes problems because often the roads are narrow and winding. Congestion is common and there isn't enough car parking available.
2) Shops that used to sell goods for local people (e.g. food, clothes) often sell gifts and outdoor clothing for tourists instead.
3) Holiday homes are usually not occupied all year round. This can lead to some services for local residents being limited, e.g. reduced bus services in off-peak seasons.

Environmental Impacts

1) Footpath erosion is often a problem due to the large numbers of walkers. Vegetation is destroyed and exposed soil is washed away — this damages the landscape and leaves large erosion scars.
2) Litter increases during the tourist season and some tourists light bonfires or BBQs, which can damage the ground.
3) Water sports (e.g. jet skiing and power boating) create noise pollution. The waves created by the boats can erode the shoreline and fuel spills can pollute the water, harming fish, birds and plants.
4) Tourists may park on grass verges, causing damage to vegetation.
5) Wildlife and livestock can be disturbed by walkers and their dogs.

Strategies are Needed to Cope with the Impact of Tourists

The impacts of tourism can be managed in different ways. Here are some examples:

1) Managing footpath erosion:
   - Resurface paths with hard-wearing materials, e.g. rocks, plastic mesh, slabs, etc.
   - Reseed vegetation to reduce the visual impact of the erosion.
   - Encourage visitors to use alternative routes by providing signposting or fencing.

2) Managing traffic congestion:
   - Increase public transport in the tourist season.
   - Improve the road network, e.g. by providing designated passing places on single-track roads.
   - Encourage people to use bikes, buses, boats and trains, e.g. by providing discounts.

3) Protecting wildlife and farmland:
   - Use signs to remind people to take their litter home and provide covered bins at the most popular sites.
   - Encourage visitors to enjoy the countryside responsibly — by closing gates and keeping dogs on leads.

Tourism can bring wealth to an area but it also causes lots of problems

Not everyone is happy with the growth of tourism — local residents can object to high prices, damage to the environment and being stuck in traffic all summer. Don't forget that tourism provides jobs and income though.

Tourism in Glacial Landscapes

The Lake District is a classic example of a glacial landscape where tourism has had impacts.

The Lake District Attracts Millions of Tourists

The Lake District is a National Park in Cumbria, which gets 16.4 million visitors every year. The attractions for visitors include:

1) Beautiful scenery — large lakes (e.g. Windermere) and mountains (e.g. Scafell Pike).
2) Cultural attractions — e.g. Beatrix Potter's house and the Wordsworth Museum.
3) Activities — e.g. rock-climbing, mountain biking, water sports, bird watching and fishing.

Lake District

Tourism is Having Big Impacts on the Area

Environmental Impacts

1) Catbells is a popular mountain for walkers, but the large number of people using the main footpath from Keswick has led to severe erosion.
2) Tourists often park on the grass verges in the popular Langdale valley, which damages the vegetation.
3) Noise, erosion and pollution of water with fuel is caused by boats and water sports on Lake Windermere.

Economic Impacts

1) Tourism employed over 16 000 people in 2014 and visitors spent over £1 billion.
2) The average price of a house in the village of Grasmere is over £350 000 (due to holiday homes etc.) but the average local household income is only £27 000, so many local people may not be able to afford to stay living in the area.

Social Impacts

1) It's estimated that 89% of visitors to the park arrive by car. Traffic is heavy on the roads linking the National Park with the motorway, especially at the end of the day when day trippers are going home.
2) Businesses in the village of Ambleside mostly cater for tourists — roughly 40% are cafés, restaurants, hotels etc. and around 10% sell outdoor clothing. Prices of everyday goods are high and local residents often travel to Windermere or Kendal to buy most of their food and clothes.
3) More than 16% of properties in the National Park are second homes or holiday homes. This means there are fewer people living in the National Park all year round, so bus services are limited, some primary schools in the Langdale valley have closed and Gosforth no longer has a doctor.

Management Strategies are Reducing the Impact of Tourism

Here are a few strategies being carried out to reduce the problems caused by tourism in the Lake District:

1) Coping with the extra traffic and lack of car parking:
   The Go Lakes Travel scheme aims to reduce car use, e.g. by introducing pay-as-you-go bikes, and Ambleside has Controlled Parking Zones within the town centre where people can park for 1 hour. This encourages a high turnover of parking spaces.
2) Helping local people cope with high property prices:
   In 2012, planning permission was granted for 134 affordable homes and 141 houses that only local people can buy (to prevent them being bought as second homes).
3) Coping with the erosion of footpaths:
   At Tarn Hows, severely eroded paths have been covered with soil and reseeded, and the main route has been gravelled to protect it.
4) Coping with the noise, erosion and pollution from water sports:
   Zoning schemes mean that some water sports are only allowed in certain areas of some lakes, e.g. Windermere has a 10 knot speed limit for all boats, which falls to 6 knots in some zones.

The Lake District is a glacial landscape that is very popular with tourists

If you've read the previous page, this one shouldn't be too tricky — just learn some facts and figures about the Lake District (or whichever example you have studied), and a few management strategies that are being used there.

Worked Exam Questions

With the answers written in, it's very easy to skim these worked examples and think you've understood. But that's not going to help you, so take the time to make sure you've really understood everything here.

1 Study **Figure 1**, a photograph showing land use in Scotland in a glacial landscape.

1.1 Name one of the land uses shown in **Figure 1** and explain why it is commonly found in glacial landscapes in the UK.

Figure 1

Land use: Forestry ....
[1]

Reason: Coniferous forests are often planted in upland areas because they can cope with the cold weather and high rainfall. The trees are used for timber, e.g. for building materials.
[2]

1.2 To what extent are the benefits from the development of UK glacial landscapes more significant than the problems?

Development of glacial landscapes can bring benefits to an area. It provides employment (e.g. in quarrying or tourism), as well as facilities for visitors and local communities. It brings money into the area, so services will improve (e.g. more frequent buses), improving the quality of life of the people who live there. However, development can also cause problems. For example, conservationists want to preserve the environmental value of the landscapes, but development can damage the environment and destroy habitats. This can make the area less attractive to tourists, reducing income to local businesses who depend on them. On balance, I think the problems caused by development outweigh the benefits.
[6]

[Total 9 marks]

2 Study **Figure 2**, a photograph showing tourists near the summit of Snowdon, in a glacial landscape in north Wales.

Figure 2

2.1 Use **Figure 2** and your own knowledge to describe the possible negative impacts of tourists visiting glacial landscapes.

Figure 2 shows that footpath erosion can be a problem due to the large numbers of walkers. Vegetation is destroyed and exposed soil is washed away. This damages the landscape and leaves large erosion scars. Also, house prices are often high in glaciated areas due to demand for holiday homes and second homes. This can mean that local people cannot afford to buy houses and are forced to move out of the area. Holiday homes are not occupied all year round. This can lead to some services for local residents being limited, for example, reduced bus services in off-peak seasons.

[Total 4 marks]

Exam Questions

1 Study **Figure 1**, an Ordnance Survey® map of part of the Lake District.

Figure 1

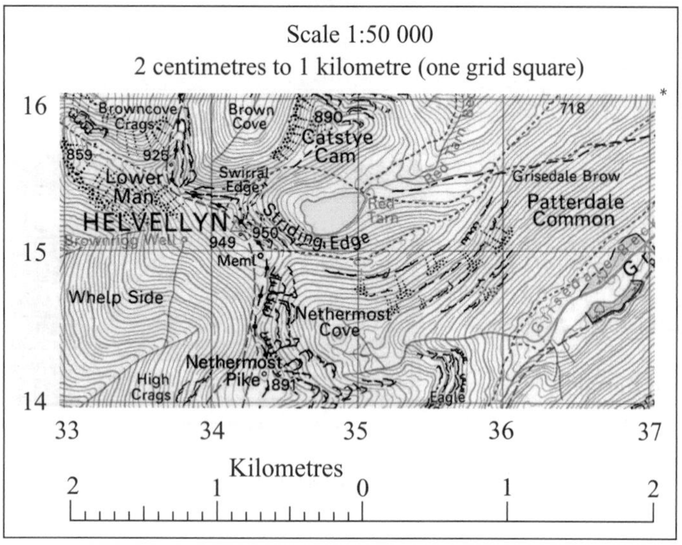

Scale 1:50 000
2 centimetres to 1 kilometre (one grid square)

1.1 Give the four figure grid reference of a grid square that contains a glacial trough and explain how they are formed.

Grid reference:......................................

Formation:...

....

....

....

....

[2]

1.2 Using **Figure 1**, how far is it between the summits of Catstye Cam and Nethermost Pike?

.... km

[1]

[Total 3 marks]

2 Study **Figure 2**, a diagram showing features of glacial deposition.

Figure 2

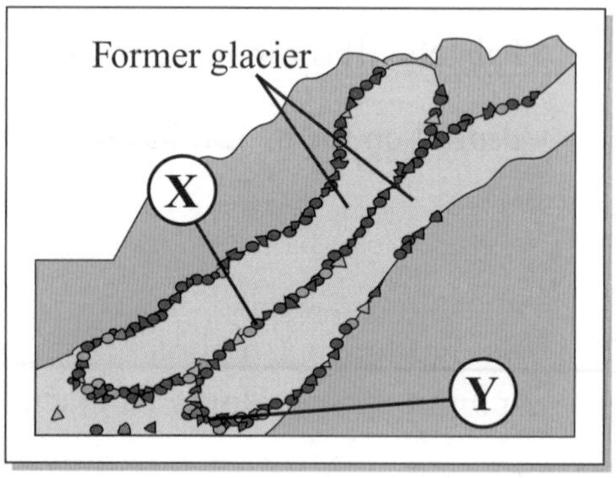

2.1 Identify the depositional feature labelled X on **Figure 2**.
Shade **one** oval only.

A Medial moraine ⬭

B Erratic ⬭

C Ground moraine ⬭

D Snout ⬭

[1]

2.2 Outline **one** way in which glaciers transport material.

....

....

[1]

2.3 Explain the formation of the feature labelled Y on **Figure 2**.

....

....

....

....

[3]

[Total 5 marks]

*Reproduced with permission by Ordnance Survey®
© Crown copyright 2016 GV-198903

Revision Summary

Right, you've reached the end of <u>Glacial Landscapes</u> — time to see how much of it you can <u>remember</u>.
- Try these questions and <u>tick off each one</u> when you <u>get it right</u>.
- When you've done <u>all the questions</u> for a topic and are <u>completely happy</u> with it, tick off the topic.

Glacial Erosion and Glacial Landforms (p.81-82) ☑

1) Describe the maximum extent of ice in the UK during the last ice age.
2) Describe two ways that ice erodes the landscape.
3) What is rotational slip?
4) Explain what freeze-thaw weathering is.
5) What is a corrie?
6) How does a pyramidal peak form?
7) Give an example of a pyramidal peak.
8) Explain how a hanging valley forms.
9) What is a glacial trough?
10) What is bulldozing?
11) Describe the formation of outwash.

Glacial Deposition (p.83) ☑

12) Give one difference between lateral and ground moraine.
13) Where is medial moraine deposited?
14) Describe the formation of terminal moraine.
15) Describe what a drumlin looks like.
16) What is an erratic?

Identifying Glacial Landforms (p.84-85) ☑

17) How would you identify a pyramidal peak on a map?
18) How would you identify an arête on a map?
19) Describe what a glacial trough looks like on a map.
20) Give an example of a glacial trough.
21) What does a ribbon lake look like on a map?
22) a) Give an example of a glaciated upland area in the UK.
    b) Name some of its major features of erosion.
23) How would you identify a corrie in a photograph?
24) Describe what an arête looks like.

Land Use in Glacial Landscapes (p.86-88) ☑

25) Describe the types of farming that commonly take place in glacial landscapes.
26) Name three economic activities, other than farming, that take place in glacial landscapes.
27) Give two examples of conflicts that might be caused by quarrying in glacial landscapes.
28) Describe the conflicts caused by a type of land use other than quarrying in glacial landscapes.
29) Describe the economic impacts of tourism on glaciated upland areas.
30) Give two strategies that might be used to manage the social impacts of tourism.
31) Explain why tourists are attracted to one glacial area you have studied.
32) Using a named example, describe the social impacts of tourism on a glaciated area.
33) For a named upland area, describe one way that environmental impacts of tourism have been managed.

Urbanisation

Urban areas (towns and cities) are <u>popular places</u> to be and getting <u>ever more so</u>. You need to know <u>why</u>...

Urbanisation is Happening **Fastest** in **Poorer Countries**

1) <u>Urbanisation</u> is the <u>growth</u> in the <u>proportion</u> of a country's population living in <u>urban areas</u>.

2) It's happening in countries <u>all over the world</u> — more than <u>50%</u> of the world's population currently live in <u>urban areas</u> (<u>3.9 billion</u> people) and this is <u>increasing</u> every day.

3) The <u>rate</u> of urbanisation <u>differs</u> between countries that are <u>richer</u> and those that are <u>poorer</u>.

4) <u>High Income Countries (HICs)</u> are <u>more</u> economically developed, e.g. UK, Japan and Germany. Urbanisation happened <u>earlier</u> in HICs than in LICs and NEEs, e.g. during the <u>Industrial Revolution</u>, and <u>most</u> of the population now <u>already live</u> in urban areas.

5) HICs have very <u>slow rates</u> of urban growth, and many people desiring a <u>better quality of life</u> are moving <u>away</u> from overcrowded cities to rural areas. Good <u>transport</u> and <u>communication networks</u> mean that people in HICs can <u>live</u> in <u>rural areas</u> and <u>commute</u> to cities, or <u>work from home</u>.

6) <u>Low Income Countries (LICs)</u> are <u>less</u> economically developed, e.g. Ethiopia, Nepal and Afghanistan. <u>Not many</u> of the population in LICs <u>currently live</u> in urban areas. In general, the <u>fastest rates</u> of urbanisation in the world are in LICs.

7) <u>Newly Emerging Economies (NEEs)</u> are those where economic development is increasing <u>rapidly</u>, e.g. Brazil, China, Russia, India. The percentage of the population living in urban areas <u>varies</u>. Some NEEs such as <u>Thailand</u>, <u>Nigeria</u> and <u>China</u> are experiencing <u>rapid urban growth</u>.

Urbanisation is **Caused** by **Rural-Urban Migration** and **Natural Increase**

1) <u>Rural-urban migration</u> is the <u>movement</u> of people from the <u>countryside</u> to the <u>cities</u>. The <u>rate</u> of rural-urban migration is affected by <u>push factors</u> (things that <u>encourage</u> people to <u>leave</u> an area) and <u>pull factors</u> (things that <u>encourage</u> people to <u>move to</u> an area). It's usually a <u>combination</u> of push and pull factors that <u>causes</u> people to migrate.

Push factors	**Pull factors**
1) <u>Natural disasters</u>, e.g. floods and earthquakes, can <u>damage</u> property and farmland, which people <u>can't afford</u> to repair.	1) There are <u>more jobs</u> in urban areas that are often <u>better paid</u>.
2) <u>Mechanisation</u> of agricultural equipment — farms require <u>fewer workers</u> so there are <u>fewer jobs</u>.	2) Access to better <u>health care</u> and <u>education</u>.
3) <u>Desertification</u> can make land <u>unproductive</u> (see p.44), so people can no longer <u>support</u> themselves.	3) To join other <u>family members</u> who have already moved.
4) <u>Conflict</u> or <u>war</u> can cause people to <u>flee</u> their homes.	4) People think they will have a better <u>quality of life</u>.

2) Urbanisation is also caused by <u>natural increase</u>. Natural increase is when the <u>birth rate</u> is <u>higher</u> than the death rate, i.e. more people are being <u>born</u> than are <u>dying</u>, so the <u>population grows</u>.

3) It's normally <u>young people</u> that <u>move</u> to cities to <u>find work</u>. These people then <u>have children</u> in the cities, which <u>increases</u> the <u>proportion of the population</u> living in <u>urban areas</u>. Also, <u>better healthcare</u> in <u>urban areas</u> means <u>people live longer</u>, again <u>increasing</u> the <u>proportion of people in urban areas</u>.

4) <u>High rates</u> of <u>urbanisation</u> are leading to the growth of <u>megacities</u>. A megacity is an urban area with <u>over 10 million people</u> living there, e.g. Mumbai in India. There are now <u>34 megacities</u> — more than two thirds are in <u>LICs</u> and <u>NEEs</u>, and more new megacities are expected to emerge in <u>Asia</u> and <u>Africa</u> by 2030.

People usually move to cities to look for better jobs and services

Nothing too difficult on this page — richer countries have a high percentage of their population in urban areas, but urbanisation in poorer countries is happening fast. Try scribbling down the reasons for the migration.

Urban Growth — Opportunities and Challenges

The lure of the city lights can be strong, but there are plenty of challenges to urban growth.

Urban Growth in NEEs and LICs Creates Opportunities...

Social Opportunities

1) There is better access to services, e.g. health care and education, compared to rural areas.

2) There is also better access to resources, such as a clean water supply and electricity.

Economic Opportunities

1) The growth of urban industrial areas can increase economic development.

2) As industries develop, more people move to urban areas to work in the factories — there are more jobs and better wages than in rural areas.

3) Industries sell the goods they produce on the international market. Manufactured goods make greater profits than unprocessed goods (e.g. agricultural products) so industrialised countries get wealthier.

...but it also Brings Challenges

Social and Economic Challenges

Many people who move to the city from rural areas end up in squatter settlements (slums) — settlements that are built illegally in and around the city, by people who can't afford proper housing.

1) They are often badly built and overcrowded.

2) People often don't have access to basic services, e.g. clean running water, proper sewers or electricity.

3) The unclean conditions and lack of access to medical services mean people often have poor health.

4) People may not have access to education so they are unable to develop the skills needed to get better jobs. They often work long hours for little pay.

5) There can be high levels of unemployment and crime.

Environmental Challenges

If cities grow rapidly waste disposal services, sewage systems and environmental regulations for factories can't keep pace with the growth.

1) Rubbish often isn't collected or it may end up in big rubbish heaps. This can damage the environment, especially if it's toxic.

2) Air pollution comes from burning fuel, vehicle exhaust fumes and factories.

3) Sewage and toxic chemicals can get into rivers, harming wildlife.

4) The road system may not be able to cope with all the vehicles. Congestion causes increased greenhouse gas emissions.

The Favela-Bairro Project Helps Poor People in Rio de Janeiro's Favelas

EXAMPLE

Often the poorest people in urban areas are the worst affected by the problems of urban growth. Urban planning schemes can help reduce the impact of these problems and improve the quality of life for the urban poor. An example of an urban planning scheme is the Favela-Bairro Project in Rio de Janeiro:

1) Rio de Janeiro is in south east Brazil. It has more than 600 squatter settlements (called favelas), housing one-fifth of the city's population (more than one million people).

2) The Favela-Bairro project ran from 1995-2008 and involved 253 000 people in 73 favelas. It has led to:

   • Social improvements — e.g. there are now day care centres for children, adult education classes and services to help people with drug or alcohol addictions.

   • Economic improvements — e.g. the project is helping people get legal ownership of their properties and running training schemes to help people find better jobs.

   • Environmental improvements — e.g. wooden buildings are being replaced with brick buildings, streets have been widened and paved, and there are now rubbish collection services.

Learn the major challenges caused by urban growth

This is important stuff — the opportunities and challenges of urban growth can be applied to most fast-growing cities. You also need to know how urban planning can help improve things for the poor. So get learning.

Urban Growth

Lagos is a great example of the <u>attraction</u> of cities and the <u>problems</u> caused by <u>rapid urban growth</u>.

Lagos is the Biggest City in Africa

1) <u>Lagos</u> is a city in <u>Nigeria</u> — Nigeria is a <u>Newly Emerging Economy</u> (<u>NEE</u>) and the <u>richest</u> country in <u>Africa</u>. The city's population is over <u>21 million</u>, and is one of the <u>fastest-growing</u> urban areas in the world.

2) It was the <u>national capital</u> until 1991, and it remains the <u>main financial centre</u> for the whole of <u>West Africa</u>.

3) More than <u>275 000 migrants</u> arrive <u>every year</u>, creating an outwards <u>urban sprawl</u> of the city into the surrounding countryside. <u>Natural increase</u> is also causing population growth but not as much as migration.

Lagos Offers People Better Jobs and a Better Quality of Life...

Social Opportunities

Lagos has <u>better access</u> to <u>services</u> and <u>resources</u> than <u>rural</u> Nigeria:

1) There are <u>more healthcare centres</u> and <u>hospitals</u> and a <u>better range</u> of <u>medicines</u> in Lagos.

2) <u>68%</u> of the population of Lagos have <u>secondary</u> education (<u>40%</u> don't even attend <u>primary</u> school in rural areas in the north of the country).

3) In Lagos, people can use <u>electricity</u> for <u>cooking</u> and <u>lighting</u>. Access to electricity also means people can <u>develop businesses</u>.

4) <u>Water treatment plants</u> provide <u>safe water</u> piped directly to areas of the city.

Economic Opportunities

1) Rural Nigeria is very poor — <u>most</u> people come to Lagos in search of <u>better jobs</u>.

2) <u>Rapid growth</u> of the city means there are lots of <u>construction</u> jobs, e.g. building the new commercial centre, Eko Atlantic.

3) Lagos is home to many of the country's <u>banks</u>, <u>government departments</u> and <u>manufacturing industries</u> (e.g. making food and drink). There are two major <u>ports</u> and a <u>fishing industry</u>.

4) Lagos also has a thriving <u>film</u> and <u>music industry</u> — 'Nollywood' films are very popular.

...But Rapid Growth has Led to Loads of Problems

Planners have been <u>unable</u> to keep up with <u>rapidly expanding population</u>. The average population density is <u>20 000 people per km²</u> — this puts pressure on the supply of <u>housing</u>, <u>services</u> and <u>infrastructure</u>.

Social Challenges

Over <u>60%</u> of the city's population live in <u>slums</u>, e.g. Makoko.

1) Houses in Makoko are <u>flimsy</u>, <u>wooden huts</u> built on <u>stilts</u> in the lagoon. There is only <u>one primary school</u> in Makoko and many families <u>can't afford</u> to send their children to school.

2) <u>Communal toilets</u> are shared by <u>15 households</u> and most of the waste goes <u>straight</u> into the <u>lagoon</u> below — it's always full of <u>rubbish</u> and <u>raw sewage</u>. This <u>causes health problems</u>, e.g. cholera.

3) Water can be bought in Makoko from a <u>communal water point</u> but that can be up to <u>3 km away</u> and the only <u>electricity</u> comes from <u>illegal connections</u> that often <u>cut out</u>.

4) There are high levels of <u>crime</u> in Makoko — the slum is <u>self-policed</u> by gangs called '<u>Area Boys</u>'.

Environmental Challenges

1) Only about <u>40% of rubbish</u> is officially collected and there are <u>large rubbish dumps</u> containing <u>toxic waste</u>.

2) <u>Waste disposal</u> and <u>emissions</u> from factories are <u>not controlled</u>, leading to <u>air</u> and <u>water pollution</u>.

3) Traffic congestion is <u>really bad</u> — many face <u>2 hour commutes</u> in rush hours known as the '<u>go slow</u>'.

Economic Challenges

There aren't enough <u>formal jobs</u> for all the <u>migrants</u> — people have to make money <u>any way they can</u>, e.g. by <u>scavenging</u> in the Olususun rubbish dump for items to sell.

Include lots of facts and figures when you write about a case study

If you've studied a different example of urban growth in class and you'd rather write about that instead, then no problem — just make sure you have enough information to cover the key points on this page.

Worked Exam Questions

Here's the first lot of worked exam questions for this section — for an extra bit of practice, try covering the answers and thinking about how you would answer each question before you read the suggested answer.

1 Study **Figure 1**, a photograph of some students in a city in Indonesia.

1.1 Using **Figure 1** and your own knowledge, outline **two** opportunities created by urban growth in a lower income country (LIC) or a newly emerging economy (NEE).

Figure 1

Opportunity 1: Figure 1 shows children in school uniform — cities offer better access to services such as education compared to rural areas.

Opportunity 2: There are motorbikes parked outside the buildings in Figure 1, showing that people are reasonably wealthy — cities offer more jobs and better wages than rural areas.

[2]

1.2 Describe **two** environmental challenges caused by urban growth in an LIC or NEE.

Challenge 1: Sewage and toxic chemicals from factories can get into rivers, harming wildlife

Challenge 2: Traffic congestion from rapidly increasing numbers of cars causes increased greenhouse gas emissions.

[2]

1.3 Explain how an urban planning scheme in an LIC or NEE has had a positive effect on people living in the area.

Around one-fifth of the population of Rio de Janeiro live in squatter settlements (favelas).

The Favela-Bairro project was a scheme designed the improve quality of life for people in 73 favelas.

It set up day care centres for children and adult education classes, improving people's social situation.

It also improved people's economic situation, for example by helping them to get legal ownership

of their homes and by running training schemes so they could find better jobs and earn more.

Environmental changes, such as setting up rubbish collection services, made the area more pleasant for

people to live in.

[4]

[Total 8 marks]

Exam Questions

1   Study **Figure 1**, a graph showing the change in the urban population of lower income countries (LICs) and higher income countries (HICs) between 1950 and 2000.

1.1   Complete the graph to show that the urban population of LICs in 2000 was 2 billion.

[1]

Figure 1

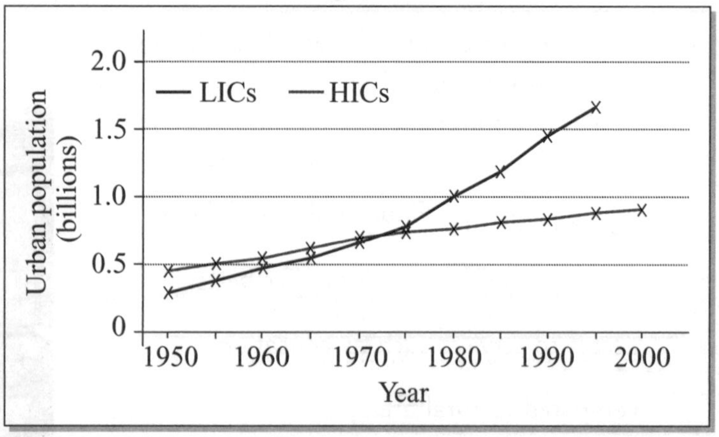

1.2   Describe the trends shown in **Figure 1**.

....

....

....

....

....

....

....

[3]

1.3   Suggest **two** pull factors that encourage people to move to cities.

1:..

....

2:..

....

[2]

1.4   Suggest reasons for the difference in the rate of urbanisation in HICs and LICs shown in **Figure 1**.

....

....

....

....

....

....

....

....

[6]

[Total 12 marks]

UK Cities

Cities don't just spring up in any old place — most of them are where they are for a reason. If you know your physical landscapes of the UK (see page 54), the urban areas should slot nicely into place.

Most Cities are in **Lowland Areas** with Good Access to **Natural Resources**

The population distribution in the UK is very uneven. Many of the major cities have developed into conurbations — towns that have merged to form continuous urban areas. These areas have the highest population density. The relief (change in the height of the land) affects where most people live:

Upland regions such as the north of Scotland are sparsely-populated — they are difficult to farm and have few natural resources.

Mineral wealth (especially of coal and iron ore) has often led to rapid population growth because this was where industries developed. Many of the UK's cities developed on major coalfields, e.g. Newcastle and Leeds.

Many coastal areas have attracted human settlement — especially where there are sheltered bays and river estuaries suitable for building harbours. Key ports (e.g. Liverpool and Cardiff) have grown into major cities.

Most urban areas developed in lowland areas (e.g. Birmingham) — these are easy to build on and have a milder climate than upland areas.

Edinburgh, Glasgow, Belfast, Newcastle, Leeds, Manchester, Liverpool, Cardiff, Birmingham, London

Population density (100s per km^2)
- 23.7+
- 3.3 – 23.7
- 0 – 3.3

London is the UK's biggest city — it has over 8.6 million people, which is 10% of the country's total population. It is the national capital and has many industries (e.g. it is one of the global financial centres).

Cities Have Different **Zones**

Most UK cities have distinct areas called zones. You might be asked to spot one of them on a map, so here are the four main zones and what to look out for:

The Central Business District (CBD) is usually in the middle of a town or city. It has its main public buildings, train and bus stations, hotels, shops, offices, restaurants and entertainment facilities — you can see some of these on maps. The CBD is often surrounded by a ring road — so look out for one of these as well.

The suburbs are found towards the edge of the city. They are mainly residential areas, often with semi-detached houses. Look for lots of short, curved streets and cul-de-sacs on the map.

LEICESTER

The rural-urban fringe is on the edge of the city. It has farmland and open spaces as well as new housing developments and large retail and business parks. Look for white spaces showing fields mixed with more built-up areas.

The inner city area often has a mix of land uses — mainly residential (including old terraced houses, high-rise tower blocks and modern housing built in redevelopment programmes) but with some businesses and recreational parks. Lots of short, parallel roads often show areas of terraced housing in the inner city.

You might have to identify UK cities from a map in the exam

If you think anywhere south of Manchester is basically London, it's probably a good idea to take a long, hard look at the map at the top of this page. Urban zones will come in useful over the next few pages too.

Unit 2A — Urban Issues and Challenges

Change in UK Cities

UK cities have always been <u>changing</u>. These changes lead to <u>opportunities</u> and <u>challenges</u>.

Urban Change Creates Opportunities and Challenges...

1) During the <u>Industrial Revolution</u> there was <u>growth</u> of <u>manufacturing industries</u> and <u>rapid urbanisation</u>.
2) This was followed by industrial <u>decline</u> — many industries relocated <u>overseas</u> or to the <u>rural-urban fringe</u>.
3) Lots of people moved to the <u>suburbs</u>, and the <u>inner city areas</u> and <u>CBDs declined</u>.
4) <u>Regeneration</u> projects have helped to make city centres more <u>attractive</u> again.
5) These changes have created various <u>opportunities</u> and <u>challenges</u>:

Opportunities

1) <u>Immigrant</u> communities were attracted by <u>low cost</u> inner city housing. Many UK cities are now very <u>multicultural</u> — offering a range of <u>food</u> and <u>festivals</u>, e.g. the Notting Hill Carnival in London.
2) <u>Redevelopment</u> presents opportunities for <u>new investment</u>. Hotels, restaurants and entertainment venues can be <u>upgraded</u> to make the city centre <u>more attractive</u>.
3) CBDs have been redeveloped with <u>offices</u> and <u>entertainment facilities</u> — creating employment opportunities in, for example, <u>finance</u>, <u>tourism</u> and the <u>creative industries</u>.
4) Cities dealing with <u>congestion problems</u> and high numbers of <u>commuters</u> coming into CBD have developed <u>innovative transport solutions</u>.
5) The importance of <u>green space</u> in cities is being increasingly <u>recognised</u> by planners. <u>Parks</u>, <u>gardens</u> and <u>open spaces</u> are being incorporated into <u>regenerated areas</u> of UK cities.

Challenges

1) <u>Industrial decline</u> in cites caused a <u>decrease</u> in <u>wealth</u>. People <u>moved away</u>, leaving <u>derelict buildings</u> that became a <u>target</u> for <u>crime</u>, and areas in many inner cities became deprived.
2) Deprived areas are linked to <u>poor access</u> to <u>health care</u>, <u>education</u> and <u>job opportunities</u> compared to other areas — these inequalities can lead to social unrest.
3) <u>Derelict</u> land in inner cities provides <u>brownfield sites</u> (sites that have previously been developed), which can be used for new <u>development</u>. However, high demand for housing means that <u>new estates</u> also sprawl onto rural <u>greenfield sites</u> (land which has remained free from development).
4) The <u>rural-urban fringe</u> is under <u>pressure</u> from the development of <u>business parks</u> and large <u>shopping centres</u> — the land here is <u>attractive</u> because of good <u>transport links</u> and its <u>lower cost</u>.

New Islington has Been Regenerated

<u>Regeneration</u> is the <u>improvement</u> of an area. Here's how an <u>inner city area</u> in <u>Manchester</u> was regenerated:

The old estate needed regenerating...

1) The <u>Cardroom Estate</u> was built in <u>Manchester</u> in the <u>1960s</u>, just east of the city centre. It replaced the <u>old</u>, <u>cramped terraces</u> that had housed <u>factory workers</u>.
2) By the mid <u>1990s</u> the estate had become <u>run-down</u> and had a <u>bad reputation</u>. <u>50%</u> of the houses were <u>empty</u> or being used as <u>squats</u>.
3) The area had many <u>economic</u> and <u>social</u> <u>problems</u> including <u>high unemployment</u>, <u>joyriding</u>, <u>burglary</u>, <u>drug problems</u>, <u>graffiti</u> and <u>vandalism</u>.

...so people took action

1) The government's <u>regeneration agency</u> worked with <u>private companies</u> and <u>local residents</u> to <u>improve</u> the area — renamed <u>New Islington</u>.
2) <u>1700 new homes</u> were built in consultation with local residents, and a <u>new tram stop</u> improved public transport links.
3) New <u>community facilities</u> include a <u>health centre</u>, <u>village hall</u>, and <u>restaurants</u> and <u>cafés</u>.
4) The project provided an <u>orchard</u>, an <u>eco-park</u> and a <u>community football pitch</u> — these have made the area a more <u>attractive</u> place to live.

REVISION TIP

Draw a table of urban opportunities and challenges

Make sure you're familiar with the opportunities and challenges caused by change in urban areas of the UK. Try making a table or highlighting them in different colours to help you remember them.

Change in UK Cities

Right, that's enough about <u>urban change</u> in general — it's time to get into the details with a case study. <u>Liverpool</u> is a classic example of how changes in a city provide both <u>opportunities</u> and <u>challenges</u>.

Liverpool is a **Port City** in **North West England**

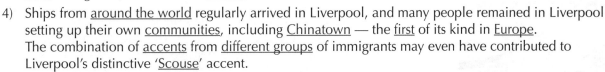

1) <u>Liverpool</u> developed on the <u>River Mersey estuary</u> and became an important <u>port</u> for cotton, sugar and slave ships coming from <u>Africa</u> and the <u>West Indies</u>.

2) It also developed a thriving <u>manufacturing industry</u>, with large factories <u>employing</u> many people, e.g. making cars and ships.

3) <u>Immigration</u> has played a large role in shaping the <u>character</u> of Liverpool. People from <u>Wales</u> moved to the city as it started to develop, attracted by <u>jobs</u> building <u>canals</u> and <u>railways</u>. By 1850, around a quarter of Liverpool's population were <u>Irish</u> immigrants, who had fled <u>famine</u> in Ireland.

4) Ships from <u>around the world</u> regularly arrived in Liverpool, and many people remained in Liverpool setting up their own <u>communities</u>, including <u>Chinatown</u> — the <u>first</u> of its kind in <u>Europe</u>. The combination of <u>accents</u> from <u>different groups</u> of immigrants may even have contributed to Liverpool's distinctive 'Scouse' accent.

5) The <u>decline</u> of the <u>docks</u> in the 1960s led to the closure of 350 factories, causing large scale <u>unemployment</u> and <u>deprivation</u>. Lots of people <u>left</u> the city — especially the <u>young</u> and <u>skilled</u>.

6) More recently, Liverpool has attracted huge <u>investment</u> for <u>regeneration</u>, and was chosen as <u>European Capital of Culture</u> in 2008.

Urban Change has Brought **Social** and **Economic Opportunities** to Liverpool...

Liverpool has <u>changed</u> from a busy <u>port</u> and <u>manufacturing</u> centre to a modern <u>tourist destination</u> and centre for <u>creative industries</u>. This change has led to many <u>opportunities</u>.

1) <u>Cultural mix</u> — <u>ethnic diversity</u> from repeated migrations has brought a range of <u>foods</u>, <u>festivals</u> and <u>cultural experiences</u> to the city, which <u>attract</u> lots of people, e.g. Liverpool's <u>Chinatown</u> is a popular <u>tourist destination</u> and has a thriving Chinese <u>community</u>.

2) <u>Recreation and entertainment</u> — the Albert Dock has been <u>restored</u> and developed to include many <u>shops</u>, <u>restaurants</u> and <u>museums</u> (e.g. the Beatles Story and Merseyside Maritime Museum). The <u>Echo Arena</u> sport and concert venue was built on a brownfield site at <u>Kings Dock</u>. <u>£1 billion</u> was spent <u>regenerating</u> the city centre to create Liverpool ONE — a large <u>shopping and leisure complex</u>.

3) <u>Employment</u> — the <u>tourism</u> and <u>service sectors</u> (e.g. health and finance) now offer many jobs, along with new business developments, e.g. <u>Liverpool Science Park</u>. Development of the 'Baltic Triangle' area of the city has seen the conversion of derelict <u>factories</u> and <u>warehouses</u> into spaces for <u>creative industries</u>, such as <u>art</u>, <u>film making</u> and <u>digital design</u>. Some industry does remain — there is a <u>car manufacturing</u> plant at Halewood, and <u>Liverpool2</u>, a new <u>container port</u>, is opening in 2016.

4) <u>Integrated transport systems</u> — one company (<u>Merseytravel</u>) operate the city's <u>bus</u>, <u>train</u> and <u>ferry</u> networks. A <u>prepaid</u> card can be used across all the different <u>networks</u>, making <u>transfers easier</u>.

Change in UK Cities

CASE STUDY

...but it has also Brought Social and Economic **Challenges**

1) <u>Industrial decline</u> in the 20th century left much of Liverpool's <u>inner city</u> very <u>deprived</u>. Areas of the inner city such as <u>Anfield</u> and <u>Toxteth</u> are among the <u>most deprived</u> areas in England.

2) <u>Regeneration</u> of parts of the city has lead to <u>increased inequality</u> — people in <u>wealthier</u> areas have better access to <u>housing</u>, education, <u>employment</u> and <u>healthcare</u>.

3) Some <u>inner city areas</u> have been <u>redeveloped</u> — existing housing has been <u>cleared</u> and replaced with <u>modern housing</u>. The new housing is often <u>too expensive</u> for the former residents, who are <u>forced out</u>.

4) Many children in deprived areas of Liverpool leave school <u>without basic qualifications</u>, leading to <u>low incomes</u> and <u>high unemployment</u> — about 9% of adults in Anfield are <u>unemployed</u>.

5) <u>Unhealthy lifestyles</u>, e.g. drinking, smoking and poor diets, are <u>more common</u> in <u>deprived areas</u>. Life expectancy in Toxteth is over <u>10 years lower</u> than it is in <u>wealthier</u> areas of the city.

Urban Change has Brought **Environmental Opportunities...**

1) The decline of industry left many areas of Liverpool <u>run down</u> and <u>open spaces</u> as <u>wasteland</u>. <u>Urban greening</u> is forming part of the city's <u>regeneration</u>. Planners are trying to <u>increase</u> and <u>preserve</u> open spaces such as <u>public parks</u> and <u>gardens</u>.

2) More <u>cycle</u> and <u>pedestrian routes</u> are being created and <u>wasteland</u> is being converted into usable <u>parks</u>.

3) Liverpool ONE includes a five acre <u>park</u>, called <u>Chavasse Park</u>, right in the middle of the <u>city centre</u>.

Change in UK Cities

...and **Environmental Challenges**

1) As people <u>left inner city areas</u>, buildings were left <u>empty</u>. <u>Derelict</u> buildings were targets for <u>graffiti</u> and <u>vandalism</u>. Many areas, e.g. Toxteth, became <u>run down</u>.

2) The <u>growth</u> of the city and <u>movement</u> of people to the <u>suburbs</u> means there is <u>pressure</u> to build on <u>greenfield sites</u>. This has <u>destroyed natural habitats</u>. Building on <u>brownfield sites</u> is better for the environment but the land needs <u>clearing</u> and <u>decontaminating</u> first.

3) <u>Waste disposal</u> is becoming an increasing issue as the city's <u>population grows</u>.

4) Plans are in place to build a <u>new waste and recycling centre</u> in the Old Swan area.

Scrap metal is recycled and shipped overseas at this plant at Gladstone Docks.

Urban Sprawl Puts **Pressure** on the **Rural-Urban Fringe**

<u>Urban sprawl</u> is the unplanned <u>growth</u> of <u>urban areas</u> into the <u>surrounding countryside</u>. The <u>rural-urban fringe</u> is an area of <u>transition</u> where there's a <u>mix</u> of urban and rural <u>land use</u>.

1) As Liverpool has <u>grown</u>, it has <u>sprawled</u> outwards, merging with surrounding urban areas to create the <u>Merseyside conurbation</u>. This has affected the <u>rural-urban fringe</u>:

- <u>Large housing estates</u>, e.g. Croxteth Park, have been built on rural <u>greenfield land</u>. This provides a <u>pleasant environment</u> for people to live in but means that <u>open spaces</u> are <u>lost</u> and <u>ecosystems damaged or destroyed</u>.

- <u>Out-of-town developments</u>, e.g. <u>Knowsley Business Park</u> and <u>New Mersey Shopping Park</u>, take advantage of <u>cheaper land</u> outside the city and are <u>easily accessible</u> to lots of people. But <u>large areas</u> of rural land are <u>lost</u> when they are built and they can lead to <u>air</u> and <u>noise pollution</u> and <u>traffic congestion</u>, as people often travel to them by <u>car</u>.

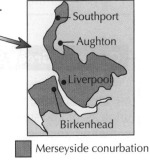

Merseyside conurbation

2) <u>Commuter settlements</u>, e.g. Aughton, are places in the <u>rural-urban fringe</u> where the <u>majority</u> of the population leaves the <u>town</u> each day to work elsewhere. This can cause <u>challenges</u>.

- <u>New housing developments</u> can affect the <u>character</u> of rural settlements and <u>damage</u> the <u>environment</u>.
- <u>Demand</u> for houses increases <u>house prices</u>. Prices in Aughton are among the highest in the region. Locals may not be able to <u>afford</u> to remain in the area.
- <u>Businesses</u> in commuter settlements may <u>suffer</u>, as the majority of the population are absent a lot of the time and may spend their money where they <u>work</u> rather than where they <u>live</u>.
- Large numbers of <u>commuters</u> can increase <u>pollution</u> and cause <u>traffic congestion</u> and <u>parking problems</u>.

Revise the details of Liverpool or another UK city

Right, loads of stuff here... Make sure you're clear on how urban change has created both opportunities and challenges in Liverpool — or another place you've studied. Keep going over the details 'til you know them inside out.

Sustainable Urban Living

It's the 's' word again — it wouldn't be a geography topic without it. This time it's sustainable cities.

Urban Areas Need to Become More Sustainable

1) Sustainable living means doing things in a way that lets the people living now have the things they need, but without reducing the ability of people in the future to meet their needs.

2) Basically, it means behaving in a way that doesn't irreversibly damage the environment or use up resources faster than they can be replaced.

3) Big cities need so many resources that it's unlikely they'd ever be truly sustainable. But things can be done to make a city (and the way people live there) more sustainable:

Water Conservation Schemes

Only as much water should be taken from the environment as can be naturally replaced. Water conservation schemes reduce the amount of water used. For example:

- collecting rainwater for use on gardens or for flushing toilets.
- installing toilets that use less water to flush.
- installing water meters so that people have to pay for the water that they use.
- encouraging people to use less water, e.g. by turning off taps whilst brushing teeth.

Creating Green Space

Cities can be noisy, dirty, busy and hot — they are unsustainable because people find them unpleasant and stressful. Creating green space within urban areas helps to make sure that they remain places where people want to live and work. This is because:

- they provide naturally cooler areas where people can relax in very hot weather.
- they encourage people to exercise more and to use alternative transport, e.g. bikes. This makes people healthier and less stressed.
- they make people feel happier by providing a break from the noise and bustle of the city.

Green spaces also have environmental benefits. For example:

- they reduce the risk of flooding by reducing surface runoff from rainfall.
- they reduce air pollution by creating pockets of clean air.

Energy Conservation Schemes

Burning fossil fuels to generate power isn't sustainable because they'll run out. Burning them also increases the rate of climate change because it produces greenhouse gases (see p.22). Energy conservation schemes reduce the use of fossil fuels. For example by:

- promoting renewable energy sources (wind, solar, tidal etc.) over traditional coal or gas fired power stations.
- government incentives to make homes more energy efficient, e.g. allowing homeowners who generate electricity from renewable sources (such as solar panels) to sell any excess energy to the national grid.
- making sure that new homes that are built meet minimum energy efficiency requirements.
- encouraging people to use less energy at home, e.g. by turning off lights when they're not needed.

Waste Recycling

More recycling means fewer resources are used, e.g. metal cans can be melted down and used to make more cans. Less waste is produced, which reduces the amount that goes to landfill. Landfill is unsustainable as it wastes resources that could be recycled and eventually there'll be nowhere left to bury the waste. Decomposing landfill also releases greenhouse gases.

Waste recycling schemes include:

- collection of household recycling boxes.
- recycling facilities for larger items, e.g. fridges.
- websites, e.g. Freecycle™ and Freegle™, where items are offered for free so they can be used by others instead of being thrown away.

A lot of these strategies are common sense

If you're asked about how cities can be made more sustainable in the exam and you can't remember, don't panic — start off by thinking about how people can use less water or energy in their homes.

Traffic Management

Everyone wants a car but everyone hates being stuck in a traffic jam. Cities have so many people and so many cars that traffic congestion is a massive problem. Fortunately, there are some schemes in place to manage it.

Traffic Congestion is a Big Problem for Urban Areas

Many people have to travel to work in urban areas, often by car. Businesses also use lorries and vans for deliveries. Having so many vehicles on the road leads to lots of traffic congestion, which causes problems:

- Environmental problems — lots of traffic increases air pollution and the release of greenhouse gases contributes to climate change (see page 22).

- Economic problems — congestion can make people late for work or meetings and delay deliveries by lorries, which causes companies to lose money.

- Social problems — there is a higher chance of accidents (with other cars, cyclists, or pedestrians). Congestion also causes frustration for drivers, health issues for pedestrians and cyclists (from breathing in polluted air) and can delay emergency vehicles.

Using Public Transport Reduces Traffic Congestion

Many urban transport strategies encourage people to use public transport instead of travelling by car. London is a good example of the strategies used but similar schemes are also used in many other cities.

1) The Docklands Light Railway is an automatic train system that connects east London with the city centre. It operates mostly on tracks raised above street level, though parts are underground. It is used by 110 million people each year.

2) London's Underground system takes 3 million passengers off the roads every day. A new underground line, Crossrail, is being built east to west across the city to increase rail capacity in central London by 10%.

3) Self service bicycles are available to hire for as little as 30 minutes at a time, and are cheaper than other forms of public transport. Bike lanes and special bike signals at junctions can improve safety.

4) Electronic 'Oyster Cards' allow people to travel on buses, trains, the Underground and some boats without buying separate tickets. They can be automatically topped up and are simply swiped on entry and exit from stations and buses, making them quick and easy to use.

5) Many cities (although not London) also have park-and-ride facilities on the outskirts of the city, which allow people to drive to a large car park, then get the bus into the city centre.

Traffic Flow Can Also be Managed

Traffic congestion can also be reduced by managing the flow of traffic through the city. For example:

1) Ring roads and pedestrianised shopping streets keep traffic away from the city centre, making it safer and less polluted, and preventing congestion on narrow city centre roads.

2) Bus priority lanes stop buses being held up in traffic, making them more attractive than driving.

3) Parking restrictions make sure parked cars don't block traffic flow on narrow roads. 'Urban clearways' are major roads along which stopping or parking is very limited.

4) Congestion charging discourages drivers from entering the city centre at peak times. A scheme in Durham cut the number of cars entering the historic city centre by 85%.

5) Car sharing schemes connect people with similar commutes so that fewer cars are needed. Carpool lanes encourage more people to use car shares. These are traffic lanes where only cars with 2 or more occupants can go — reducing journey times.

6) Promoting flexible working hours means workers aren't all working the standard hours of 9am to 5pm. This helps to spread traffic out through the day, avoiding congestion at rush hour.

Getting people to use public transport is a major traffic management scheme in cities

Basically, the aim is to get as many people as possible out of their cars and onto public transport, then cleverly manage the flow of the traffic that's left. Something for you to think over next time you're waiting in a queue of traffic.

Worked Exam Questions

And here's the second lot of worked exam questions for this section. Remember, these answers are just suggestions — there are other correct answers — but they should give you an idea of the kinds of things to write.

1   Study **Figure 1**, a photograph of a street in Northern Ireland.

Figure 1

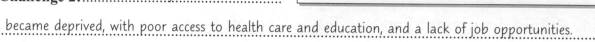

1.1   Using **Figure 1** and your own knowledge, outline **two** challenges caused by industrial decline in UK cities.

Challenge 1: Derelict buildings became a target for crime and graffiti.

Challenge 2: Areas in many inner cities became deprived, with poor access to health care and education, and a lack of job opportunities.

[2]

1.2   Using a named example, explain how the rural-urban fringe has been affected by urban sprawl.

As Liverpool has grown, it has sprawled outwards, creating the Merseyside conurbation. This has had positive effects. For example, housing estates such Croxteth Park provide a pleasant environment for people to live in, while out-of-town developments, e.g. New Mersey Shopping Park, create jobs and provide services. However, development of the rural-urban fringe also means that open spaces are lost and ecosystems damaged or destroyed. In addition, villages such as Aughton have become commuter settlements; such areas may suffer from lack of parking and increased house prices, which may mean that local people can no longer afford to live there.

[4]

1.3   Explain how the sustainability of urban areas can be improved through energy conservation schemes.

Urban areas have lots of homes and businesses, which use a lot of energy. Much of this energy comes from fossil fuels, which are not sustainable because they will run out. Energy conservation schemes include encouraging people to use less energy, e.g. by turning off lights, and making homes more energy-efficient, e.g. ensuring that new homes and office buildings meet minimum energy efficiency requirements, so they use less power. Energy conservation schemes can also promote renewable energy sources (wind, solar, tidal etc.) over fossil fuels. All these schemes mean that fossil fuels will be used less, so there will be less pollution and energy sources won't run out as quickly.

[4]

[Total 10 marks]

Exam Questions

1   Study **Figure 1**, a map showing the plans for a new town.

Figure 1

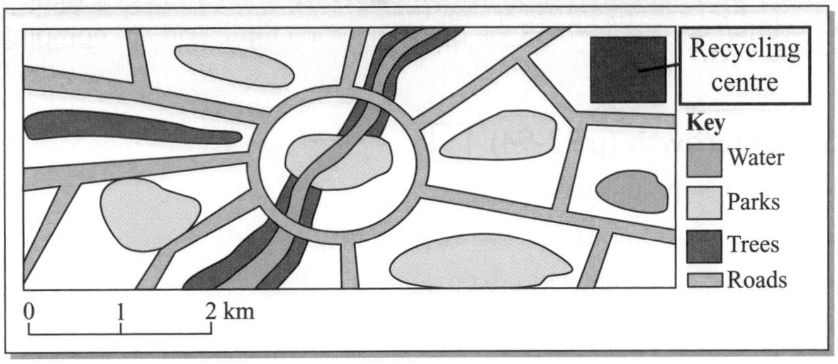

1.1   Give **two** features of the town that could make it a model for sustainable living.

Feature 1:......................................

....

Feature 2:...

[2]

1.2   Explain how the houses built in the new town in **Figure 1** could be designed to use water more sustainably.

....

....

....

....

....

[4]

[Total 6 marks]

Figure 2

2   Study **Figure 2**, an area of Newcastle quayside that has been regenerated. The area declined when industry relocated.

2.1   Using **Figure 2**, give **two** features of the regeneration project.

Feature 1:...

....

Feature 2:...

....

[2]

2.2   For a UK urban regeneration project that you have studied, explain how the area has been improved.

....

....

....

....

....

[4]

[Total 6 marks]

Revision Summary

Have a go at these questions to check you really know your megacities from your commuter settlements.
- Try these questions and <u>tick off each one</u> when you <u>get it right</u>.
- When you've done <u>all the questions</u> for a topic and are <u>completely happy</u> with it, tick off the topic.

Urban Growth (p.92-94) ☑

1) What is urbanisation?
2) Where is urbanisation taking place most rapidly?
3) Describe the trend in urbanisation in HICs.
4) Give three push factors that lead to rural-urban migration.
5) Give one factor, other than migration, that causes urbanisation.
6) What is a megacity?
7) Describe how industrialisation can lead to economic development.
8) a) Using a case study of a city in an LIC or NEE, describe the economic opportunities offered by urban growth.

   b) Describe the social challenges that have been caused by rapid urban growth in that city.

Change in UK Cities (p.97-101) ☑

9) Describe the distribution of population in the UK.
10) Why are most cities in the UK found in lowland areas?
11) Describe how you could identify the rural-urban fringe on a map.
12) Explain how urban change in the UK can lead to opportunities.
13) Explain how urban change in the UK can lead to deprivation.
14) a) Give the reasons why regeneration was needed in a named urban area.

    b) List the main features of an urban regeneration scheme in that area.

15) a) Explain how migration has influenced the character of a named UK city.

    b) Describe the economic opportunities that urban change has created in that city.

    c) Describe two challenges that urban change has created in that city.

16) What is urban sprawl?
17) Give two environmental impacts of urban sprawl on the rural urban fringe.
18) What is a commuter settlement?
19) How might businesses in a village be affected if the village becomes a commuter settlement?

Urban Sustainability (p.102-103) ☑

20) What does sustainable urban living mean?
21) Describe how water conservation schemes can help make a city more sustainable.
22) Explain the importance of green space for sustainable living in an urban environment.
23) Describe how waste recycling can help make cities more sustainable.
24) Give two economic problems caused by traffic congestion in urban areas.
25) Describe two different ways that public transport can be used to reduce traffic congestion in urban areas.
26) Give three strategies for managing traffic flow in urban areas, and explain how they work.

Measuring Development

This topic is a little <u>tricky</u> — but this <u>page</u> will set you up well, so make sure you take a <u>good look</u> at it.

Development is when a **Country is Improving**

1) <u>Development</u> is the <u>progress</u> in <u>economic growth</u>, use of <u>technology</u> and improving <u>welfare</u> that a country has made. When a country <u>develops</u> it basically <u>gets better</u> for the people living there — their <u>quality of life improves</u> (e.g. their <u>wealth</u>, <u>health</u> and <u>safety</u>).

2) The level of development is different in <u>different countries</u>, e.g. France is more developed than Ethiopia. The <u>difference in development</u> between more and less developed countries is called the <u>global development gap</u>.

There Are Loads of **Measures of Development**

Development is <u>pretty hard to measure</u> because it <u>includes so many things</u>. But you can <u>compare</u> the development of different countries using 'measures of development'.

Name	What it is	A measure of...	As a country develops, it gets...
<u>Gross National Income (GNI)</u>	The <u>total value</u> of <u>goods</u> and <u>services</u> produced by a <u>country</u> in a <u>year</u>, including income from <u>overseas</u>. It's often given in <u>US$</u>.	Wealth	Higher
<u>GNI per head</u>	The GNI <u>divided</u> by the <u>population</u> of a <u>country</u>. It's also often given in <u>US$</u> and is sometimes called <u>GNI per capita</u>.	Wealth	Higher
<u>Gross Domestic Product (GDP)</u>	The <u>total value</u> of <u>goods</u> and <u>services</u> a <u>country produces</u> in a <u>year</u>. It's often given in US$.	Wealth	Higher
<u>Birth rate</u>	The number of <u>live babies born per thousand</u> of the population <u>per year</u>.	Women's rights	Lower
<u>Death rate</u>	The number of <u>deaths per thousand</u> of the population <u>per year</u>.	Health	Lower
<u>Infant mortality rate</u>	The number of <u>babies</u> who <u>die under 1 year old</u>, <u>per thousand babies born</u>.	Health	Lower
<u>People per doctor</u>	The <u>average number</u> of people <u>for each doctor</u>.	Health	Lower
<u>Literacy rate</u>	The <u>percentage</u> of <u>adults</u> who <u>can read and write</u>.	Education	Higher
<u>Access to safe water</u>	The <u>percentage</u> of people who can <u>get clean drinking water</u>.	Health	Higher
<u>Life expectancy</u>	The <u>average age</u> a person can <u>expect to live to</u>.	Health	Higher
<u>Human Development Index (HDI)</u>	This is a number that's calculated using <u>life expectancy</u>, <u>literacy rate</u>, <u>education level</u> (e.g. average number of years of schooling) and <u>income per head</u>. Every country has an HDI value between <u>0</u> (<u>least developed</u>) and <u>1</u> (<u>most developed</u>).	Lots of things	Higher

1) <u>Individual</u> indicators can be <u>misleading</u> if they are used <u>on their own</u> because as a country develops, some aspects <u>develop before others</u>. So it might seem that a country's <u>more developed</u> than it <u>actually is</u>.

2) Using <u>more than one measure</u> of development (i.e. wealth and something else), or using the <u>Human Development Index</u> avoids these problems.

There are lots of ways of measuring development

These measures of development could well come up in the exam, so make sure you know what each of them means and whether it gets higher or lower as a country develops. In fact, shut the book and test yourself now.

Economic Development

Development isn't just about money. But when it comes to classifying HICs and LICs, well, it pretty much is.

Some Countries are More Developed than Others

1) Countries used to be classified into just two categories based on how economically developed they were.

2) Richer countries were classed as More Economically Developed Countries (MEDCs) and poorer countries were classed as Less Economically Developed Countries (LEDCs).

3) MEDCs were generally found in the north. They included the USA, European countries, Australia and New Zealand.

4) LEDCs were generally found in the south. They included India, China, Mexico, Brazil and all the African countries.

5) But using this simple classification you couldn't tell which countries were developing quickly and which weren't really developing at all. Nowadays, countries are classified into more categories.

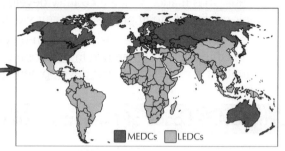

Countries can be Classified based on How Wealthy they Are...

A simple way to find a country's level of development is to look at its wealth.

Higher Income Countries (HICs)

HICs are the wealthiest countries in the world, where the GNI per head is high and most citizens have a high quality of life.
For example: UK, USA, Canada, France.

Lower Income Countries (LICs)

LICs are the poorest countries in the world, where the GNI per head is very low and most citizens have a low quality of life.
For example: Afghanistan, Somalia, Uganda and Nepal.

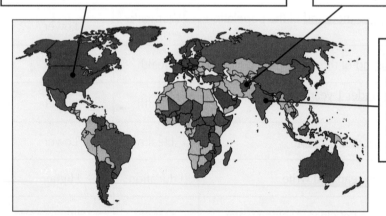

Newly Emerging Economies (NEEs)

NEEs are rapidly getting richer as their economy is moving from being based on primary industry (e.g. agriculture) to secondary industry (manufacturing).
Quality of life for many citizens is improving.
For example: China, Brazil, Russia, India.

...But Using Wealth On Its Own Can Cause Problems

GNI per head can be misleading when used on its own because it is an average — variations within the country don't show up.

1) It can hide variation between regions in the country, and between classes — the rich in big cities may have much higher measures of development than the poor in rural areas.

2) For example, if you looked at the GNI per head of Russia it might seem quite developed (because it is high enough to be an HIC), but in reality there are a small number of extremely wealthy people and a lot very poor people.

Economic development can improve people's quality of life

You don't need to learn how every country is classified but you should have a general understanding of the characteristics of HICs, LICs and NEEs. It might help to learn a few examples of each too.

Development and the DTM

The Demographic Transition Model can be used to show how countries develop over time.

Development is Linked to the Demographic Transition Model

1) The Demographic Transition Model (DTM) shows how changing birth rates and death rates affect population growth.

2) When the birth rate is higher than the death rate, more people are being born than are dying, so the population grows — this is called natural increase. It's called natural decrease when the death rate's higher than the birth rate.

3) Birth rates and death rates differ from country to country. This means that population growth is faster in some countries than others, especially in less developed countries.

4) Population growth also changes within a country over time as it develops.

5) Changing birth and death rates are linked to a country's economic development (see p.107).

6) So the five stages of the DTM are linked to a country's level of development.

Stage 1 is the least developed — the birth rate is high because there's no use of contraception. People also have lots of children because poor healthcare means that many infants die.

The death rate is also high due to poor healthcare or famine, and life expectancy is low (few people reach old age).

Income is very low.

	Stage 1	Stage 2	Stage 3	Stage 4	Stage 5
Birth rate	High and fluctuating	High and steady	Rapidly falling	Low and fluctuating	Slowly falling
Death rate	High and fluctuating	Rapidly falling	Slowly falling	Low and fluctuating	Low and steady
Population growth rate	Zero	Very high	High	Zero	Negative
Population size	Low and steady	Rapidly increasing	Increasing	High and steady	Slowly falling
Example countries	No countries, some tribes in Brazil	Gambia (HDI = 0.4)	India (HDI = 0.6)	UK (HDI = 0.9)	Japan (HDI = 0.9)

DEVELOPMENT

Stage 2 is not very developed — many LICs are in stage 2.

The economy is based on agriculture so people have lots of children to work on farms, which means that birth rates are high. Death rates fall due to improved healthcare and diet so life expectancy increases.

Stage 3 is more developed — most NEEs are at stage 3. The birth rate falls rapidly as women have a more equal place in society and better education.

The use of contraception increases and more women work instead of having children.

The economy also changes to manufacturing, so income increases and fewer children are needed to work on farms. Healthcare improves so life expectancy increases.

Stages 4 and 5 are the most developed — most HICs are at one of these stages.

Birth rates are low because people want possessions and a high quality of life, and may have dependent elderly relatives, so there is less money available for having children.

Healthcare is good, so the death rate is low and life expectancy is high. Income is also high.

Population often increases rapidly as countries start to develop

Lots of information here, but don't panic — you don't have to memorise all the information on the diagram. Just make sure you understand what's happening at each stage and how population and development are connected.

Causes of Uneven Development

You need to know the <u>reasons why</u> there are <u>global inequalities</u> — i.e. why <u>countries differ</u> in how <u>developed</u> they are. There are a fair few, but take it steady and you'll be OK...

Physical Factors can Affect How Developed a Country is

A country is more likely to be <u>less</u> developed if it has...

1 A Poor Climate

1) If a country has a poor climate (<u>really hot</u> or <u>really cold</u> or <u>really dry</u>) not much will grow. This <u>reduces</u> the amount of <u>food produced</u>. In some countries this can lead to <u>malnutrition</u>, e.g. in Chad and Ethiopia. People who are malnourished have a <u>low quality of life</u>.

2) People also have <u>fewer crops to sell</u>, so <u>less money</u> to <u>spend on goods and services</u>. This also <u>reduces</u> their <u>quality of life</u>.

3) The government gets <u>less money from taxes</u> (as less is sold and bought). This means there's <u>less to spend</u> on <u>developing the country</u>, e.g. to spend on <u>improving healthcare</u> and <u>education</u>.

2 Poor Farming Land

If the land in a country is <u>steep</u> or has <u>poor soil</u> (or no soil) then they <u>won't produce a lot of food</u>. This has the same effect as a poor climate (see above).

3 Few Raw Materials

1) Countries <u>without</u> many <u>raw materials</u> like <u>coal</u>, <u>oil</u> or <u>metal ores</u> tend to <u>make less money</u> because they've got <u>fewer products to sell</u>.

2) This means they have <u>less money</u> to <u>spend on development</u>.

3) Some countries <u>do</u> have a lot of raw materials but still <u>aren't very developed</u> because they don't have the <u>money</u> to <u>develop</u> the <u>infrastructure</u> to <u>exploit them</u> (e.g. roads and ports).

4 Lots of Natural Hazards

1) A natural hazard is a <u>natural process</u> which <u>could</u> cause <u>death</u>, <u>injury</u> or <u>disruption</u> to humans or to <u>destroy property</u> and possessions. A <u>natural disaster</u> is a natural hazard that has actually <u>happened</u>.

2) Countries that <u>have a lot of natural disasters</u> (e.g. Bangladesh, which floods regularly) have to <u>spend a lot of money rebuilding</u> after disasters occur.

3) So natural disasters <u>reduce quality of life</u> for the people affected, and they <u>reduce</u> the amount of <u>money</u> the government has to spend on <u>development projects</u>.

There can also be Historical Reasons for Uneven Development

Colonisation

1) Countries that were <u>colonised</u> (<u>ruled</u> by a <u>foreign country</u>) are often at a <u>lower</u> level of development when they gain <u>independence</u> than they <u>would be</u> if they had <u>not been colonised</u>.

2) <u>European countries</u> colonised much of Africa in the 19th century. They controlled the economies of their colonies, <u>removed raw materials</u> and <u>slaves</u>, and sold back expensive <u>manufactured goods</u>. This was <u>bad</u> for African <u>development</u> as it made parts of Africa <u>dependent</u> on Europe, and led to <u>famine</u> and <u>malnutrition</u>.

Conflict

1) <u>War</u>, especially <u>civil wars</u>, can <u>slow</u> or <u>reduce</u> levels of development even <u>after</u> the war is <u>over</u>. E.g. <u>healthcare</u> becomes much <u>worse</u> and things like <u>infant mortality increase</u> a <u>lot</u>.

2) <u>Money</u> is spent on <u>arms</u> and <u>fighting</u> instead of <u>development</u>, people are <u>killed</u> and <u>damage</u> is done to <u>infrastructure</u> and <u>property</u>.

3) For example, <u>10 years</u> after the civil war in <u>Uganda</u> ended in 1986, levels of development had <u>barely returned</u> to pre-war levels.

Learn these physical and historical causes of uneven development

Basically, if a country is rubbish for farming or it's a hotspot for natural disasters then it's going to struggle to develop. There are a few exceptions though, e.g. Japan gets battered by natural hazards but is developed.

Causes of Uneven Development

Countries have a tough time trying to develop. It's not just things like earthquakes and conflicts that hold them back — things like <u>trade</u>, <u>debt</u> and <u>primary-product based economies</u> are to blame too...

Economic Factors can cause Uneven Development

A country is more likely to be at a <u>lower level</u> of development if it has...

1 Poor Trade Links

1) Trade is the <u>exchange</u> of <u>goods</u> and <u>services</u> <u>between countries</u>.
2) <u>World trade patterns</u> (who trades with whom) seriously influence a country's <u>economy</u> and so affect their <u>level of development</u>.
3) If a country has <u>poor trade links</u> (it trades a small amount with only a few countries) it <u>won't make a lot of money</u>, so there'll be <u>less to spend on development</u>.

2 Lots of Debt

1) Very poor countries <u>borrow money</u> from <u>other countries</u> and <u>international organisations</u>, e.g. to help cope with the aftermath of a natural disaster.
2) This money has to be <u>paid back</u> (sometimes with <u>interest</u>).
3) Any <u>money</u> a country makes is <u>used to pay back</u> the debt, so <u>isn't used to develop</u>.

3 An Economy Based On Primary Products

1) Countries that mostly export <u>primary products</u> (raw materials like wood, metal and stone) tend to be <u>less developed</u>.
2) This is because you <u>don't make much profit</u> by selling primary products. Their <u>prices</u> also <u>fluctuate</u> — sometimes the <u>price falls below</u> the <u>cost of production</u>.
3) This means people <u>don't make much money</u>, so the government has <u>less to spend on development</u>.
4) Countries that export <u>manufactured goods</u> tend to be <u>more developed</u>.
5) This is because you usually make a <u>decent profit</u> by selling manufactured goods. Wealthy countries can also <u>force down</u> the <u>price of raw materials</u> that they buy from poorer countries.

Uneven Development has Consequences

Uneven development leads to <u>great differences</u> in <u>wealth</u> and <u>health</u>, and has caused <u>large flows</u> of <u>international migration</u>.

Wealth

1) People in <u>more developed countries</u> have a <u>higher income</u> than those in <u>less developed</u> countries.
2) For example, GNI per head in the <u>UK</u> is over <u>40 times higher</u> than in <u>Chad</u>.

Health

1) <u>Healthcare</u> in <u>more developed countries</u> is <u>better</u> than in <u>less developed countries</u>.
2) People in HICs <u>live much longer</u> — e.g. the UK's life expectancy is <u>81</u>, but in Chad it's only <u>51</u>.
3) <u>Infant mortality</u> is also <u>much higher</u> in <u>less developed countries</u> — e.g. it is <u>85 per 1000 births</u> in <u>Chad</u>, compared to <u>4 per 1000 births in the UK</u>.

International Migration

1) If neighbouring or nearby countries have a <u>higher</u> level of development, people will seek to <u>enter</u> that country to make use of the <u>opportunities</u> it provides to <u>improve</u> their <u>quality of life</u>.
2) For example, <u>Mexico</u> (an <u>NEE</u>) <u>borders</u> the <u>USA</u> (an <u>HIC</u>). Every year <u>over 130 000</u> Mexicans move to the USA <u>legally</u> (and <u>thousands more</u> enter <u>illegally</u>) to seek <u>better paid jobs</u> and a <u>higher quality of life</u>.

Less money made = less to spend on development

EXAM TIP If you get a long answer question (6-9 marks) about the causes of uneven development, scribble down a quick plan with the key points before starting your answer — examiners are looking for a good structure.

Reducing the Global Development Gap

Reducing the global development gap is a <u>massive task</u> — but there are <u>quite a few ways</u> to go about it...

There are **Lots** of **Strategies** that can **Reduce** the **Development Gap**

Aid

1) Aid is <u>given</u> by one country to another as <u>money</u> or <u>resources</u> (e.g. food, doctors).

2) It is spent on development projects, for example constructing <u>schools</u> to <u>improve literacy</u> rates, building <u>dams</u> and <u>wells</u> to <u>improve clean water supplies</u> and providing <u>farming knowledge</u> and <u>equipment</u> to <u>improve agriculture</u>.

3) Aid can definitely help, but sometimes it is wasted by <u>corrupt governments</u>. Or once the <u>money runs out</u>, projects can <u>stop working</u> if there isn't enough <u>local knowledge</u> and <u>support</u> to keep the projects going.

Fair Trade

1) The <u>fair trade movement</u> is all about farmers getting a <u>fair price</u> for goods produced in <u>LICs</u>, e.g. <u>coffee</u> and <u>bananas</u>, allowing them to <u>provide</u> for their <u>families</u>.

2) Companies who want to <u>sell products</u> labelled as 'fair trade' have to <u>pay producers</u> a <u>fair price</u>.

3) <u>Buyers</u> also pay <u>extra</u> on top of that to <u>help develop</u> the area where the goods come from, e.g. to <u>build schools</u> or <u>health centres</u>.

4) But there are problems — only a <u>tiny proportion</u> of the extra money reaches the original producers. Much goes to <u>retailers' profits</u>.

Using Intermediate Technology

1) <u>Intermediate technology</u> includes tools, machines and systems that <u>improve quality of life</u> but are also <u>simple</u> to <u>use</u>, <u>affordable</u> to <u>buy</u> or <u>build</u> and <u>cheap</u> to <u>maintain</u>.

2) For example, <u>solar powered LED lightbulbs</u> are used in parts of <u>Nepal</u> where the only other lighting options are polluting and dangerous <u>kerosene lamps</u> or <u>wood fires</u>.

3) This allows people to <u>work</u> in their <u>homes</u> or <u>businesses</u>, and <u>children</u> to <u>study</u>, after <u>dark</u>. As a result, <u>skills</u>, <u>incomes</u> and <u>industrial output</u> can increase, which helps <u>reduce</u> the <u>development</u> gap.

Debt Relief

1) <u>Debt relief</u> is when some or all of a country's debt is <u>cancelled</u>, or <u>interest rates</u> are <u>lowered</u>. This means they have <u>more money</u> to <u>develop</u> rather than to <u>pay back the debt</u>.

2) For example, <u>Zambia</u> (in southern Africa) had <u>$4 billion</u> of <u>debt cancelled</u> in <u>2005</u>. In 2006, the country had enough money to start a <u>free healthcare</u> scheme for <u>millions of people</u> living in <u>rural areas</u>, which <u>improved</u> their <u>quality of life</u>.

Investment

1) <u>Foreign-direct investment</u> (<u>FDI</u>) is when <u>people</u> or <u>companies</u> in one country buy <u>property</u> or <u>infrastructure</u> in <u>another</u>.

2) FDI leads to better access to <u>finance</u>, <u>technology</u> and <u>expertise</u>, and improved <u>infrastructure</u>, <u>improved industry</u> and an increase in <u>services</u>.

Industrial Development

In countries with a <u>very low</u> level of development, <u>agriculture</u> makes up a <u>large portion</u> of the economy. Developing industry <u>increases GNI</u> and helps improve levels of development as <u>productivity</u>, <u>levels of skill</u> and <u>infrastructure</u> are <u>improved</u>.

Tourism

<u>Tourism</u> can also provide <u>increased income</u> as there will be <u>more money</u> entering the country. Countries like <u>Kenya</u> are using <u>tourism</u> to <u>increase</u> their <u>level of development</u> (see next page).

Microfinance Loans

1) <u>Microfinance</u> is when <u>small loans</u> are given to people in LICs who may not be able to get loans from <u>traditional banks</u>. The loans enable them to <u>start</u> their own <u>businesses</u> and become <u>financially independent</u>.

2) Although microfinance <u>works</u> for <u>some people</u>, it's <u>not clear</u> that microfinance can <u>reduce poverty</u> on a <u>large scale</u>.

There are lots of ways to help poor countries develop

Poorer countries can improve their own level of development through industry or tourism. Other countries can also help by providing aid or trading more fairly. Small scale schemes, e.g. microfinance, can be effective too.

Increasing Development — Tourism

As you've already seen, <u>tourism</u> can be used to help poor countries to <u>develop</u>. Here is an example of how <u>Kenya</u> has turned itself into a <u>popular tourist destination</u> and how that has <u>reduced</u> the <u>development gap</u>.

Tourism is Helping Kenya to Increase its Development

1) <u>Kenya</u> is a low-income country in <u>East Africa</u>. It attracts <u>tourists</u> because of its <u>tribal culture</u>, <u>safari wildlife</u>, <u>warm climate</u> and <u>beautiful unspoilt scenery</u>. Kenya's <u>government</u> is trying to <u>boost tourism</u> as a way of <u>increasing</u> its <u>development</u>.

2) <u>Visa fees</u> for <u>adults</u> were <u>cut by 50%</u> in <u>2009</u> to make it <u>cheaper to visit</u> the country. They were also <u>scrapped</u> for <u>children under 16</u> to encourage <u>more families</u> to visit.

3) <u>Landing fees</u> at airports on the Kenyan <u>coast</u> have been <u>dropped</u> for charter airlines.

4) Tourism has increased from <u>0.9 million</u> visitors per year in <u>1995</u> to <u>1.8 million</u> in <u>2011</u>.

Effectiveness — Benefits

1) Tourism now contributes <u>over 12%</u> of Kenya's <u>GDP</u> — money that can be spent on <u>development</u> and <u>improving quality of life</u>.
2) Nearly <u>600 000 people</u> are <u>directly</u> or <u>indirectly employed</u> by the <u>tourism industry</u> — that's 10% of <u>all employment</u> in Kenya.
3) The <u>24 national parks</u> charge <u>entry fees</u> to tourists. This money is used to <u>maintain</u> the national parks, which helps to protect the <u>environment</u> and <u>wildlife</u>.
4) Since 2000, Kenya's score on the <u>Human Development Index</u> has <u>increased</u> from <u>0.45</u> to <u>0.55</u>.

Effectiveness — Negatives

1) Only a <u>small proportion</u> of the money earned goes to <u>locals</u>. The rest goes to <u>big companies</u>, often based in <u>HICs overseas</u>, so <u>doesn't</u> help to <u>close</u> the development gap.
2) Some Maasai tribespeople were <u>forced off their land</u> to create national parks for tourists.
3) Tourist vehicles <u>damage</u> the <u>environment</u>, e.g. <u>safari vehicles</u> destroying vegetation and disturbing animals.

Tourism has brought wealth and jobs to Kenya

Things have generally improved for people in Kenya — many people now have a better quality of life, but things aren't perfect for everyone. If you've studied a different example in class, feel free to learn that one instead.

Increasing Development — TNCs

Right, last little bit about <u>increasing development</u> — and something you are probably <u>familiar</u> with already, though you may not have <u>realised</u> it... Don't think you can get away without studying <u>trans-national corporations</u>.

Trans-National Corporations Work in More Than One Country

1) TNCs (trans-national corporations) are <u>companies</u> that are located in, or <u>produce and sell products</u> in, <u>more than one country</u>. E.g. Sony is a TNC — it makes electronic products in China and Japan.

2) TNC <u>factories</u> are usually located in <u>poorer countries</u> because <u>labour is cheaper</u>, and there are fewer environmental and labour regulations, which means they make <u>more profit</u>.

3) They can <u>improve</u> the <u>development</u> of countries they work in by <u>transferring jobs</u>, <u>skills</u> and <u>money</u> to less developed countries, <u>reducing</u> the <u>development gap</u>.

4) TNC <u>offices</u> and <u>headquarters</u> are usually located in <u>richer countries</u> because there are <u>more people</u> with <u>administrative skills</u> (because <u>education is better</u>).

Trans-National Corporations have Advantages and Disadvantages

Advantages

1) TNCs <u>create jobs</u> in all the countries they're located in.

2) <u>Employees in poorer countries</u> get a <u>more reliable income</u> compared to jobs like farming.

3) TNCs <u>spend money</u> to <u>improve</u> the <u>local infrastructure</u>, e.g. airports and roads.

4) <u>New technology</u> (e.g. computers) and <u>skills</u> are <u>brought to poorer countries</u>.

Disadvantages

1) <u>Employees in poorer countries</u> may be <u>paid lower wages</u> than employees in <u>richer countries</u>.

2) <u>Employees in poorer countries</u> may have to work <u>long hours</u> in <u>poor conditions</u>.

3) Most TNCs <u>come from richer countries</u> so the <u>profits go back there</u> — they <u>aren't reinvested</u> in the <u>poorer countries</u> the TNC operates in.

4) The <u>jobs created in poorer countries aren't secure</u> — the TNC could relocate the jobs to another country at any time.

TNCs are everywhere — and I mean everywhere

TNCs are companies that do business in more than one country — walk down your local high street and you'll see plenty of examples. They can help poorer countries to develop industry and become richer but there are often downsides too. Close the book and see if you can scribble down the advantages and disadvantages of TNCs.

Worked Exam Questions

Here are some handy worked exam questions to get you in the exam mood. Use them wisely.

1 Study **Figure 1**, which shows measures of development for Canada, Malaysia and Angola.

1.1 "Canada is the most developed of these three countries." Do you agree with this statement? Justify your answer using **Figure 1**.

Figure 1

	Canada	Malaysia	Angola
GNI per head	$41 170	$21 430	$6560
Birth rate	10.28	19.71	38.78
Death rate	8.42	5.03	11.49
Infant mortality rate	4.65	13.27	78.26
Life expectancy	81.76	74.75	55.63
Literacy rate	97.1%	94.6%	71.1%

I agree that Canada is the most developed of the

three countries. It has a much greater GNI per

head than the other countries, which indicates

that its citizens are wealthier and can probably

afford a high quality of life. Measures of health,

such as infant mortality rate and life expectancy, both indicate that Canada is more developed than

Malaysia and Angola. Canada's literacy rate is higher than Malaysia's, and much higher than Angola's,

suggesting that there is a formal education system, and that children have the time to go to school.

This also suggests that Canada is the most developed of the three countries.

[4]

1.2 Outline **one** limitation of only using GNI per head as a measure of development.

GNI per head is an average, so it can hide variation between regions in the country, and between classes.

[2]

[Total 6 marks]

2 Study **Figure 2**, which shows the annual income of a farmer in Mali between 2006 and 2014. He joined a fair trade cooperative in 2008.

2.1 Calculate the increase in the farmer's annual income from 2008 to 2014.

£490 – £230 = £260

[1]

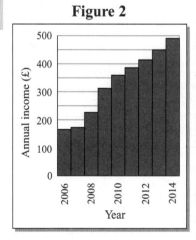

Figure 2

2.2 Using evidence from **Figure 2**, suggest how fair trade schemes can affect a country's development.

The farmer's income in Figure 2 rose quickly after he joined the

fair trade cooperative, and continued to rise after that. His income

may have increased because fair trade schemes involve paying farmers a fair price for goods produced.

Receiving a fair price for goods means people have more money to spend on improving their quality of

life, which can help to increase development. The income of the state increases too through taxes,

so there may be more investment, for example in infrastructure and healthcare.

[4]

[Total 5 marks]

Exam Questions

1 Study **Figure 1**, which shows damage caused by fighting in Libya's civil war, which has been ongoing since 2011.

Figure 1

1.1 Using **Figure 1** and your own knowledge, suggest how the conflict may have affected Libya's level of development.

....

....

....

....

[3]

1.2 Libya is a former Italian colony. Explain how being a former colony may affect a country's economic development.

....

....

....

[3]

[Total 6 marks]

2 Study **Figure 2**, which shows the Demographic Transition Model (DTM).

Figure 2

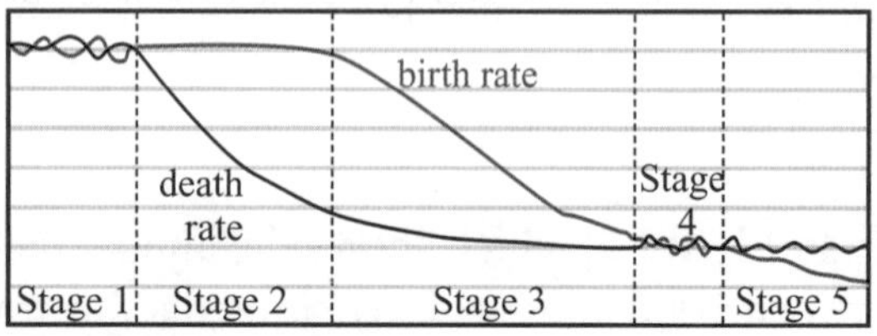

2.1 Using **Figure 2**, which **two** of the statements below are true? Shade **two** ovals only.

A Countries in Stage 5 experience natural population decrease. ⬭

B Population growth is fastest in Stage 1. ⬭

C The death rate in countries in Stage 3 is rapidly falling. ⬭

D Population size is stable in Stage 4. ⬭

E Countries in Stage 2 have low population growth. ⬭

[2]

2.2 **Figure 3** shows birth and death rates in Morocco.

Using **Figure 2** and **Figure 3**, assess Morocco's level of economic development. Justify your answer.

Figure 3

Birth rate	18.2
Death rate	4.81

....

....

....

[3]

[Total 5 marks]

Economic Development in India

India is a <u>newly emerging economy</u> (<u>NEE</u>) with a <u>huge population</u> and <u>lots of potential</u>. Its level of development is <u>fairly low</u>, but <u>increasing</u>. Like many other <u>LICs</u> and <u>NEEs</u>, its growth is causing lots of <u>change</u>.

India is a **Newly Emerging Economy** in Southern Asia

1) <u>India</u> is a rapidly developing <u>NEE</u>. It has the <u>second largest</u> population in the world (approx. 1.3 billion) and is <u>still growing</u>.

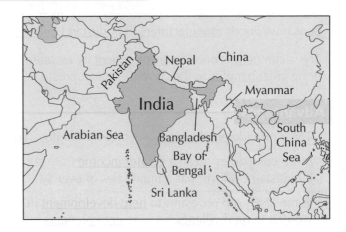

2) India was a <u>British colony</u> until <u>1947</u>, but now has its own <u>democratically elected government</u>.

3) India has a <u>medium</u> level of development (<u>HDI = 0.61</u>). There are <u>large inequalities</u> — some people are <u>very wealthy</u>, but the <u>majority</u> are <u>poor</u>, and <u>over 20%</u> of the population live in <u>poverty</u>. <u>Education</u> is <u>improving</u>, but the <u>adult literacy rate</u> is still <u>less than 70%</u>.

4) It <u>exports services</u> and <u>manufactured goods</u> across the <u>world</u>.

India's **Rapid Development** means its **Industrial Structure** is Changing

1) <u>Primary industry</u> (e.g. <u>agriculture</u>) employs <u>50%</u> of the working population, but is becoming a <u>smaller</u> part of India's economy. It makes up only <u>17%</u> of its GDP.

2) <u>Secondary industry</u> (manufacturing) has <u>grown</u> to employ <u>22%</u> of the workforce. Secondary industries are <u>stimulating economic development</u>. They provide people with <u>reliable jobs</u> (compared to <u>seasonal agricultural work</u>), and selling <u>manufactured</u> goods overseas brings <u>more income</u> into India than selling raw materials.

3) <u>Tertiary</u> (services) and <u>quaternary</u> (knowledge) industries have become a <u>much larger</u> part of the economy, employing <u>29%</u> of the workforce. Lots of this is due to <u>growth</u> in IT firms (especially in the city of <u>Bangalore</u>) and in supplying <u>services</u> for <u>foreign companies</u>, such as customer service centres. <u>Tertiary</u> and <u>quaternary</u> industries contribute the most to India's GDP — <u>53%</u>.

India is experiencing rapid change

You may not have studied India in class, but you do need to learn a case study from an LIC or NEE. This case study covers lots of different aspects of India's development over the next few pages. Make sure you learn lots of details — you could be asked about anything that's covered here in your exam.

Economic Development in India

CASE STUDY

Right, now you've got a bit of background on <u>economic development</u> in <u>India</u>, it's time to move on to the next lot of information. This time we're focusing on <u>TNCs</u> and India's <u>relationship</u> with the rest of the <u>world</u>.

Lots of Trans-National Corporations Operate in India

1) Many TNCs (see page 114) operate in India, including <u>Unilever</u> — one of the world's biggest <u>food</u> and consumer goods <u>manufacturers</u>. <u>Hindustan Unilever Limited</u> is its Indian division.

2) TNCs can <u>help</u> economic <u>development</u> by increasing the amount of manufacturing industry and they can bring great <u>benefits</u> to the countries they operate in, but they also have <u>disadvantages</u>.

Advantages

1) TNCs provide <u>employment</u> — Unilever employs <u>16 000 people</u> in India.

2) More companies mean a <u>greater income</u> from tax for <u>India</u>.
   Hindustan Unilever has annual sales of over $4.5 billion.

3) Some TNCs run programs to <u>help development</u> in India. E.g. Unilever's <u>Project Shakti</u> helps <u>poor women</u> in <u>rural villages</u> become <u>entrepreneurs</u> by providing <u>loans</u> and <u>products</u> for them to <u>sell</u> in places that Unilever would otherwise struggle to <u>supply</u>. There are now about <u>45 000 women</u> in the scheme.

4) Unilever also works with charities to help run <u>hygiene education programs</u> and provide <u>sanitation</u> to <u>115 million</u> people in India. This improves <u>health</u> (and also increases sales).

Disadvantages

1) Some profits from TNCs <u>leave India</u>, e.g. Unilever is a Dutch-British company.

2) TNCs can cause <u>environmental problems</u>, e.g. <u>mercury</u>-contaminated glass from a Unilever factory in <u>Kodaikanal</u> ended up in a <u>waste dump</u> instead of being <u>safely</u> disposed of.
   Mercury is a poisonous chemical that can cause <u>environmental damage</u> and <u>health problems</u>, e.g. <u>brain damage</u>. Unilever did <u>remove</u> the waste and dispose of it safely, and now monitors the area and those affected. However, <u>environmental</u> and <u>public interest groups</u> remain <u>unhappy</u>.

3) TNCs may <u>move</u> around India to take <u>advantage</u> of local <u>government incentives</u>. Unilever have been accused of closing factories in <u>Dharwad</u> and <u>Mumbai</u> once local <u>tax breaks</u> ended.

India's Relationship with the Wider World is Changing

India is playing a <u>larger role</u> in <u>regional</u> and <u>global politics</u> as it develops. In recent years the Indian government has <u>improved relations</u> with its immediate <u>neighbours</u> and <u>global trading partners</u>. <u>International trade</u> is also <u>growing</u>:

1) India is <u>reducing barriers</u> to trade and encouraging <u>foreign direct investment</u>.

2) Trade with <u>foreign businesses</u>, particularly those who get companies in India's <u>large service sector</u> to do <u>office jobs</u> for them, is also <u>increasing</u>.

3) India is also working with its <u>neighbours</u> to build the <u>TAPI pipeline</u> to carry <u>natural gas</u> from <u>Turkmenistan</u>, through <u>Afghanistan</u> and <u>Pakistan</u> to <u>India</u>.

There are pros and cons to TNCs in India

Political and trading relationships may seem rather complicated, but basically, good relationships mean more trade and the arrival of foreign businesses. This leads to more money and more influence in the region.

Economic Development in India

CASE STUDY

This is the last bit about India — I promise. You need to know about the different types of aid that India (or the country you have chosen for your case-study) receives, as well as the impacts of economic development.

India Receives **Different Types** of Aid

Short-term Aid

1) Intended to help recipient countries cope with emergencies. Can come from foreign governments or non-governmental organisations (NGOs).

2) The UK sent £10m, a rescue team and 1200 tents to India after an earthquake in 2001. NGOs like Oxfam provided supplies and temporary buildings.

3) Helps with immediate disaster relief, but often not able to help longer-term recovery efforts.

Long-term Aid

1) Intended to help the recipient countries funded to become more developed.

2) E.g. until 2015, India received over £200m each year from the UK to tackle poverty.

3) Impact can vary — India has had problems with corruption and aid does not always reach the poorest people.

'Top-down' Aid

1) When an organisation or government receives the aid and decides where it should be spent.

2) Often large infrastructure projects like dams for hydroelectric power or irrigation schemes.

3) Can improve a country's economy, but may not improve the quality of life of the poorest people.

'Bottom-up' Aid

1) Money is given directly to local people, e.g. to build or maintain a well.

2) E.g. WaterAid trains local people to maintain village handpumps in rural India.

3) Can have a large impact — schemes are generally supported by local people and can improve health, skills and income.

Economic Development Impacts **Quality of Life** and the **Environment**

Quality of Life

1) There are more jobs and India's daily wages have increased by about 42 Rupees since 2010. This means that people have more money to improve their life, for example by securing access to clean water, a higher quality home and medical care when they need it

2) But some jobs in industry, e.g. coal mining, can be dangerous or include poor conditions, which can reduce workers' quality of life.

Environment

1) India's energy consumption has increased with economic development. Fossil fuels like coal and oil are the most readily available and affordable fuels, but release lots of pollution and greenhouse gases. The capital, Delhi, is the most polluted city in the world.

2) Demand for resources can lead to destruction of habitats, e.g. mining in Karnataka.

3) But increased income from economic development means people can afford to protect the environment. For example, since 1990 India's forest cover has stopped decreasing and started to grow.

Foreign aid and development are bringing benefits and problems to India

Try to get your head around the different types of aid and remember, aid isn't a perfect solution to ending poverty — it may not help those who need it most. You need to be able to give a balanced account of the impacts of aid.

Economic Development in the UK

Changes in the economy of the UK are affecting employment patterns and regional growth.

The UK's Economy is Changing

Key causes of economic change include:

1) De-industrialisation and the decline of the UK's industrial base — fewer jobs are available in manufacturing and heavy industries (such as coal mining and steel production). These industries were once a primary source of employment and income for the UK GDP.

2) Globalisation — a lot of manufacturing has moved overseas, where labour costs are lower, though headquarters have often remained in the UK. Trade with other countries is an increasingly important part of UK GDP.

3) Government policies — government decisions on investment in new infrastructure and technology and support for businesses (e.g. tax breaks) affect how well the economy grows. Membership in government groups, e.g. World Trade Organisation, make it easier for companies in the UK to operate across the world.

Services are More Important as the Economy becomes Post-Industrial

Tertiary and quaternary industries are growing as secondary manufacturing is declining in the UK. In 2011, they employed 81% of the UK's workforce — and this proportion is increasing. Important industries include:

1) Services — e.g. retail, entertainment and personal services (e.g. hairdressers).
    Retail is the UK's largest sector, employing 4.4 million people.

2) Information technology — this is now an important part of the UK's economy. Over 60 000 people are employed in the IT sector by companies like Microsoft® and IBM®.

3) Finance — the UK, and especially the City of London, is home to many global financial institutions. Some, like HSBC, have their global headquarters in the UK.

4) Research — research and development (R&D) is increasing in the UK, making use of the UK's skilled university graduates. In 2013, nearly £30 billion was spent on R&D in the UK.

Science and Business Parks

Quaternary industries are increasingly found in science parks or business parks. These are often:

1) On the outskirts of cities near to good transport links, e.g. motorways, A-roads and airports.

2) Close to housing to accommodate the workforce.

3) Near universities so that research businesses in science parks can have access to university research, allowing them to develop cutting edge technology.

The number of them has grown because:

- There is a large and growing demand for high-tech products. Science parks can help develop new technology for these products.

- The UK has a high number of strong research universities for businesses on science parks to form links with.

- Clusters of related businesses in one place can boost each other.

IT, services and finance are becoming more important in the UK
You might have to use the information here to interpret a map or photograph — make sure you understand the sorts of changes that are occurring in the UK and don't just memorise the stats.

Economic Development in the UK

Apparently the UK has a bit of <u>split across the middle</u> when it comes to <u>economic development</u>. And <u>rural</u> areas are experiencing quite a lot of <u>changes</u> too.

There is **Some Evidence** for a **North-South Divide** in the **UK**

The <u>decline</u> of <u>heavy industry</u> has had a <u>greater negative impact</u> on the <u>north</u> of the UK, but the <u>growth</u> of the <u>post-industrial service industry</u> has mostly benefited the <u>south</u>. In general, <u>economic</u> and <u>social</u> indicators tend to be <u>better</u> in the <u>south</u> than the <u>north</u>. This is the <u>north-south divide</u>.

- <u>Wages</u> are generally <u>lower</u> in the <u>north</u> than the south, e.g. the 2014 <u>average weekly wage</u> was <u>40% lower</u> in <u>Huddersfield</u> than <u>London</u>.

- <u>Health</u> is generally <u>worse</u> in the <u>north</u> than the south, e.g. <u>life expectancy</u> for male babies born in <u>Glasgow</u> in 2012 was <u>72.6 years</u>, but in <u>East Dorset</u> it was <u>82.9 years</u>.

- <u>Education</u> — <u>GCSE results</u> are generally <u>better</u> in the <u>south</u> of England than the <u>Midlands</u> or the <u>north</u>.

There are <u>exceptions</u> — some cities <u>don't fit</u> the trends, and <u>not everything is worse</u> in the north.

Changes in the **UK Economy** are Changing **Rural Areas**

Changes in the UK economy are causing changes in rural landscapes.

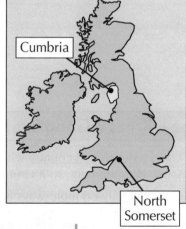

1) In <u>Cumbria</u> (a rural area in <u>north west England</u>, which includes the <u>Lake District National Park</u>) the <u>population</u> of some villages has <u>decreased</u> recently, especially in <u>western Cumbria</u>. This is mainly due to there being <u>fewer jobs</u> — <u>agriculture</u> and <u>manufacturing</u> are big industries in Cumbria but they're both in <u>decline</u>.

2) In <u>North Somerset</u> (a mainly rural area in the <u>west of England</u>, close to <u>Bristol</u>), the <u>population</u> of some North Somerset towns and villages have <u>increased</u> a lot in recent years, particularly close to <u>Bristol</u>. People are moving to <u>quieter towns</u> and <u>villages</u> with <u>easy access</u> to the centre of <u>Bristol</u>.

3) These changes have social and economic effects:

- As the population has <u>dropped</u> it's caused a <u>decrease in services in Cumbria</u>. Schools, shops and other businesses in some areas are <u>closing</u>. <u>Unemployment</u> is <u>above</u> the national <u>average</u> in <u>two</u> of the seven <u>districts</u> in Cumbria.

- In <u>North Somerset</u>, house prices are <u>rising</u> which risks <u>pricing out locals</u>. Roads are <u>congested</u> with people <u>commuting</u> to Bristol, and services like schools are <u>oversubscribed</u>.

There are regional differences in development in the UK

Make sure you know why lots of people are moving to some rural areas and the reasons why they are leaving other areas. Then swot up on the evidence for a north-south divide — but remember, there are exceptions.

Economic Development in the UK

If you've read the previous page, you'll know all about the north-south divide in the UK. Well, that's not the end of the story — the government has various schemes to try and make economic development more even.

The Government is Trying to Resolve Regional Differences

The UK government is trying to reduce the north-south divide by:

1 Devolving More Powers

1) Scotland, Wales and Northern Ireland have their own devolved governments, and some powers are being devolved to local councils in England too.

2) This allows them to use money on schemes they feel will best benefit the local community, e.g. better public transport or regeneration projects to turn disused buildings into modern office spaces to attract business to the area.

3 The Northern Powerhouse

The Northern Powerhouse is the government's plan to reduce the inequality between the north and south by attracting investment into the north and improving transport links between northern cities. It has been criticised for being more of a concept than an actual plan.

2 Creating Enterprise Zones

1) 55 Enterprise Zones have been created across England, Scotland and Wales.

2) These offer companies a range of benefits for locating in enterprise zones, including:

- Reduced taxes — business rates are reduced by up to 100%.

- Simpler planning rules — certain developments (e.g. new industrial buildings) are automatically allowed within enterprise zones.

- Financial benefits — in some enterprise zones, businesses who invest in buildings or equipment can reduce future tax bills.

- Improved infrastructure — the government ensures superfast broadband is available.

These measures can be used to encourage companies to locate in areas of high unemployment, bringing jobs and income which could help to reduce the north-south divide.

The UK has a Good but Improving Transport Network

The UK is a developed country with a good transport network. But congested transport networks can slow economic development, so it's important to improve them to ensure continued economic growth:

Roads — capacity on motorways is being increased by upgrading to "smart motorways" with extra lanes, e.g. the M4. A new road is being built to link the port of Heysham in Lancashire to the M6.

Railways — Crossrail (currently under construction) will increase central London's rail capacity by 10% when it opens in 2018. The proposed HS2 line linking London, Birmingham, Leeds and Manchester will increase capacity and allow faster journeys between major English cities if it is built.

Airports — the UK government has agreed that a new runway is needed in the south east as existing airports are full or filling up.

Ports — a new port, London Gateway, is operating at the mouth of the River Thames. It is able to handle the world's largest container ships and hopes to become a hub for global trade.

Investing in transport can help economic development

Some complicated sounding stuff here but if you keep the basic ideas in mind you won't go too far wrong — the government wants poorer areas to get richer, so is trying to get more businesses and industry to move there.

Economic Development in the UK

Almost there, I promise — just this last page on the UK then a few questions to test your knowledge.
First up, a bit about how the UK is connected to the wider world...

The UK has Strong Links to Other Countries

The UK has formed strong links with other countries as it has developed.

Trade — the UK trades globally, with links to the USA, Europe and Asia being particularly significant.
  The UK's overseas exports are worth over £250 billion per year.

Culture — the UK's strong creative industries mean that UK culture is exported worldwide,
  e.g. the Shaun the Sheep™ TV series made by Aardman Animations in Bristol
  is shown in 170 countries.

Transport — the Channel Tunnel links the UK to France by rail, providing a route for
  goods and people to access mainland Europe. Large airports like
  Heathrow act as a hub and provide links to hundreds of countries
  around the world.

Electronic Communications — as well was being home to offices for many global IT firms, most of the
  trans-Atlantic cables (carrying phone lines and internet connections)
  linking Europe with the USA are routed via the UK.

European Union (EU) — the EU is an economic and political partnership of 28 countries. Membership of the
  EU gives UK citizens and businesses access to a large market without trade or political
  barriers. It's an important part of the UK's economy — over £130 billion of the UK's
  exports were to the EU in 2015.

The Commonwealth — the Commonwealth is an association of 53 independent states, including the UK.
  It exists to improve the well being of everyone in Commonwealth countries.

The Effect of Industry on the Physical Environment can be Reduced

EXAMPLE

1) Industry can have negative effects on the environment, for example by releasing pollutants,
   greenhouse gases or by damaging the environment through raw material extraction.

2) Modern industrial developments are more environmentally sustainable
   than older plants as a result of more strict environmental regulations, better
   environmental awareness and increasing energy and waste disposal costs.

3) For example, Jaguar Land Rover opened a new engine manufacturing centre in
   Wolverhampton in 2014. The factory is designed to operate more sustainably
   — it was built to maximise natural cooling and natural light to reduce energy use, and
   has solar panels in the roof that can generate 30% of the plant's electricity. Almost all
   of the waste from the plant is recycled, with only a small proportion going to landfill.

Make sure you know how the UK is connected to the rest of the world

It's easy to assume you know everything on these four pages because it's about the UK and you probably know the
UK quite well. But you might need to know details for the exam, so don't be tempted to cut corners.

Worked Exam Questions

Another set of worked exam questions to look at here. It's tempting to skip over them without thinking, but it's worth taking time to look carefully — similar questions might just come up in your own exams...

1   Study **Figure 1**, photographs of Chadderton, a northern town, and Bath, a southern city.

Figure 1

Chadderton   Bath

1.1   Using **Figure 1**, outline **one** piece of evidence for a north-south divide.

The quality of housing in the photograph of Bath is higher than that in the photograph of Chadderton.

[1]

1.2   Give **one** reason for the development of the north-south divide.

The growth of post-industrial service industries has mostly benefited the south.

[1]

1.3   Explain how the north-south divide can be reduced.

Devolving more powers to Scotland, Wales, Northern Ireland and some local councils in the north of

England can help to reduce the development gap by providing money that can be used on schemes

they feel will best help the development of the local area. Creating Enterprise Zones could help to

reduce the north-south divide by encouraging companies to locate in areas of high unemployment,

bringing jobs and income to areas that need them. Transport links between the north and the south of

the country could be improved, e.g. the development of the HS2 line, which will allow faster journeys.

[4]

[Total 6 marks]

2   Study **Figure 2**, a photograph showing vehicles boarding a shuttle at the Channel Tunnel terminal in the UK.

Figure 2

2.1   Using **Figure 2**, describe how the UK's transport links help it to connect to the wider world.

Links such as the Channel Tunnel make it quick and easy for people

to get to and from other countries in Europe. Goods can also be

transported easily, increasing the UK's potential for trade with other countries.

[Total 2 marks]

Exam Questions

1   Study **Figure 1**, an article about an aid project in Ghana.

Figure 1

UK Government Support for Ghana

The UK is the second largest aid donor to Ghana. The UK Government's Department for International Development (DFID) gave over £205 million between 2005 and 2007 towards Ghana's poverty reduction plans. This level of aid continues, with donations of around £85 million per year. The aid is used in several ways, including to improve healthcare, education and sanitation.

About 15% of the UK's funding in 2008 was used to support the healthcare system in Ghana —

£42.5 million was pledged to support the Ghanaian Government's 2008-2012 health plan. On top of that, in 2008 the UK gave nearly £7 million to buy emergency equipment to reduce maternal deaths.

Thanks to a £105 million grant from the UK in 2006, Ghana has been able to set up a ten year education strategic plan. It was the first African country to do this. The UK pledged additional money to help 12 000 children in North Ghana to get a formal basic education.

1.1   Outline one potential advantage and one potential disadvantage for the recipient country of long-term aid projects.

Advantage:..

....

Disadvantage: ....

....

[2]

1.2   To what extent do trans-national corporations (TNCs) improve economic development and quality of life in LICs and NEEs? Reference at least one country you have studied.

[9 + 3 SPaG]

[Total 14 marks]

2   Study **Figure 2**, a map of central Newcastle in 2016.

Figure 2

2.1   Suggest two reasons why the Stephenson Quarter may be a desirable location for a computing business.

Reason 1: ....

....

....

Reason 2: ....

....

....

[Total 2 marks]

To Newcastle International Airport

Key
- ～ motorway
- ～ A-road
- ～ B-road
- ～ other road
- — railway
- ● railway station
- Ⓤ university
- ⬢ Stephenson Quarter
- ▮ River Tyne

Scale
0 m   500 m

Stephenson Quarter

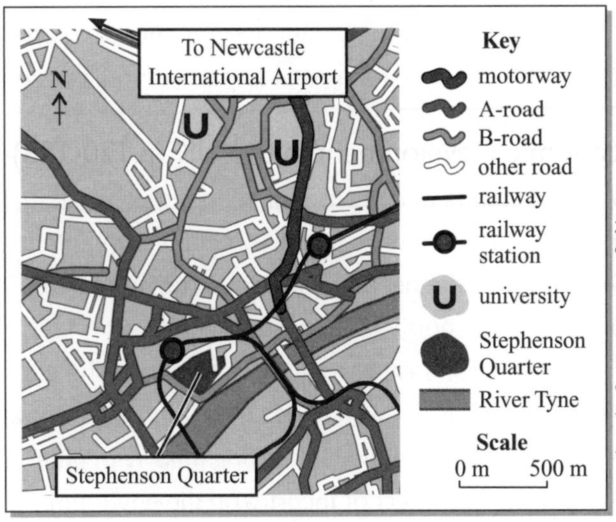

Contains OS data © Crown copyright and database right (2016)

Revision Summary

Hurrah, you've finally reached the end of <u>Unit 2B</u> — time to see how good your <u>understanding</u> of this topic is.
- Try these questions and <u>tick off each one</u> when you <u>get it right</u>.
- When you've done <u>all the questions</u> for a topic and are <u>completely happy</u> with it, tick off the topic.

Development (p.107-109) ☑

1) What is development?
2) What is meant by the development gap?
3) List five measures of development.
4) Give one way countries can be classified.
5) What do HIC, LIC and NEE stand for?
6) Describe the five stages of the demographic transition model.
7) How is a country's level of development linked to the different stages of the DTM?

Uneven Development (p.110-114) ☑

8) Give four physical factors that can affect how developed a country is.
9) Give two historical factors that can affect how developed a country is.
10) Give three economic factors that can affect how developed a country is.
11) What are the consequences of uneven development?
12) a) Explain how debt relief can reduce the global development gap.
    b) Give six other strategies to reduce the global development gap.
13) a) Name one country that is trying to grow tourism to close the development gap.
    b) Describe how it is doing this.
14) What is a TNC?
15) Give two advantages and two disadvantages for poorer countries of TNCs locating there.

Economic Development in India (p.117-119) ☑

16) What is India's current level of development?
17) How is India's industrial structure changing?
18) Name a TNC that operates in India.
19) What is the difference between short-term and long-term aid?
20) Explain the difference between top-down and bottom-up aid.
21) Describe the impact of India's economic development on quality of life.
22) Describe the environmental impacts of India's economic development.

> If you've learned about a different country, try answering these questions for the country you've studied instead.

Economic Development in the UK (p.120-123) ☑

23) What are the main causes of economic change in the UK?
24) What sort of industry has become more important as the UK becomes post-industrial?
25) Why has there been an increase in the number of science parks in the UK?
26) What is the north-south divide?
27) Give two contrasting ways that changes in the UK's economy are affecting rural areas.
28) Give two ways in which the UK is improving its transport network.
29) Give examples of the UK's strong links with other countries.
30) How can the effect of industry on the environment be reduced?

Global Distribution of Resources

Resources are just all the things that we use — and in this case we're talking about food, water and energy.

Everyone Needs Food, Water and Energy

1) Resources, such as food, water and energy, are needed for basic human development.

2) People need food and water to survive and stay healthy. Energy is needed for a basic standard of living, e.g. to provide lighting and heat for cooking.

3) Access to food, water and energy affects the economic and social well-being of people and countries:

Food

1) Without access to enough safe, nutritious food people can become malnourished — not have the right balance of nutrients, e.g. iron deficiency causes tiredness and can affect children's development. Malnourishment includes undernourishment — where people don't get enough food of any kind.

2) Malnourishment increases the likelihood of getting diseases — one third of all under-5s globally die from diseases linked to malnourishment.

3) People who aren't getting enough to eat may not perform as well at school, meaning that they lack skills needed to help a country's economic development. Malnourishment can also prevent people from working, harming their personal economic well-being, and also harming the economy of their country.

Water

1) People need clean, safe water for drinking, cooking and washing.

2) Without proper sanitation, water sources get polluted by raw sewage.

3) Water-borne diseases such as cholera and typhoid kill many people each year.

4) Having to walk long distances to fetch clean water can also have an economic impact on people and on a country's economy — people are able to spend less time working, and children may not be able to go to school.

5) Water is needed to produce food, clothes and many other products — it has a big impact on people's lifestyles.

Energy

1) Countries need energy for industry and transport, as well as for use in homes.

2) Electricity can allow industries to develop, creating jobs and making countries wealthier.

3) The way of life in high income countries (HICs) depends on having a large, stable supply of energy.

4) Without electricity, people may burn wood or kerosene for cooking and to provide light and heat for their homes. Using fuelwood can lead to local deforestation, meaning people have to walk further and further to find fuel. Kerosene stoves can release harmful fumes and may start fires.

5) Electricity can also power pumps for wells and provide more safe water for communities.

The Global Supply and Consumption of Resources is Uneven

1) The global distribution of resources is very uneven. Some countries don't have their own energy reserves. Others have dry climates or environments that are not suitable for food production.

2) To access more resources, these countries have to import them or find technological solutions to produce more, e.g. build desalination plants to produce fresh water from saltwater. This is expensive.

3) So consumption of resources depends on a country's wealth, as well as their availability.

4) Consumption of resources is greater in more developed HICs because they can afford to buy the resources they need and expect a higher standard of living.

5) Consumption is increasing rapidly in newly emerging economies (NEEs), e.g. China. Industry is developing very fast (which requires lots of energy) and population and wealth are also increasing rapidly.

6) Consumption is lower in low income countries (LICs) because they either can't afford to exploit the resources that they have, or to import resources if they're lacking their own.

People in richer countries consume more food, water and energy

That was a quick dash through some pretty big ideas. Don't worry, there's more coming up on managing resources — but if you can get your head round this lot, it'll really help with the rest of the topic, so go back and read it again.

Food in the UK

The production and availability of food in the UK is changing.

People Want **Seasonal** Food **All Year Round**

1) The types of food that are in demand in the UK have changed. Before the 1960s, most of the fruit and vegetables on sale in the UK were locally produced and seasonal. Seasonal food isn't available all year round — you can only buy it during the months that it grows.

2) Since the 1960s, there has been a growing demand for seasonal products all year round. So fruit and vegetables are being imported, e.g. apples from South Africa, and strawberries from Mexico.

3) There has also been an increasing demand for high-value foods, such as exotic fruits and vegetables, coffee and spices — they have become more popular in the UK as people's incomes have increased. These are often grown in lower income countries, e.g. Peru and Ivory Coast, and exported to the UK.

4) Organic produce is becoming increasingly popular — organic foods are produced according to strict regulations, e.g. banning the use of artificial fertilisers. Demand is growing as people are becoming more concerned about the environmental impacts of food production and the effect of chemicals on their health. Some organic food is produced in the UK, but lots of it is imported too.

The **Carbon Footprint** of Our Food is **Growing**

1) The growing, processing and packaging of food produces CO_2 and other greenhouse gases (see p.22). Up to 9% of the UK's total greenhouse gas emissions in 2013 came directly from the growing of food.

2) Transporting food from where it is grown to where it is sold also produces CO_2. The distance food is transported to the market is called its food miles. The higher the food miles, the more CO_2 is produced.

3) The amount of greenhouse gas produced during growing, packing and transporting a food is called its carbon footprint. A larger carbon footprint means more greenhouse gases and more global warming.

4) Imported foods have to be transported a long way so have high food miles and a large carbon footprint.

5) People are becoming aware of the environmental issues caused by transporting food over long distances. Environmentalists are encouraging people to buy food grown locally. Farmers' markets, farm shops and locally-produced vegetable boxes are becoming more and more popular.

Farming is Becoming More **Industrialised**

1) Since the 1960s, there has been a growth in agribusiness in the UK. Agribusiness is large-scale, industrial farming where processes from the production of seeds and fertilisers, to the processing and packaging of the food are controlled by large firms.

2) This means that farms in the UK have been changing, for example:

> • Farm sizes have been increasing — many small farms have been taken over and field sizes increased so that food can be produced more cheaply.
>
> • The amount of chemicals used in food production has been increasing — large quantities of artificial fertilisers and pesticides are applied to crops, and animals are given special feed to encourage growth.
>
> • The number of workers employed has been falling because of greater use of machinery, e.g. in planting and harvesting.

3) Industrial farming also has environmental impacts. Increasing farm size has meant hedgerows have been removed, leading to a loss in biodiversity, and heavy machinery is causing soil erosion.

EXAM TIP

Food variety and availability are increasing, but there are problems too

You might have to interpret information on food production in your exam — learn the main trends, so you know the sorts of things to look out for. Back up your answer with any evidence you are given.

Managing the UK's Water

The UK may be famous for being <u>grey</u> and <u>wet</u>, but apparently the <u>rain</u> doesn't fall in the <u>right places</u>...

The **Demand** for **Water Varies** Across the **UK**

In the UK, the places with a <u>good supply</u> of water <u>aren't the same</u> as the places with the <u>highest demand</u>:

<u>UK average annual rainfall</u>   <u>UK population density</u>

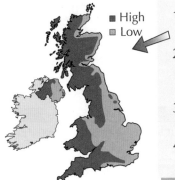

■ High
□ Low

1) The <u>north</u> and <u>west</u> of the UK have <u>high rainfall</u>, which means there's a <u>good supply</u> of water.

2) The <u>south east</u> and <u>Midlands</u> have <u>high population densities</u>, which means there's a <u>high demand</u> for water.

3) The <u>south east</u> and <u>Midlands</u> are areas of <u>water deficit</u> (there's a <u>greater demand</u> than <u>supply</u>).

4) The <u>north</u> and <u>west</u> are areas of <u>water surplus</u> (there's a <u>greater supply</u> than <u>demand</u>).

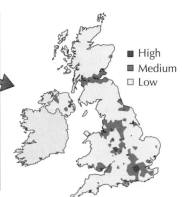

■ High
■ Medium
□ Low

The <u>demand</u> for water in the UK is <u>increasing</u>:

1) Since 1975, the amount of water <u>used</u> by households in the UK has <u>gone up</u> by about <u>70%</u>. This is partly because people have more <u>appliances</u> that use <u>lots of water</u>, e.g. dishwashers and washing machines.

2) The <u>UK population</u> is predicted to <u>increase</u> by around <u>10 million</u> people by <u>2040</u>.

3) Population <u>densities</u> are also <u>changing</u> — lots of <u>new homes</u> are planned to be built in the <u>south east</u> where there is already a water deficit.

Water **Pollution** Needs to be **Managed**

1) <u>Polluted</u> or <u>low quality</u> water <u>reduces</u> the amount <u>available</u> for use. This puts more <u>pressure</u> on <u>water resources</u>, especially in areas with a water deficit.

Groundwater is water found underground in soil and in cracks in rock.

2) Overall, the <u>quality</u> of <u>river water</u> in the UK has been <u>improving</u>. However, there are still some <u>problems</u>:

• <u>Nitrates</u> and <u>phosphates</u> from <u>fertilisers</u> used on crops are being <u>washed</u> into <u>rivers</u> and <u>groundwater</u>.

• <u>Pollutants</u> from <u>vehicles</u> are being washed into water sources through <u>runoff</u> when it rains.

• Accidental <u>chemical</u> and <u>oil spills</u> at factories are <u>polluting local water sources</u> and <u>groundwater supplies</u>.

3) Up to <u>80%</u> of water in some parts of <u>southern England</u> comes from groundwater, but <u>pollution</u> is affecting the water quality of nearly <u>50%</u> of <u>groundwater</u> used for public supply in the UK. Many groundwater sources have been <u>closed</u> or have had to have <u>expensive treatment</u> to make them <u>safe to use</u>.

4) <u>Strategies</u> to manage water quality include <u>improving drainage systems</u> (e.g. by slowing down the movement of rainwater to rivers so that pollutants can be broken down in the soil) and imposing <u>regulations</u> on the amount and types of <u>fertilisers</u> and <u>pesticides</u> used.

Water **Transfers** Can Help **Maintain Supplies**

1) One way to deal with the <u>supply and demand problem</u> is to <u>transfer water</u> from areas of <u>surplus</u> to areas of <u>deficit</u>. For example, <u>Birmingham</u> (an area of <u>deficit</u>) is supplied with water from the <u>middle of Wales</u> (an area of <u>surplus</u>).

2) However, water transfer can cause a variety of <u>issues</u>:

• The <u>dams</u> and <u>aqueducts</u> (bridges used to <u>transport water</u>) that are needed are <u>expensive</u> to build.

• It can <u>affect the wildlife</u> that lives in the rivers, e.g. <u>fish migration</u> can be disrupted by dams.

• There might be <u>political issues</u>, e.g. people <u>may not want</u> their <u>water transferred to another area</u>.

The demand for water is increasing and there's not always enough available

Remember, the availability of water depends on how much there is and how many people want to use it. If there's a deficit, one way to solve the problem is to transfer water from somewhere else. Get this page thoroughly learnt.

Energy in the UK

We get most of our energy from underground as coal, oil and gas and it's been that way for a long time now. However, there is a general trend towards using more energy from renewable sources.

The UK's Energy Mix Has Changed

1) Traditionally, the UK has relied on fossil fuels (coal, oil and gas) to supply its energy. In 1970, 91% of our energy came from coal and oil.

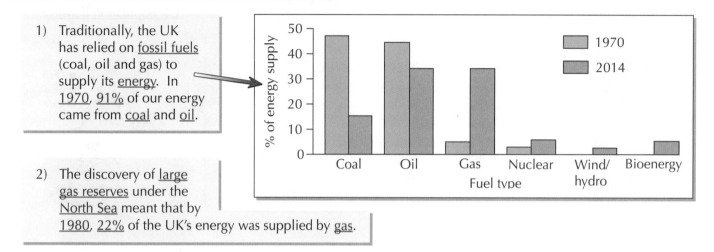

2) The discovery of large gas reserves under the North Sea meant that by 1980, 22% of the UK's energy was supplied by gas.

3) The use of nuclear energy to produce electricity also increased during the 1990s.

4) Recently there has been a shift away from burning fossil fuels, and towards renewable energy sources (i.e. ones that won't run out). All coal fired power stations in the UK are due to close by 2025, and in 2014, 19% of all electricity in the UK was generated from renewable sources.

5) Wind and bioenergy (energy from the break down or burning of biological sources) are the biggest sources of renewable energy, but the use of solar and hydroelectric power has also increased.

The UK's Supplies of Coal, Oil and Gas are Running Out

1) North Sea oil and gas reserves are being rapidly used up and production has been declining since 2000.
2) The UK still has coal reserves but coal production has fallen hugely since the mid-20th century. There has been a decline in demand due to an effort to reduce CO_2 emissions, and the cost of mining the remaining reserves is increasing. The last deep coal mine in the UK closed in December 2015.

3) The use of shale gas from underground is being considered in the UK, as a way of adding to resources. It's extracted using a process called fracking: fluid is pumped into shale rock at high pressure, causing it to crack. This forces gas trapped in the rock to flow back out of a well, where it is collected.

EXAM TIP

The UK uses a wide variety of energy sources — not just fossil fuels

Don't panic if you're asked to interpret data on energy in the exam — just read it carefully and try to link it to what you know from this page. That does, however, require learning this page, so read it again.

Energy in the UK

We need energy to <u>heat</u> our homes, <u>cook</u> food and drive <u>cars</u>, but unfortunately that's not the end of the story — there's a whole host of <u>issues</u> relating to <u>exploiting energy sources</u> that you need to know...

Exploiting Energy Sources Causes Economic Issues...

Energy <u>resources</u> are very important — exploiting energy sources <u>creates jobs</u> and <u>wealth</u> for the UK. However, the <u>extraction of fossil fuels</u> and <u>production of electricity</u> can cause <u>problems</u>:

Economic Issues

1) <u>Extracting fossil fuels</u> can be <u>expensive</u> and the cost of extraction <u>increases</u> as reserves are <u>used up</u>.

2) <u>North Sea oil</u> is <u>especially expensive</u> to produce. If the <u>price of oil</u> on the world market <u>drops</u>, it may cost <u>more to produce</u> than it can be <u>sold</u> for.

3) The cost of producing electricity from <u>nuclear</u> and <u>renewable</u> energy sources is <u>relatively high</u>.

4) Money is needed for <u>research</u> into <u>alternative energy sources</u>, e.g. shale gas, and for <u>initial investment</u>, e.g. building the new nuclear power station at Hinkley Point.

5) Many <u>renewable</u> sources <u>don't provide</u> a <u>reliable enough</u> supply of energy, so the UK still has to <u>pay</u> to <u>import energy</u> from other countries.

...as well as Environmental Problems

Exploiting both <u>renewable</u> and <u>non-renewable</u> energy sources can <u>harm</u> the <u>environment</u>.

Environmental Issues

1) The <u>burning</u> of <u>fossil fuels</u> releases <u>carbon dioxide</u> and other <u>greenhouse gases</u>.

2) <u>Fracking</u> may <u>pollute groundwater</u> and cause <u>mini-earthquakes</u> — some people in the UK are <u>campaigning</u> to <u>ban it</u>.

3) <u>Accidents</u>, such as oil spills or nuclear disasters, can leak <u>toxic chemicals</u> into <u>water sources</u>, <u>soils</u> and the <u>atmosphere</u>.

4) <u>Natural ecosystems</u> can be <u>damaged</u> by <u>renewable</u> energy generators like large <u>wind farms</u> or the <u>tidal barrage</u> system planned for Swansea in Wales.

5) <u>Power stations</u> and <u>wind farms</u> are often considered to be <u>eyesores</u>.

Exploiting energy sources can bring wealth, but it causes problems too

Everything has advantages and disadvantages, and exploiting energy sources is no exception — make sure you're able to write about both sides of the issue. Learn these economic and environmental problems and remember that renewable energy sources aren't a magic solution — there are issues with using them to supply energy too.

Worked Exam Questions

Take your time going through these worked exam questions — something similar might come up in the exam...

1   Study **Figure 1** and **Figure 2**, which show rainfall and population density in the UK.

Figure 1

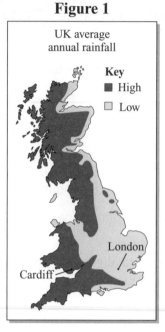

UK average annual rainfall

Key
- ■ High
- □ Low

London

Cardiff

Figure 2

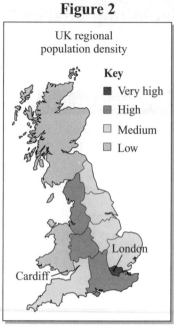

UK regional population density

Key
- ■ Very high
- ■ High
- □ Medium
- □ Low

London

Cardiff

1.1   Using **Figure 1** and **Figure 2**, describe the pattern of water supply and demand across the UK.

The north and the west of the UK
have high rainfall, which means there's
a good supply of water. The south east
and west Midlands have high population
densities, which means there's a high
demand for water.

[2]

1.2   Are the following places likely to have a water deficit or surplus? Explain your answers.

Cardiff: Water surplus because it has high annual rainfall and a low regional population density.

London: Water deficit because it has low annual rainfall and a very high regional population density.

[4]

1.3   Explain why the water deficit in some areas of the UK is increasing.

Since 1975, the amount of water used by households in the UK has gone up. This is partly because
people have more appliances that use lots of water, e.g. dishwashers and washing machines.
Also, the UK population is predicted to increase by around 10 million people over the next 25 years,
so the demand for water is increasing. This is increasing the water deficit in areas that don't receive
much rainfall because there isn't enough water to replace the amount being extracted for use.
The water deficit can also increase when population densities increase. For example, lots of new homes
are planned to be built in the south east. There is already a water deficit there, and more homes and
more people will increase the deficit.

[4]

1.4   Explain **one** way in which water quality in the UK can be managed.

Drainage systems can be improved, for example by slowing down the movement of rainwater
to rivers, so that pollutants can be broken down in the soil.

[2]

[Total 12 marks]

Exam Questions

1 Study **Figure 1**, pie charts showing the proportion of UK energy from different sources in 1970 and 2014.

1.1 Which source of energy did the UK most rely on in 1970?

....
[1]

1.2 Which energy source increased its share the most between 1970 and 2014?

....
[1]

Figure 1

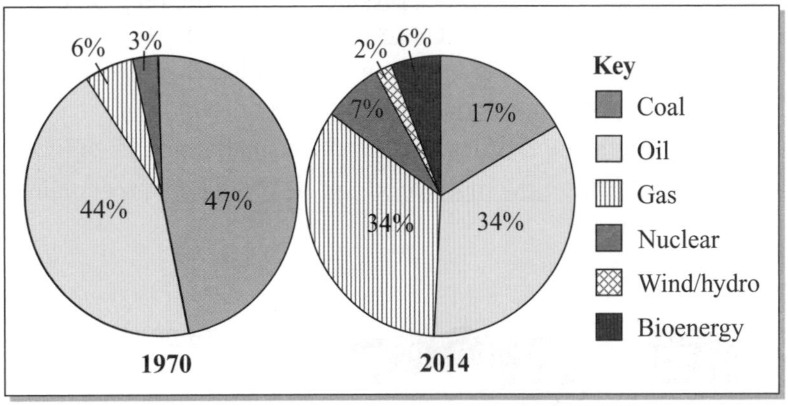

6%
3%
44%
47%
1970
2%
6%
7%
17%
34%
34%
2014
Key
Coal
Oil
Gas
Nuclear
Wind/hydro
Bioenergy

1.3 Using **Figure 1**, describe the changes in energy sources in the UK between 1970 and 2014.

....

....

....

....
[3]

1.4 Suggest **one** reason for the trend in the UK's use of coal shown in **Figure 1**.

....

....
[2]

1.5 Outline **one** economic issue caused by exploiting renewable energy resources.

....

....
[1]

1.6 Explain how exploiting energy resources can cause environmental issues.

....

....

....

....

....

....

....
[6]

[Total 14 marks]

Global Demand for Food

The world needs <u>more</u> and <u>more food</u>, but in some areas there just isn't <u>enough</u>.

Global **Food Supply** is **Uneven**

The <u>amount</u> of food that countries <u>produce varies</u>. The map on the right shows the production of <u>cereals</u> by country from 2012 to 2014. The production of other food follows a <u>similar pattern</u>.

1) <u>East Asia</u> and <u>North America</u> produce <u>a lot</u> of food.

2) <u>Central America</u> and <u>Africa</u> only produce <u>small</u> amounts of food.

The <u>factors</u> that affect <u>how much food</u> can be <u>produced</u> are explained on the next page.

Metric tonnes (millions)
■ >410   ■ 50-90   □ 2.8-16   ■ No data
■ 90-410   ■ 16-50   □ <2.8   available

Daily calorie (kcal) intake per person (2011-2013)
■ Over 3539   ■ 3266 to 3358   □ 2546 to 3095
■ 3358 to 3539   □ 3095 to 3266   □ Less than 2546
□ No data available

The <u>amount</u> of food people <u>eat</u> also <u>varies</u> across the world. The map on the left shows the <u>daily calorie intake</u> of people in different countries.

1) <u>More developed</u> areas like <u>North America</u> and <u>Europe</u> eat <u>a lot</u>. They can <u>afford</u> to <u>import</u> a large variety of foods and many people have a <u>high income</u> so can buy more food.

2) <u>Less developed</u> areas like <u>Africa</u>, <u>Central America</u> and parts of <u>Asia</u> consume <u>less</u> food per person as they <u>can't afford</u> as much and less food is <u>available</u>.

3) <u>China</u> and other <u>newly industrialised</u> countries are consuming <u>more</u> as their <u>wealth increases</u>.

- <u>Food security</u> is when people are able to eat enough <u>nutritious food</u> to stay <u>healthy</u> and <u>active</u>. Countries that can <u>produce a lot</u> of food or are <u>rich</u> enough to <u>import</u> the food they need have <u>food security</u>.

- <u>Food insecurity</u> is when people <u>aren't</u> able to get enough food to stay healthy or lead an active life. Countries that <u>don't grow enough</u> to feed their population and <u>can't afford to import</u> the food they need have <u>food insecurity</u>.

Global **Food Consumption** is **Increasing**

Food <u>consumption</u> around the world is <u>increasing</u>. This is down to <u>two</u> main reasons:

1 Rising Population

The global population is <u>increasing</u> and is expected to reach 9 billion by 2040 — <u>more people</u> require <u>more food</u>.

2 Economic Development

1) <u>Economic development</u> means that countries are getting <u>wealthier</u>.

2) Some <u>Newly Emerging Economies</u> are experiencing <u>high</u> population growth rates and <u>lots</u> of people are getting a lot <u>richer</u>, very <u>quickly</u>.

3) Wealthier people have <u>more disposable income</u> to spend on <u>food</u>. They often buy a greater <u>variety</u> of food and <u>more</u> than they <u>need</u>.

4) Wealthy <u>countries</u> can afford to <u>import</u> food <u>all year round</u> so people no longer eat just what is <u>seasonally available</u>.

5) <u>Industrialisation</u> of <u>agriculture</u> means some countries are able to <u>produce more</u> food at <u>lower cost</u>. Food becomes <u>cheaper</u>, so people can <u>afford</u> to <u>eat more</u>.

More people and more money = more food required

If you can get this lot under your belt it'll really help with understanding the rest of the topic. Make sure you're clear on the meaning of food security and insecurity — it's all about whether people have a reliable source of food.

Food Insecurity

Food insecurity is a pretty complex issue — there are loads of factors that affect how much food is available.

Food Supply is Affected by Physical Factors...

Food insecurity occurs for two reasons — not enough food is being produced or people are unable to access food supplies. Food production and accessibility are affected by physical factors:

Climate

Countries that have climates that are unsuitable for farming (e.g. too hot, too cold, or too little rainfall) can't grow much food of their own. Extreme weather events, such as floods and droughts, can also affect food supply.

Water stress

Crops and livestock need water to survive. Areas that have low rainfall or where water for irrigation is scarce struggle to grow enough food.

Pests and diseases

Pests reduce yields by consuming crops, e.g. rats cause big problems by eating stored grain, and huge locust swarms eat all the vegetation in their path. Diseases affect most crops and livestock and can cause a lot of damage if they spread through crops and herds, e.g. 37% of the world's wheat crops are under threat from a disease called wheat rust.

...and Human Factors

Food production and accessibility are also affected by human factors:

Poverty

People living in poverty often don't have their own land where they can grow food. Poverty can also affect people's ability to farm the land effectively, e.g. they may not be able to buy the fertilisers or pesticides they need. At a global scale, poverty means that countries which can't grow enough can't afford to import food from countries with a surplus.

Technology

The mechanisation of farm equipment (e.g. use of tractors) increases the amount of food that can be grown by making the process more efficient. New technologies (e.g. genetic engineering — see p. 137) can help protect plants from disease, increase their yields and help them grow better in harsh climates.

Conflict

Conflict — fighting may damage agricultural land or make it unsafe, making it difficult to grow enough food. Access to food becomes difficult for people who are forced to flee their homes. Conflicts also make it difficult to import food because trade routes are disrupted and political relationships with supply countries may break down.

Learn these six factors that can lead to food insecurity

Food insecurity is a complex issue, and is usually caused by a combination of these factors. Knowing the factors listed on this page won't help solve world hunger I'm afraid, but it will help you to write great exam answers.

Food Insecurity

Time to delve into what happens when there isn't enough food to go round... There's a lot more to it than you might think, but don't worry — as long as you can remember these impacts of food insecurity you'll be fine.

Food Insecurity has Negative Impacts

Food insecurity doesn't just mean that people go hungry — it can lead to a whole load of other problems too:

Famine

A serious lack of food across a large area is known as a famine. During a famine people are unable to get enough food of any sort, which leads to starvation and death if the situation continues.

Undernutrition

To stay healthy, people need to eat a balanced diet. Undernutrition is when you don't get enough nutrients of a particular sort to keep your body healthy.

Soil erosion

If people are struggling to get enough food, they may not use the best agricultural practices, e.g. they may over-cultivate the land (grow crops repeatedly, without allowing time for the soil to recover its nutrients). Pressure to get enough to eat may also lead to overgrazing, when there are more animals than the land can support. Over-cultivation and overgrazing lead to soil erosion.

Rising prices

When there isn't enough food available, food prices usually increase. This is because shops don't have to lower their prices to compete for customers — people will pay any price to get the food they need. Rising prices mean that the poorest people can't afford to feed themselves properly.

Refugees from a civil war receiving food aid

Social unrest

People expect governments to help them get enough food during times of food insecurity, e.g. during a drought. If governments don't appear to be doing enough, make the situation worse or distribute aid unfairly, it can cause rioting and even turn into a bigger conflict, e.g. a civil war.

EXAM TIP

Food insecurity can cause a variety of problems

Some of the impacts of food insecurity are not particularly obvious. If you're asked about them in the exam, bear in mind things like soil erosion, rising food prices and social unrest, and don't try to answer an essay question entirely about people being hungry. You'll need more than that to get top marks.

Increasing Food Production

If you've read the previous page you'll know why <u>food insecurity</u> can make things <u>difficult</u>. We need to <u>produce more</u> food — and there are some pretty interesting ways people are doing just that.

New **Technologies** can **Increase Food Supply**

With the global <u>demand</u> for food <u>increasing</u>, new ways of <u>increasing food supplies</u> are urgently needed. Trying to increase <u>yields</u> (how much food is produced in a given area) is <u>important</u>. Solutions exist at a <u>range of scales</u> from a <u>complete change</u> in agricultural methods, to smaller, <u>local</u> techniques to improve crop growth using <u>existing technology</u>. Here are some <u>examples</u>:

Irrigation

<u>Irrigation</u> is <u>artificially watering</u> the land so crops can grow. It can be used to make <u>dry</u> areas more <u>productive</u>, or to increase the <u>number</u> of <u>harvests</u> and the <u>yield</u> of <u>crops</u>.

There are three main types of irrigation:

1) <u>Gravity flow</u> — digging <u>ditches</u> and <u>channels</u> to <u>transport</u> ground or surface water to fields.

2) <u>Sprinklers</u> — <u>spraying</u> water across fields.

3) <u>Drip systems</u> — <u>dripping</u> water from <u>small holes</u> in pipes <u>directly</u> onto the soil around the <u>roots</u> of crop plants.

Hydroponics and Aeroponics

<u>Hydroponics</u> and <u>aeroponics</u> are methods of growing plants <u>without soil</u>:

1) In <u>hydroponics</u> plants are grown in a <u>nutrient solution</u>, supported by a <u>material</u> such as rockwool, gravel, or clay balls.

2) In <u>aeroponics</u> plants are <u>suspended</u> in air and a <u>fine mist</u> of water containing <u>nutrients</u> is <u>sprayed</u> onto the <u>roots</u>. The water drips off the roots and is <u>used again</u>.

3) Plants are <u>monitored</u> closely and nutrients <u>adjusted</u> to <u>maximise</u> the <u>yield</u> of crops.

4) <u>Less water</u> is required than plants grown in soil and <u>reduced risk</u> of <u>disease</u> and <u>pests</u> means less need for pesticides.

5) Hydroponics and aeroponics are very <u>expensive</u>, so these methods are currently only used for <u>high value crops</u>.

Biotechnology

Biotechnology involves <u>genetically engineering</u> crops to improve <u>production</u>. Genetically modified (GM) crops allow <u>more food</u> to be grown in <u>smaller areas</u> with <u>fewer resources</u>.

For example, GM crops can be designed to have:

1) <u>Higher yields</u>, e.g. C4 rice is a breed of rice that is being developed to produce high yields.

2) <u>Resistance</u> to <u>drought</u>, <u>disease</u> or <u>pests</u> (which reduces the need for pesticides).

3) <u>Higher nutritional values</u>, e.g. potatoes with more protein, rice with more vitamin A.

However, there are <u>ethical</u> and <u>environmental concerns</u>:

• They may <u>reduce biodiversity</u> because fewer varieties of crops are planted.

• GM plants may <u>interbreed</u> with wild plants and pass on their <u>genes</u> or <u>disrupt ecosystems</u>.

The New Green Revolution

The Green Revolution (1960s-70s) involved using <u>mechanisation</u>, <u>chemicals</u> and <u>new strains</u> of plants to <u>increase</u> the <u>yield</u> of crops. However, it caused lots of <u>environmental problems</u> and mainly benefited <u>large-scale producers</u> and <u>richer</u> farmers. The <u>new</u> green revolution aims to improve yields in a more <u>sustainable</u> way (see page 139). This will involve using a combination of:

1) <u>GM varieties</u>, including varieties with pest and disease resistance.

2) <u>Traditional</u> and <u>organic</u> farming methods, including <u>soil nutrient recycling</u>, <u>crop rotation</u> and <u>natural predators</u> to control pests.

Increasing Food Production

Appropriate Technology

1) The high-tech methods discussed on the previous page all have disadvantages. They also all tend to be extremely expensive, so aren't a practical choice to use in less-wealthy countries. For these countries, appropriate technologies are a much better option.

2) Using appropriate technologies involves choosing ways of increasing food production that are suited to local environments and the needs, skills, knowledge and wealth of the people in those areas.

3) For example, in LICs:

- Individual wells with easy to maintain, mechanical pumps are more suitable than larger, diesel powered pumps.

- A drip irrigation system constructed from local materials is more appropriate than an imported, high-tech sprinkler system.

- Planting a variety of local species that can cope with local environmental conditions and have seeds that can be collected and re-planted may be more appropriate than planting a single GM variety that may have to be repurchased each year.

Thanet Earth Grows Crops in Huge Greenhouses

1) Thanet Earth is a large-scale agricultural development in Kent, in south-east England.

2) 4 greenhouses, each the size of 10 football pitches, are used to grow salad vegetables — tomatoes, cucumbers and peppers — using hydroponics, nearly all year round.

3) The development aims to be sustainable. Each greenhouse has its own power station to provide heat and lighting, and rainwater collected from the roofs is used to provide the water supply. Hot air and carbon dioxide from the power stations is pumped back into the greenhouses.

4) The scheme has many advantages, but not everyone is happy with it:

Advantages

- More than 500 jobs have been created in an area with relatively high unemployment.

- British salad vegetables can be grown nearly all year round, reducing reliance on foreign imports. This gives the UK better food security. Reducing the number of air miles on our food is also better for the environment.

- Bees are used for pollination and natural predators are used to reduce pest numbers, reducing the need for artificial pesticides.

- The hydroponic system is completely automated so each plant gets the right amount of nutrients, limiting the amount of fertiliser needed.

Disadvantages

- A large area of farmland has been built on.

- Natural habitats have been lost and ecosystems disrupted.

- The money generated goes mostly to the large companies that have invested in it, rather than to local communities.

- The greenhouses are built on high land and are artificially lit, causing visual and light pollution.

- A large amount of energy is required to power the greenhouses, as well as to package and deliver the produce to the supermarkets.

There are pros and cons to large-scale agricultural developments

You might be asked to write about a named example of a large-scale agricultural development — Thanet Earth is a good example, but if you've learnt a different one in class then go ahead and use that instead. If you're asked about how successful it is, make sure you cover both its advantages and disadvantages.

Sustainable Food Supply

It's no good if we just go around destroying the environment — we have to look after it, if we want to eat.

Industrial Agriculture is Bad for the Environment

1) There are two challenges in making sure that food supplies are sustainable:
   - Growing enough food now to feed a rising population.
   - Making sure that the environment isn't damaged in the process, so that enough food can continue to be grown to feed future generations.

2) Industrial agriculture does a good job of producing lots of food now. But it has a large negative impact on the environment, affecting our ability to produce food in the future.

3) Irrigation for agriculture uses 70% of the world's fresh water supply and industrial agriculture also relies on added chemical pesticides and artificial fertilisers, which can pollute waterways and disrupt ecosystems. It can permanently remove nutrients from the soil, making it less and less productive.

4) Transporting food long distances from where it's grown is also affecting the environment — planes and lorries used to transport food release huge amounts of greenhouse gases into the air (see p.22).

Low Impact Farming Makes Food Supplies More Sustainable

To make food supplies sustainable, alternatives to industrial agriculture are needed, which don't damage the environment. Here are some different approaches that people are taking:

Organic Farming

1) Organic farming uses natural processes to return nutrients to the soil, so that crops can continue to be grown. E.g. crops, animals and empty (fallow) areas are rotated and natural fertilisers, such as cow manure, are used, which can be less damaging to the environment.

2) Artificial herbicides and pesticides are restricted and animals aren't given extra supplements or vaccinations. This reduces the reliance on unsustainable resources and can protect biodiversity.

3) Organic farmers are encouraged to sell their produce as close to where it is produced as possible, reducing the amount of road and air transport required.

Permaculture

1) Permaculture is a way of living sustainably. It includes trying to produce food in a way that recreates natural ecosystems in an effort to protect the soil, insects and other wildlife.

2) People are encouraged to grow their own food and change their eating habits — eating fewer animal products and more fruit and vegetables, and buying local, organic or fair trade food wherever possible.

3) The production of food is designed to be low maintenance and to keep soils healthy so that crops can continue to be grown. For example, mixed cropping is used which involves having plants of different heights and lots of different types in one area. This means the available space and light are used better, there are fewer pests and diseases and less watering is required.

Urban Farming Initiatives

1) Urban farming initiatives use empty land, roof tops and balconies to grow food and raise animals in towns and cities, e.g. allotments are often used by urban residents to grow fruit and vegetables for their families.

2) Urban farming makes food locally available, reducing the need to transport food long distances. This means it is often fresher and more nutritious and can also be cheaper — improving the food security of poorer residents.

3) It adds greenery to cities, making them healthier and more attractive places to live and makes urban areas less dependent on industrial agriculture.

Some alternatives to industrial agriculture aim to be more sustainable

Sustainable agriculture is all about using as few resources as possible and trying to keep things natural — after all, if you don't use much, you'll have more left to use later and you'll probably do less damage to the environment.

Sustainable Food Supply

Right, just a few more ways to help make <u>food supplies</u> more <u>sustainable</u> and an <u>example</u> of a sustainable scheme.

Eating **Seasonally** and **Reducing Waste** is More **Sustainable**

Making food supplies more sustainable is not just about using <u>better growing techniques</u> — <u>changing</u> how we <u>consume food</u> can also have an effect.

Fish and Meat from Sustainable Sources

1) Many fish species are at risk from <u>over-fishing</u>, due to <u>increased consumption</u>. Sustainable fishing includes <u>catch quotas</u> that limit the amount of fish taken and fishing methods that are <u>less harmful</u> to the environment. <u>Labelling</u> allows consumers to <u>choose</u> to eat fish that have been <u>fished sustainably</u>.

2) The raising of <u>cattle</u> is <u>bad</u> for the <u>environment</u> — forests are often <u>cleared</u> to make space for them and they produce a lot of <u>methane</u> (a greenhouse gas). However, eating <u>grass-fed</u> meat is much more <u>sustainable</u>. These animals are raised on <u>natural grassland</u> — they don't need feeding on <u>grain</u> (which requires lots of space and artificial fertilisers to grow) and they provide <u>natural manure</u> for the soil.

Seasonal Food Consumption

1) In many <u>wealthy countries</u>, people expect to be able to get the foods they like to eat <u>all year round</u>. However, this means that these foods have to be <u>imported</u> during the part of the year that they are not available locally, e.g. <u>peaches</u> are harvested in the <u>UK</u> from July to September, but are <u>imported all year round</u> from warmer countries, such as <u>Spain</u>, <u>Italy</u> and <u>Greece</u>.

2) Importing lots of food is <u>not sustainable</u> because transport <u>pollutes</u> the <u>environment</u>.

3) <u>Eating seasonally</u> means <u>only</u> eating the foods that <u>grow locally</u> at that time of year, <u>reducing</u> the amount of food that is <u>imported</u>.

Reduced Waste and Losses

1) Globally, <u>one third</u> of food that is produced is <u>lost</u> or <u>wasted</u> — reducing this will make <u>more food available</u>, so <u>less</u> needs to be <u>grown</u> to feed the world's population.

2) Schemes such as '<u>Think.Eat.Save</u>' and '<u>Love Food Hate Waste</u>' encourage <u>individuals</u>, <u>businesses</u> and <u>governments</u> to be <u>less wasteful</u> with food. E.g. by helping people <u>plan</u> their meals better and sharing recipe ideas for <u>using up leftovers</u>. They also encourage people to <u>compost waste</u> rather than putting it in the <u>bin</u> (food in <u>landfill</u> sites produces <u>methane</u>, which is a greenhouse gas).

Agroforestry Schemes in **Mali** are Producing a **Sustainable Food Supply**

1) In the <u>Koutiala</u> region of <u>Mali</u> (an LIC), many <u>local farmers</u> have begun to use <u>agroforestry</u> techniques to make sure that their food supply is <u>sustainable</u>.

2) Mali is a very <u>dry</u> country. <u>Intensive use</u> of land for farming is causing <u>desertification</u> of the land (see p.44), making it <u>less fertile</u>.

3) Farmers were shown how to plant <u>staple crops</u> like maize in amongst <u>trees</u> and <u>nitrogen-fixing plants</u>.

4) The plants add <u>nitrogen</u> to the soil so <u>artificial fertilisers</u> aren't needed. The trees provide <u>shade</u> and <u>prevent soil erosion</u>. They also <u>increase</u> the <u>nutrient</u> and <u>water content</u> of the soil — leaf fall increases the <u>organic content</u> of the soil so that it holds <u>water</u> better. The trees can also be used for <u>building materials</u>.

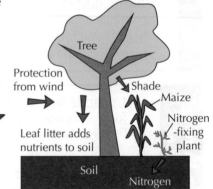

5) This system <u>increases</u> the <u>yield</u> of <u>maize</u> at the same time as <u>protecting</u> the <u>soil</u>. The system is <u>sustainable</u> because farmers can provide the <u>food</u> they need <u>without damaging</u> the local <u>environment</u>, so they can <u>continue</u> to produce food using these methods in the <u>future</u>.

Consumers' food choices can affect how sustainable food supplies are

It's not just farmers and agricultural companies that affect how sustainable food supplies are — what people choose to buy and eat is important too. You need to learn why that is, plus an example of a local scheme in an LIC or NEE.

Worked Exam Questions

You know the routine by now — work carefully through these examples and make sure you understand them. Then it's on to the real test of doing some exam questions yourself.

1 Study **Figure 1**, which shows corn production in Canada (a high-income country) and Zimbabwe (a low-income country) between 1961 and 2013.

1.1 Compare corn production in Canada and Zimbabwe over the time period shown in **Figure 1**.

Canada increased its corn production from roughly

1 million tonnes per year in 1961 to about 14 million

tonnes per year in 2013. However, there was no overall

increase in corn production in Zimbabwe, with production

varying between about 0.5 and 3 million tonnes.

[2]

Figure 1

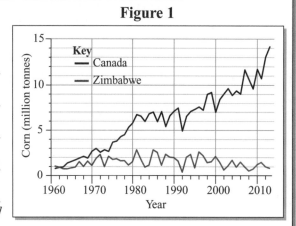

1.2 Outline **one** way in which appropriate technologies could be used to increase corn production in Zimbabwe.

Water supply could be improved by using individual wells with easy-to-maintain, mechanical pumps.

[1]

1.3 Evaluate the success of a large-scale agricultural development you have studied.

Thanet Earth uses hydroponics to grow salad vegetables in large greenhouses nearly all year round.

This has created more than 500 jobs in an area with relatively high unemployment. The hydroponic

system is automated so each plant gets the right amount of nutrients. This limits the amount of fertiliser

needed, making food production more sustainable. However, a large area of farmland has been built on,

so natural habitats have been lost and ecosystems disrupted. Also, a large amount of energy is required

to power the greenhouses, as well as to deliver the produce to shops, which releases greenhouse gases.

In conclusion, the benefits of the scheme outweigh the downsides, so it has been generally successful.

[4]

[Total 7 marks]

2 Study **Figure 2**, a photograph of an arid landscape in Namibia, Africa.

Figure 2

2.1 Using **Figure 2**, explain how climate might be affecting food production in Namibia.

Arid landscapes, such as Namibia, have too little rainfall, which

can reduce the amount of food that can be grown because crops

and livestock need water to survive. High temperatures may

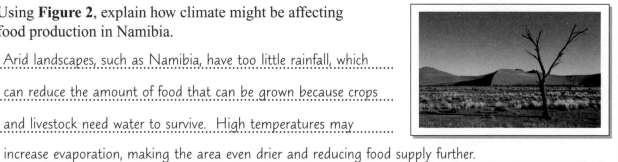

increase evaporation, making the area even drier and reducing food supply further.

[Total 2 marks]

Exam Questions

1   Study **Figure 1**, which gives information about an urban farming initiative in Singapore.

Figure 1

> As an island nation, Singapore has a limited amount of land. In total, there are only 250 acres of farmland available to feed a population of 5 million people, and more than 90% of Singapore's food is imported. This leaves the country vulnerable to disruptions to food supply and increases in price.
>
> In 2009, a company called Sky Greens came up with the idea for a vertical farm that would produce vegetables all year round using minimal space, energy and water. Each A-shaped tower holds up to 26 tiers of plants, and the greenhouses in which they are housed provide protection for the plants from heavy monsoon rainfall.
>
> Singapore's climate is warm, which means that no energy is needed to heat the greenhouses. Rainwater is collected in overhead reservoirs and any run-off from the plants is filtered and reused. Water is used to rotate each tower to ensure that each plant receives the same amount of sunlight.

1.1   Using **Figure 1**, explain the advantages of vertical farming for Singapore.

....

....

....

....

....

....

....

[6]

1.2   Other than urban farming initiatives, describe **one** way in which farming can be made more sustainable.

....

....

....

[3]

1.3   For a lower income country (LIC) or newly emerging economy (NEE) you have studied, explain how a local farming scheme has made food supplies more sustainable.

....

....

....

....

....

[4]

[Total 13 marks]

Revision Summary

Well, that's it for <u>Resource Management</u> and <u>Food</u>. Remember, you only have to study <u>one</u> topic out of <u>Food</u>, <u>Water</u> and <u>Energy</u>, so the good news is that if you <u>haven't</u> studied Food, you only have half a page of questions to answer. The bad news is that after that, you need to keep on <u>reading</u>.

- Try these questions and <u>tick off each one</u> when you <u>get it right</u>.
- When you've done <u>all the questions</u> for a topic and are <u>completely happy</u> with it, tick off the topic.

Global Distribution of Resources (p.127) ☑

1) How might a lack of access to water affect the economic development of a country?
2) Give two ways that food is important to people's social well-being.
3) Give two ways that energy is important to people's economic well-being.
4) Which category of country consumes the most resources?

Resources in the UK (p.128-131) ☑

5) Describe how demand for seasonal food has changed in the UK.
6) Why has demand for organic food increased in the UK?
7) What are food miles?
8) Describe three ways that farming in the UK has changed.
9) True or false: the south east UK has a high demand for water.
10) True or false: demand for water in the UK is decreasing.
11) Why does water pollution need managing?
12) Give one solution to problems of water deficit.
13) How has the use of renewable energy sources in the UK changed since 1970?
14) Why has coal production in the UK declined?
15) Give two environmental issues caused by the exploitation of energy resources.

Food Demand, Supply and Insecurity (p.134-136) ☑

16) Give a definition of food security.
17) Explain why global food consumption is increasing.
18) Give two physical factors that affect the availability of food.
19) Explain how conflict can affect food security.
20) List five impacts of food insecurity.

Increasing Food Supplies (p.137-140) ☑

21) Explain how irrigation can increase food production.
22) What is hydroponics?
23) Give two ways that biotechnology can increase food production.
24) What is the new green revolution?
25) What is appropriate technology?
26) Describe the key features of a named large-scale agricultural development.
27) Describe three different methods of sustainable farming.
28) Give three ways that changing consumption can help make food supplies more sustainable.
29) a) Give an example of a local scheme to increase sustainable food supply in an LIC or NEE.
    b) Explain why the scheme is needed.

Global Demand for Water

The <u>availability</u> of water <u>varies</u> from place to place and the world keeps requiring <u>more</u> and <u>more</u>...

Water Insecurity is **Not** Having Enough **Clean Water**

1) <u>Water security</u> means having a <u>reliable</u> and <u>sustainable</u> source of enough <u>good quality water</u> to meet <u>everyone's needs</u> — for industry, agriculture and personal health.

2) <u>Water security</u> depends on the <u>amount</u> of water available (e.g. from rainfall, rivers, groundwater etc.) and the <u>number of people</u> who need to use the water. It also depends on being able to <u>access the water</u> — which can be hard if you're <u>poor</u>.

3) Having <u>more water</u> than is needed is known as a <u>water surplus</u>. When there's not <u>enough water</u> to meet people's needs it's called a <u>water deficit</u>.

4) A water deficit can lead to <u>water insecurity</u> — when there's <u>not enough clean water</u> to keep everyone <u>healthy</u>, or enable them to make a <u>living</u> (e.g. to water their crops, provide energy etc.).

5) When <u>demand</u> for water <u>exceeds supply</u> during a certain period, or when water is not of high enough <u>quality</u> to use, places are said to experience <u>water stress</u>.

Global Patterns of Water **Security** and **Insecurity Vary**

This map shows the <u>global patterns</u> of water <u>insecurity</u>. A <u>high percentage</u> means that there are <u>more people</u> competing for <u>less water</u> — causing <u>water stress</u>.

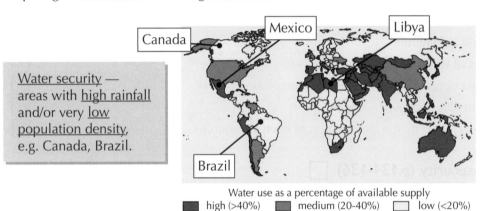

Water security — areas with <u>high rainfall</u> and/or very <u>low population density</u>, e.g. Canada, Brazil.

Water insecurity — areas with <u>low rainfall</u> and/or <u>high population density</u>, e.g. Libya, Mexico.

Water use as a percentage of available supply
high (>40%)   medium (20-40%)   low (<20%)

Water Demand is **Rising** because there are **More People** with **More Money**

The <u>global demand</u> for water is <u>rising</u> for two main reasons:

1 Rising population

1) Global <u>population</u> is <u>increasing</u> — each person needs water for <u>drinking</u>, <u>washing</u>, <u>preparing food</u> etc.

2) <u>More people</u> also means that <u>more food</u> needs to be grown — <u>irrigation</u> for agriculture uses <u>70%</u> of the world's freshwater resources.

2 Economic development

The world is becoming <u>increasingly developed</u>.

1) <u>Industrialisation</u> — as countries become more developed, they <u>produce</u> more goods. <u>Manufacturing</u> uses <u>a lot of water</u>.

2) <u>Energy production</u> — <u>15%</u> of all water withdrawn globally is used to produce energy, e.g. in cooling thermal power plants.

3) <u>Rising living standards</u> — as countries develop, people's <u>wealth increases</u> and they can afford a <u>higher standard of living</u>. This <u>increases water use</u>, as more people can afford flushing toilets, showers, dishwashers, etc.

Make sure you understand all these terms

Test yourself on these definitions before you move on — knowing them will help you with the rest of the topic. You need to know the global patterns of water security too, so take a good look at the map.

Water Insecurity

Loads of <u>factors</u> come together to <u>cause</u> water insecurity. Here are the ones you need to <u>know</u> about...

Water Availability is Affected by Many Factors

<u>Water availability</u> isn't just about how much <u>rainfall</u> you get — there are a load of <u>other factors</u> that affect it too.

Physical Factors

1) <u>Climate</u> — most places rely on <u>rainfall</u>, which feeds <u>lakes</u> and <u>rivers</u>, for their <u>water supply</u>. If climates are <u>hot</u>, lots of water is also lost from lakes and rivers due to <u>evaporation</u>. <u>Climate change</u> is altering the <u>total amount</u> of rainfall in places, as well as <u>how often</u> it rains and <u>how heavy</u> it is. Many <u>dry areas</u> are getting <u>drier</u>, increasing the <u>risk</u> of <u>droughts</u>.

2) <u>Geology</u> — when rain falls on <u>impermeable rock</u>, e.g. clay, it can't soak in, so <u>flows off</u> into <u>rivers</u> and <u>lakes</u>. These are <u>easy</u> to get water from. When rain falls on <u>permeable rock</u>, e.g. sandstone, it <u>flows down</u> through them and can form <u>underground water stores</u> (aquifers), which are <u>harder</u> to get to. However, <u>groundwater</u> can make <u>water available</u> in very <u>dry</u> places, e.g. the Sahara desert.

Economic and Social Factors

1) <u>Over-abstraction</u> is when <u>more water</u> is being used than is being <u>replaced</u>. It is caused by:
   - <u>Population growth</u> and <u>economic development</u> (see previous page).
   - <u>Improvements</u> in <u>sanitation</u> and <u>personal hygiene</u> — e.g. people take more frequent showers.
   - <u>High demand</u> from <u>businesses</u> — tourism and recreation can put <u>water stress</u> on places during peak holiday seasons, e.g. keeping golf courses in arid regions green.

2) The <u>pollution</u> of water sources, e.g. rivers, lakes and groundwater, reduces the amount of <u>clean water</u> that is <u>available</u>. Water pollution is a major problem in <u>rapidly industrialising countries</u>, where a lot of <u>industrial waste</u> is dumped into rivers without being <u>treated</u>. Human and animal <u>waste</u> are a <u>hazard</u> where people <u>share water sources</u> with animals and don't have access to sanitation.

3) <u>Limited infrastructure</u> — <u>rapid urbanisation</u> means that <u>water pipes</u> and <u>sewers</u> can't be built <u>quickly enough</u> to supply the population and prevent sewage from <u>contaminating</u> the supply.

4) <u>Poverty</u> — water providers charge a <u>fee</u> for <u>supplying water</u> to homes. People who are <u>too poor</u> to pay for it have to find <u>other sources</u> of water, which may not be treated to make them <u>safe</u> to drink.

Water Insecurity Can Have a Wide Range of Impacts

<u>Water insecurity</u> leads to lots of <u>problems</u>. For example:

1) <u>Pollution and disease</u> — where water is scarce, supplies of <u>drinking water</u> can become polluted by <u>sewage</u>, <u>industrial chemicals</u> or <u>nitrogen</u> from <u>fertilisers</u>. Some diseases, e.g. <u>cholera</u> and <u>typhoid</u>, are caused by <u>microorganisms</u> that are <u>passed on</u> through water <u>containing</u> untreated <u>sewage</u>. Without access to <u>alternative</u> water supplies, people may be <u>forced</u> to drink <u>polluted water</u>, which can cause <u>death</u> or <u>disease</u>.

2) <u>Food production</u> — <u>irrigation</u> for <u>agriculture</u> uses a lot of water. A shortage of water means that <u>less food</u> can be grown, which could lead to <u>starvation</u>.

3) <u>Industrial output</u> — <u>manufacturing</u> industries are hugely water-intensive so they can't <u>produce as much</u> during <u>water shortages</u>, reducing people's <u>wages</u> and affecting the <u>economy</u> of the country.

4) <u>Conflict</u> — when areas of water insecurity <u>share</u> the <u>same water supplies</u>, e.g. a <u>river</u> or an <u>aquifer</u>, water shortages can trigger <u>conflicts</u>. For example, if one country tries to <u>improve</u> its water security by taking <u>more water</u> from a <u>river</u>, it can <u>reduce</u> the water security of countries <u>downstream</u>.

Learn the causes and impacts of water insecurity

In the exam, you might be asked to identify the causes or impacts of water insecurity from a photo or a diagram — it'll be much easier to spot them if you know what you're looking for, so learn them...

Increasing Water Supply

There are some pretty <u>large-scale technological solutions</u> that can <u>improve water supply</u>...

Water Supplies Can be **Increased**

1) Water is often not <u>where</u> it is most <u>needed</u>. <u>Water diversion schemes</u> transfer water from areas of <u>surplus</u> to areas of <u>deficit</u>.

2) <u>Seasonal variations</u> in rainfall or <u>unpredictable</u> rainfall can cause a <u>water deficit</u> at certain points during the year. One way of coping with this problem is by <u>increasing storage</u>. Rainfall can be <u>stored</u> in large <u>tanks</u> or <u>trapped</u> in <u>reservoirs</u> (see below). This means that there can be a <u>reliable</u> source of water <u>all year round</u>.

Water Transfer

1) <u>Water transfers</u> are <u>large-scale engineering projects</u> that move water from a river that has <u>surplus</u> water to a river that has a water <u>shortage</u>.

2) The water is usually transferred in <u>canals</u> and <u>pipes</u>, but the original river channel can also be <u>dredged</u> (deepened) to improve water flow.

3) Water transfer has the potential to reduce water insecurity in the <u>receiving basin</u> but can cause massive <u>environmental</u>, <u>social</u> and <u>economic</u> problems (see page 148).

Dams and Reservoirs

1) Building a dam across a river <u>traps</u> a large amount of water behind the dam, creating a <u>reservoir</u>.

2) During times of water <u>surplus</u> the <u>reservoir</u> will be <u>filled</u>. The water can then be <u>released</u> when there's a water <u>deficit</u>. This means that there can be a <u>consistent</u> flow of water in the river <u>all year round</u>.

3) Water <u>transfer</u> from reservoirs is usually along <u>pipelines</u>, but it can involve building <u>tunnels</u>, <u>aqueducts</u> and <u>pumping stations</u>. These are <u>expensive</u> to construct and maintain.

4) E.g. most of <u>Birmingham's</u> water supply comes from the Elan valley in <u>mid-Wales</u>, where a series of dams and reservoirs provide a continuous supply for the city.

5) Reservoirs can cause <u>conflict</u> because they <u>flood</u> agricultural land. They may also <u>drown settlements</u> so people are forced to <u>move</u> and find new <u>jobs</u>.

Desalination allows Seawater to be Used as a Water Source

1) <u>Desalination</u> is the removal of <u>salt</u> from <u>seawater</u> so that it can be <u>used</u>. There are two main processes that are used — either the seawater can be <u>heated</u> to <u>evaporate</u> it and then <u>condensed</u> to collect the freshwater or the seawater can be passed through a <u>special membrane</u> to remove the salt.

2) It is <u>expensive</u> because <u>energy</u> is needed to <u>heat</u> the water or to <u>force</u> it through the membrane. Most plants are also powered by <u>fossil fuels</u>, though Saudi Arabia is building the world's first <u>large scale</u>, <u>solar powered</u> desalination plant.

3) In the <u>UK</u>, desalination is mainly used during <u>droughts</u>, rather than being the <u>main source of water</u>. E.g. London has a <u>desalination plant</u> on the banks of the River Thames. It can <u>supply</u> enough water for 400 000 homes in times of <u>water shortage</u>.

4) However, <u>wealthy desert countries</u> often use desalination as their main source of clean, drinking water. <u>Dubai</u> supplies <u>98.8%</u> of its water through desalination. It has the <u>largest supply plant</u> in the region, which can produce <u>140 million gallons</u> of desalinated water every day.

5) Desalination plants in countries that are more dependent on them, have developed more <u>efficient technology</u>, e.g. Dubai's new plant is <u>82% efficient</u> compared to about 45% for plants in Europe.

Water transfer moves water from an area of surplus to an area of deficit

You need to be able to describe some of the strategies to increase water supply in the exams, so get revising. Remember, large-scale schemes like these often cost a lot of money and come with social and environmental costs.

Sustainable Water Supply

Massive engineering works aren't always the answer to water insecurity. We can all do our bit to make sure that we use water resources sustainably, to help make sure that there's enough for everyone.

Sustainable Water Supplies — Use Less and Re-Use More

Water needs to be used more sustainably to make sure there is enough to meet everyone's current needs without preventing future generations from meeting their needs.

Water Conservation

Water conservation is about trying to use less water. For example by:

1) Fixing leaking reservoirs, pipes and dripping taps to stop water being wasted.

2) Fitting dual-flush toilets, as they use less water, or using devices in the cistern (the toilet water tank) that can save up to 3.5 litres of water for every flush.

3) Buying efficient washing machines and dishwashers and only running them with full loads.

4) Irrigating farmland using drip pipes and sprays that direct the water exactly where it is needed, so use less water than traditional irrigation channels and ditches.

5) Fitting homes and businesses with water meters. Charging for metered water makes people more aware of how much they use are using, so are more likely to reduce their usage.

6) Educating people to take shorter showers and turn off taps when not in use.

Groundwater Management

1) The amount of groundwater being extracted can be monitored to ensure it is not extracted faster than it is naturally replaced. Laws can be passed to prevent too much groundwater being extracted.

2) To prevent pollution of groundwater making it unusable, farmers can be encouraged to apply less artificial fertiliser and pesticides to farmland and companies that leak toxic industrial waste can be fined.

3) When groundwater supplies are shared between countries, international agreements are needed to make sure one country doesn't take an unsustainable amount of water from the aquifer, leaving other countries unable to meet the needs of their population. Agreeing how much water each country should take from the aquifer can be very difficult.

Recycling and 'Grey' Water

1) Recycling water means taking water that has already been used and using it again rather than returning it to a river or the sea straight away. This makes water use more sustainable because less water needs to be extracted from rivers or from groundwater to meet people's needs.

2) Water from homes and industries can be piped to water treatment plants where it is treated to make it safe enough to reuse.

3) Most recycled water is used for irrigation, industry, power plants and toilet flushing, though it can also be treated enough to make it safe to drink.

4) 'Grey' water is a type of recycled water — it is usually reused immediately rather than being treated first. It is mostly waste water from peoples homes, e.g. from washing machines, showers, or sinks. (It doesn't include water from toilets though, as this water is contaminated.)

5) Because it is relatively clean, it can be safely used for irrigating gardens or farmland, washing cars and flushing toilets. It's not safe for washing hands or drinking though.

6) These methods have the benefit of also conserving energy, as less energy is needed for treating water unnecessarily.

Water needs to be managed sustainably

As you've probably figured out by now, sustainability is a bit of a buzz word. Remember, sustainable solutions are often quite cheap and can be done on a local scale. Study these water examples until you know them inside out.

Increasing Water Supply

Solutions to water insecurity can be a <u>large scale</u> and expensive, or <u>local</u> and <u>sustainable</u>.

China is Transferring Water from the Wetter South to the Drier North

To cope with water insecurity, the Chinese government has planned a <u>$62 billion project</u> that will transfer <u>44.8 billion cubic litres</u> of water <u>every year</u> from the <u>south</u> to the <u>north</u> of the country. <u>Two</u> out of <u>three</u> planned routes have been <u>completed</u> — the <u>Central</u> and <u>Eastern Routes</u>.

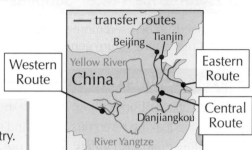

The water transfer project has <u>advantages</u>:

1) It provides water to the people in the cities of <u>Beijing</u> and <u>Tianjin</u>.
2) It allows <u>industry</u> to continue to <u>develop</u>, bringing <u>wealth</u> to the country.
3) It provides <u>water</u> for <u>irrigating farmland</u> so crops can be grown.

However, the project has lots of <u>disadvantages</u>:

1) Large areas have been <u>flooded</u>, destroying natural <u>habitats</u>.
   The huge <u>construction works</u> are <u>damaging</u> fragile <u>ecosystems</u>.
2) Raising the <u>dam</u> of the Danjiangkou Reservoir <u>flooded</u> productive <u>farmland</u> and forced <u>345 000 people</u> to <u>move</u>. Most of them now have <u>less land</u> and <u>poorly built housing</u>. Many received <u>little compensation</u> and are now <u>unemployed</u>.
3) The water it supplies to Beijing is <u>very expensive</u> for consumers as the project has <u>cost so much</u>. The project only supplies <u>urban areas</u> and those who can <u>afford it</u> — the <u>urban poor</u> and many people in <u>rural areas</u> have <u>no access</u> to the diverted water.
4) <u>Water stress</u> in the <u>south</u> will <u>increase</u>, because so much water is diverted. During severe <u>droughts</u>, there won't be enough <u>drinking</u> or <u>irrigation</u> water for <u>30 million</u> local people. E.g. a drought in 2010-2011 significantly <u>reduced</u> China's <u>wheat yields</u>.

Kenya is Using Sand Dams to Create a Sustainable Water Supply

Kenya is an LIC with a <u>hot, dry</u> climate. Most rain falls in just a <u>few heavy downpours</u> each year. Most <u>rivers</u> only flow during the <u>rainy season</u> — during the <u>dry season</u> the water <u>evaporates</u>. It is difficult for rural communities to <u>store</u> water for <u>future</u> use. People in Kenya's <u>Machakos District</u> have been helped to build <u>sand dams</u>, which now give them access to water <u>all year round</u>:

1) A <u>low dam</u> (about 1 m high) is built across the river.
2) During the <u>rainy season</u>, when water is <u>flowing</u> in the river, <u>coarse</u> material (e.g. sand) is <u>trapped</u> behind the dam.
3) <u>Water</u> gets <u>trapped</u> between the sand particles (about a <u>third</u> of what is trapped behind the dam is actually water).
4) The <u>sand</u> prevents the water from being <u>evaporated</u> by the hot sun during the <u>dry season</u>.
5) When the river <u>stops flowing</u>, water can be <u>extracted</u> from the sand by digging a <u>well</u>, <u>piping</u> the water through the dam to a <u>tap</u> or simply <u>digging holes</u> and scooping out the water.
6) The dams are <u>cheap</u> to build, use <u>local materials</u> and don't require much <u>maintenance</u>.
7) The <u>height</u> of the dam can be <u>raised</u> each year to trap <u>more sand</u>, and <u>more water</u>.

Make sure you learn two examples of increasing water supply

You need to know an example of a water transfer scheme and an example of a scheme to increase water supply in an LIC or NEE — make sure you know the ins and outs of both so you can produce a top answer in the exam.

Worked Exam Questions

These worked answers show you the kind of answers you should be writing in the exam.

1 Study **Figure 1**, which shows population density in Huffland and average monthly rainfall at two settlements in the region.

Figure 1

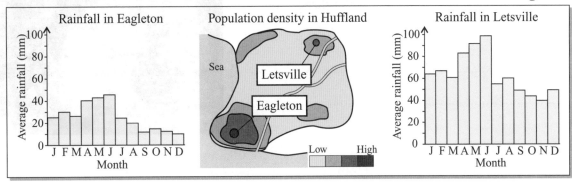

1.1 Using **Figure 1**, describe the amount and pattern of rainfall at Eagleton.

Rainfall is relatively low all year round (less than 50 mm on average per month). Rainfall generally increases between January and June and is at its lowest levels between July and December.

[2]

1.2 Using **Figure 1**, explain why a water transfer scheme might be necessary in Huffland.

In Eagleton the population density is high but rainfall is low, so there is likely to be a water deficit. In Letsville the population density is lower and rainfall is higher, so it's likely to have a water surplus that could be transferred to Eagleton.

[2]

1.3 Other than water transfer, describe **one** large-scale way of increasing water supply and explain how it could help make water supply in Eagleton more reliable.

Desalination could be used to remove salt from seawater so that it can be used. The seawater can either be heated to evaporate it and then condensed to collect the freshwater, or passed through a membrane to remove the salt. This could be used to provide a reliable supply of water all year round.

[3]

1.4 Using an example of a local scheme from an LIC or NEE, explain how water supply has been made more sustainable.

Water supply in Kenya is irregular because most rivers only flow during the rainy season. In the Machakos District, low dams have been built across rivers. During the rainy season, these dams trap coarse material such as sand. Water is trapped between particles, so it doesn't evaporate when the river stops flowing. During times of water shortage, water can be extracted from the sand. The stored water is replenished during each rainy season, and the dams can be raised to trap more sand and water. This means they will continue to provide water in the future, making water supply sustainable.

[6]

[Total 13 marks]

Exam Questions

1   Study **Figure 1**, a photo showing children
        collecting water in Kenya, Africa.

Figure 1

1.1   Give **one** piece of evidence from **Figure 1** that
        indicates that this is an area of water insecurity.

        ....

        ....

        ....
        [1]

1.2   Using **Figure 1** and your own knowledge, give
        one physical factor and explain how it may limit water availability in this region.

        ....

        ....

        ....
        [2]

1.3   Describe **two** human factors that can affect the availability of water.

        Factor 1:..

        ....

        Factor 2:..

        ....
        [2]

1.4   Using **Figure 1**, suggest **one** impact of water insecurity on the people in this community.

        ....

        ....
        [1]

1.5   Outline **one** possible effect of water insecurity on industry.

        ....

        ....

        ....
        [2]

1.6   Explain how water insecurity could lead to conflict.

        ....

        ....

        ....
        [2]

        [Total 10 marks]

Global Demand for Energy

Energy is a pretty important resource — it's needed for lighting and heating homes, cooking, producing goods and so on. But some countries have a better energy supply than others...

Energy Security Depends on Energy **Production** and **Consumption**

1) Energy security means having a reliable, uninterrupted and affordable supply of energy available.

2) It depends on the supplies available (either produced or imported), the size of the population, and the amount of energy that a typical person uses.

3) Producing more energy than is required by the population is an energy surplus (this can then be exported to other countries). Having too little energy to meet people's needs is a deficit.

Global **Energy Production** is **Unevenly Distributed**

The map below shows the total amount of energy produced, per country, in 2012.

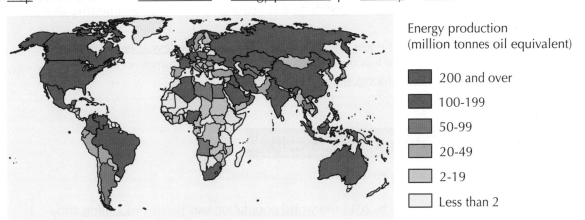

Energy production
(million tonnes oil equivalent)

- 200 and over
- 100-199
- 50-99
- 20-49
- 2-19
- Less than 2

1) Some countries produce lots of energy because they have large energy reserves and the money to exploit them. For example:

- Iran, Saudi Arabia — large oil reserves.
- China, Australia — large coal reserves.
- UK, Russia — large oil and gas reserves.

2) Some countries produce little energy because they have few resources or are unable to exploit their resources due to lack of money or political instability.

- Sudan — politically unstable and little money.
- Ireland — few resources that can be exploited.

Energy insecurity is not having a reliable source of energy

You don't have to learn every detail of the map but have a good look just in case you have to describe the global patterns of energy production. Having a few example countries up your sleeve won't hurt either.

Global Demand for Energy

It's not just energy <u>production</u> that <u>varies</u> across the world — energy <u>consumption</u> does too.
And the <u>demand</u> for <u>energy</u> just keeps <u>increasing</u> as people get <u>wealthier</u>...

Global **Energy Consumption** is also **Unevenly Distributed**

The map below shows the <u>energy consumption per person</u> across the world in 2014.

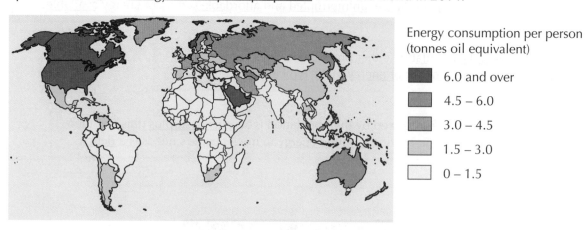

Energy consumption per person
(tonnes oil equivalent)

- ■ 6.0 and over
- ■ 4.5 – 6.0
- ■ 3.0 – 4.5
- ■ 1.5 – 3.0
- □ 0 – 1.5

There's a <u>strong relationship</u> between <u>wealth</u> and <u>energy consumption</u>:

1) <u>Wealthy</u>, <u>developed</u> countries tend to consume <u>lots of energy</u> per person because they <u>can afford to</u>. <u>Most people</u> in these countries have <u>access</u> to <u>electricity</u> and <u>heating</u>, and use <u>energy-intensive devices</u> like cars. E.g. <u>Australia</u>, <u>Sweden</u>, <u>USA</u>.

2) <u>Poorer</u>, <u>less developed</u> countries consume <u>less energy</u> per person as they are <u>less able to afford it</u>. <u>Less energy</u> is <u>available</u> and lifestyles are less dependent on high energy consumption than in wealthier countries. E.g. <u>Burkina Faso</u>, <u>Mongolia</u>.

The **Global Demand** for **Energy** is **Increasing**

There are <u>three main reasons</u> why the global demand for energy is increasing:

1) The world's population is increasing — in <u>2011</u> the <u>world population</u> was just over <u>7 billion</u> and it's <u>projected</u> to increase to <u>over 9 billion</u> in <u>2040</u> — <u>more people</u> means <u>more energy</u> is needed.

2) Recent <u>economic development</u> has <u>increased the wealth</u> of some poorer countries so people are <u>buying more things</u>. A lot of these things <u>use energy</u>, e.g. <u>cars</u>, <u>fridges</u> and <u>televisions</u>.

3) <u>Technological advances</u> have created loads of <u>new devices</u> that all <u>need energy</u>, e.g. <u>computers</u>, <u>mobile phones</u> and <u>tablets</u>. These are becoming <u>more popular</u> so <u>more energy</u> is needed.

Energy consumption increases as people get wealthier

Countries that consume lots of energy don't necessarily produce a lot of energy — they often rely on imports, which are expensive. Make sure you know the reasons for the increasing energy demand across the world.

Energy Supply

You may remember from page 151 that <u>energy supply varies</u> across the world — well, here's <u>why</u>...

Energy Supply is Affected by **Many Factors**

Physical Factors

1) There is <u>unequal distribution</u> of <u>fossil fuels</u> (oil, gas and coal) in the world, so some countries have <u>fewer resources</u> than others and some resources are <u>harder</u> to access, e.g. Antarctic oil reserves.

2) Fossil fuels are <u>non-renewable</u> so supplies will <u>run out</u> eventually.

3) Variations in <u>climate</u> and <u>geography</u> affect the potential for use of <u>solar</u>, <u>wind power</u>, <u>hydroelectric power</u>, <u>wave</u> and <u>tidal power</u>.

4) The likelihood of <u>natural disasters</u> that could <u>damage energy infrastructure</u> affects what energy sources can be developed and used.

Technological Factors

Some countries are <u>not able</u> to <u>exploit</u> their energy resources as the <u>technology</u> required is <u>unavailable</u> or too <u>expensive</u>:

1) <u>Niger</u> has large uranium reserves but does not have the <u>technology</u> to develop nuclear power plants.

2) Some <u>oil reserves</u> in the USA are <u>trapped</u> in <u>rocks</u> and do not <u>flow freely</u>.

Economic Factors

1) The non-renewable energy sources that are left in the world are becoming <u>increasingly difficult</u> to <u>reach</u>, so are <u>more costly</u> to <u>extract</u>.

2) The <u>prices</u> of fossil fuels such as oil and gas are <u>very volatile</u> — they can <u>vary</u> a great deal due to complex <u>economic</u> and <u>political</u> factors. Countries that <u>rely</u> on <u>energy imports</u> might <u>not</u> always be able to <u>afford</u> them.

3) Some LICs may have <u>potential energy sources</u> but <u>cannot afford</u> to <u>exploit</u> them.

4) The <u>cost</u> of <u>building</u> new <u>energy infrastructure</u> (e.g. new nuclear power stations, wind farms, solar powered technology) can be <u>very high</u>.

Political Factors

1) <u>Wars</u> and <u>political instability</u> in countries with <u>large energy reserves</u> can affect their ability to <u>export</u> their <u>resources</u>, e.g. during the <u>Gulf War</u> (1990-1991) exports of <u>oil</u> from the <u>Middle East decreased</u>.

2) <u>Climate change</u> linked to burning <u>fossil fuels</u> (p.20-22) has resulted in <u>international agreements</u> (e.g. the <u>Kyoto Protocol</u> — see p.24) to reduce the amount of CO_2 emissions. In some countries, this means that they <u>can't burn fossil fuels</u> as much as they <u>used to</u>.

3) Concerns over the <u>safety</u> of <u>nuclear power</u> and nuclear <u>waste disposal</u> have resulted in <u>stricter regulations</u>. This means it's become <u>harder</u> to <u>build</u> nuclear power stations to generate <u>electricity</u>.

Energy Insecurity has a Range of **Impacts**

1) As fossil fuels get <u>used up</u>, reserves in <u>more difficult</u> and <u>environmentally sensitive</u> areas are exploited. This increases the <u>cost</u> of <u>producing energy</u> and <u>risks environmental damage</u>.

2) Demand for <u>cleaner</u> and <u>cheaper</u> energy sources increases demand for <u>biofuels</u>. Growing <u>crops</u> for biofuels has <u>negative impacts</u> on the <u>environment</u> and takes up <u>land</u> that could be used for <u>growing food</u>.

3) Energy shortages and higher energy costs <u>reduce industrial output</u> — factories have to <u>produce less</u> (e.g. by only using power at certain times) or <u>relocate</u> to somewhere with <u>better</u> energy security.

4) There is the <u>potential</u> for <u>political instability</u> or <u>conflict</u> between countries with an <u>energy surplus</u> and countries with an <u>energy deficit</u>, e.g. gas supplies from <u>Russia</u> to <u>Ukraine</u> and on to <u>Europe</u> have been <u>disrupted</u> several times due to <u>political conflict</u> between Russia and Ukraine.

Learn all the factors affecting energy supply

Be careful — political instability and conflict can be both a cause <u>and</u> an impact of energy insecurity. Get the details clear in your head so you don't get muddled up if you're asked about it in the exam.

Increasing Energy Supply

Finding ways to <u>increase energy supply</u> is <u>really important</u>, given all the problems on the previous page...

Renewable Energy Sources will Never Run Out

<u>Renewable energy</u> can be a good option for <u>increasing energy supply</u> — the sources <u>won't run out</u>, they produce <u>little</u> or <u>no waste products</u>, and generally requires <u>less maintenance</u> than non-renewable power stations.

There are <u>lots</u> of <u>renewable</u> energy sources — these are the ones you <u>need to know</u> about:

1) **BIOMASS** — <u>wood</u>, <u>plants</u> or <u>animal waste</u> burnt for <u>power</u> or used to <u>produce biofuels</u>. Simply burning biomass <u>doesn't</u> require much <u>technology</u>, so it's a good choice for <u>LICs</u>. But it's <u>only</u> renewable if the biomass used is <u>managed sustainably</u>.

2) **WIND** — turbines use the <u>energy of the wind</u> to <u>generate electricity</u>, either <u>on land</u> or <u>out at sea</u>, often in <u>large windfarms</u> with <u>lots</u> of turbines. There are <u>no</u> greenhouse gas emissions once the turbines have been built. Wind is <u>variable</u> though, so wind farms <u>can't generate</u> electricity <u>all the time</u>.

3) **SOLAR** — energy from the Sun is used to <u>heat water</u> and <u>solar cookers</u> or to generate <u>electricity</u> using <u>photovoltaic cells</u>. Solar cookers and water heaters can be a <u>cheap</u> source of heat energy for LICs, but the cells for generating electricity are <u>much more expensive</u>.

4) **HYDRO** — uses the <u>energy</u> of <u>falling water</u>. Water is <u>trapped</u> by a <u>dam</u> and allowed to <u>fall</u> through tunnels, where the pressure of the falling water turns turbines to generate electricity. Building dams for hydroelectric power can <u>destroy environments</u> and <u>communities</u>, and they may be <u>too expensive</u> for LICs.

5) **TIDAL** — <u>currents</u> or <u>changes in water level</u> caused by <u>tides</u> are used to turn turbines and generate electricity. It <u>can't generate</u> power <u>all day long</u>, but it can <u>reliably predicted</u> because tidal cycles are very <u>regular</u>.

6) **WAVE** — wind blowing across water makes <u>waves</u>, which <u>drive turbines</u> to <u>generate electricity</u>. The turbines are currently quite <u>expensive</u> and don't produce much energy in <u>calm conditions</u>.

7) **GEOTHERMAL** — water is <u>pumped</u> into the <u>ground</u>, where <u>heat</u> deep in the Earth's <u>crust</u> turns it into <u>steam</u>, which drives a <u>turbine</u> to <u>generate electricity</u>. The steam may be <u>piped</u> to <u>homes</u> for <u>hot water</u> and <u>heating</u>. It's a <u>cheap</u> source of energy to <u>set up</u>, but works <u>best</u> in <u>tectonically active</u> areas, which <u>not every country</u> has.

Non-renewable Energy Sources Will Run Out Eventually

<u>Fossil fuels</u> (coal, oil and natural gas) have traditionally supplied <u>most</u> of our <u>energy</u>, but the supply of fossil fuels will eventually <u>run out</u> or become <u>too difficult</u> to <u>extract</u>. The use of <u>nuclear energy</u> has been <u>increasing</u> since the 1950s but nuclear energy comes from <u>uranium</u>, which will eventually <u>run out</u> too.

However, there are ways that we can <u>increase energy supplies</u> from <u>non-renewable</u> sources:

1) **FOSSIL FUELS** — the <u>supply</u> of <u>fossil fuels</u> can be <u>increased</u> by <u>searching</u> for <u>new reserves</u> to exploit, or by exploiting reserves that have been <u>discovered</u> but <u>not yet used</u>. As technology <u>develops</u>, it has become <u>possible</u> to <u>extract resources</u> that were previously too <u>difficult</u> or <u>costly</u> to use, e.g. by fracking (see page 156).

2) **NUCLEAR** — <u>nuclear</u> power can be used to generate a <u>large</u> amount of <u>energy</u> from a <u>small</u> amount of <u>fuel</u>. However, nuclear power plants are <u>very expensive</u> to <u>build</u> and <u>decommission</u>, <u>nuclear waste</u> must be <u>safely stored</u> for <u>1000s of years</u> and <u>accidents</u> can be <u>catastrophic</u>. More energy can be extracted by improving the <u>efficiency</u> of reactors by developing <u>new technology</u>. New <u>breeder reactors</u> can also generate <u>more fuel</u> during the reaction — making nuclear energy more like a <u>renewable</u> energy source.

There are lots of strategies to increase energy supply

This stuff is a hot topic at the moment — turn on the news and there's likely to be something about fracking, wind farms or nuclear power stations. Examiners love relevant geographical topics, you know. Just sayin'...

Sustainable Energy

If we go on using <u>energy</u> as we are, <u>non-renewable</u> resources will soon <u>run out</u>. However, there are lots of ways that can help us use <u>less energy</u> and use it more <u>efficiently</u>, which you need to know about.

Sustainable Energy means Future Generations can Meet their Energy Needs

1) <u>Sustainable energy</u> provides energy <u>today</u> without preventing <u>future generations</u> from <u>meeting their energy needs</u>.

2) It's important because <u>demand</u> for <u>energy</u> is <u>increasing</u> as the world's <u>population</u> is <u>increasing</u>, but <u>non-renewable</u> energy resources (such as coal, oil and gas) are <u>running out</u>.

3) Humans need to find <u>new renewable energy sources</u> and use energy <u>more efficiently</u> so that future generations can meet their energy needs.

A Carbon Footprint is a Measure of Energy Use

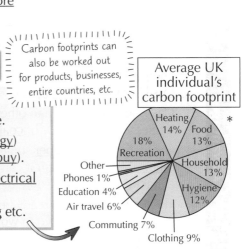

Carbon footprints can also be worked out for products, businesses, entire countries, etc.

Average UK individual's carbon footprint

1) A <u>carbon footprint</u> is a measure of the <u>amount</u> of greenhouse gases (<u>carbon dioxide</u> and <u>methane</u>) an individual's <u>activities</u> produce.

2) It includes <u>direct emissions</u> (those produced from things that <u>use energy</u>) as well as <u>indirect emissions</u> (those produced making things that we <u>buy</u>).

3) <u>Examples</u> of direct emissions include having the <u>heating</u> on, using <u>electrical appliances</u>, <u>commuting</u> and <u>air travel</u>. <u>Examples</u> of an individual's <u>indirect</u> emissions are those produced making their <u>food</u> and <u>clothing</u> etc.

Energy can be Conserved in Various Ways

There are <u>lots of ways</u> that <u>energy</u> use can be <u>reduced</u>:

Sustainable Design

<u>Homes</u>, <u>workplaces</u> and <u>transport</u> can be designed to use energy more sustainably, for example:

1) <u>Insulation</u> — by insulating <u>walls</u>, <u>roofs</u> and <u>floors</u>, less energy is required to <u>heat</u> homes and workplaces.

2) <u>Modern boilers</u> — new boilers are <u>more efficient</u> than older models, so will use <u>less energy</u> in homes and workplaces.

3) <u>Switching</u> to <u>electric</u> — electric cars, vans and trains are <u>more efficient</u> than <u>petrol</u> or <u>diesel</u> versions.

4) <u>Solar panels</u> can be fitted to the <u>roofs</u> of homes and workplaces providing <u>renewable</u>, <u>low-carbon</u> energy.

Increasing Efficiency

Doing the <u>same job</u> but using <u>less fuel conserves</u> energy:

1) <u>Hybrid</u> cars, vans and trains combine <u>diesel</u> and <u>electric</u> power to increase efficiency. E.g. <u>hybrid trains</u> between London and the south west will use <u>electricity when possible</u> and <u>diesel</u> when there are <u>no overhead electric wires</u>.

2) <u>Regenerative braking</u> — road vehicles and trains can be fitted with devices to <u>store</u> the <u>energy lost under braking</u> to be used <u>later</u> or return it to the national grid.

3) <u>Engine manufacturers</u> are making <u>more efficient engines</u> in response to <u>laws</u> and <u>rising fuel costs</u>.

4) <u>Power stations</u> are becoming more efficient by switching to <u>gas</u> and using <u>Gas Turbine Combined Cycle</u> technology.

Demand Reduction

<u>Demand reduction</u> can reduce the amount of electricity that needs to be <u>generated</u>:

1) <u>Demand</u> can be reduced by, e.g. encouraging people to <u>turn off</u> lights when they're not needed, boiling only the water <u>needed</u> and using <u>more efficient appliances</u>.

2) <u>Improving public transport</u> and <u>encouraging walking</u> or <u>cycling</u> reduces <u>demand</u> for <u>energy</u> used for <u>transport</u>.

Energy use can be made more sustainable — learn how

Lots to learn here but don't panic — you don't have to learn every detail of how energy can be conserved, but a few examples from each box would impress the examiners. Make sure you're clear on what sustainability is too.

*Pie chart based on the data from a study by the government-funded Carbon Trust.

Unit 2C — Energy

Increasing Energy Supply

In <u>high-income countries</u>, we're finding new and <u>more technologically advanced</u> ways of getting to the very <u>last reserves</u> of <u>fossil fuels</u>. In many other parts of the world, they're going in a <u>different direction</u> altogether...

Extracting Fossil Fuels has **Advantages** and **Disadvantages**

1) <u>Fracking</u> is a way of extracting <u>shale gas</u> — natural gas that is trapped underground in <u>shale rock</u>.

2) <u>Liquid</u> is <u>pumped</u> into the shale rock at <u>high pressure</u>. This causes the rock to <u>crack</u> (fracture), releasing the <u>gas</u>, which is then <u>collected</u> as it comes back out the well.

3) There are a range of advantages and disadvantages to fracking for shale gas:

Advantages

1) There appears to be <u>lots of shale gas</u> available in the UK. Fracking <u>increases</u> the <u>energy</u> <u>security</u> of the UK as supplies of other <u>fossil fuels</u> start <u>running out</u>.

2) <u>Gas</u> is <u>less polluting</u> than <u>other</u> fossil fuels. It releases <u>half</u> the CO_2 of <u>coal</u>.

3) Fracked gas is a <u>cheaper</u> source than <u>some</u> <u>renewables</u> — although it can cost <u>more</u> to extract than gas from some other sources.

4) The <u>technology</u> has already been <u>tested</u> (in the <u>USA</u>) and shown to <u>work</u>, unlike some <u>renewable</u> sources.

Disadvantages

1) Gas is not a <u>sustainable</u> energy source. It's <u>non-renewable</u>, and releases CO_2 when it's burned — contributing to <u>global warming</u>.

2) There's a risk of <u>pollution</u> of <u>groundwater</u>, <u>drinking water</u> and <u>air</u>.

3) It uses <u>lots</u> of <u>water</u> (a limited resource).

4) It's known to cause <u>small earthquakes</u>.

5) It's an issue that people feel <u>strongly</u> about. <u>Public opposition</u> has stopped it from being used yet in the UK.

6) Investment in fracking may <u>slow down</u> the investment in <u>renewable</u> energy.

Rice Husks are used to **Generate Sustainable Power** in **Bihar**

<u>Bihar</u> is a rural state in north-east India (an NEE). Around <u>85%</u> of people who live in Bihar are <u>not connected</u> to the <u>electricity grid</u>, particularly those in <u>rural areas</u>. Those that <u>are</u> connected often have an <u>unreliable supply</u>. In 2007, a scheme began to use <u>local biomass</u> (a <u>renewable</u> energy source) to supply homes in <u>rural</u> parts of <u>Bihar</u> with <u>electricity</u>. The scheme uses <u>rice husks</u> — a <u>waste product</u> from producing rice for <u>food</u>.

1) <u>Rice husks</u> are collected and used to generate <u>electricity</u> in <u>small</u>, <u>local power plants</u>. Each power plant has a <u>simple design</u> and contains a <u>rice husk gasifier</u>, <u>filters</u> to <u>clean</u> the gas, a <u>gas turbine</u>, a <u>generator</u> and a <u>distribution system</u> that can supply electricity to homes within a <u>1.5 km range</u>.

2) By 2015, <u>84</u> rice husk powered plants were <u>operating</u> in Bihar, supplying <u>electricity</u> to around <u>200 000 people</u>.

3) Producing electricity <u>locally</u> is very <u>efficient</u>, as the <u>energy sources</u> do not have to be <u>transported long distances</u> and the <u>electricity produced</u> does not need to be transferred over <u>long distances</u> to <u>homes</u>.

4) Providing electricity from <u>biomass</u> has reduced the need for <u>small diesel generators</u> and <u>kerosene lamps</u> in rural homes — and so <u>reduced</u> the use of <u>fossil fuels</u>.

5) As well as supplying <u>electricity</u>, the power plants provide <u>employment</u> for <u>local people</u>. They are <u>trained</u> in <u>management</u>, <u>operation</u> or <u>maintenance</u>. This keeps the scheme <u>sustainable</u> as it reduces <u>reliance</u> on <u>external organisations</u> and <u>expertise</u>.

6) The <u>government</u> now offers <u>financial support</u> to help <u>set up</u> biomass plants.

There are pros and cons to using fossil fuels for energy supply

You don't have to use these examples but you do need to be able to argue the case for and against the extraction of a fossil fuel and describe details of a local renewable scheme in an LIC or NEE.

Worked Exam Questions

Exams can be pretty scary, but the best preparation you can do is practise answering exam questions.
Read this page to get an idea of how to answer them, then turn over and have a go at the next lot yourself.

1   Study **Figure 1**, a map showing energy consumption per person in 2007 by country.

Figure 1

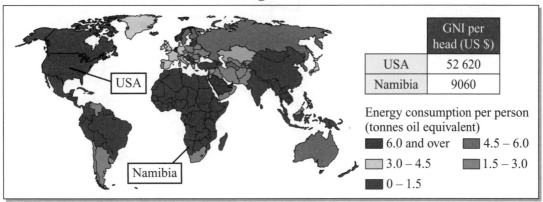

	GNI per head (US $)
USA	52 620
Namibia	9060

Energy consumption per person (tonnes oil equivalent)
- 6.0 and over
- 4.5 – 6.0
- 3.0 – 4.5
- 1.5 – 3.0
- 0 – 1.5

1.1   Using **Figure 1**, suggest one reason for the difference in energy consumption between the USA and Namibia.

> The USA has a much larger GNI per head than Namibia, so people
>
> there are likely to own more energy-intensive appliances.

You could also write that there is likely to be more industry in the USA than in Namibia, which uses lots of energy.

[2]

1.2   Explain what might happen to Namibia's energy consumption if its GNI per head increased.

> If Namibia's GNI per head increased, its energy consumption would also increase. Increased wealth
>
> means that people can afford to buy more goods, e.g. cars, fridges and televisions that use a lot of energy.

[3]

1.3   Using an example from a lower income country (LIC) or newly emerging economy (NEE), explain how a renewable energy supply is improving energy security and sustainability.

> The electricity supply in Bihar in north-east India is unreliable and around 85% of the population of
>
> are not even connected to it. However, a scheme was started in 2007 that uses rice husks (a waste
>
> product from producing rice for food) to generate electricity in small, local power plants. This is
>
> improving energy security in the area because the reliability of the energy supply is much better.
>
> Producing electricity locally is also very efficient, as the energy sources and electricity produced do not
>
> have to be transported long distances. Providing electricity from biomass has reduced the need for
>
> small diesel generators and kerosene lamps in rural homes, and so reduced the use of fossil fuels.
>
> This makes it more sustainable because biomass is a renewable resource. As well as supplying
>
> electricity, the power plants provide employment for local people, which keeps the scheme sustainable
>
> as it reduces reliance on external organisations and expertise.

[6]

[Total 11 marks]

Exam Questions

1 Study **Figure 1**, a map of Barmouth Bay, Wales.

Figure 1

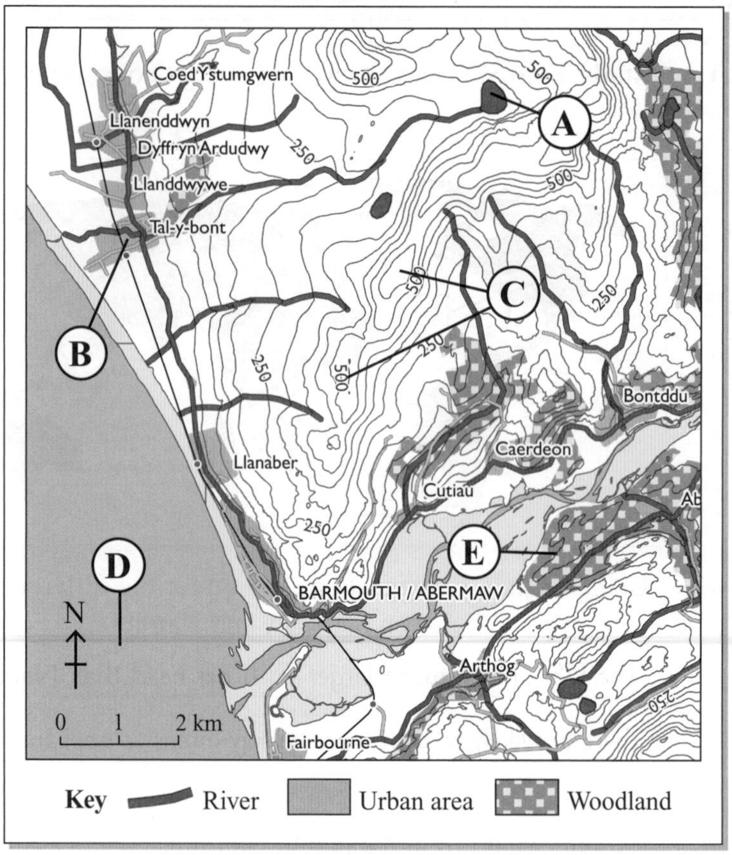

1.1 Which location, A-E, would be the best site for an onshore wind farm? Give one reason for your choice.

Location:.. *[1]*

Reason: ....

....

....

....

.... *[1]*

1.2 Suggest why location E is not suitable for a solar power plant.

....

....

....

.... *[2]*

1.3 Outline one advantage of using hydropower to increase energy supply.

....

.... *[1]*

1.4 Discuss the advantages and disadvantages of the extraction of a fossil fuel you have studied.

....

....

....

....

....

....

.... *[6]*

[Total 11 marks]

Revision Summary

You've reached the end of Unit 2C — remember, you only need to do <u>one</u> option from <u>Food</u>, <u>Water</u> and <u>Energy</u>. If you chose <u>Food</u>, then the revision summary questions you need are back on p.143, but if you're a <u>Water</u> or <u>Energy</u> sort of person, you've come to exactly the <u>right place</u>.

- Try these questions and <u>tick off each one</u> when you <u>get it right</u>.
- When you've done <u>all the questions</u> for a topic and are <u>completely happy</u> with it, tick off the topic.

Water Demand, Supply and Insecurity (p.144-145) ☑

1) Give a definition of water security.
2) Describe the global pattern of water insecurity.
3) Explain how economic development is increasing the demand for water.
4) Explain how geology can affect water availability.
5) Explain how pollution can lead to water insecurity.
6) Describe how water insecurity can affect food production.

Increasing Water Supply (p.146-148) ☑

7) Describe how dams and reservoirs increase water supply.
8) How might creating reservoirs lead to conflict?
9) Name the process by which seawater can be made suitable for drinking.
10) List six ways that water can be conserved.
11) Describe how managing groundwater can provide more sustainable water supplies.
12) a) What is 'grey' water?
    b) How is using 'grey' water sustainable?
13) a) Give an example of a large scale water transfer scheme.
    b) Give two advantages and two disadvantages of the scheme.

Energy Demand, Supply and Insecurity (p.151-153) ☑

14) Give a definition of energy insecurity.
15) Describe the global distribution of energy production.
16) Why is global energy consumption unevenly distributed?
17) Give three reasons why the global demand for energy is changing.
18) Give two physical, economic, political and technological factors that affect energy security.
19) What are the impacts of energy insecurity?

Increasing Energy Supply (p.154-156) ☑

20) Give seven renewable energy sources that could be used to increase energy supply.
21) Describe one way that the energy supply from non-renewable energy sources can be increased.
22) What does 'sustainable use of energy' mean?
23) What does a person's carbon footprint measure?
24) How can energy be conserved by sustainable design?
25) How can demand for energy be reduced?
26) Give examples of improvements in efficiency that have helped to conserve energy.
27) What is fracking?
28) a) Give a named example of local renewable energy scheme in an LIC or NEE.
    b) Explain why the scheme is needed.

Issue Evaluation

The <u>issue evaluation</u> makes up about <u>half</u> of the third exam you'll have to sit — here's what you need to know.

Issue Evaluation is All About Analysing and Interpreting Information

<u>Part A</u> of <u>Paper 3</u> is <u>issue evaluation</u>. You have to answer questions based on a <u>geographical issue</u>. But you get loads of information <u>in advance</u> to help you.

1) You'll be given a <u>resource booklet 12 weeks before the exam</u> to let you get your head round the topic. It will contain <u>loads</u> of <u>material</u> about a <u>geographical issue</u>:

- The issue could be based in the <u>UK</u> or <u>elsewhere</u> and could vary in scale from <u>local</u> to <u>international</u>.
- It might be about <u>physical</u> or <u>human</u> geography topics, or a <u>mix of the two</u>.
- It could cover <u>any</u> of the <u>compulsory content</u> you've studied during the course.
- It might extend into <u>new contexts</u> that you <u>haven't studied before</u>.

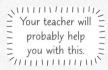
Your teacher will probably help you with this.

2) You need to study <u>all</u> the information <u>carefully</u>, work out <u>what it all means</u> and how it <u>fits together</u>.

3) In the <u>exam</u> you'll have to answer <u>questions</u> about the <u>issue</u>, using the <u>resources</u> you've been given, as well as your <u>existing knowledge</u> of Geography.

4) You'll also have to write a <u>longer answer</u> where you'll have to <u>make a decision</u> about something related to the issue you've been presented with, and <u>justify</u> that decision (see below).

There'll be Lots of Different Information Sources on the Resource Booklet

1) The booklet could include <u>several</u> different types of information, such as <u>maps</u>, <u>graphs</u>, <u>photographs</u>, <u>diagrams</u>, <u>statistics</u>, <u>newspaper articles</u> and <u>quotes</u> from people involved.

2) All the information will be <u>related</u> in some way — e.g. you might be given a <u>newspaper article</u> on a non-governmental organisation, <u>photos</u> of a city in an LIC and a <u>data table</u> about measures of development in that LIC.

3) The information you're given will give you some <u>clues</u> about the <u>type of questions</u> that might come up. E.g. if the booklet has a <u>table</u> of development indicators in <u>two</u> countries, it's <u>pretty likely</u> that you'll have to <u>compare them</u> in some way.

4) You <u>won't</u> be able to take your copy of the resource booklet <u>into the exam</u> with you — you'll get a <u>fresh</u>, <u>clean</u> copy. You can <u>write notes</u> about the topics covered on your copy of the booklet but you'll need to <u>learn</u> them for the exam.

Use All the Information to Form Opinions About the Issue

1) You'll be asked to <u>argue</u> a <u>point of view</u> using the <u>information</u>, e.g. <u>suggesting</u> how an area could best be <u>managed</u> to meet the needs of <u>everyone</u> involved. <u>There's no single right or wrong answer</u> — but you need to be able to <u>justify</u> your argument, so make sure you can use the <u>data</u> to <u>support it</u>.

2) <u>Whatever</u> your view is, you need to give a <u>balanced argument</u>. Try to think of potential <u>economic</u>, <u>political</u>, <u>social</u> and <u>environmental impacts</u> of the different sides of the argument, and how any <u>negative impacts</u> could be <u>reduced</u>.

3) It's likely to be a <u>complex issue</u> with <u>lots</u> of <u>different parties involved</u>. So think about <u>possible conflicts</u> that your solution might cause <u>between different groups</u> of people, or between <u>people</u> and the <u>environment</u>, and how they could be <u>resolved</u>.

REVISION TIP

Think about what questions might come up in the exam

You have 12 weeks to study your resource booklet and work out what might come up, so there's no excuse for not being prepared. Try writing some questions based on the material — and then try answering them.

Fieldwork

For your Geography GCSE you need to complete <u>two</u> bits of <u>fieldwork</u>, and you'll be asked about them in the exam.

You have to Write About **Two Geographical Enquiries** in the Exam

1) Fieldwork is <u>assessed</u> in the second part (<u>Part B</u>) of <u>Paper 3</u>. There's no assessed <u>coursework</u>, but you need to be able to <u>write about</u> fieldwork that you have done in the exam.

2) You need to have done at least one <u>human</u> and one <u>physical</u> geographical enquiry. You could be asked about <u>both</u> in the exam.

'Geographical enquiry' is just fancy exam-speak for fieldwork.

3) The fieldwork part of the exam is <u>split</u> into <u>two parts</u>:

- In one part you'll be asked about fieldwork techniques in <u>unfamiliar</u> situations. You might have to answer questions about <u>techniques</u> for <u>collecting data</u>, how to <u>present data</u> you've been given or how <u>useful</u> the <u>different techniques</u> are.

- In the other part you have to answer questions about <u>your investigation</u> — you might be asked about your <u>question</u> or <u>hypothesis</u>, <u>methods</u>, what <u>data</u> you <u>collected</u> and <u>why</u>, how you <u>presented</u> and <u>analysed</u> it, how you could <u>extend your research</u> and so on.

For **Each** of your **Enquiries**, You'll **Need to Know...**

1 Why You Chose Your Question

You'll need to explain <u>why</u> the question or hypothesis you chose is <u>suitable</u> for a <u>geographical enquiry</u>.

You'll also need to know the <u>geographical theory</u> behind your question.

Make sure you know what the <u>risks associated</u> with <u>collecting</u> your data were, how they were <u>reduced</u>, and why the <u>location</u> you chose was <u>suitable</u>.

2 How and Why You Collected Data

You need to <u>describe</u> and <u>justify</u> what data <u>you collected</u>. This includes whether it was <u>primary data</u> (data that you collected <u>yourself</u>) or <u>secondary</u> data (data that <u>someone else</u> collected and you <u>used</u>), <u>why</u> you collected or used it, <u>how</u> you <u>measured</u> it and <u>how</u> you <u>recorded</u> it.

3 How You Processed and Presented Your Data

The way you <u>presented</u> your data, and <u>why</u> you <u>chose</u> that option, could come up.

You'll need to <u>describe what you did</u>, <u>explain</u> why it was <u>appropriate</u>, and <u>how</u> you <u>adapted</u> your presentation method for <u>your data</u>.

You might also be asked for a <u>different way</u> you <u>could</u> have presented your data.

There's more on analysing, concluding and evaluating on the next two pages.

4 What Your Data Showed

You'll need to know:

- A <u>description</u> of your data.
- How you <u>analysed</u> your data.
- An <u>explanation</u> of your data.

This might include <u>links</u> between your <u>data sets</u>, the <u>statistical techniques</u> you used, and any <u>anomalies</u> (odd results) in the data that you spotted.

There's more on graphs and statistical techniques on pages 172-175.

5 The Conclusions You Reached

This means you'll need to <u>explain how</u> your data provides <u>evidence</u> to <u>answer</u> the <u>question</u> or <u>support</u> the <u>hypothesis</u> you set at the <u>beginning</u>.

6 What Went Well, What Could Have Gone Better

You might be asked to <u>evaluate</u> your fieldwork:

- Were there <u>problems</u> in your <u>data collection methods</u>?
- Were there <u>limitations</u> in your <u>data</u>?
- What <u>other data</u> would it have been <u>useful</u> to have?
- How <u>reliable</u> are your <u>conclusions</u>?

Plan your fieldwork before you start...

... but don't worry if it doesn't quite go to plan. It's more important that you can write about it and say why things went wrong. It does help if you at least attempt to make it work though — so have another read through the page.

Analysing and Concluding

Analysing your data and drawing conclusions from it can be pretty tricky — here's a summary of what you need to do, and there's some more help with analysing data on pages 172-175.

You need to Describe and Explain what the Data Shows

When you analyse data you need to:

Describe

1) Describe what the data shows — you need to describe any patterns and correlations (see pages 172-174) and look for any anomalies.

2) Make sure you use specific points from the data and reference what graph, table etc. you're talking about.

3) You might also need to make comparisons between different sets of data.

4) Statistical techniques (see page 175) help make the data more manageable, so it's easier to spot patterns and make comparisons.

Explain

1) Explain what the data shows — you need to explain why there are patterns and why different data sets are linked together.

2) Use your geographical knowledge to help you explain the results and remember to use geographical terms.

Here's an example:

> 38% of people who visited Cliffthorpe Valley in 2016 visited the tarn — 40 000 people (see Diagram 1). The tarn area may attract visitors due to its beauty and services such as a free car park, café and tourist information centre (see Leaflet 1). However, the largest amount of litter was found at the valley head (see Graph 1), which was the fourth most popular attraction (9.5% of visitors). There are fewer bins at the valley head, and more people tend to picnic there (see Table 1), which could be why there's more litter.

Conclusions are a Summary of the Results

A conclusion is a summary of what you found out in relation to the original question. It should include:

> Be careful when drawing conclusions. Some results show a link or correlation, but that doesn't mean that one thing causes the other.

1) A summary of what your results show.

2) An answer for the question you are investigating, and an explanation for why that is the answer.

3) An explanation of how your conclusion fits into the wider geographical world — think about how your conclusion and results could be used by other people or in further investigations.

You'll have to analyse your own data and data you're given

In the exam, you'll need to write about how you analysed your data and your conclusion, so make sure you have some points ready before you hit the exam. You might also be asked to analyse some data that you're given and draw conclusions from it — the more practice you get now, the easier that'll be.

Evaluating

Evaluating data is all about working out how <u>accurate</u> it is, and whether it lets you <u>answer</u> your research question. You also need to think about how your investigation could be <u>improved</u> if you were to do it again.

Evaluations Identify **Problems** in the Investigation

Evaluation is all about <u>self assessment</u> — looking back at how <u>good or bad</u> your study (or the data you are given in the exam) was. You need to be able to:

1) Identify any <u>problems</u> with the <u>methods</u> used and suggest how they could be <u>improved</u>. Think about things like the <u>size</u> of the <u>data sets</u>, if any <u>bias</u> (unfairness) slipped in and if <u>other methods</u> would have been <u>more appropriate</u> or <u>more effective</u>.

2) Describe how <u>accurate</u> the results are and <u>link</u> this to the methods used — say whether any <u>errors</u> in the methods affected the results.

3) Comment on the <u>validity</u> of your <u>conclusion</u>. You need to talk about how <u>problems</u> with the methods and the <u>accuracy</u> of the results affect the <u>validity</u> of the conclusion. Problems with methods lead to <u>less</u> reliable and accurate results, which affects the validity of the conclusion.

Accurate	**Reliable**	**Valid**
<u>Accurate</u> results are <u>as near</u> as possible to the <u>true answer</u> — they have <u>few errors</u>.	<u>Reliable</u> means that data can be <u>reproduced</u>.	<u>Valid</u> means that the data <u>answers</u> the <u>original question</u> and is <u>reliable</u>.

For example:

I <u>concluded</u> that the river <u>flowed faster</u> further <u>downstream</u>. However, one <u>problem</u> with my data collection method was that it was <u>difficult</u> to put the float in at <u>exactly</u> the <u>same point</u> each time. This <u>reduced</u> the <u>accuracy</u> of my measurements. To make my investigation <u>more accurate</u>, I could have placed a tape measure across the river to <u>mark the exact point</u> of entry. Another <u>problem</u> was that I only took <u>two readings</u> at each site and I only used <u>one upstream site</u> and <u>one downstream site</u>. To make my data <u>more reliable</u> I could have taken <u>more readings</u> at each site, and used a larger <u>number of sites</u> both upstream and downstream. These <u>improvements</u> would have produced a more <u>valid</u> conclusion.

Be critical of your results — if you think some are unreliable, then say so

You can do some preparation for this bit as you're going along. While you're collecting your data, think about whether your results would be different if you'd chosen a different day or time, or if you were in a different location. Explain how they'd be different, and why. And don't forget to discuss the validity of your conclusions.

Answering Questions

This section is filled with lots of <u>techniques</u> and <u>skills</u> that you need for your <u>exams</u>. It's no good learning the <u>content</u> of this book if you don't learn the skills you need to pass your exam too. First up, answering questions properly...

Make Sure you **Read the Question Properly**

It's dead easy to <u>misread</u> the question and spend five minutes writing about the <u>wrong thing</u>.
Four simple tips can help you <u>avoid</u> this:

1) Figure out if it's a <u>case study question</u> — if the question wording includes 'using <u>named examples</u>' or 'with reference to one <u>named</u> area' you need to include a case study or an example you've learnt about.

2) <u>Underline</u> the <u>command words</u> in the question (the ones that tell you <u>what to do</u>):

Answers to questions with 'explain' in them often include the word '<u>because</u>' (or '<u>due to</u>').

When writing about differences, '<u>whereas</u>' is a good word to use in your answers, e.g. 'HICs have a high level of development whereas LICs have a lower level'.

Command word	Means write about...
Describe	what it's <u>like</u>
Explain	<u>why</u> it's like that (i.e. give <u>reasons</u>)
Compare	the <u>similarities</u> AND <u>differences</u>
Discuss	give <u>both sides</u> of an argument
Suggest why	give <u>reasons</u> for
Outline	give <u>main</u> points

If a question asks you to describe a <u>pattern</u> (e.g. from a map or graph), make sure you identify the <u>general pattern</u>, then refer to any <u>anomalies</u> (things that <u>don't</u> fit the general pattern).

E.g. to answer 'describe the global distribution of volcanoes', <u>first</u> say that they're mostly on plate margins, <u>then</u> mention that a few aren't (e.g. in Hawaii).

3) <u>Underline</u> the <u>key words</u> (the ones that tell you what it's <u>about</u>), e.g. volcanoes, tourism, immigration, rural-urban fringe, development gap.

4) If the question says '<u>using Figure 2</u>', <u>make sure</u> you've talked about <u>what Figure 2 shows</u>. <u>Don't</u> just write out all of your <u>geographical knowledge</u> and forget all about the photo you're <u>supposed</u> to be <u>talking about</u>. <u>Re-read</u> the <u>question</u> and your <u>answer</u> when you've <u>finished</u>, just to check.

Some **Questions** are **Level Marked**

Questions worth <u>4 marks or more</u> with longer written answers are <u>level marked</u>, which means you need to do these <u>things</u> to get the <u>top level</u> and a <u>high mark</u>:

1) <u>Read</u> the question properly and figure out a <u>structure</u> for your answer before you start. Your answer needs to be well <u>organised</u> and <u>structured</u>, and written in a <u>logical</u> way.

2) If it's a <u>case study</u> question, include plenty of <u>relevant details</u>:

- This includes things like <u>place names</u>, <u>dates</u>, <u>statistics</u>, names of <u>organisations</u> or <u>companies</u>.
- Don't forget that they need to be <u>relevant</u> though — it's no good including the exact number of people killed in a flood when the question is about the <u>causes</u> of a flood.

3) <u>9 mark</u> questions sometimes have <u>3 extra marks</u> available for <u>spelling</u>, <u>punctuation</u> and <u>grammar</u>. To get <u>top marks</u> you need to:

- Make sure your <u>spelling</u>, <u>punctuation</u> and <u>grammar</u> are <u>consistently correct</u>.
- Write in a way that makes it <u>clear</u> what you mean.
- Use a <u>wide range</u> of <u>geographical terms</u> (e.g. sustainable development) <u>correctly</u>.

Answers to level marked questions should be well structured

It may all seem a bit simple to you, but it's really important to understand what you're being asked to do. This can be tricky — sometimes the differences between the meanings of the command words are quite subtle.

Labelling

These next few pages give you some advice on what to do for specific types of questions.
Some of these skills will be helpful for your fieldwork investigation too (see pages 161-163).

You Might have to Label Photos, Diagrams or Maps

If you're asked to label something:

1) Figure out from the question what the labels should do, e.g. describe the effects of an earthquake, label the characteristics of a waterfall, describe the coastal defences, etc.

2) Add at least as many labels as there are marks.

3) When describing the features talk about things like the size, shape and relief. Make sure you use the correct geographical names of any features, e.g. arête, wave cut platform, meander.

Q: Label the characteristics of this coastline

A:

Stack formed from a collapsed arch.

Some vegetation on top of the cliffs.

Arch caused by wave erosion (abrasion and hydraulic power).

Sandstone cliffs, easily eroded.

Cave

Cracks and weaknesses in the rock making it susceptible to erosion.

Q: Label the glacial landforms in the diagram below

A:

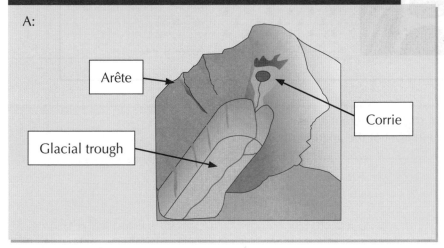

Arête

Corrie

Glacial trough

Read the question carefully

EXAM TIP — Check what the question is asking you to label — you might just have to write a name, or you might have to add a bit more detail. If you're just asked for a name, you won't get extra marks for writing more.

Comparing

In the exam, you could be given two resources you have to compare — not just describe.
Plans and photos are a popular choice, so here are some hints on how to go about it...

Look at Shapes When You Compare Plans and Photos

You might be given two items, like a plan and an aerial photograph, and be asked to use them together
to answer some questions. Plans and aerial photos are a bit like maps — they show places from above.
Here are some tips for questions that use plans and photos:

1) The plan and photo might not be the same way up.

2) Work out how the photo matches the plan — look for the main features on the plan like
a lake, a big road or something with an interesting shape, and find them on the photo.

3) Look at what's different between the plan and the
photo and think about why it might be different.

Example

Q: Look at the development plan for Crystal Bay (2000) and the photo
taken after development in 2009.
a) Name the area labelled A in the photo.
b) Give one difference you can see between the photo and the plan.

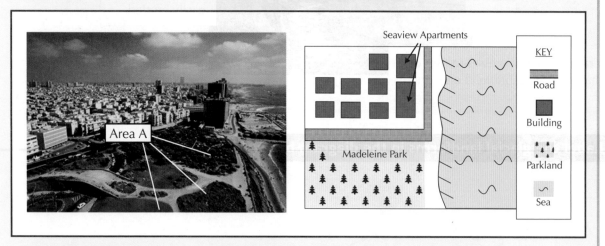

A: a) Madeleine Park
b) The roads have been built in slightly different areas.
There's a small harbour area in front of the apartments.

Look for obvious features to help you match up the plan and the photo
If you have to compare a plan and a photo in the exam, the key is to take your time, read the question
carefully and study the resources thoroughly so you know exactly what you should be doing.

Maps

Maps are a staple of most Geography exams, so make sure you know how to read them.

Latitude and Longitude are Used for Global Coordinates

1) The position of anywhere on Earth can be given using coordinates if you use latitude and longitude.

2) Lines of latitude run horizontally around the Earth. They measure how far north or south from the equator something is.

3) Lines of longitude run vertically around the Earth. They measure how far east or west from the Prime Meridian (a line of longitude running through Greenwich in London) something is.

4) Latitude and longitude are measured in degrees.

5) For example, the coordinates of London are 51° N, 0° W New York is at 40° N, 74° W.

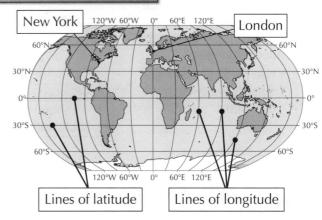

Describing Distributions on Maps — Describe the Pattern

1) In your exam you could get questions like, 'use the map to describe the distribution of volcanoes' and 'explain the distribution of deforestation'.

2) Describe the general pattern and any anomalies (things that don't fit the general pattern).

3) Make at least as many points as there are marks and use names of places and figures if they're given.

4) If you're asked to give a reason or explain, you need to describe the distribution first.

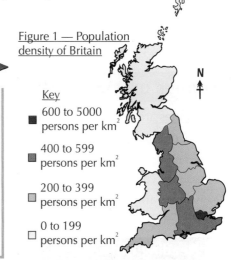

Figure 1 — Population density of Britain

Key
- 600 to 5000 persons per km²
- 400 to 599 persons per km²
- 200 to 399 persons per km²
- 0 to 199 persons per km²

Q: Use Figure 1 to explain the pattern of population density in Britain.

A: The London area has a very high population density (600 to 5000 per km²). There are also areas of high population density (400 to 599 per km²) in the south east, Midlands and north west of England. These areas include major cities (e.g. Birmingham and Manchester). More people live in and around cities because there are better services and more job opportunities than rural areas. Scotland and Wales have the lowest population densities in Britain (less than 199 per km²)...

Describing Locations on Maps — Include Details

You could be given two maps to use for one question — link information from the two maps together.

1) In your exam you could get a question like, 'describe the location of cities in ...'.

2) When you're asked about the location of something say where it is, what it's near and use compass points.

3) If you're asked to give a reason or explain, you need to describe the location first.

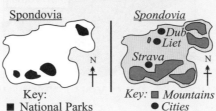

Q: Use the maps to describe the location of the National Parks.

Spondovia

Key:
■ National Parks

Spondovia
●Dub
●Liet
Strava

Key: ■ Mountains
● Cities

A: The National Parks are found in the south west and north east of Spondovia. They are all located in mountainous areas. Three of the parks are located near to the city of Strava.

Maps

Dot Maps Show Distribution and Quantity Using Identical Symbols...

1) Dot maps use identical dots to show how something is distributed across an area.

2) Use the key to find out what quantity each dot represents.

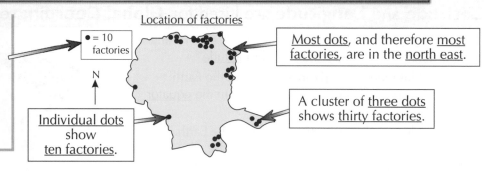

Location of factories

• = 10 factories

N

Individual dots show ten factories.

Most dots, and therefore most factories, are in the north east.

A cluster of three dots shows thirty factories.

...Proportional Symbol Maps use Symbols of Different Sizes

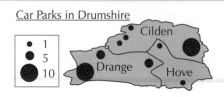

Car Parks in Drumshire

• 1
• 5
● 10

Cilden
Drange
Hove

1) Proportional symbol maps use symbols of different sizes to represent different quantities.

2) A key shows the quantity each different sized symbol represents. The bigger the symbol, the larger the amount.

3) The symbols might be circles, squares, semi-circles or bars, but a larger symbol always means a larger amount.

Q: Which area of Drumshire has the most car parks?

A: Drange, with 20.

Isolines on Maps Link up Places with Something in Common

1) Isolines are lines on a map linking up all the places where something's the same, for example:
   • Contour lines are isolines linking up places at the same altitude.
   • Isolines on a weather map (called isobars) link together all the places where the pressure's the same.

2) Isolines can be used to link up lots of things, e.g. average temperature, wind speed or rainfall.

3) Isolines are normally labelled with their value. The closer together the lines are, the steeper the gradient (how quickly the thing is changing) at that point.

① Reading Isoline Maps

1) Find the place you're interested in on the map and if it's on a line just read off the value.

2) If it's between two lines, you have to estimate the value.

Q: Find the average annual rainfall in Port Portia and on Mt. Mavis.

A: Port Portia is between the lines for 200 mm and 400 mm so the rainfall is likely to be around 300 mm per year. Mt. Mavis is on an isoline so the rainfall is 1000 mm per year.

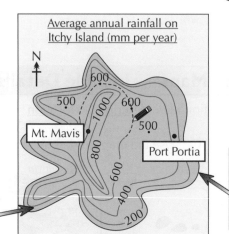

Average annual rainfall on Itchy Island (mm per year)

N

600
500
1000
600
800
500
Mt. Mavis
Port Portia
600
400
200

② Completing Isoline Maps

1) Drawing an isoline's like doing a dot-to-dot — you just join up all the dots with the same numbers.

2) Make sure you don't cross any other isolines though.

Q: Complete on the map the isoline showing an average rainfall of 600 mm per year.

A: See the red line on the map.

Maps

Choropleth Maps show How Something Varies Between Different Areas

1) <u>Choropleth maps</u> show how something varies between different areas using <u>colours</u> or <u>patterns</u>.

2) The maps in exams often use <u>cross-hatched lines</u> and <u>dot patterns</u>.

3) If you're asked to talk about all the parts of the map with a certain <u>value</u> or <u>characteristic</u>, look at the map carefully and put a <u>big tick</u> on all the parts with the <u>pattern</u> that <u>matches</u> what you're looking for. This makes them all <u>stand out</u>.

4) When you're asked to <u>complete</u> part of a map, first use the <u>key</u> to work out what type of <u>pattern</u> you need. Then <u>carefully</u> draw on the pattern, e.g. using a <u>ruler</u>.

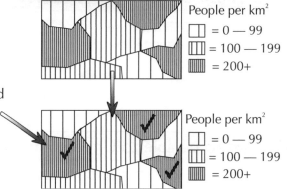

People per km²
☐ = 0 — 99
▥ = 100 — 199
▦ = 200+

People per km²
☐ = 0 — 99
▥ = 100 — 199
▦ = 200+

Flow Lines show Movement

1) <u>Flow line maps</u> have <u>arrows</u> on, showing how things <u>move</u> (or are moved) from one place to another.

2) They can also be <u>proportional symbol maps</u> — the <u>width</u> of the arrows show the <u>quantity</u> of things that are <u>moving</u>.

Q: From which <u>area</u> do the <u>greatest</u> number of people entering the UK come from?

A: <u>USA</u>, as this arrow is the largest.

Q: The number of people entering the UK from the <u>Middle East</u> is <u>roughly half</u> the number of people entering from the <u>USA</u>. Draw an <u>arrow</u> on the map to <u>show</u> this.

A: Make sure your arrow is going in the <u>right direction</u> and its <u>size</u> is appropriate (i.e. <u>half the width</u> of the USA arrow).

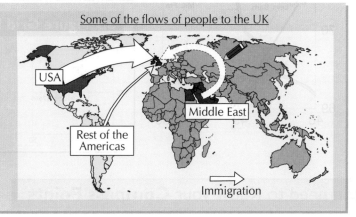

Some of the flows of people to the UK

USA
Middle East
Rest of the Americas
Immigration

Desire Lines show Journeys

1) <u>Desire line maps</u> are a type of flow line as they show <u>movement</u> too.

2) They're <u>straight lines</u> that show <u>journeys</u> <u>between</u> two <u>locations</u>, but they <u>don't follow</u> <u>roads</u> or <u>railway lines</u>.

3) <u>One line</u> represents <u>one journey</u>.

4) They're used to show <u>how far</u> all the people have <u>travelled</u> to get to a <u>place</u>, e.g. a shop or a town centre, and <u>where</u> they've <u>come from</u>.

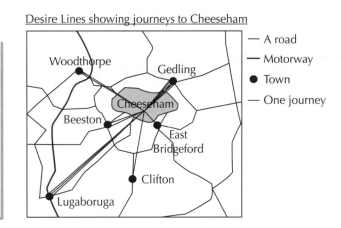

Desire Lines showing journeys to Cheeseham

Woodthorpe
Gedling
Cheeseham
Beeston
East Bridgeford
Clifton
Lugaboruga

— A road
— Motorway
● Town
— One journey

Make sure you study the key for any map

If you have to complete a map, check all the info on the map before you start drawing — that way you're less likely to muck it up. Make sure you do it in pencil too, so if you do make a mistake you can rub it out.

Ordnance Survey Maps

Next up, the dreaded <u>Ordnance Survey</u>® maps. Don't worry, they're easy once you know how to use them.

Learn These **Common Symbols**

Ordnance Survey (OS®) maps use lots of <u>symbols</u>. It's a good idea to learn some of the most <u>common ones</u> — like these:

- ▬ Motorway
- ▬ Main (A) road
- ▬ Secondary (B) road
- ⌣ Bridge
- ▬ Railway
- – · – County boundary
- National Park boundaries
- ▭ Building
- ● Bus station
- ⌁ Footpaths
- ⩔ Viewpoint
- 𝒊 Tourist information centre
- Ⓟ Parking
- + ⛪ ⛪ Places of worship

You have to be able to Understand **Grid References**

You need to be able to use <u>four figure</u> and <u>six figure</u> <u>grid references</u> for your exam.

Q: Give the four figure and six figure grid reference for the place of worship.

Place of worship

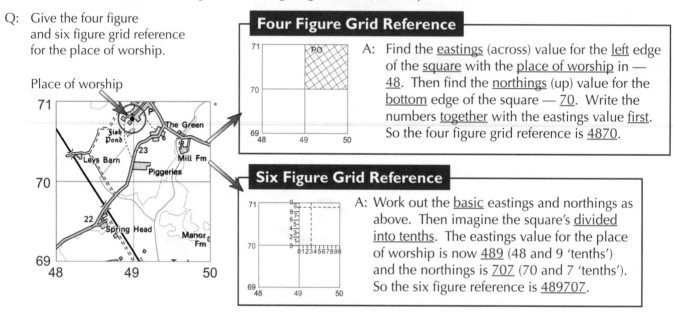

Four Figure Grid Reference

A: Find the <u>eastings</u> (across) value for the <u>left</u> edge of the <u>square</u> with the <u>place of worship</u> in — <u>48</u>. Then find the <u>northings</u> (up) value for the <u>bottom</u> edge of the square — <u>70</u>. Write the numbers <u>together</u> with the eastings value <u>first</u>. So the four figure grid reference is <u>4870</u>.

Six Figure Grid Reference

A: Work out the <u>basic</u> eastings and northings as above. Then imagine the square's <u>divided</u> <u>into tenths</u>. The eastings value for the place of worship is now <u>489</u> (48 and 9 'tenths') and the northings is <u>707</u> (70 and 7 'tenths'). So the six figure reference is <u>489707</u>.

You need to Know your **Compass Points**

You've got to know the compass — for giving <u>directions</u>, saying <u>which way</u> a <u>river's flowing</u>, or knowing what they mean if they say 'look at the river in the <u>NW</u> of the map' in the exam. Read it <u>out loud</u> to yourself, going <u>clockwise</u>.

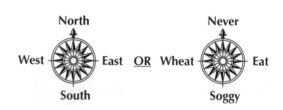

North — East — South — West **OR** Never — Eat — Soggy — Wheat

You Might have to **Work Out** the **Distance** Between **Two Places**

To work out the <u>distance</u> between <u>two places</u> on a <u>map</u>, use a <u>ruler</u> to measure the <u>distance</u> in <u>cm</u> then <u>compare</u> it to the scale to find the distance in <u>km</u>.

Q: What's the distance from the bridge (482703) to the church (489707)?

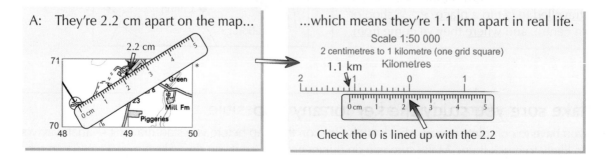

A: They're 2.2 cm apart on the map...

2.2 cm

...which means they're 1.1 km apart in real life.

Scale 1:50 000
2 centimetres to 1 kilometre (one grid square)
1.1 km Kilometres

Check the 0 is lined up with the 2.2

Geographical Skills

Ordnance Survey Maps

The **Relief** of an Area is Shown by **Contours** and **Spot Heights**

1) <u>Contour lines</u> are the <u>browny-orange lines</u> drawn on maps — they join points of <u>equal height</u> above sea level (<u>altitude</u>).

2) They tell you about the <u>relief</u> of the land, e.g. whether it's hilly, flat or steep.

3) They show the <u>height</u> of the land by the <u>numbers</u> marked on them. They also show the <u>steepness</u> of the land by how <u>close together</u> they are (the <u>closer</u> they are, the <u>steeper</u> the slope).

4) For example, if a map has <u>lots</u> of contour lines on it, it's probably <u>hilly</u> or <u>mountainous</u>. If there are only a <u>few</u> it'll be flat and often <u>low-lying</u>.

5) A <u>spot height</u> is a <u>dot</u> giving the height of a particular place. A <u>trigonometrical point</u> (trig point) is a <u>blue triangle</u> plus a height value. They usually show the <u>highest point</u> in that area (in metres).

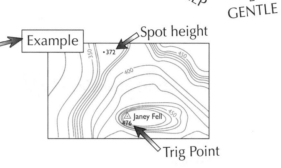

Sketching Maps — Do it Carefully

1) In the <u>exam</u>, they could give you a <u>map</u> or <u>photograph</u> and tell you to <u>sketch</u> part of it.

2) Make sure you figure out <u>what bit</u> they want you to sketch out, and <u>double check</u> you've <u>got it right</u>. It might be only <u>part</u> of a lake or a wood, or only <u>one</u> of the roads.

3) If you're <u>sketching</u> an <u>OS</u>® map, it's a good idea to <u>copy</u> the <u>grid</u> from the map onto your sketch paper — this helps you to copy the map <u>accurately</u>.

4) Draw your sketch <u>in pencil</u> so you can <u>rub it out</u> if it's <u>wrong</u>.

5) Look at how much <u>time</u> you have and <u>how many marks</u> it's worth to decide how much <u>detail</u> to add.

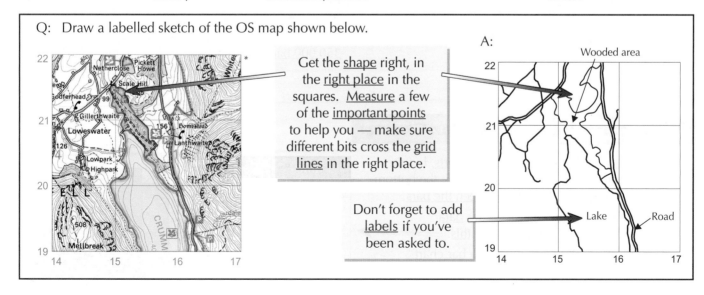

Q: Draw a labelled sketch of the OS map shown below.

Get the <u>shape</u> right, in the <u>right place</u> in the squares. <u>Measure</u> a few of the <u>important points</u> to help you — make sure different bits cross the <u>grid lines</u> in the right place.

Don't forget to add <u>labels</u> if you've been asked to.

Make your sketch maps as accurate as possible

When you're sketching a copy of a map or photo see if you can lay the paper over it — then you can trace it (sneaky). Go back over these pages and check you're comfortable with everything map-related.

Geographical Skills

Charts and Graphs

Stand by for <u>charts</u> and <u>graphs</u>. Make sure you can <u>interpret</u> (read) and <u>construct</u> (draw) each of them...

Describing what **Graphs** Show — **Include Figures** from the Graph

When <u>describing</u> graphs make sure you mention:

1) The general pattern — when it's <u>going up</u> and <u>down</u>, and any <u>peaks</u> (highest bits) and <u>troughs</u> (lowest bits).

2) Any <u>anomalies</u> (odd results).

3) Specific <u>data points</u>.

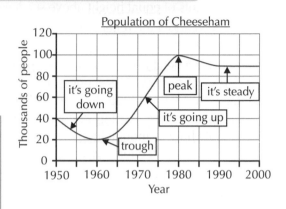

Population of Cheeseham

Q: Use the graph to describe population change in Cheeseham.

A: The population halved between 1950 and 1960 from 40 thousand people to 20 thousand people. It then increased to 100 thousand by 1980, before falling slightly and staying steady at 90 thousand from 1990 to 2000.

Bar Charts — Draw the Bars **Straight** and **Neat**

To <u>read</u> a bar chart:

1) Read along the <u>bottom</u> to find the <u>bar</u> you want.

2) To find out the <u>value</u> of a bar in a <u>normal</u> bar chart — go from the <u>top</u> of the bar <u>across</u> to the <u>scale</u>, and <u>read off</u> the number.

3) To find out the <u>value</u> of <u>part</u> of the bar in a <u>divided</u> bar chart — find the <u>number at the top</u> of the part of the bar you're interested in, and <u>take away</u> the <u>number at the bottom</u> of it.

To <u>complete</u> a bar chart:

1) First find the number you want on the <u>vertical scale</u>.

2) Then <u>trace</u> a line across to where the <u>top</u> of the bar will be with a <u>ruler</u>.

3) Draw in a bar of the <u>right size</u> using a <u>ruler</u>.

Oil production

2014
2015
Line across from 350

Q: How many barrels of oil did Hoxo Plc. produce per day in 2015?

A: 500 000 – 350 000 = <u>150 000 barrels</u> per day

Q: Complete the chart to show that Froxo Inc. produced 200 000 barrels of oil per day in 2015.

A: 150 thousand (2014) + 200 thousand = <u>350 000 barrels</u>. So draw the bar up to this point.

Histograms are a Lot Like **Bar Charts**

1) <u>Histograms</u> are very <u>similar</u> to <u>bar charts</u>, but they have a <u>continuous scale</u> of <u>numbers</u> on the <u>bottom</u> and there <u>can't</u> be any <u>gaps between the bars</u>.

2) You can use <u>histograms</u> when your <u>data</u> can be divided into <u>intervals</u>, like this:

3) You <u>draw</u> and <u>plot</u> them just like a <u>bar chart</u>, but you have to make sure that the bars are all the <u>correct width</u>, as well as the <u>correct height</u>.

Time	Cars
0700-0800	334
0800-0900	387
0900-1000	209
1000-1100	121
1100-1200	?

Number of cars passing a point

Q: How many cars were recorded between 1100 and 1200?

A: Trace a line from the top of the 1100-1200 bar and read the answer off — <u>200 cars</u>.

Charts and Graphs

Line Graphs — the Points are Joined by Lines

To read a line graph:

1) Read along the <u>correct scale</u> to find the <u>value</u> you want, e.g. 20 thousand tonnes or 1920.

2) Read <u>across</u> or <u>up</u> to the line you want, then read the value off the <u>other</u> scale.

To complete a line graph:

1) Find the value you want on <u>both scales</u>.

2) Make a <u>mark</u> (e.g. ×) at the point where the <u>two values meet</u> on the graph.

3) Using a <u>ruler</u>, <u>join</u> the <u>mark</u> you've made to the <u>line</u> that it should be <u>connected to</u>.

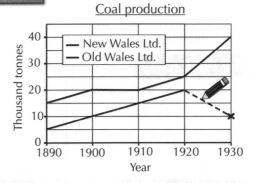

Coal production

Q: Complete the graph to show that Old Wales Ltd. produced 10 thousand tonnes of coal in 1930.

A: Find 1930 on the bottom scale, and 10 thousand tonnes on the vertical scale. Make a mark <u>where they meet</u>, then join it to the <u>blue</u> line <u>with a ruler</u>.

Scatter Graphs Show Relationships

<u>Scatter graphs</u> tell you how <u>closely related</u> two things are, e.g. altitude and air temperature. The fancy word for this is <u>correlation</u>. <u>Strong</u> correlation means the two things are <u>closely</u> related to each other. <u>Weak</u> correlation means they're <u>not very</u> closely related. The <u>line of best fit</u> is a line that goes roughly through the <u>middle</u> of the scatter of points and tells you about what <u>type</u> of correlation there is. Data can show <u>three</u> types of correlation:

1) <u>Positive</u> — as one thing <u>increases</u> the other <u>increases</u>.

2) <u>Negative</u> — as one thing <u>increases</u> the other <u>decreases</u>.

3) <u>None</u> — there's <u>no relationship</u> between the two things.

Line of best fit

Positive   Negative   None

1 Reading Scatter Graphs

1) If you're asked to <u>describe</u> the <u>relationship</u>, look at the <u>slope</u> of the graph, e.g. if the line's moving <u>upwards</u> to the <u>right</u> it's a <u>positive correlation</u>. You also need to look at how <u>close</u> the points are to the <u>line of best fit</u> — the <u>closer</u> they are the <u>stronger</u> the correlation.

2) If you're asked to read off a <u>specific point</u>, just follow the <u>rules</u> for a <u>line graph</u> (see above).

Relationship between river discharge and rainfall

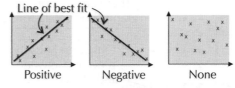

Line of best fit

2 Completing Scatter Graphs

1) You could be asked to <u>draw</u> a <u>line of best fit</u> — just draw it roughly through the <u>middle</u> of the scatter of points.

2) If you're asked to <u>add a point</u> — just follow the <u>rules</u> for adding a point to a <u>line graph</u> (see above).

Q: Describe the relationship shown by the scatter graph.

A: Altitude and rainfall show a strong, positive correlation — as altitude increases, so does the amount of rainfall.

- You can use your <u>line of best fit</u> to make <u>predictions</u> by <u>reading off values</u> from the graph.
- If you're confident your best fit line will <u>continue</u>, you can <u>extend</u> it <u>beyond</u> the data you have collected. This means you can make <u>predictions outside the range</u> of data you <u>collected</u>.

Charts and Graphs

Pie Charts Show Amounts or Percentages

The important thing to remember with pie charts is that <u>the whole pie = 360°</u>.

1 Reading Pie Charts

1) To work out the <u>%</u> for a wedge of the pie, use a <u>protractor</u> to find out how large it is in <u>degrees</u>.

2) Then <u>divide</u> that number by <u>360</u> and <u>times</u> by <u>100</u>.

3) To find the <u>amount</u> a wedge of the pie is <u>worth</u>, work out your <u>percentage</u> then turn it into a <u>decimal</u>. Then times the <u>decimal</u> by the <u>total amount</u> of the pie.

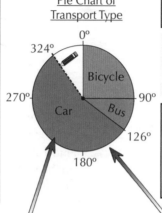

Pie Chart of Transport Type

2 Completing Pie Charts

1) To <u>draw</u> on a <u>new wedge</u> that you know the <u>%</u> for, turn the % into a <u>decimal</u> and <u>times</u> it by <u>360</u>. Then draw a wedge of that many <u>degrees</u>.

Q: Out of 100 people, 25% used a bicycle. Add this to the pie chart.

A: 25 ÷ 100 = 0.25, 0.25 × 360 = <u>90°</u>.

2) To add a <u>new wedge</u> that you know the <u>amount</u> for, <u>divide</u> your amount by the <u>total amount</u> of the pie and <u>times</u> the answer by <u>360</u>. Then <u>draw</u> on a wedge of that many <u>degrees</u>.

Q: Out of 100 people, how many used the bus?

A: 126 – 90 = 36°, so (36 ÷ 360) × 100 = 10%, so 0.1 × 100 = <u>10 people</u>.

Q: Out of 100 people, 55 used a car. Add this to the pie chart.

A: 55 ÷ 100 = 0.55, 0.55 × 360 = <u>198°</u> (198° + 126° = <u>324°</u>).

Dispersion Diagrams Show the Frequency of Data

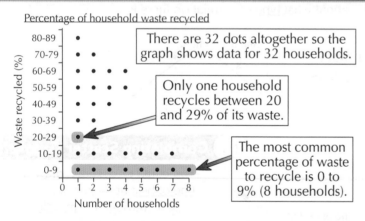

Percentage of household waste recycled

There are 32 dots altogether so the graph shows data for 32 households.

Only one household recycles between 20 and 29% of its waste.

The most common percentage of waste to recycle is 0 to 9% (8 households).

1) Dispersion diagrams are a bit like a cross between a <u>tally chart</u> and a <u>bar chart</u>.

2) The <u>range</u> of <u>data that's measured</u> goes on one axis. <u>Frequency</u> goes on the other axis.

3) <u>Each dot</u> represents <u>one piece</u> of <u>information</u> — the <u>more dots</u> there are in a particular category, the <u>more frequently</u> that event has happened.

4) The dispersion diagram on the left shows the <u>percentage</u> of <u>household waste</u> that's <u>recycled</u> for <u>households</u> in a <u>particular village</u>.

Population Pyramids Show the Structure of a Population

1) <u>Population pyramids</u> are a bit like <u>two bar charts</u> on their <u>sides</u>.

2) It's way of showing the <u>population</u> of a country by <u>age</u> and <u>gender</u>.

3) The <u>number of people</u> goes on the <u>horizontal axis</u>, and the <u>age groups</u> go on the <u>vertical axis</u>. The <u>left side</u> is the <u>male population</u> and the <u>right side</u> is the <u>female population</u>.

There are a few people over 80.

There are lots of people aged 0-9.

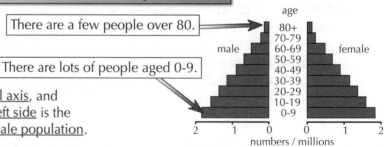

Lines, bars and crosses should be neat and legible

If you're asked to read a value off a graph, or add some data to it, remember to read the scale carefully — it's easy to assume that each division is worth one, but sadly that's not always the case.

Statistics

You might be asked to do a bit of <u>maths</u> in the exam — it should all be <u>familiar</u> from your <u>maths lessons</u>.

Learn the Definitions for **Mode, Median, Mean** and **Range**...

<u>Mode</u>, <u>median</u> and <u>mean</u> are measures of <u>average</u> and the <u>range</u> is how <u>spread out</u> the values are:

> <u>MODE</u> = <u>MOST</u> common
>
> <u>MEDIAN</u> = <u>MIDDLE</u> value (when values are in order of size)
>
> <u>MEAN</u> = <u>TOTAL</u> of items ÷ <u>NUMBER</u> of items
>
> <u>RANGE</u> = <u>DIFFERENCE</u> between highest and lowest

> <u>REMEMBER</u>:
>
> <u>Mode</u> = <u>most</u> (emphasise the 'mo' in each when you say them)
>
> <u>Median</u> = <u>mid</u> (emphasise the m*d in each when you say them)
>
> <u>Mean</u> is just the <u>average</u>, but it's <u>mean</u> 'cos you have to work it out.

Sample	1	2	3	4	5	6	7
River discharge (cumecs)	184	90	159	142	64	64	95

Q: Calculate the mean, median, mode and range for the river discharge data shown in the table above.

A: • The mode is the most common value = <u>64</u>.

• To find the median, put all the numbers in order and find the middle value:
64, 64, 90, <u>95</u>, 142, 159, 184. So the median is <u>95</u>.

When there are two middle numbers, the median is halfway between the two.

• Mean = $\dfrac{\text{total of items}}{\text{number of items}} = \dfrac{184 + 90 + 159 + 142 + 64 + 64 + 95}{7} = \dfrac{798}{7} = \underline{114}$

• The range is the difference between highest and lowest value, i.e. 184 − 64 = <u>120</u>

As well as finding the <u>median</u> (the middle value in a list), you can also find the <u>upper</u> and <u>lower quartiles</u> — the values a <u>quarter</u> (25%) and <u>three-quarters</u> (75%) of the way through the <u>ordered data</u>.

Q: The number of shoppers in each shop in a village were counted. Find the median and the quartiles of the data set.

A: 2, 3, ⑥, 6, 7, ⑨, 13, 14, ⑰, 22, 22

| Lower quartile | Median | Upper quartile |

The <u>interquartile range</u> is the <u>difference between</u> the <u>upper quartile</u> and the <u>lower quartile</u>. It contains the middle <u>50%</u> of values.

Q: Find the interquartile range of the number of shoppers.

A: 17 − 6 = <u>11</u>

You Need to be Able to **Calculate Percentages** and **Percentage Change**...

To give the amount X as a <u>percentage</u> of a sample Y, you need to <u>divide</u> X by Y and <u>multiply by 100</u>.

Q: This year, 35 out of the 270 houses in Foxley were burgled. Calculate the percentage of houses burgled in Foxley.

A: 35 ÷ 270 × 100 = <u>13%</u>

Calculating <u>percentage change</u> lets you work out <u>how much</u> something has <u>increased</u> or <u>decreased</u>. You use this <u>formula</u>:

$$\text{Percentage change} = \frac{\text{final value} - \text{original value}}{\text{original value}} \times 100$$

A <u>positive</u> value shows an <u>increase</u> and a <u>negative</u> value shows a <u>decrease</u>.

Q: Last year in Foxley, only 24 houses were burgled. Calculate the percentage change in burglaries in Foxley.

A: $\dfrac{35 - 24}{24} \times 100 = \underline{46\% \text{ increase}}$ in the number of burglaries in Foxley.

Read the question carefully and check your answer

There are some easy marks up for grabs here as long as you calculate the right figure — don't miss out on them by working out the median rather than the mean, or typing the wrong number into your calculator.

Practice Exams

Once you've been through all the questions in this book, you should feel pretty confident about the exams.
As final preparation, here is a mini set of **practice exams** to give you a taste of what the exams will be like.
Each of your real exam papers will be longer than these, but they will follow a very similar structure.

GCSE Geography

Paper 1: Living with the Physical Environment

In addition to this paper you should have:
• A pencil.
• A ruler.

Centre name				
Centre number				
Candidate number				

Time allowed:
• 40 minutes

Surname	
Other names	
Candidate signature	

Instructions to candidates
• Write your name and other details in the spaces provided above.
• Answer **all** questions in Section A and Section B in the spaces provided.
• Answer **one** question in Section C in the spaces provided.
• Do all rough work on the paper.

Information for candidates
• The marks available are given in brackets at the end of each question.
• There are 38 marks available for this paper.
• You are allowed to use a calculator.
• You should use good English and present your answers in a clear and organised way. There are 3 marks available for spelling, punctuation, grammar and terminology in Question 2.4.

Advice to candidates
For multiple choice questions:
• Clearly shade the oval next to your chosen answer. For example: ⬤
• If you wish to change your answer, put a cross through your original answer. For example: ✖
• If you wish to change your answer to one that you have previously crossed out, draw a circle around the answer. For example: ⊗

For examiner's use

Q	Attempt Nº			Q	Attempt Nº		
	1	2	3		1	2	3
1				4			
2							
3							
			Total				

Section A: The Challenge of Natural Hazards
Answer **all** the questions in this section

1   Study **Figure 1**, which shows the maize yield and annual rainfall
for a low latitude farm in Central Africa.

Figure 1

1.1   Using **Figure 1**, describe how climate change may
be affecting crop yields in low latitude areas.

....

....

....

....

....

....

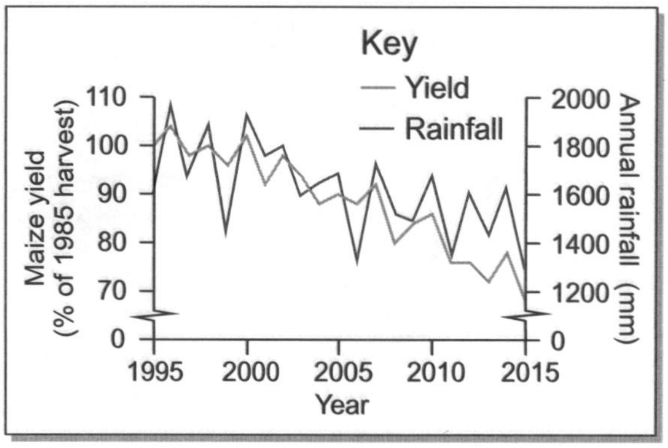

[2 marks]

1.2   Suggest **one** possible effect on people of the trends in crop yield shown in **Figure 1**.

....

....

[1 mark]

1.3   Outline **one** effect, other than changing crop yields, that climate change may have on people.

....

....

[1 mark]

Figure 2 shows Naples, a city in Italy. Naples is close to Mount Vesuvius, an active volcano,
and the area is also prone to earthquakes.

1.4   Explain how planning for tectonic hazards might
help to reduce the effects of an earthquake or
volcanic eruption in Naples.

Figure 2

....

....

....

....

....

....

....

[4]

[Total 8 marks]

Turn over ▶

Section B: The Living World
Answer **all** the questions in this section

2   Study **Figure 3**, a map showing the distribution of some of the world's ecosystems.

Figure 3

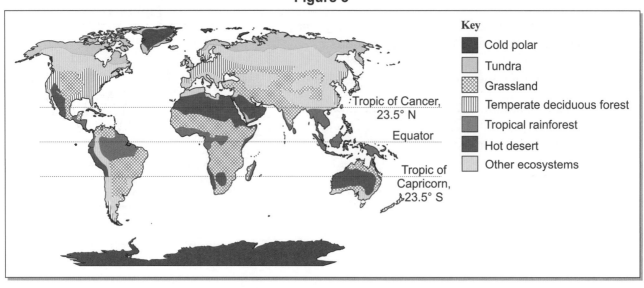

2.1   Using **Figure 3**, describe the global distribution of tropical rainforests.

....

....

....

[2 marks]

2.2   Fill in the gaps to complete the passage.

Tundra is found at .... latitudes, including areas such as ....

The .... winters and .... rainfall mean that vegetation is sparse.

[4 marks]

2.3   Explain how ecotourism can be part of a sustainable management strategy for a tropical rainforest.

....

....

....

....

....

....

....

[4 marks]

2.4   For a named hot desert environment **OR** a named cold environment,
discuss the opportunities and challenges for development.

[9 marks + 3 SPaG]

[Total 22 marks]

Section C: Physical Landscapes in the UK
Answer **one** from: Question 3 (Rivers) and Question 4 (Glacial)

3   Study **Figure 4**, which shows part of the upper course of a river.

Figure 4

3.1   Give **two** features that show that **Figure 4** is the upper course of a river.

Feature 1: ....

....

....

Feature 2: ....

....

....

[2 marks]

3.2   Outline **two** processes of erosion that are likely to be deepening the river channel in the upper course of the river shown in **Figure 4**.

Process 1: ....

....

Process 2: ....

....

[2 marks]

Study **Figure 5**, which shows a photograph of a river landform, in Snowdonia, Wales.

3.3   Explain the processes involved in the formation of the landform shown in **Figure 5**.

Figure 5

....

....

....

....

....

....

....

....

....

....

[4 marks]

[Total 8 marks]

Turn over ▶

4 Study **Figure 6**, a photograph of a glacial landscape in the Scottish Highlands.

Figure 6

4.1 Identify the glacial landform labelled X in **Figure 6**. Shade **one** oval only.

A   Truncated spur   ⬭

B   Glacial trough   ⬭

C   Arête   ⬭

D   Hanging valley   ⬭

[1 mark]

4.2 Describe **two** ways in which moving ice erodes the landscape to create the change in gradient between points Y and Z in **Figure 6**.

1: ....

....

....

....

2: ....

....

....

....

[4 marks]

Study **Figure 7**, a sketch map of a typical drumlin.

Figure 7

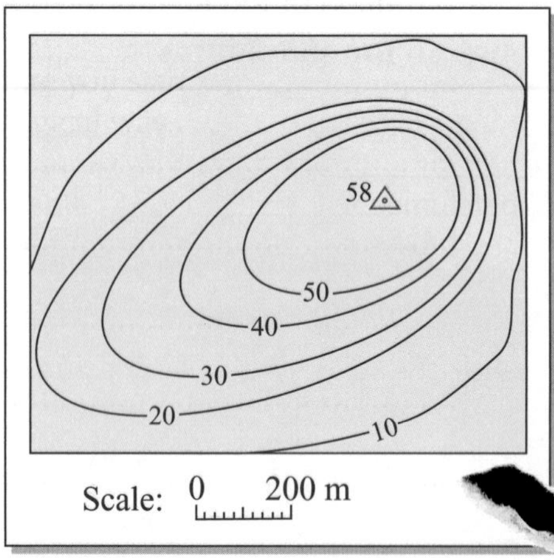

4.3 Label the sketch map to show the direction of ice flow.
[1 mark]

4.4 Using **Figure 7**, describe the characteristics of a drumlin.

....

....

....

....

....

....

....

[2 marks]

[Total 8 marks]

END OF QUESTIONS

Practice Paper 3

You may study Figure 1 on page 188 and Figure 2 on page 189 for as long as you like before you begin answering the questions in this practice paper.
In the real exam, you will be given a resource booklet to study 12 weeks before you sit the exam.

AQA GCSE Geography
Paper 3: Geographical Applications

In addition to this paper you should have:
• A pencil.
• A ruler.

Centre name				
Centre number				
Candidate number				

Time allowed:
• 1 hour for the questions
• You may study Figure 1 and Figure 2 before your time starts.

Surname	
Other names	
Candidate signature	

Instructions to candidates
• Write your name and other details in the spaces provided above.
• Answer **all** questions in the spaces provided.
• Do all rough work on the paper.

Information for candidates
• The marks available are given in brackets at the end of each question.
• There are 55 marks available for this paper.
• You are allowed to use a calculator.
• You should use good English and present your answers in a clear and organised way. There are 3 marks available for spelling, punctuation, grammar and terminology in Question 2.4.

For examiner's use

Q	Attempt Nº			Q	Attempt Nº		
	1	2	3		1	2	3
1				4			
2				5			
3							
		Total					

Figure 1
Causes and possible effects of climate change

The Earth's climate constantly changes due to variations in the Earth's orbit, changes in the output of the Sun, volcanic activity and the concentration of greenhouse gases in the Earth's atmosphere.

The greenhouse effect is when greenhouse gases in the atmosphere absorb some of Earth's outgoing heat, so less is lost to space. This is essential for keeping the planet warm — without the greenhouse effect, the Earth would have an average surface temperature of –19 °C.

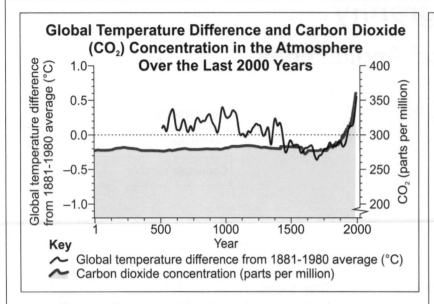

Global Temperature Difference and Carbon Dioxide (CO₂) Concentration in the Atmosphere Over the Last 2000 Years

Key
~ Global temperature difference from 1881-1980 average (°C)
~ Carbon dioxide concentration (parts per million)

Deforestation and greenhouse gas emissions

- Greenhouse gas emissions from deforestation account for about 12% of the CO_2 emitted by human activities.
- Most deforestation takes place in LICs and NEEs, especially in Brazil and Indonesia. Since 1978, more than 750 000 km² of the Amazon rainforest has been deforested.
- The majority of this deforestation is driven by demand for meat from cattle farmed on deforested land, and for rainforest products such as hardwoods (e.g. teak and mahogany). Much of this demand comes from HICs.

Carbon footprint (tonnes per person)

	USA (an HIC)	Malawi (an LIC)
2011	17.0	0.1

DAILY NEWS
APRIL 2014
GREENHOUSE GAS EMISSIONS INCREASING

The Intergovernmental Panel on Climate Change (IPCC) released a report today revealing that emissions of greenhouse gases grew more quickly between 2000 and 2010 than in each of the three previous decades — despite attempts by many countries to reduce emissions.

The IPCC state that this will lead to significant global warming, but the report suggests that this could be limited to 2 °C if global greenhouse gas emissions are reduced by 40-70% by 2050, and eliminated almost completely by 2100. Meeting this target will require social, economic and technological change to reduce emissions from transport, buildings, land use and settlements, and to make electricity production nearly emission-free.

In addition to switching to less polluting sources of energy, the IPCC also suggest that we will need to reduce overall energy usage to help limit warming to 2 °C.

Models suggest that climate change could cause temperatures to rise by 1-2 °C by 2100, if not more. This is expected to cause precipitation patterns to change, with some areas seeing an increase in droughts and others seeing more frequent and extreme flooding. Tropical storms are also predicted to increase in intensity. In addition, a rise in temperature will cause permafrost and ice to melt.

The melting of ice on land could cause sea levels to rise by up to by 1 m by 2100 and by as much as 3 m by 2300, according to some predictions.

Figure 2
Reducing the impacts of climate change

We can reduce the effects of climate change in two main ways. We can try to tackle the causes, for example by decreasing greenhouse gas emissions in order to minimise the warming that occurs. This can be done both at a large scale, by governments and industry, and at a smaller scale, by individuals.

Alternatively, we can accept the changes to climate and adapt to them, for example by improving flood defences in low-lying areas and increasing water storage capacity in areas at risk from drought.

Global Electricity Sources

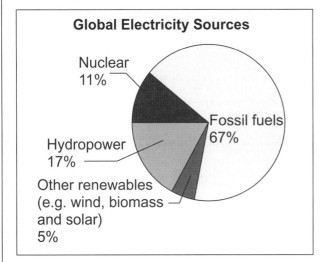

- Nuclear 11%
- Fossil fuels 67%
- Hydropower 17%
- Other renewables (e.g. wind, biomass and solar) 5%

Renewable Energy Sources in the UK

Biomass

Some power stations in the UK have been converted to run on biomass. Like conventional power stations, biomass plants can generate large amounts of power reliably.

> Currently, half the Drax power station in Yorkshire has been converted from coal to run on sustainably-sourced biomass.
>
> Using biomass emits 86% less carbon dioxide than using coal, even though biomass is often imported from the US and Canada.

Wind

The UK has a number of onshore and offshore wind farms. In total, they generate 6% of the UK's electricity.

Solar

The amount of energy generated by solar power is increasing, but as of 2012 it provided only 0.4% of the UK's electricity.

Carbon Capture and Storage (CCS)

- CCS involves capturing carbon dioxide produced during electricity generation and storing it deep underground instead of releasing it into the air.
- The technology is still at the developmental stage and several problems have been identified:
  › It's expensive — in 2015 the UK government withdrew funding for CCS demonstrations because it is 'not regarded as affordable'.
  › Stored carbon dioxide could leak out over time.

Percentage of Country Covered by Forest

	UK	USA	China	Malawi
1990	11.5%	33.0%	16.7%	41.3%
2013	12.9%	33.8%	21.9%	33.8%

Proposed Schemes

Scheme 1

An international agreement signed by the vast majority of countries, that requires all new vehicles to meet a minimum level of fuel efficiency. Additionally, the vehicles must emit fewer pollutants and less carbon dioxide than current models.

Scheme 2

A project run by an international charity that aims to educate people in countries with a large carbon footprint about the need to reduce their energy usage. It will offer advice about ways to save energy, such as improving home insulation and driving less.

Scheme 3

Governments and NGOs will work together to ensure those most affected by climate change receive help. A response team will be formed to deliver aid to affected areas, and a fund will be available to support farmers affected by changing weather patterns.

Turn over for Question 1

Turn over ▶

190

Section A: Issue Evaluation
Answer **all** questions in this section.

1   Study **Figure 1** on page 188, 'Causes and possible effects of climate change'.

1.1   What was the concentration of carbon dioxide in the year 1400?

.... ppm

[1 mark]

1.2   Suggest why it may be difficult to reduce global greenhouse gas emissions by 40-70% by 2050.

....

....

....

....

....

....

....

[4 marks]

1.3   'Human activities are the main cause of climate change over the last 200 years.'

With the help of **Figure 1**, discuss this statement.

....

....

....

....

....

....

....

....

....

....

....

[6 marks]

[Total 11 marks]

2   Study **Figure 2** on page 189, 'Reducing the impacts of climate change.'

2.1   What impact might the changes in percentage forest cover shown in **Figure 2** have on climate change?

....

....

....

[2 marks]

2.2   Using evidence from **Figure 2**, suggest how carbon capture and storage might help to reduce climate change.

....

....

....

[2 marks]

2.3   'Renewable energy sources are always small-scale and unreliable. They are not a viable alternative to fossil fuels.'

Use **Figure 2** and your own knowledge to discuss this statement.

....

....

....

....

....

....

....

....

[6 marks]

2.4   **Figure 2** describes three schemes that have been proposed to reduce the effects of climate change.

Which of the three schemes do you think will best reduce the effects of climate change on people and the environment?

Use **Figure 1**, **Figure 2** and your own knowledge to explain your choice.

[9 marks + 3 SPaG]

[Total 22 marks]

Turn over ▶

Section B: Fieldwork

Answer **all** questions in this section.

3 A group of students sent a questionnaire to a random selection of residents in Suninsky to find out how many houses had solar panels. The results for each district are shown in **Figure 3**.

Figure 3

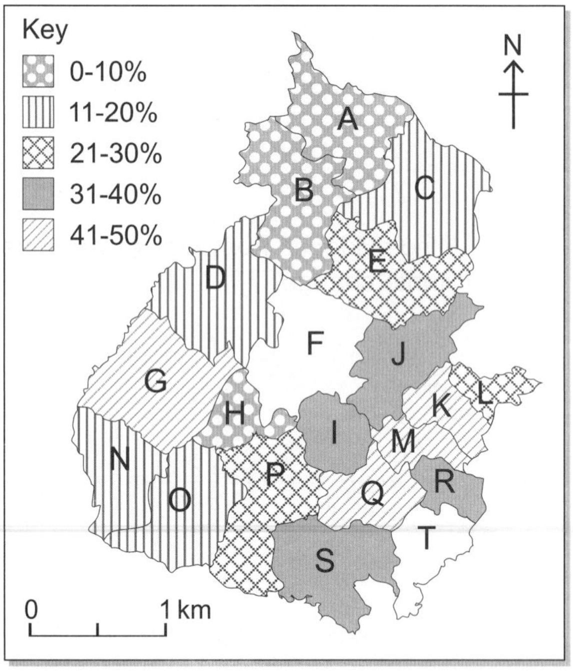

Key
0-10%
11-20%
21-30%
31-40%
41-50%
N
A
B
C
D
E
F
G
H
I
J
K
L
M
N
O
P
Q
R
S
T
0
1 km

3.1 Complete **Figure 3** to show that 17% of the houses in district F have solar panels.

[1 mark]

3.2 Complete **Figure 3** to show that 43% of the houses in district T have solar panels.

[1 mark]

3.3 What is the percentage range of houses in district E that have solar panels?

....

[1 mark]

3.4 Describe the pattern in the use of solar panels in Suninsky shown in **Figure 3**.

....

....

....

....

....

[3 marks]

3.5 Evaluate the data presentation technique used in **Figure 3**.

....

....

....

....

....

....

[4 marks]

3.6 Suggest **one** other way in which the students could have presented the data.

....

....

[1 mark]

[Total 11 marks]

4   This question is about your fieldwork enquiry that involved
the collection of **physical geography** data.

Give the title of your enquiry that involved the collection of physical geography data.

Title of enquiry: ....

....

4.1   Identify **one** risk that you needed to manage in your fieldwork location.

....

....

[1 mark]

4.2   Justify the statistical techniques you used to analyse your data.

....

....

....

....

....

....

[4 marks]

[Total 5 marks]

5   This question is about your fieldwork enquiry that involved
the collection of **human geography** data.

Give the title of your enquiry that involved the collection of human geography data.

Title of enquiry: ....

....

5.1   Assess the effectiveness of your data collection methods in helping you to answer your
original question.

....

....

....

....

....

....

....

....

[Total 6 marks]

END OF QUESTIONS

Answers

Unit 1A — Tectonic Hazards

Page 10

1.1 This question is level marked. How to grade your answer:

Level 0: There is no relevant information. *[0 marks]*

Level 1: There is a basic description of one or two building features. *[1-2 marks]*

Level 2: There is a clear description of specific building features and a detailed explanation of how they might help to reduce the effects of tectonic hazards. *[3-4 marks]*

Here are some points your answer may include:

- Buildings, bridges etc. might have been designed to withstand earthquakes, e.g. by using materials like reinforced concrete or building special foundations that absorb an earthquake's energy.
- Existing buildings and bridges might have been strengthened (e.g. by wrapping pillars in steel frames) so they're less likely to collapse under the weight of falling ash or due to shaking from an earthquake.
- Adaptations like these would make buildings less likely to collapse during a tectonic hazard, so fewer people would be killed, injured or trapped. Also, less rebuilding would be necessary, so the economic effects would also be reduced.
- Automatic shut-off switches that can turn off gas and electricity supplies if an earthquake is detected by a monitoring system might have been installed. This prevents fires and therefore could reduce the death toll and damage to the city.

1.2 E.g. earth movements and volcanoes can be monitored *[1 mark]*, so that people have time to evacuate the area or prepare before an earthquake or eruption occurs *[1 mark]*.

2.1 Volcanic eruptions — any two from: e.g. buildings and roads are destroyed or buried by ash *[1 mark]*. / Buildings may collapse if enough ash falls on them *[1 mark]*. / Vegetation is damaged when ash falls on it *[1 mark]*.

Earthquakes — any two from: e.g. buildings and bridges collapse, and homes are destroyed *[1 mark]*. / Roads are damaged *[1 mark]*. / Electricity cables and communications networks are damaged, cutting off supplies *[1 mark]*.

Unit 1A — Weather Hazards

Page 19

1.1 Any two from: e.g. lightning can cause death if it strikes a person *[1 mark]*. / Lightning can cause fires that damage property or the environment *[1 mark]*. / Thunderstorms can cause flooding due to torrential rain *[1 mark]*. / Thunderstorms can damage buildings due to strong winds *[1 mark]*.

1.2 Any two from: e.g. people can experience health problems such as heat exhaustion *[1 mark]*. / Transport can be disrupted from rails buckling or roads melting *[1 mark]*. / Disruption to transport can delay people or goods, which can cause companies to incur more costs *[1 mark]*. / The tourism industry may benefit from people spending money on holidays and leisure in warm weather *[1 mark]*. / Droughts may result in water shortages *[1 mark]*.

2.1 Predicting where and when a tropical storm will hit gives people in Miami time to evacuate, so fewer people will be injured or killed *[1 mark]*. It also gives people time to protect their homes and businesses, e.g. by boarding up windows, so there will be less damage to property *[1 mark]*.

2.2 This question is level marked. How to grade your answer:

Level 0: There is no relevant information. *[0 marks]*

Level 1: There is a basic explanation of how immediate and/or long-term responses reduced the effects of a named tropical storm. *[1-2 marks]*

Level 2: There is a clear explanation of how immediate and/or long-term responses reduced the effects of a named tropical storm. *[3-4 marks]*

Level 3: There is a detailed explanation of how immediate and/or long-term responses reduced the effects of a named tropical storm. *[5-6 marks]*

Your answer must refer to a named example.

Here are some points your answer may include:

- The immediate responses to the event, e.g. evacuation before the hurricane reached land; setting up control centres and emergency shelters; stockpiling supplies; the coastguard, police, fire service and army rescuing people; charities providing aid.
- How the immediate responses helped to reduce the effects of the storm, e.g. rescuing people from affected areas prevented deaths.
- The long-term responses to the event, e.g. government funds to rebuild homes and repair other essential infrastructure; not rebuilding on high risk areas; placing new buildings on stilts in high risk areas; repairing and improving flood defences.
- How the long-term responses helped to reduce the effects of the storm, e.g. aid to rebuild houses meant that people were not left homeless.
- Answers may refer to tropical storm events such as Hurricane Katrina, which struck the Gulf of Mexico in 2005. Although 1800 people were killed and hundreds of thousands made homeless, the majority of residents were evacuated before it arrived. The US government provided $16 billion for rebuilding homes and funded other infrastructure repairs to help speed up the recovery.

Unit 1A — Climate Change

Page 26

1.1 0.85 °C (accept 0.8-0.9 °C) *[1 mark]*

1.2 The temperature stayed between about 13.5 and 13.8 °C between 1860 and 1930 *[1 mark]*, and then rose fairly steadily to around 14.4 °C by 2000 *[1 mark]*.

2.1 Ice sheets are made up of layers of ice, with one new layer formed each year *[1 mark]*. By analysing the gases trapped in the layers of ice, scientists can tell what the temperature was in each year *[1 mark]*.

2.2 Any two from: the path of the Earth's orbit around the Sun changes from an almost perfect circle to an ellipse *[1 mark]*. This affects the amount of solar radiation/energy that the Earth receives. If the Earth receives more energy, it gets warmer *[1 mark]*. / The Sun's output of energy changes in short cycles of about 11 years *[1 mark]*. Periods when solar output is reduced may cause the Earth's climate to become cooler in some areas *[1 mark]*. / Major volcanic eruptions eject large quantities of material into the atmosphere *[1 mark]*. Some of these particles reflect the Sun's rays back out to space, so the Earth's surface cools *[1 mark]*.

Unit 1B — Tropical Rainforests

Page 38

1.1 Any two from: e.g. as the population in the area increases, trees are cleared to make land for new settlements *[1 mark]*. / Some areas have deposits, e.g. of gold or iron ore, so trees are cleared to make space for mines *[1 mark]*. / Building dams to generate hydro-electric power floods large areas of forest *[1 mark]*. / Trees are felled to be sold *[1 mark]*. / Road building for logging requires tree clearance *[1 mark]*. / The forest may be cleared for commercial farming, such as cattle grazing, palm oil or soya plantations *[1 mark]*. / The forest may be cleared for subsistence farming so farmers can grow food for themselves and their families *[1 mark]*.

1.2 Any one from: e.g. logging, mining and farming create jobs *[1 mark]*. / A lot of money is made from selling timber, extracted minerals and animals/crops *[1 mark]*.

1.3 Any one from: e.g. with no trees to hold the soil together, heavy rain washes away the soil *[1 mark]*. This can lead to landslides and flooding *[1 mark]*. / Without a tree canopy to intercept rainfall and tree roots to absorb it, more water reaches the soil *[1 mark]*. This reduces soil fertility as nutrients in the soil are washed away, out of reach of plants *[1 mark]*. / Trees remove CO_2 from the atmosphere and burning vegetation to clear the forest produces CO_2 *[1 mark]*. So deforestation means more CO_2 in the atmosphere, which adds to the greenhouse effect *[1 mark]*.

1.4 Only some trees are felled — most trees are left standing, so the forest is less damaged *[1 mark]*. The overall forest structure is kept — the canopy is still there and the soil isn't exposed, so the soil remains fertile and is able to support plant growth *[1 mark]*. This means that the forest will be able to regenerate so it can be used in the future *[1 mark]*.

1.5 The country may be allowing logging, farming and mining in its rainforests to make money to pay its debt *[1 mark]*. Reducing the debt would mean the country wouldn't have to do this, so the rainforest would be conserved for the future *[1 mark]*.

Unit 1B — Hot Deserts
Page 46

1.1 E.g. low rainfall means that soils are dry *[1 mark]*, while high temperatures mean that evaporation rates are high so soils are dry and salty *[1 mark]*. Dry soils are easily eroded and can form dust clouds, which inhibit rainfall *[1 mark]*.

1.2 Any two from: e.g. extracting groundwater by digging wells means people are able to grow more crops in the short-term, so human populations in the area may increase *[1 mark]*. / In the long-term, extracting water reduces soil moisture, leaving soil drier and more easily eroded *[1 mark]*. / Drier soil means that plants will die, so vegetation cover decreases *[1 mark]*.

2.1 This question is level marked. How to grade your answer:

Level 0: There is no relevant information. *[0 marks]*

Level 1: There is a basic description of at least one human cause of desertification. *[1-2 marks]*

Level 2: There is a clear description of some of the ways that humans contribute to the process of desertification. *[3-4 marks]*

Level 3: There is a detailed description of a number of ways that humans contribute to the process of desertification. *[5-6 marks]*

Here are some points your answer may include:

- People living in the area may have removed vegetation for firewood. Removal of trees leaves the soil exposed so it is more easily eroded.
- Keeping too many animals in a small area can cause overgrazing of vegetation, whilst trampling can contribute to erosion.
- Over-cultivation of the land can mean that nutrients are used up. This means that plants can no longer be grown in those soils and, without plants, soil erosion increases because their roots no longer hold the soil together.
- Population growth puts pressure on the land, leading to more deforestation (for firewood), more over-grazing and more over-cultivation.
- Human activities are also contributing to climate change.
- Climate change is expected to reduce rainfall in areas that are already quite dry. Less rain means that less water is available for plant growth, so plants begin to die. Plant roots hold the soil together. If the plants die, the soil is easily eroded.

- Climate change is expected to increase global temperature. Higher temperatures would mean that more water would evaporate from the land and from plants. This would make soils drier and mean that plants would die (so their roots would no longer hold the soil together).

Unit 1B — Cold Environments
Page 52

1.1 Any one from: e.g. the Arctic fox has a light-coloured coat to camouflage it against the snow *[1 mark]* so it can sneak up on prey *[1 mark]*. / It has thick fur *[1 mark]* to reduce the amount of energy needed to keep warm *[1 mark]*.

1.2 E.g. warming may cause Arctic foxes to move towards the poles, where it is cooler *[1 mark]*. If warming leads to loss of the polar environment, or if the Arctic foxes can't move further towards the poles, they may be at risk of decline or extinction *[1 mark]*.

2.1 Economic opportunities at location A include fishing and tourism *[1 mark]*. The settlement is on the coast with easy access to fishing areas *[1 mark]*. The nearby airport and roads make the settlement accessible to tourists, who may visit to go whale-watching *[1 mark]*.

2.2 E.g. the only access route to location B by land is a long, twisty ice road that may not be usable all year round *[1 mark]*. This could make it difficult for people to access the area, which could limit the development of e.g. tourism *[1 mark]*.

The question tells you to use evidence from the map, so make sure your answer refers to features you can see on the map.

Unit 1C — Coastal Landscapes in the UK
Page 64

1.1 991802 *[1 mark]*

1.2 2.0 km (accept between 1.9 km and 2.1 km) *[1 mark]*

1.3 Longshore drift transported sand and shingle north east past a sharp bend in the coastline *[1 mark]* and deposited it in the sea, forming a spit *[1 mark]*.

2.1 Any one from: e.g. beach nourishment is when sand and shingle from elsewhere or from lower down the beach is added to the upper part of beaches *[1 mark]*. / Dune regeneration is when sand dunes are created or restored by nourishment, or by planting vegetation to stabilise the sand *[1 mark]*.

2.2 **Advantage:** Any one from: e.g. beach nourishment creates wider beaches which slow the waves, giving greater protection from flooding and erosion *[1 mark]*. / Dune regeneration restores or creates sand dunes that provide a barrier between the land and the sea. This means wave energy is absorbed, which prevents flooding and erosion *[1 mark]*.

Disadvantage: Any one from: e.g. taking material from the sea bed for beach nourishment can kill organisms like sponges and corals *[1 mark]*. / Beach nourishment is a very expensive defence that has to be repeated *[1 mark]*. / Dune regeneration only protects a small area *[1 mark]*. / Nourishment of existing dunes is very expensive *[1 mark]*.

Unit 1C — River Landscapes in the UK
Page 79

1.1 18 hours *[1 mark]*

1.2 Any one from: the River Seeton is more likely to flood *[1 mark]* because it has a higher peak discharge, meaning that there is more water in the channel *[1 mark]*. / The River Seeton is more likely to flood *[1 mark]* because it has a shorter lag time, meaning that discharge increases more quickly *[1 mark]*.

1.3 Built-up areas contain lots of impermeable surfaces and drains *[1 mark]*. Impermeable surfaces increase runoff and drains quickly take runoff to rivers, so the hydrograph will have a higher peak discharge and a shorter lag time *[1 mark]*.

2.1 This question is level marked. How to grade your answer:
Level 0: There is no relevant information. *[0 marks]*
Level 1: There is a basic explanation of the formation of interlocking spurs. *[1-2 marks]*
Level 2: There is a detailed explanation of the formation of interlocking spurs, which uses geographical terms accurately. *[3-4 marks]*
Here are some points your answer may include:
- In the upper course of a river most of the erosion is vertically downwards, creating steep-sided, V-shaped valleys.
- In the upper course, rivers aren't powerful enough to erode laterally (sideways), so they wind around the high hillsides that stick out into their paths on either side.
- The hillsides interlock with each other as the river winds around them, forming interlocking spurs.

Unit 1C — Glacial Landscapes in the UK

Page 90

1.1 **Grid reference:** 3614 *[1 mark]*.
Formation: Glacial troughs start off as V-shaped river valleys *[1 mark]*. Glaciers erode the sides and bottom of the valley, forming a U-shaped glacial trough *[1 mark]*.

1.2 1.7 km (allow 1.6-1.8km) *[1 mark]*

2.1 A *[1 mark]*
Medial moraine is a ridge of material deposited along the centre of a valley.

2.2 Any one from: the material can be frozen in the glacier *[1 mark]*. / The material can be carried on the surface of the glacier *[1 mark]*. / The material can be transported by bulldozing, when the ice pushes loose material in front of it *[1 mark]*.

2.3 Terminal moraine forms at the snout of the glacier *[1 mark]*. Material is abraded and plucked from the valley floor and transported at the front of the glacier *[1 mark]*. When the ice retreats, the material is deposited as semicircular mounds *[1 mark]*.

Unit 2A — Urban Issues and Challenges

Page 96

1.1

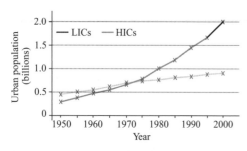

[1 mark]

1.2 The urban population of HICs increased gradually from about 0.5 billion to 0.9 billion *[1 mark]*. The urban population of LICs was less than that of HICs in 1950 but much greater by 2000 *[1 mark]*. It increased rapidly from about 0.3 billion to 2 billion *[1 mark]*.

1.3 Any two from: e.g. there are more jobs in urban areas, and they are often better paid *[1 mark]*. / To get access to better health care and education *[1 mark]*. / To join other family members who have already moved *[1 mark]*. / People think they will have a better quality of life in cities *[1 mark]*.

1.4 This question is level marked. How to grade your answer:
Level 0: There is no relevant information. *[0 marks]*
Level 1: There are a few points about the rate of urbanisation in either HICs or LICs. *[1-2 marks]*
Level 2: There is a clear explanation of the rate of urbanisation in HICs and LICs. *[3-4 marks]*
Level 3: There is a detailed explanation of the rate of urbanisation in HICs and LICs. *[5-6 marks]*
Here are some points your answer may include:
- Urbanisation happened earlier in HICs than in LICs, e.g. during the industrial revolution, so most of the population now already live in urban areas. This means that there are fewer people moving into cities in HICs than in LICs.
- Good transport and communication networks mean that people in HICs can live in rural areas and commute to cities, or work from home. This means that many people in HICs are moving away from cities.
- Decline of heavy industry in cities in HICs caused mass unemployment. People desiring a better quality of life moved away from overcrowded cities to rural areas, meaning that urban population growth slowed.
- A lower proportion of the population in LICs currently live in urban areas, so there are more people living in rural areas who might move to cities.
- Many people in LICs are moving to cities to get a better quality of life, e.g. access to better healthcare, jobs and education. This causes rapid urban growth in LICs.

Page 105

1.1 E.g. there is lots of green space, including parks, wooded areas, rivers and lakes *[1 mark]*. / There is a big recycling centre *[1 mark]*.

1.2 This question is level marked. How to grade your answer:
Level 0: There is no relevant information. *[0 marks]*
Level 1: There is a basic explanation of how water can be conserved in people's homes. *[1-2 marks]*
Level 2: There is a clear explanation of how water can be conserved in people's homes. *[3-4 marks]*
Here are some points your answer may include:
- Houses could be fitted with water butts to collect rainwater for use on gardens or for flushing toilets, which reduces the amount of piped water needed.
- Toilets that use less water to flush could be installed.
- Water meters could be installed so that people have to pay for the water that they use. This is likely to reduce their water usage.
- Efficient dishwashers and washing machines that use less water for each load could be installed.

2.1 Any two from: e.g. the buildings have been improved *[1 mark]*. / A walkway has been developed along the river *[1 mark]*. / New homes/offices have been built *[1 mark]*. / The environment has been made more attractive *[1 mark]*.

2.2 This question is level marked. How to grade your answer:
Level 0: There is no relevant information. *[0 marks]*
Level 1: There is a basic explanation of the improvements made to a named UK regeneration project. *[1-2 marks]*
Level 2: There is a clear explanation of the improvements made to a named UK regeneration project. *[3-4 marks]*
Your answer must refer to a named example.
Here are some points your answer may include:
- A brief description of the regeneration project and why the area needed regenerating.
- Social improvements, such as better (and affordable) housing, community facilities (health care centres, community centres etc.) and the introduction of cafés and restaurants.
- Economic improvements, such as the creation of jobs and improved transport links.

- Environmental improvements, such as the development of parks and community sports fields, and the cleaning up of waste land.
- Your answer may refer to the regeneration of the Cardroom Estate in Manchester, now known as New Islington, where new homes have been built and public transport links and community facilities have been improved.

Unit 2B — The Changing Economic World
Page 116
1.1 E.g. conflict is likely to decrease Libya's level of development *[1 mark]*. This is because damage is done to infrastructure and property, such as the building in Figure 1 *[1 mark]*, and money is spent on arms and fighting instead of development *[1 mark]*.

1.2 Countries that were colonised often have a lower level of development when they gain independence than they would if they had not been colonised *[1 mark]*. This is because colonisers control the economies of their colonies, e.g. by exploiting raw materials *[1 mark]*. The money made goes to the colonising country, so it is not used to develop the colonised country, which remains relatively undeveloped *[1 mark]*.

2.1 A *[1 mark]* and D *[1 mark]*.
In Stage 5, birth rate is lower than death rate, so population decreases. In Stage 4, birth rate and death rate are equal, so population remains stable.

2.2 Morocco has a relatively high birth rate and a low death rate *[1 mark]*, so it is likely to be at Stage 3 of the demographic transition model *[1 mark]*. Countries at Stage 3 are poorer countries, but with increasing levels of economic development *[1 mark]*.

Page 125
1.1 Advantage: e.g. helps to improve the level of development of the recipient country (by improving health, education and agriculture) *[1 mark]*.
Disadvantage: e.g. the aid may not reach the poorest people *[1 mark]* / aid may be lost through corruption *[1 mark]*.

1.2 This question is level marked. There are 3 extra marks available for spelling, punctuation and grammar.
How to grade your answer:
Level 0: There is no relevant information. *[0 marks]*
Level 1: There is a basic description of how TNCs can affect economic development and quality of life in LICs and NEEs. *[1-3 marks]*
Level 2: There is a clear description of the advantages and disadvantages of TNCs for economic development and quality of life in LICs and NEEs, and a basic judgement of the extent of improvements in a named country. *[4-6 marks]*
Level 3: There is a detailed description of the advantages and disadvantages of TNCs for economic development and quality of life in LICs and NEEs, and a clear judgement of the extent of improvements in a named country. *[7-9 marks]*
Make sure your spelling, punctuation and grammar is consistently correct, that your meaning is clear and that you use a range of geographical terms correctly *[0-3 marks]*.
Your answer must outline ways in which TNCs can improve economic development and quality of life, and ways in which they do not generate improvements, using examples of TNCs in at least one country. You must come to a conclusion about how far they can improve economic development and quality of life, and explain your decision.

Here are some points your answer may include:
- TNCs help increase economic development and improve quality of life by employing people, which provides an income for workers and tax income for the state. Some TNCs also run programs to help development, and work with charities to help improve quality of life.
- TNCs may not help to improve economic development and quality of life as profits made by the company normally leave the country in which they were made. TNCs may also move around within countries or internationally to take advantage of local government incentives, which can reduce the income from TNCs or prevent long-term development.
- Some TNCs may also cause environmental damage, particularly if environmental regulations are not strict or not enforced. This can affect places where people live, which negatively affects quality of life.
- Answers may refer to TNCs in India, for example Unilever, which employs 16 000 people in India and runs development initiatives, but which has been accused of causing environmental damage and moving factories to take advantage of government incentives.

2.1 Any two from: e.g. near to the central business district (CBD) for easy access to banks etc. *[1 mark]* / close to good road and rail links for easy access *[1 mark]* / close to Newcastle International Airport for international travel *[1 mark]* / near to two universities for collaborations with researchers *[1 mark]*.

Unit 2C — Resource Management
Page 133
1.1 coal *[1 mark]*
1.2 gas *[1 mark]*
1.3 E.g. the proportion of energy from coal and oil decreased from 91% in 1970 to 51% in 2014 *[1 mark]*. The proportion of energy from gas increased hugely from 6% in 1970 to 34% in 2014 *[1 mark]*. Between 1970 and 2014 a variety of renewable sources of energy were introduced *[1 mark]*.
1.4 Any one from: e.g. there has been a decline in demand *[1 mark]* due to efforts to reduce CO_2 emissions *[1 mark]*. / Less coal is being mined *[1 mark]* because the cost of mining is increasing as the reserves of coal are decreasing *[1 mark]*.
1.5 Any one from: e.g. the cost of producing electricity from renewable energy sources is relatively high *[1 mark]*. / Research into renewable energy sources and the initial cost of setting up the means of producing them is expensive *[1 mark]*. / Many renewable sources don't provide a reliable supply of energy, so the UK still has to import energy from other countries *[1 mark]*.
1.6 This question is level marked. How to grade your answer:
Level 0: There is no relevant information. *[0 marks]*
Level 1: There are a few points about the effect of exploiting energy reserves on the environment. *[1-2 marks]*
Level 2: There is a basic explanation of the effect of exploiting energy reserves on the environment. *[3-4 marks]*
Level 3: There is a detailed explanation of the effect of exploiting energy reserves on the environment. *[5-6 marks]*
Here are some points your answer may include:
- Burning fossil fuels releases carbon dioxide and other greenhouse gases, which contribute to global warming.
- Fracking may pollute groundwater, damaging natural ecosystems. It also causes mini-earthquakes, which could impact local wildlife.

- Accidents, such as oil spills or nuclear disasters, can leak toxic chemicals into water sources, soils and the atmosphere. This affects local ecosystems and may reduce the number of species living in the area.
- Natural ecosystems can be damaged by the installation of renewable energy generators such as tidal barrage systems or large wind farms.
- Power stations and wind farms are often considered to be eyesores because they alter the look of the natural environment.

Unit 2C — Food

Page 142

1.1   This question is level marked. How to grade your answer:

Level 0:   There is no relevant information. *[0 marks]*

Level 1:   There is a basic explanation of the advantages of vertical farming in Singapore. *[1-2 marks]*

Level 2:   There is a clear explanation of the advantages of vertical farming in Singapore. *[3-4 marks]*

Level 3:   There is a detailed explanation of the advantages of vertical farming in Singapore. *[5-6 marks]*

Here are some points your answer may include:

- Singapore is densely populated and only has 250 acres available for farming. Vertical farming takes up much less space than conventional farming, so more food can be grown in a smaller area.
- Over 90% of Singapore's food is imported. Increasing locally grown crops improves food security because it makes Singapore less reliant on imports, which could be affected by conflict, increasing prices etc.
- Singapore has a monsoon climate that can damage outdoor crops. Growing crops under shelter, as in vertical farming, reduces crops damaged by the weather and so allows food to be grown all year round.
- Vertical farming allows the recycling of water, which means that it is a more sustainable form of agriculture because it doesn't use as many natural resources.

Make sure you refer to Figure 1 in your answer — you're asked to use it in the question and it gives lots of clues about what you should include.

1.2   Any one from: e.g. organic farming uses natural processes that return nutrients to the soil *[1 mark]*. Artificial herbicides and pesticides that are made from unsustainable resources are banned *[1 mark]*. This reduces damage to the environment and means that food can continue to be grown to feed future generations *[1 mark]*. / Permaculture tries to recreate natural ecosystems to protect the soil, insects and other wildlife *[1 mark]*. It's designed to need low energy inputs and to be long lasting *[1 mark]*. This reduces damage to the environment and doesn't use up as many resources, so food can continue to be grown to feed future generations *[1 mark]*.

1.3   This question is level marked. How to grade your answer:

Level 0:   There is no relevant information. *[0 marks]*

Level 1:   There is a basic explanation of how a local farming scheme in an LIC or NEE has made food supplies more sustainable. *[1-2 marks]*

Level 2:   There is a clear explanation of how a local farming scheme in an LIC or NEE has made food supplies more sustainable. *[3-4 marks]*

Your answer must refer to a specific example.

Here are some points your answer may include:

- A brief description of the scheme.
- How it has made food supplies more sustainable, e.g. by increasing yields and decreasing the amount of resources (e.g. water, fertiliser) needed.
- Other ways in which the scheme is sustainable, e.g. protecting against environmental damage (e.g. desertification) and preserving the land/soil for future generations to use.

- Answers may refer to agroforestry schemes in Mali where crops like maize are planted between trees and nitrogen-fixing plants. This reduces the need for fertilisers, helps prevent soil erosion, and increases the nutrient and water content of the soil. As a result, yields are higher and the soil is protected.

Unit 2C — Water

Page 150

1.1   Any one from: e.g. the children are collecting water from an open pool, suggesting that there's no piped water supply *[1 mark]*. / The children are collecting water that looks unclean/unsafe to drink *[1 mark]*.

1.2   E.g. the climate looks dry and hot *[1 mark]* so there may not be much rainfall and lots of water may be lost due to evaporation *[1 mark]*.

1.3   Any two from: e.g. population growth increases the amount of water used, which decreases availability *[1 mark]*. / Industry uses a lot of water, so industrial development can decrease water availability *[1 mark]*. / The pollution of water sources, e.g. rivers, lakes and groundwater, can reduce the amount of clean water that is available *[1 mark]*. / Limited infrastructure, e.g. lack of water pipes and sewers, might mean that sewage contaminates the water supply, decreasing water availability *[1 mark]*. / People may not be able to afford to have water supplied to their home and may not have a water source nearby *[1 mark]*.

1.4   E.g. people may become ill from drinking contaminated water *[1 mark]*. / A shortage of water means that less food can be grown, which could lead to starvation *[1 mark]*.

1.5   Manufacturing industries are very water-intensive, so they can't produce as much during water shortages *[1 mark]*. This may force industries to close *[1 mark]*.

1.6   E.g. when countries in areas of water insecurity share the same water supplies *[1 mark]*, water shortages may trigger one country to take more water from the shared supplies, causing conflict *[1 mark]*.

Unit 2C — Energy

Page 158

1.1   Location: C *[1 mark]*

Reason: C is exposed on all sides, so turbines will be powered by wind from all directions *[1 mark]*. / It is high up, where winds are stronger *[1 mark]*.

Locations A, B and E are ruled out because they are sheltered by hills, buildings or trees. Location D is ruled out because it is offshore.

1.2   E.g. E would not be suitable for a solar plant because it is in a forest in a valley *[1 mark]*, where trees and the valley sides would block the sunlight *[1 mark]*.

1.3   Any one from: e.g. it's a renewable energy source so it won't run out *[1 mark]*. / It produces no waste products *[1 mark]*.

1.4   This question is level marked. How to grade your answer:

Level 0:   There is no relevant information. *[0 marks]*

Level 1:   There is a basic discussion of the benefits or costs of extracting a named fossil fuel. *[1-2 marks]*

Level 2:   There is a clear discussion of the benefits and costs of extracting a named fossil fuel. *[3-4 marks]*

Level 3:   There is a detailed discussion of the benefits and costs of extracting a named fossil fuel. *[5-6 marks]*

Your answer must refer to a specific fossil fuel.

Here are some points your answer may include:
- A brief description of the fossil fuel and how it is extracted.
- A discussion of the benefits of extracting it, e.g. it may be a readily available source of energy, it may cause less pollution than other fossil fuels, it may be cheaper to extract than investing in the technology needed to get energy from other renewable resources.
- A discussion of the costs of extracting it, e.g. there is not an unlimited supply of it so it will run out if it continues to be extracted, using it releases greenhouse gases so extracting it may contribute to global warming, its extraction may cause environmental damage.
- Answers may refer to the extraction of shale gas by fracking. The UK appears to have large shale gas resources, shale gas is less polluting than coal or oil and is cheaper than some renewables. But extracting it risks polluting groundwater and air, could cause small earthquakes, and local people are often against it.

Practice Exam Paper 1: Living with the Physical Environment

Pages 177-180

1.1 The overall decrease in rainfall from 1995 to 2015 corresponds to a decrease in maize yield *[1 mark]*. This suggests that climate change may be causing crop yields to decrease *[1 mark]*.

1.2 Any one from: e.g. farmers' incomes may decrease if it becomes too dry for farming *[1 mark]*. / Less food being grown could lead to malnutrition, ill health and death from starvation *[1 mark]*.

1.3 Any one from: e.g. in some places deaths due to heat may increase, but deaths due to cold may decrease *[1 mark]*. / Some areas could become so hot and dry that they're difficult or impossible to inhabit so people are forced to move *[1 mark]*. / Low-lying coastal areas could be lost to the sea or flood so often that they become impossible to inhabit, so people have to move *[1 mark]*. / Migration due to changing environmental conditions may cause overcrowding in other areas *[1 mark]*. / Some areas may struggle to supply enough water for their residents due to problems with water availability caused by changing rainfall patterns *[1 mark]*. / Problems with water availability may lead to political tensions, especially where rivers cross borders *[1 mark]*. / Climate change may make the weather more extreme, so more money may need to be spent on predicting extreme weather events, reducing their impacts and rebuilding after them *[1 mark]*.

1.4 This question is level marked. How to grade your answer:
Level 0: There is no relevant information. *[0 marks]*
Level 1: There is a basic description of one or two planning strategies. *[1-2 marks]*
Level 2: There is a clear description of several planning strategies and an explanation of how they might help to reduce the effects of tectonic hazards. *[3-4 marks]*
Here are some points your answer may include:
- Future developments can be planned to avoid the areas most at risk from tectonic hazards, so that future hazards affect a smaller area.
- Emergency services can train and prepare for disasters, e.g. by practising rescuing people from collapsed buildings or setting up shelters. This will reduce the number of people killed or injured.
- People can be educated so that they know what to do if an earthquake or eruption happens. This will mean that they know how to respond, so deaths and injuries will be reduced.

- Governments can plan evacuation routes to get people out of dangerous areas quickly and safely in case of an earthquake or volcanic eruption. This reduces the number of people killed or injured by hazards such as fires, pyroclastic flows or mudflows.
- Emergency supplies, like blankets, clean water and food, can be stockpiled. If a natural hazard is predicted, the stockpiles can be moved close to areas likely to be affected, so they are quickly accessible when they are needed.

2.1 Tropical rainforests are found around the equator *[1 mark]*, in areas such as central America / northeast South America / central Africa / south east Asia *[1 mark]*.

2.2 Tundra is found at **high** *[1 mark]* latitudes, including areas such as **northern Canada** *[1 mark]* / **northern Russia** *[1 mark]* / **the coast of Greenland** *[1 mark]* / **northern Europe** *[1 mark]*. The **cold** *[1 mark]* winters, and **low** *[1 mark]* rainfall mean that vegetation is sparse.

2.3 This question is level marked. How to grade your answer:
Level 0: There is no relevant information. *[0 marks]*
Level 1: There is a basic explanation of how ecotourism helps in the sustainable management of tropical rainforests. *[1-2 marks]*
Level 2: There is a clear explanation of how ecotourism helps in the sustainable management of tropical rainforests. *[3-4 marks]*
Here are some points your answer may include:
- Ecotourism minimises environmental impacts, e.g. by making sure waste and litter are disposed of properly to prevent land and water contamination. This helps to make sure that the tropical rainforest isn't damaged.
- Ecotourism provides a source of income for local people, e.g. they act as guides, and provide accommodation and transport. If local people are employed in tourism, they don't have to log or farm to make money, meaning fewer trees are cut down.
- Ecotourism can bring in more money for rainforest conservation. This money can be used to e.g. monitor conservation areas to make sure that restrictions on damaging activities are kept to.
- If a country's economy relies on ecotourism, there's an incentive to conserve the environment. This means that it is more likely to be protected for the future.

2.4 This question is level marked. There are 3 extra marks available for spelling, punctuation and grammar.
How to grade your answer:
Level 0: There is no relevant information. *[0 marks]*
Level 1: There is a basic description of the opportunities and challenges for development in a named hot desert or cold environment. *[1-3 marks]*
Level 2: There is a clear description and explanation of opportunities and challenges for development in a named hot desert or cold environment. *[4-6 marks]*
Level 3: There is a detailed description and explanation of the opportunities and challenges for development in a named hot desert or cold environment. *[7-9 marks]*
Make sure your spelling, punctuation and grammar is consistently correct, that your meaning is clear and that you use a range of geographical terms correctly *[0-3 marks]*.
Your answer must refer to a named example.
Here are some points your answer may include:
Hot desert environments:
- Hot deserts may provide opportunities for development, including farming, mineral extraction, energy production and tourism.
- However, there are also challenges to development, for example extreme temperatures, inaccessibility and limited water supply.

200

- Development can also damage fragile hot desert environments, which can take a long time to recover.
- Answers may refer to development in the Sahara, which is the world's largest hot desert. It offers numerous opportunities for development, such as extraction of phosphate in Morocco, and the construction of the Aswan Dam, which enabled farming in Egypt. Because of its challenges, the population of the Sahara is low and development is limited.

Cold environments:
- Cold environments may include opportunities for development, for example oil and gas extraction, mineral resource mining, fishing and tourism.
- There are also significant challenges to development, for example extreme temperatures, inaccessibility and the difficulty of constructing permanent buildings and infrastructure.
- Development such as oil extraction and mineral mining can damage fragile cold environments, which can take a very long time to recover.
- Answers may refer to development in Alaska, where oil and gas extraction makes up over half the state's income but where the main oil field, around Prudhoe Bay, is very inaccessible and very cold with a mean annual temperature of –9 °C. The trans-Alaska oil pipeline had to be built across the tundra due to the inaccessibility of Prudhoe Bay to large shipping.

3.1 Any two from: the gradient of the river channel is steep *[1 mark]*. / The valley has steep sides *[1 mark]*. / The valley is V-shaped *[1 mark]*. / The river channel is narrow *[1 mark]*. / The river valley has interlocking spurs *[1 mark]*.

3.2 Any two from: hydraulic action may deepen the river channel because the force of the water breaks rock particles away from the river bed *[1 mark]*. / Abrasion may deepen the river channel because eroded rocks picked up by the river scrape and rub against the river bed, wearing it away *[1 mark]*. / Solution may deepen the river channel because river water dissolves some types of rock, e.g. chalk and limestone *[1 mark]*.

3.3 This question is level marked. How to grade your answer:
Level 0: There is no relevant information. *[0 marks]*
Level 1: There is a basic explanation of the formation of an estuary. *[1-2 marks]*
Level 2: There is a clear explanation of the formation of an estuary, which uses some geographical terms. *[3-4 marks]*
Here are some points your answer may include:
- Estuaries are found at the mouth of a river, where the land is close to sea level.
- The water is tidal, so the river level rises and falls each day.
- When the tide comes in, the water floods over the banks of the river and deposits silt and sand on the valley floor.
- Over time, more and more mud builds up, creating large areas of mudflats.

4.1 D *[1 mark]*
Hanging valleys are smaller valleys that are left at a higher level than the main valley when the ice melts, appearing to 'hang' above them.

4.2 1: Plucking occurs when meltwater at the base, back or sides of a glacier freezes onto the rock *[1 mark]*. As the glacier moves forward it pulls pieces of rock off the mountain face, making the back wall steeper *[1 mark]*.
2: Abrasion occurs when bits of rock stuck in the ice grind against the rock below the glacier, wearing it away *[1 mark]*. Abrasion wears away rock at the base of the glacier, making the base deeper and forming the hollow between X and Y (which is now a tarn) *[1 mark]*.
You may have also described how the glacier moves in a circular motion (called rotational slip) as part of your answer. This erodes hollows in the landscape like the one shown in the photo.

4.3

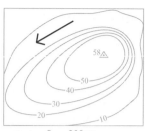

Scale: 0   200 m
[1 mark]

4.4 Drumlins are elongated hills *[1 mark]* which are round, blunt and steep at the upstream end and tapered, pointed and gently sloping at the downstream end *[1 mark]*.

Practice Exam Paper 2: Challenges in the Human Environment
Pages 182-186

1.1 The west and north of the UK generally have a low population density *[1 mark]*. Population density is highest in the south east and the midlands *[1 mark]*.

1.2 A: Glasgow *[1 mark]*
B: London *[1 mark]*

1.3 Upland regions such as the north of Scotland are difficult to farm and have few natural resources *[1 mark]*.

1.4 The number of megacities increased from three in 1975 to twenty-eight in 2014 *[1 mark]*. By 2014 there were a few more megacities in HICs and LICs *[1 mark]*. However, most of the new megacities that had developed by 2014 are in NEEs *[1 mark]*.

1.5 This question is level marked. There are 3 extra marks available for spelling, punctuation and grammar.
How to grade your answer:
Level 0: There is no relevant information. *[0 marks]*
Level 1: There is a basic description of the challenges created by urban growth. *[1-3 marks]*
Level 2: There is a clear discussion of the challenges of urban growth. *[4-6 marks]*
Level 3: There is a detailed discussion of the challenges created by urban growth. *[7-9 marks]*
Make sure your spelling, punctuation and grammar is consistently correct, that your meaning is clear and that you use a range of geographical terms correctly *[0-3 marks]*.
Your answer must refer to a named example.
Here are some points your answer may include:
- A brief description of the city in an LIC or NEE that you have chosen and how it is growing.
- A discussion of the social challenges caused by urban growth, e.g. the growth of squatter settlements with poorly built, overcrowded housing. Your answer should describe some of the problems this creates, including limited access to healthcare, education, clean water, electricity and sanitary facilities and high levels of crime.
- A discussion of the economic challenges caused by urban growth, including a lack of formal jobs and high levels of unemployment. Many formal jobs (e.g. in factories) have long working hours and low pay.
- A discussion of the environmental challenges caused by urban growth, including lack of proper sewage systems and waste collection services, air pollution from traffic congestion and unregulated waste disposal and emissions from factories.
- Your answer may refer to the city of Lagos, Nigeria, which is experiencing rapid urban growth. 60% of the population live in squatter settlements without access to basic services or resources.

2.1 US $2.1 million *[1 mark]*
5 100 000 ÷ 100 × 41.4 = US $2 111 400.

Answers

2.2 If a country has poor trade links (it trades a small amount with only a few countries) its GNP will be lower than if it had good trade links *[1 mark]*. This means there will be less to spend on development, so development will be slow *[1 mark]*.

2.3 Nicaragua's largest exports are agricultural products (which are primary products), and manufactured goods make up less of its exports than in the UK *[1 mark]*. Primary products don't generate as much money as manufactured goods, which means there is less money to spend on development in Nicaragua *[1 mark]*.

2.4 The health of people in the UK is likely to be better than in Nicaragua *[1 mark]*. Life expectancy is normally higher in more developed countries, and infant mortality is generally lower *[1 mark]*. Health improves with development, so the difference is likely to be a result of more investment in healthcare in the UK *[1 mark]*.

2.5 Any one from: e.g. tourism can provide extra employment *[1 mark]*, providing people with an income they might not have had otherwise *[1 mark]*. / Tourism contributes to a country's income *[1 mark]*, allowing it to invest in improving development and quality of life *[1 mark]*. / Entry fees can be charged *[1 mark]*, which fund preservation or protection schemes, e.g. national parks *[1 mark]*.

3.1 C *[1 mark]*

3.2 Food insecurity is when people aren't able to get enough food to stay healthy or lead an active life *[1 mark]*. If daily calorie intake is low, it may indicate that people aren't able to get enough food *[1 mark]*.

3.3 Any two from: e.g. there may be a famine, causing starvation and death, if the lack of food becomes serious *[1 mark]*. / People may experience poor health due to undernutrition *[1 mark]*. / Soil erosion due to unsustainable agricultural practices (e.g. over-cultivation) may increase *[1 mark]*. / Rising food prices due to shortages mean that the poorest can't afford to feed themselves properly *[1 mark]*. / Social unrest caused by food shortages and lack of help from governments *[1 mark]*.

3.4 The risk of food insecurity in the area will probably increase because the arrival of refugees will increase the demand for food *[1 mark]*. Access to food will be difficult for the refugees, who have had to flee their homes and may not have money to buy food *[1 mark]*. The refugees may be forced to rely on handouts like those shown in Figure 5, and the host country may struggle to provide handouts if it is a poor country or if imports have been disrupted because of the conflict *[1 mark]*.

4.1 Canada *[1 mark]*

4.2 Mexico *[1 mark]*

4.3 Increased wealth is related to increased water consumption *[1 mark]*.

4.4 Canada has a low population density, so demand for water is relatively low *[1 mark]*. Although Canada receives less rainfall than the USA or Mexico, the climate there is cooler *[1 mark]*, so less water is lost to evaporation *[1 mark]*.

4.5 Any one from: e.g. the amount of groundwater being extracted can be monitored *[1 mark]* to ensure it is not extracted faster than it is naturally replaced *[1 mark]*. / Farmers can be encouraged to apply less artificial fertiliser and pesticide to farmland *[1 mark]* to prevent groundwater supplies from becoming polluted *[1 mark]*. / Companies which leak toxic industrial waste can be fined *[1 mark]* to discourage them from polluting groundwater supplies *[1 mark]*.

5.1 150-199 million tonnes oil equivalent *[1 mark]*

5.2 E.g. Venezuela produces around twice as much energy as it consumes each year *[1 mark]*.

5.3 E.g. the demand for energy in Chile is higher than the energy that it produces *[1 mark]*. Chile consumes 35 million tonnes of oil equivalent per year, but produces only 0-19 million tonnes of oil equivalent per year *[1 mark]*. Chile also has very low oil reserves (3 million tonnes), which limits its ability to produce energy *[1 mark]*.

5.4 0.8 tonnes (accept between 0.75 and 0.85) *[1 mark]*

5.5 Any two from: e.g. insulating walls, roofs and floors *[1 mark]* / fitting a modern, more efficient boiler *[1 mark]* / fitting solar panels to the roof to provide renewable, low-carbon energy *[1 mark]* / fitting more efficient appliances, e.g. energy-efficient washing machines and televisions *[1 mark]* / turning off lights when not in use *[1 mark]*.

Practice Exam Paper 3: Geographical Applications
Pages 190-193

1.1 280 ppm (accept 270-290 ppm) *[1 mark]*

1.2 This question is level marked. How to grade your answer:
Level 0: There is no relevant information. *[0 marks]*
Level 1: There is a basic explanation of why it may be difficult to reduce greenhouse gas emissions. *[1-2 marks]*
Level 2: There is a clear explanation of why it may be difficult to reduce greenhouse gas emissions by 40-70%. *[3-4 marks]*
Here are some points your answer may include:
- Reducing greenhouse gas emissions will require social change. This will require people to change their behaviour, e.g. decreasing their energy use or travelling less, which they may be unable or unwilling to do.
- Reducing greenhouse gas emissions will also require technological change. This is likely to be expensive, and it may take time to develop and test.
- Electricity production will need to become nearly emission-free, but most electricity generation is from fossil fuels. Switching to renewable sources would require a lot of investment, which many countries may not be able to afford.
- The IPCC say reducing emissions by 40-70% will also require an overall reduction in energy use, but LICs and NEEs are still developing, which will cause large increases in energy use. This is likely to increase greenhouse gas emissions.

1.3 This question is level marked. How to grade your answer:
Level 0: There is no relevant information. *[0 marks]*
Level 1: There is a basic discussion of the statement with limited reference to the figure and some use of knowledge. *[1-2 marks]*
Level 2: There is a clear discussion of the statement with analysis of the figure and use of knowledge. *[3-4 marks]*
Level 3: There is a detailed discussion of the statement with extensive analysis of the figure and appropriate use of knowledge. *[5-6 marks]*
Your answer should come to a conclusion about whether human activities are the main cause of climate change or not. Here are some points your answer may include:
- The climate changes naturally due to variations in the Earth's orbit, changes in the output of the Sun and volcanic activity.
- Climate change may also be related to changing concentrations of greenhouse gases in the atmosphere, as they trap heat and create a warming effect.

- CO_2 concentration in the atmosphere was almost constant from year 1 to 1800, and then increased rapidly from 280 parts per million in 1800 to 360 parts per million in 2000. This rapid increase coincided with a rapid increase of about 0.7 °C in global temperature over the same period.
- This increase in CO_2 occurred at the same time as humans began to burn large amounts of fossil fuels, which releases greenhouse gases into the atmosphere.
- Deforestation has also been extensive during this period, for example over 750 000km² of the Amazon rainforest had been lost since 1978. Deforestation reduces the amount of CO_2 that is removed from the atmosphere by trees, and if the trees are burnt, CO_2 is added to the atmosphere.
- The evidence suggests that humans have caused the increase in atmospheric CO_2 concentration. This increase coincides with increasing temperature, which may suggest that humans are the main cause of climate change.

2.1 The UK, USA and China have seen small increases in percentage forest cover, which may help to limit climate change *[1 mark]*. However, Malawi has seen a significant decrease in forest cover, which is likely to increase climate change *[1 mark]*.

2.2 Carbon capture and storage removes the CO_2 produced in fossil fuel combustion and stores it underground *[1 mark]*. This means it is not released into the atmosphere, where it could increase the concentration of greenhouse gases and increase warming *[1 mark]*.

2.3 This question is level marked. How to grade your answer:
Level 0:   There is no relevant information. *[0 marks]*
Level 1:   There is a basic discussion of whether renewable energy sources are always small-scale and unreliable. *[1-2 marks]*
Level 2:   There is a clear discussion of whether renewable energy sources are always small-scale and unreliable, which uses evidence from Figure 2 and other knowledge. *[3-4 marks]*
Level 3:   There is a detailed discussion of whether renewable energy sources are always small-scale and unreliable, which uses evidence from Figure 2 and other knowledge. *[5-6 marks]*

Your answer must come to a conclusion about whether renewable energy sources are always small-scale and unreliable. Here are some points your answer may include:
- Fossil fuels have traditionally supplied most of our energy and are likely to be able to do so for some years yet.
- Renewable energy sources currently produce 22% of the world's electricity. Most (17%) of this is hydropower.
- Hydropower can be reliable and large scale. However, it requires a constant supply of flowing water, so it is not a viable alternative to fossil fuels in all areas. Its viability may also be affected by changing precipitation patterns and water supply.
- Biomass is a reliable renewable energy source that can be used on a large scale, for example in converted coal-fired power stations such as Drax in Yorkshire. However, it requires a constant supply of biomass, which in some cases has to be imported, contributing to greenhouse gas emissions. It may therefore not be a viable alternative to fossil fuels in all areas.
- Wind generates 6% of the UK's electricity, and large offshore windfarms can generate significant amounts of power. But the wind does not always blow, so they are unreliable as they cannot generate electricity all the time.

- Solar is a growing source of renewable energy in the UK, but it is not yet used on a large scale and provides only 0.4% of the UK's electricity needs. It needs quite intense sunlight to produce significant amounts of power, so although it may be a viable alternative to fossil fuels in some countries, it is not suitable for all.

2.4 This question is level marked. There are 3 extra marks available for spelling, punctuation and grammar.
How to grade your answer:
Level 0:   There is no relevant information. *[0 marks]*
Level 1:   There is a basic view stated and a simple justification. *[1-3 marks]*
Level 2:   There is a clear view stated and an adequate justification using at least one figure and other knowledge. *[4-6 marks]*
Level 3:   There is a thorough evaluation of the effectiveness of each scheme at reducing the social, economic and environmental consequences of climate change, and a clear argument for a chosen scheme. The answer draws on evidence from both figures. *[7-9 marks]*

Make sure your spelling, punctuation and grammar is consistently correct, that your meaning is clear and that you use a range of geographical terms correctly *[0-3 marks]*.
You must use your own knowledge and information from Figure 1 and Figure 2 to decide which of the schemes you think will best reduce the social, economic and environmental consequences of climate change. You will need to examine the pros and cons of each scheme and produce evidence to support your choice.
Here are some points your answer may include:
- Schemes 1 and 2 in Figure 2 aim to reduce the effects of climate change by reducing the CO_2 emissions, which Figure 1 suggests contribute to global warming. The schemes may help to make the effects of climate change on people and the environment less severe, but do not directly help those affected.
- Scheme 3 reduces the effects of climate change by directly helping those worst affected, but does not help to reduce climate change itself.
- Scheme 1 aims to reduce emissions from cars, which would lead to a slower increase in atmospheric greenhouse gases and therefore reduced climate change. It is an international agreement, which means it is likely to reduce emissions in most countries around the world. However, it may make new vehicles more expensive, which may cause economic problems for poorer people and encourage people to keep using older, dirtier vehicles. It also only aims to reduce emissions from cars, not from other major sources.
- Scheme 2 aims to reduce carbon emissions from countries with a large carbon footprint, e.g. the USA, which has a carbon footprint of 17 tonnes per person, by encouraging people to change their behaviour. It aims to reduce emissions from a range of sources, such as homes and transport, and it targets a broader range of sources of emissions than Scheme 1, so it could deliver large reductions in carbon emissions. However, it relies on individuals to make changes, which they may be unable or unwilling to do. By targeting individuals it seems to ignore large sources of emissions, such as industry. It is also aimed at countries that already have a large carbon footprint, so it won't prevent developing countries from expanding their carbon footprints.

- Scheme 3 offers aid to those who are worst affected by climate change so they can overcome its effects. For example, Figure 1 states that droughts could become more frequent in some areas. This could reduce crop yields in affected areas, so food packages could be delivered to these areas to help to prevent starvation in the case of crop failure. However, aid does not offer a long-term, sustainable solution to the problem. The scheme also makes no attempt to reduce climate change, it just reduces some of its effects. Without tackling the underlying causes, some effects may continue to get worse, and will therefore need ever-more aid or funding to mitigate their impacts. In addition, the scheme focuses only on people and makes no attempt to relieve the environmental effects of climate change.

3.1-3.2

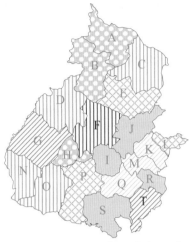

[1 mark for each area shaded correctly]

3.3   21-30% *[1 mark]*

3.4   The north and west of the town has the lowest proportion of houses with solar panels, with less than 20% of the houses having them *[1 mark]*. However, there is an anomaly in District G, where 41-50% of the houses have solar panels even though it is in the west of the town *[1 mark]*. The south and east of the town has a much higher proportion of houses with solar panels, with 21-50% of houses having solar panels *[1 mark]*.

3.5   This question is level marked. How to grade your answer:
Level 0:   There is no relevant information. *[0 marks]*
Level 1:   There is a basic description of at least one problem and at least one benefit of the choropleth map shown. *[1-2 marks]*
Level 2:   There is a detailed evaluation considering both the problems and benefits of the choropleth map shown. *[3-4 marks]*
Here are some points your answer may include:
Benefits
- The data is summarised into districts so the diagram isn't cluttered by too much detail, which might make it difficult to read.
- It is easy to see the patterns in the data.
- The map doesn't take too long to draw.
Problems
- The shading/patterns used for each section can make it difficult to distinguish between the different categories shown on the map.
- It only shows the information at a district scale — there may be variations within each district.
- The groupings for each category are quite broad so it's possible that too much detail has been lost.

3.6   Any one from: e.g. the students could have used a dot map, using identical symbols to show the distribution of houses with solar panels *[1 mark]*. / Proportional symbols could have been used to show the relative number of panels in different areas *[1 mark]*.

4.1   Any one from: e.g. water hazards, such as drowning *[1 mark]* / weather hazards, for example getting too cold, too hot or sunburnt *[1 mark]* / potential for slips and falls *[1 mark]* / being hit by falling rocks etc. *[1 mark]*.

4.2   This question is level marked. How to grade your answer:
Level 0:   There is no relevant information. *[0 marks]*
Level 1:   There is a basic description of at least one technique used and an attempt to support its use in the investigation. *[1-2 marks]*
Level 2:   There is a detailed description of at least two techniques used and clear evidence to support their use in the investigation. *[3-4 marks]*
Here are some points your answer may include:
- Measures of average, e.g. mean, median or mode, can be used to summarise the data collected to make it easier to spot patterns and draw conclusions.
- Measures of spread, e.g. range or interquartile range, can be used to show how far the data is spread out or how consistent the results are. This can give an indication of the precision/repeatability of the data.
- Lines of best fit can be used to identify correlation between sets of data and to help draw conclusions about the relationship of one set of data to another.
- Percentage increase and decrease can be used to show how much something has changed over time. They are useful when comparing two data sets with different amounts of data in each, because a percentage shows a proportion rather than an absolute value.
- Calculating percentiles can tell you if a data point is very big or small compared to the rest of the data set.

Try to include specific details about why you used each technique or how it helped you to identify patterns in your data.

5.1   This question is level marked. How to grade your answer:
Level 0:   There is no relevant information. *[0 marks]*
Level 1:   There are a few points about the effectiveness of the data collection techniques used. *[1-2 marks]*
Level 2:   There is a clear evaluation of the effectiveness of the data collection methods used and the answer attempts to come to a conclusion. *[3-4 marks]*
Level 3:   There is a detailed evaluation of the effectiveness of the data collection methods used and the answer comes to a clear conclusion. *[5-6 marks]*
Here are some points your answer may include:
- An outline of the data sets collected and the conclusions that could be drawn. Whether these conclusions answered the original question.
- An outline of the limitations of the data collection methods used, and how they may have affected the validity of the conclusion.
- An overall conclusion about the effectiveness of the techniques used in answering the research question.

Acknowledgements

Photograph of Nepal earthquake damage on page 4 © Rajan Journalist; photograph of Nepal on page 10 © Krish Dulal both licensed under the Creative Commons Attribution-Share Alike 4.0 International license (https://creativecommons.org/licenses/by-sa/4.0/deed.en)

Photograph of Montserrat on page 6 © Dr. Richard Roscoe, Visuals Unlimited/Science Photo Library

Photograph on p.10 (Montserrat) © Wailunip licensed under the Creative Commons Attribution-Share Alike 2.5 Generic license.

Satellite images on page 13 and page 17: Jeff Schmaltz, MODIS Rapid Response Team, NASA/GSFC

Photograph of flood defences on page 15: US Army Corps of Engineers

Photograph on p.16 (UK flooding) © Rose and Trev Clough/p.17 (snow in UK) © John Brightley/p.21 (tree rings) © Albert Bridge/ p.17 (Wrabness Point) © Zorba the Geek/p.54 (River Avon) © Clive Giddis/p.54 (Snowdonia) © Bill Boaden/p.54 (Fens) © Hugh Venables/p.60 (Old Harry) © Raymond Knapman/p.60 (Lulworth Cove) © Nick Macneill/p.60 (Chesil Beach) © Eugene Birchall/ p.61 (Alkborough Flats) © Chris/p.62 (beach defences) © JThomas/p.64 (coastal defences) © Rob Farrow/p.68 (interlocking spurs) © Bob Bowyer/p.72 (Erskine from the air) © Thomas Nugent/p.72 (Corra Lin and gorge) © Iain Thompson/p.72 (meander) © G Laird/ p.77 (Boscastle flood prevention) © Trevor Rickard/p.77 (new footbridge over River Valency) © Steve Daniels/p.77 (River Valency) © Rod Allday/p.79 (interlocking spurs near Church Stretton) © Bob Bowyer/p.83 (erratic) © Gordon Brown/p.85 (Llyn Ogwen) © Ivan Hall/p.85 (Nant Ffrancon valley) © Meirion/p.85 (Llyn Idwal moraine) © N Chadwick/p.85 (Llyn Idwal) © Dudley Smith/ p.85 (truncated spur) © John Smith/p.87 (paved path) © Katy Waters/p.88 (speed buoy) © Anthony Parkes/p.89 (Quarry, Whitelee Forest) © Richard Webb/p.89 (Snowdon summit) © John S Turner/p.100 (derelict buildings in Toxteth) © Nigel Cox/p.100 (modern buildings) © Sue Adair/p.100 (cycle path) © Peter Holmes/p.100 (Chavasse Park) © Rept0n1x/p.101 (scrap metal recycling) © Roger May/ p.104 (derelict street in Northern Ireland) © Albert Bridge/p.105 (Newcastle quayside) © Robert Graham/p.116 (damaged building in Libya) © Al Jazeera English/p.118 (office building in Bangalore) © Eirik Refsdal./p.120 (office building) © Bob Jones/p.124 (Chadderton) © Jza84/p.124 (Channel Tunnel) © Helmut Zozmann p.128 (crop spraying) © Walter Baxter/p.136 and p.184 (refugees) © Magharebia/ p.137 (crop irrigation) © John Spivey/p.138 (Thanet Earth) © David Anstiss/p.163 (river fieldwork in Garrachra Glen) © Robbie Livingstone/p.179 (Afon Doethie) © Trevor Littlewood/p.179 (Barmouth Estuary) © Janine Forbes/p.180 (Lochan a' Choire) © Dave Moir. Licensed under the Creative Commons Attribution-Share Alike 2.0 Generic Licence (http://creativecommons.org/licenses/by-sa/2.0/)

Image of Slidell, Louisiana on page 18 © FEMA/Liz Roll

Figure 2 on page 18: Global annual average near-surface temperature anomalies (difference from 1961-1990 average). Data are from HadCRUT.4.4.0.0 which is produced by the Met Office Hadley Centre in collaboration with the University of East Anglia Climatic Research Unit

Short term climate graph on pages 20 and 26 adapted from Crown Copyright data supplied by the Met Office; data on UK emissions on page 24; map of population distribution on pages 97, 129 and 182; wage data on page 121; life expectancy data for the UK on page 121 from Office for National Statistics; information used in article on p.125 provided by Department for International Development; data used to compile graph of UK energy mix on page 130; pie charts of UK energy sources in 1970 and 2014 on p.133 all contain public sector information licensed under the Open Government Licence v3.0.

Scientist analysing ice core on page 21 © NASA/Lora Koenig; photograph of hand pump on page 138 courtesy of Vicki Francis/ Department for International Development; photograph of desalination plant on page 146 © Octal. All licensed under the Creative Commons Attribution 2.0 Generic license (https://creativecommons.org/licenses/by/2.0/deed.en)

Graph of sea level rise on p.25 adapted from Climate Change 2001: The Scientific Basis. Contribution of Working Group I to the Third Assessment Report of the Intergovernmental Panel on Climate Change. Figure 5. Cambridge University Press.

Photograph of buttress roots on page 32 ©iStock.com/Morley Read; p.37 (periwinkle) © iStock.com/pmrco; p.95 (Indonesian students) © iStock.com/Artush; p.150 (children collecting water in Kenya) © iStock.com/journalturk

Photograph of Morocco on p.46 by Anderson sady; topographic map of the United Kingdom on page 54 by Captain Blood and photograph of growing tomatoes on page 138 © Goldlocki. All licensed under the Creative Commons Attribution-Share Alike 3.0 Unported license (https://creativecommons.org/licenses/by-sa/3.0/deed.en).

Map extracts on pages 59, 64, 71, 84, 90, 97, 170 and 171 reproduced with permission by Ordnance Survey® © Crown copyright 2016 OS GV-198903

Map extracts on pages 72, 85, 125 created from OS Open Data. Contains OS data © Crown copyright and database right 2016.

Data used to construct HIC/LIC/NEE map on pages 108 and 182 from The World Bank: Country and Lending Groups.

HDI values, mean time in education values and life expectancies on page 111 from: 2015 Human Development Report, United Nations Development Programme from hdr.undp.org. HDI data on pages 113 and 115 provided by the UNDP. These data licensed under the Creative Commons Attribution 3.0 IGO license (http://creativecommons.org/licenses/by/3.0/igo/legalcode)

Infant mortality rates on page 111 from The World Bank: Mortality rate, infant (per 1,000 live births): Estimates developed by the UN Inter-agency Group for Child Mortality Estimation (UNICEF, WHO, World Bank, UN DESA Population Division) at www.childmortality.org.

GNI per capita values for UK and Chad on page 111 from The World Bank: GNI per capita, Atlas method (current US$): World Bank national accounts data, and OECD National Accounts data files.

Data on tourism in Kenya on page 113 from The World Bank: International tourism, number of arrivals: World Tourism Organization, Yearbook of Tourism Statistics, Compendium of Tourism Statistics and data files.

Acknowledgements

Data used to compile Figure 1 on p.115 (except GNI and Canada literacy rate); data used to compile the table on page 116; data for water consumption per person (m3 per year) on p.185 © Central Intelligence Agency

GNI values on pages 115, 157, 185 and 186 from Global Health Observatory country views, © World Health Organisation (2016), http://apps.who.int/gho/data/node.country, accessed April 2016.

Indian employment statistics on page 117 from The World Bank: International Labour Organization, Key Indicators of the Labour Market database.

Employment data for the UK on page 120 contains Parliamentary information licensed under the Open Parliament Licence v3.0 and data from Office for National Statistics licensed under the Open Government Licence v3.0.

Photograph of Bath on p.124 © David Iliff. License: CC-BY-SA 3.0. https://creativecommons.org/licenses/by-sa/3.0/deed.en

Data used to compile the UK average rainfall map on pages 129 and 132 from the Manchester Metropolitan University.

Data used to construct the population density of the UK map on pages 132 and 167; flow map of immigration on page 169 — Source Office for National Statistics © Crown Copyright used under the terms of the Open Government Licence.

Cereal production map on page 134 © FAO 2015 Cereal production quantities by country 2012-2014 (http://faostat3.fao.org/browse/Q/QC/E 11.3.2016). This is an adaptation of an original work by FAO.

Calorie intake map on pages 134 and 184 © FAO 2015 World food supply 2011-2013 (http://faostat3.fao.org/browse/FB/FBS/E 11.3.2016)

Graph of corn production on p.141 © FAO 2015 Corn production quantities in Canada and Zimbabwe 1960 - 2010 (http://faostat3.fao.org/browse/Q/QC/E [16/03/16]). This is an adaptation of an original work by FAO.

Map of global water scarcity on pages 144 and 185 © 2014 World Resources Institute. This work is licensed under the Creative Commons Attribution 3.0 License. To view a copy of the license, visit http://creativecommons.org/licenses/by/3.0/

Data used to construct energy production map on page 151, map of energy production on page 186 and renewable energy data on page 189 from U.S. Energy Information Administration.

Global Energy Consumption map on pages 152 and 157, oil reserves data on page 186 and energy consumption data on page 186 © BP Statistical Review of World Energy 2015, BP p.l.c.

Pie chart on page 155 based on the data from a study by the government-funded Carbon Trust.

Map on p.158 by David Maliphant. Contains OS data © Crown copyright and database right (2016)

Data used to compile the graphs on p.183 © World Trade Organisation, (http://stat.wto.org/CountryProfile/WSDBCountryPFReporter.aspx?Language=E)

Page 185: The World Bank: Average precipitation in depth (mm per year): Food and Agriculture Organization, electronic files and web site.

Page 185: The World Bank: Population density (people per sq. km of land area): Food and Agriculture Organization and World Bank population estimates.

Temperature graph on page 188: Figure 5.7 (c) from Masson-Delmotte, V., M. Schulz, A. Abe-Ouchi, J. Beer, A. Ganopolski, J.F. González Rouco, E. Jansen, K. Lambeck, J. Luterbacher, T. Naish, T. Osborn, B. Otto-Bliesner, T. Quinn, R. Ramesh, M. Rojas, X. Shao and A. Timmermann, 2013: Information from Paleoclimate Archives. CO2 graph on page 188: Figure 6.11 from Ciais, P., C. Sabine, G. Bala, L. Bopp, V. Brovkin, J. Canadell, A. Chhabra, R. DeFries, J. Galloway, M. Heimann, C. Jones, C. Le Quere, R.B. Myneni, S. Piao and P. Thornton, 2013: Carbon and Other Biogeochemical Cycles. Climate projections on page 188: Summary for Policymakers; sea-level rise projections on page 188: Kirtman, B., S.B. Power, J.A. Adedoyin, G.J. Boer, R. Bojariu, I. Camilloni, F.J. Doblas-Reyes, A.M. Fiore, M. Kimoto, G.A. Meehl, M. Prather, A. Sarr, C. Schär, R. Sutton, G.J. van Oldenborgh, G. Vecchi and H.J. Wang, 2013: Near-term Climate Change: Projections and Predictability. All in: Climate Change 2013: The Physical Science Basis. Contribution of Working Group I to the Fifth Assessment Report of the Intergovernmental Panel on Climate Change [Stocker, T.F., D. Qin, G.-K. Plattner, M. Tignor, S.K. Allen, J.Boschung, A. Nauels, Y. Xia, V. Bex and P.M. Midgley (eds.)]. Cambridge University Press, Cambridge, United Kingdom and New York, NY, USA.

Article on page 188 based on the data from IPCC.

Carbon footprint data on page 188: The World Bank: CO2 emissions (metric tons per capita): Carbon Dioxide Information Analysis Center, Environmental Sciences Division, Oak Ridge National Laboratory, Tennessee, United States

Page 189: The World Bank: Forest area (% of land area): Food and Agriculture Organization, electronic files and web site.

Every effort has been made to locate copyright holders and obtain permission to reproduce sources. For those sources where it has been difficult to trace the copyright holder of the work, we would be grateful for information. If any copyright holder would like us to make an amendment to the acknowledgements, please notify us and we will gladly update the book at the next reprint. Thank you.

Index

Index

Index